THE LETTERS OF
ST. CYPRIAN OF CARTHAGE

Letters 28–54

Ancient Christian Writers

THE WORKS OF THE FATHERS IN TRANSLATION

EDITED BY

JOHANNES QUASTEN   WALTER J. BURGHARDT

THOMAS COMERFORD LAWLER

No. 44

THE LETTERS OF ST.
CYPRIAN OF CARTHAGE

TRANSLATED AND ANNOTATED

BY

G. W. CLARKE

*Professor of Classical Studies and Deputy Director, Humanities Research Centre,
Australian National University*

Volume II
Letters 28–54

NEWMAN PRESS
New York, N.Y./Ramsey, N.J.

Library of Congress
Catalog Card Number: 83-80366

ISBN: 0-8091-0342-7

Published by Paulist Press
545 Island Road, Ramsey, N.J.

PRINTED AND BOUND IN THE UNITED STATES OF AMERICA

CONTENTS

THE LETTERS OF
ST. CYPRIAN OF CARTHAGE

LETTERS 28–54

INTRODUCTION

The introduction aims to be brief. It is not designed to cover all the major topics raised by the contents of this volume, but merely to sketch a general setting and framework, imperial and ecclesiastical, against which the letters themselves (the focus of the volume) might be read and possibly appreciated a little more clearly. Attention is also drawn in a very general way to some features of Church administration and inter-church relations which the letters in this volume unusually disclose. Detailed discussion of those features is reserved for the commentary under the individual letters referred to; documentation is accordingly cut to a minimum in this introduction itself. The persecution of Decius was treated at some length in the introduction to ACW 43, and is, therefore, not touched on here. As *Ep.* 55, which reveals most of what we know of the agenda and thinking of the African Council of 251, will appear in the next volume, I defer to then a fuller discussion of the timing of that Council and its resolutions (in particular the questions of penitential discipline and the excommunication of Novatian).

IMPERIAL EVENTS

Revolt on the Danube (led by Pacatianus), with Gothic invasions into Lower Moesia in its wake, appears to have heralded the hopeful new millenium of Rome inaugurated by the emperor Philip in spring of 248. This was matched in the East by mutiny under Jopatianus in the borderlands between Cappadocia and Syria and under Uranius Antoninus at Syrian Emesa, east of the Orontes. Philip's successor and usurper Decius (established by autumn 249) was to face a similar history of unrest, insurrection, and incursion.[1]

The correspondence in this volume covers the period from approximately high summer of 250 to mid-251. It is not possible to write a full narrative of imperial events under the emperor Decius over these months—our evidence is at once too incomplete and at every step controversial. But a reasonable and skeletal reconstruction would go something like this.

For a time after seizing power, and then successfully defending it at Verona (autumn 249), Decius settled down in Rome to consolidate his regime. As likely as not, it is just as the correspondence in this volume starts up, in high summer of 250, that Decius eventually left Rome, and in anxious haste.

Whilst he had been attending to political matters in Rome (after his very recent usurpation they needed delicate handling), his son Herennius Etruscus had been attending to military affairs in the Balkans. Goths (under Kniva) had invaded in force across the Danube into Moesia (some penetrating even into Thrace) and it would appear Carpi further east had pushed far into Dacia.[2] But now to precipitate his departure, events had taken a turn for the worse. The governor in Thrace had revolted and joined forces (it seems) with the Gothic invaders. Philippopolis was offered for sacking as their reward, and its inhabitants butchered.[3] And to make matters even worse, as Decius hastened forth to the battlefront, there broke out in his rear a short-lived but popularly supported uprising.[4]

Despite the suppression of these pretenders and notable fighting especially at Nicopolis (before the year was out Decius was *restitutor Daciarum* and entitled *Dacicus Maximus*),[5] there was much fighting and military reconstruction yet to be done. The surviving invaders were still within Roman territory, laden with their captives and booty. Decius and his son wintered in the area, and it may well be that it was from their winter quarters, as Decius attended to his despatches, that letters went out to various provinces and governors recommending clemency for Christians who remained in prison or who were still in exile. Domestic division and unrest were to be avoided.[6]

Next year tough campaigning continued (details are largely lost) until Decius and his son, still in pursuit of the invaders, both fell in a second major engagement of the season, at the disastrous battle at Abrittus in marsh-lands of the Dobrudja—just as the correspondence in this volume closes, in mid-251. The dramas enacted by Christians, as disclosed by this correspondence—though set in train by actions of Decius—were well beyond the emperor's knowledge and, no doubt in the press of events, his concern.[7]

THE CHURCH IN THE WEST

We can merely surmise what has been occurring in most of the Western provinces over this period from the sequel. In Spain, for example, we hear later (*Ep.* 67) of two lapsed bishops (Martialis and Basilides) and the difficulties attendant on securing their deposition from office.[8] Christians there must now be confronting the problems of penitential discipline, the laicisation of lapsed but repentant clergy (*Ep.* 67.6.2f.), and the pollution that attends those who remain in communion with the fallen (*Ep.* 67.9.1), problems that we can perceive with greater clarity were besetting the Church elsewhere. Gaul chances to reveal parallel preoccupations over the settlement of the penitential issue. Several years later, to Cyprian's outrage as a pastor, Marcian, bishop of Arles, still continues to refuse to hold out any hope of reconciliation to the fallen (*Ep.* 68). Marcian and his colleagues will now be forming their views in the lengthy and heated debates that followed everywhere in the wake of the Decian persecution. Sicily comes with breathtaking brevity into view when the Roman presbyters and deacons mention in passing that they are sending Cyprian a copy—now lost—of a letter which they have directed there (*Ep.* 30.5.2). From the context we can discern that their letter concerned interim measures for dealing with, or rather deferring, the cases of the lapsed. The Sicilian church is facing similar problems and similar debate. But it is, of course, Rome and Carthage where our sources—notably this correspondence of Cyprian—can allow us to sketch this process in greater detail.

Initially Rome appears to be in much the stronger and more orderly shape of the two churches. When the correspondence opens in this volume we meet a group of Roman confessors in prison (*Ep.* 28) but no deaths among them have yet occurred and they do not appear anticipated when the confessors write back their reply (*Ep.* 31). Their numbers may not have been very large (eight names are known and one of them, Celerinus, appears to have been released already, *Ep.* 21). Their expressed views on the issuing of certificates of forgiveness are clear and decided; they favour restraint and are on the side of the Church authorities, or what Cyprian would call the Gospel discipline, and they are prepared to make their convictions known in no uncertain terms (*Epp.* 27.4, 28, 31).[9] The church authorities themselves—the interregnal government of presbyters and deacons (Fabian, the bishop, having died in late January of 250)—can convene together, assisted in their deliberations by bishops from Italy and abroad (*Ep.* 30.8). They have already sent to Carthage (*Ep.* 9.1) a eulogistic testimonial in memory of their dead bishop Fabian (we may suspect that the presbyter Novatian, his protégé, had a hand in this) as well as two letters addressed to the Carthaginian clergy (*Ep.* 27.4, and the unfortunate *Ep.* 8). Now come directed to Cyprian lengthy and diplomatic documents, *Epp.* 30 and 36; the interim decision they convey is clear and precise—to reconcile only the genuinely repentant lapsed *in extremis,* and otherwise to await peace and the episcopal elections. *Ep.* 21.3.2 demonstrates that this decision is being firmly put into execution. And their affairs appear to be sufficiently ordered that they can keep fraternal watch over other churches as well; they can write not only to Africa, but also to Sicily (*Ep.* 30.5.2), their letters eventually enjoying world-wide circulation (*Ep.* 55.5.2); and they are not taken in by Futurus, who turns out to be an agent of the already condemned heretic Privatus (*Ep.* 36.4).

But this apparent front of confident control and solidarity quickly disintegrates before the episcopal elections in the early spring of 251, about the time that the surviving Roman confessors (some of them have now died, *Ep.* 37) begin to emerge into daylight, released at long last from their prison. The details of those elections are unfortunately lost to our view, but we can suspect that some felt that the elections may have been held too hastily, before the church, scattered as it had been before the onslaught of persecution, could fully reassemble and comprovincial bishops could muster. At least there are repeated complaints, and they were entertained seriously, that Cornelius failed to obtain the usual general approval of assembled congregation, diocesan clergy and fellow bishops (e.g., *Epp.* 44.3.2, 55.8.4). Sixteen bishops in fact attended, but we do not know what numbers might normally be expected for a Roman election (at a municipal centre in Africa six bishops attended such a ceremony early in the year 253.[10] It was never claimed that all of the local clergy had approved (*de clericorum paene omnium testimonio, Ep.* 55.8.4). We could well believe that communications had been difficult and uncertain at the time, with some refugees (bishops had been especially vulnerable) yet to return home, or who were too preoccupied to leave home. There had been a whole year of peril and confusion.

But there was more. Grave charges were levelled against the suitability of the candidate so chosen (Cornelius): he was polluted with the contagion of idolatry himself, and he was in communion with bishops who had themselves sacrificed (*Ep.* 55.10.2). To recognize such a bishop would be to share in his vile profanation and become contaminated oneself, for he had brought corruption into the Church (cf. *eos . . . coniunxisse nobiscum, Ep.* 55.10.2). Horror of ritual impurity was genuine and real, an emotion which plays a vital role in the penitential debates of the day. On these grounds the election was void, the candidate chosen being ineligible and a rival consecration was held in favour of Novatian. It was quite some time before the African bishops could reassure themselves that the charges were false (*Epp.* 44, 45, 48), the rival bishop being therefore invalid, for the see had not in fact been vacant. It was even longer before the influential group of Roman confessors (and not all of them) were prepared solemnly to renounce their allegiance to Cornelius' opponent, Novatian (*Epp.* 46, 49 *sqq.*). Others remained firmly unconvinced, and that solidly united church (as it had appeared so shortly before) is now irretrievably splintered and severed. Rome has an anti-pope, and a long-lasting schismatic church. And as in Africa, so elsewhere: the churches were all solicited by the rival factions to declare their allegiance. Turmoil and indecision ensues, with strong sympathies and respect in evidence for the side of Novatian.[11]

So far as the testimony of this correspondence goes, disagreement over the penitential issue did not appear initially as a vital ingredient in the dispute, and Cornelius' letter to Fabius of Antioch, at least in the extracts which Eusebius quotes, does not touch on the matter,[12] but by the time our correspondence closes in this volume (mid-251 or thereabouts) Novatian and Cornelius have already identified themselves with conflicting stances (*Epp.* 52.2.5, 54.3). Novatian emphasized above all that ritual purity: the Church was holy, and that could be achieved only through the holiness of its members. And when the correspondence reopens, *Ep.* 55 reveals that the Italian Council has by then met already, the disciplinary battlelines are now well and truly defined, and Novatian has been formally outlawed (Eusebius, *H.E.* 6.43.2).

By contrast with their Roman brethren, the Carthaginian Christians entered the high summer of 250 in a state of disarray and disharmony (though the sharpness of this contrast may be due in part simply to the fact we have more detailed information for Carthage). To the continued dismay of Cyprian, still in concealment since the early months of the year, there was a significant and vociferous group of confessors vigorously espousing not the cause of the Gospel discipline (as in Rome) but the cause of laxity and indiscipline—the prompt return to communion of such apostates as they (indiscriminately) recommended. And there were Carthaginian presbyters (at least five of them, *Ep.* 43) and deacons prepared to act on such recommendations in defiance of their bishop's ruling (*Ep.* 34). For that ruling Cyprian had prudently sought and got the written support and agreement of many other fellow African bishops (*Epp.* 25 and 26); but despite those affidavits, there were now bishops in the province who were weakly succumbing before the clamorous onslaught of the lapsed as they came charging in mob attack brandishing the certificates of forgiveness issued with such abandon by the African confessors (*Ep.* 27.3). The opening letter, *Ep.* 28 (to the Roman confessors), ruefully underlines the contrasting virtues displayed by the Roman confessors—their crown is for *dominica disciplina*, the example they set is in *morum magisteria. Epp.* 33 and 35 together dramatically reveal the width of the chasm that is now dividing Cyprian and his numerous opponents (who can consider themselves to constitute "the church," *Ep.* 33), and the supreme confidence which the *libelli martyrum* could give to their recipients, lapsed though they had been (*Ep.* 35). No doubt they shared the sentiments of their fellow countryman Celerinus who evinced the aspiration to the Carthaginian confessors that "whosoever of your number is first to receive his crown should forgive these sisters of ours . . . of such a sin" (*Ep.* 21.3.2)—and seventeen Carthaginian confessors at least have so won their crowns (*Ep.* 22). They were simply laying claim to the forgiveness which they considered they had now rightfully gained (*Ep.* 35).

The effusive Roman letters (*Epp.* 30, 31, 36) brought further and most welcome support and agreement for that disciplinary ruling of Cyprian's, and strengthened him in his resolve—whatever the pressures—to maintain that *forma.* But however widely read and distributed those supportive documents were (*Ep.* 32), they did not repair the breakdown in authority with those defiant confessors and clergy, nor with significant numbers among the *maxima pars* of the laity (*Ep.* 14.1.1) who in one way or another had fallen (see *Ep.* 33).

Bishops now begin to appear in evidence, expected to turn

up in Carthage (*Ep.* 32, cf. *Ep.* 34.3.1), found conferring with
Cyprian in his place of concealment (*Epp.* 38.2.2, 39.1.1), and
then in fact seen actively and repeatedly threatening rebellious
clergy in Carthage and eventually advising the local clergy on
breaking off communion with a persistently offending presbyter and his deacon (*Ep.* 34.1; were these two *peregrini*—cf. *Ep.*
34.3.2—used as an example for warning other, i.e., Carthaginian,
presbyters?). Cyprian is mustering episcopal support, and preparing the way for tougher measures (*Ep.* 34.2). Depleted clerical ranks are restocked with three spectacularly model
confessors (*Epp.* 38–40): *verecundia, pudor, humilitas, quies, tran-
quillitas, ecclesiastica disciplina* are some of their attributes, and
mitis, humilis, submissus are some of their epithets. And divine
guidance has even been directly vouchsafed in their choice (*Epp.*
39.1.2, 40; cf. *divina suffragia, Ep.* 38.1.1). Cyprian empowers two
of those supporting bishops (one a known confessor, *Ep.* 24)
along with two presbyters (both significantly confessors) to act
for him in Carthage in the distribution of the church's charitable funds, to the exclusion, no doubt, of the disloyal and the
tainted.

The reaction to all this is not long in making itself visible.
Felicissimus threatens to break off communion with those who
comply with Cyprian's agents and accept largesse from them
(*Ep.* 41); in return, Felicissimus and six followers are formally
declared excommunicate (*Ep.* 42)—an earnest in warning to
others? Open schism is on the way, but this time on the side of
laxity. For the mutinous presbyters and lawless confessors now
emerge into full view as the source and strength of the *Felicis-
simi factio* (*Ep.* 43), effectively blocking Cyprian's longed-for
reunion with his people at the great Easter celebrations of 251.
This drastic breakdown in relations, snapped under the strain of
those many long, bitter months of tension and danger, disputa-
tion and genuine distress, comes home to us when the threat to
bait a mob against Cyprian and his followers is apparently used
as the means to stall his return (*Ep.* 43.4.2). It is not long until
Felicissimus and the five presbyters, after a hearing before
the African Council of 251, are solemnly condemned and other
churches are informed with full documentation (*Ep.* 45.4). And

not long again until one of those condemned presbyters is transformed into a schismatic bishop (*Ep.* 59.9).

When eventually Cyprian returned, the African Council of bishops, clergy and laity gathered to confront the long-awaited and lengthy debates on the issues of penitence and reconciliation (see *Ep.* 55). As if this did not provide trouble enough and as if the situation in Carthage did not provide scandal enough, they were confronted by further trouble and further scandal—there were envoys from Novatian and messages from Cornelius laying conflicting claims to the chair of Peter. There was little choice but to investigate those claims independently. One or other party was bound to be offended by the inevitable delays before they could offer recognition—and he was (*Epp.* 44, 45, 48). The procrastination of the African bishops may have been a matter of but a month or two. But in the Eastern churches agreement by the church leaders to reject the claims of Novatian was much longer in coming (Eusebius, *H.E.* 7.4 f.)—perhaps reached not long before, or even after, the end of Cornelius' pontificate itself.[13]

The Church in the East

We are not in a position to write a coherent narrative of those churches in the East. Our evidence is too haphazard and too fragmentary. But such activities as we can discern fit into the patterns that we have traced already in their western counterparts.

As the persecution dies down—its end in retrospect appeared unexpected (Dionysius of Alexandria *apud* Eusebius, *H.E.* 7.5)[14]—refugees begin to make their way back to their homes. Gregory Thaumaturgus and his companions come down to Neocaesarea in Pontus from the safety of the Pontic hills (Gregory of Nyssa, MG 46.953 ff.);[15] Dionysius of Alexandria and his companions return to Alexandria, and Egyptian fugitives (those who survived) straggle in from the wilds of the "Arabian mountain" or negotiations are started, if they are lucky, for their ransom from the clutches of their Saracen captors (Dionysius of Alexandria *apud* Eusebius, *H.E.* 6.42.2 ff.). Confessors begin to emerge from prison after their long ordeals of torture and incarceration (so Origen and his companions in Palestine, Eusebius, *H.E.* 6.39.5).[16] And churches are holding episcopal elections to replace their martyred—or apostate— bishops: so in Jerusalem, Mazabanes in place of the martyred Alexander; in Antioch, Fabius in place of the martyred Babylas; and without a doubt in Smyrna there is need to replace the renegade bishop Euctemon, (*Acta Pionii* 15.1, 19.12 ff.)[17]

And the problems which confront those returning or re- cently installed bishops, those confessors and happily reunited communities are identical with the preoccupations of their western brethren.

Firstly, penitence. Dionysius of Alexandria, for example, begins a flurry of activity and a long series of letters on the issue. He writes to the newly appointed Fabius of Antioch (amongst other things urging, on compassionate grounds, some recognition for the recommendations of confessors, *apud* Euse- bius, *H.E.* 6.42.5 f.; 6.44.1 ff.); he addresses his fellow Egyptians generally (Eusebius, *H.E.* 6.46.1), distinguishing various degrees of lapse; he writes to Conon, bishop of Hermopolis, to Thely- midres, bishop of Laodicea in Syria, and to his own Alexandri- ans (Eusebius, *H.E.* 6.46.1 f.); his communications on the subject extend as far east as the Christians in Armenia[18] and as far west as the Christians in Rome (Eusebius, *H.E.* 6.46.2 and 5). And he maintains, as did Cyprian, a correspondence with the Roman confessors both before and after their Novatianist phase, which could well have touched on penitential matters (Eusebius, *H.E.* 6.46.5). The question of the appropriate treatment of apostates had been raised throughout the Empire by the persecution of Decius—and everywhere that question urgently needed an an- swer.[19]

Secondly, Novatian. Dionysius of Alexandria, again, initi- ates another vigorous series of communications. He writes on the question to Fabius of Antioch (Eusebius, *H.E.* 6.44.1 ff.), to the people of Rome ("On Peace," Eusebius, *H.E.* 6.46.5), to Cornelius himself as well as to Novatian (Eusebius, *H.E.* 6.46.3,

6.45.1 ff.). But Alexandria, Antioch and Rome are not the only sees affected by the dispute. The Cilicians led by Helenus of Tarsus, Firmilian of Caesarea in Cappadocia, Theoctistus of Caesarea in Palestine are all concerned (Eusebius, *H.E.* 6.46.3). And opinions in the East are divided: it is not until the Council of Antioch eventually meets that, after a season of disharmony, concord is to be reached on the issue between those sees and others—Jerusalem and Tyre, the Syrias, Arabia, Mesopotamia, Bithynia and Pontus (Eusebius, *H.E.* 7.4 f.). All over the East, the churches have to face, as in the West, a testing period of indecision and disagreement.

THE CHURCHES AT WORK

In a sense we are the beneficiaries of Cyprian's continued enforced concealment. He was obliged to communicate with his congregation by letter, and copies of those letters were forwarded over to Rome not only to help rehabilitate his personal reputation there as a pastoralist but also to obtain fraternal support from overseas for his own pastoral policies at home. Hence in part (we may suspect) we have surviving today copies of that correspondence ourselves: it may descend to us in some measure *via* Roman archives. And thanks to that correspondence we are able to catch glimpses, rarely obtained for this period, of a bishop at work with his church even in the routine and mundane matters of his administration.

As the persecution's intensity eases off, we observe Christians beginning to emerge and to set about the daily business of their community; the processes of repair and reconstruction start to get under way. Cyprian can commission (*Ep.* 41) ecclesiastics acting in his stead (*vicarios*) to ensure that the physical necessities of his flock continue to be met, even assisting brethren, if necessary, in setting up their crafts (would these include refugees who had, literally, dropped their tools as they fled to the comparative safety of the anonymous crowds of Carthage?). The registers for charitable handouts are to be reviewed—just as cities had periodic purgings of their lists of recipients for corn-doles or the like—for Christians' individual *aetates, condiciones* and *merita* are to be noted not only for Cyprian's general infor-mation but also for drawing his attention to possible recruits for his depleted clergy. Trouble follows, and it is centered on the lapsed (*Epp.* 41 and 43): and lapsed of whatever degree—as a class altogether officially unreconciled as yet except *in extre-mis*—would have to be expunged from such registers. Cyprian was insistent that the church's poor should be the meritorious poor (*his tamen qui in fide stantes . . . Christi castra non reliquerunt, Ep.* 12.2.2). We can see in operation one of the practical effects of Cyprian's "closed community" definition of the Church (the *hortus conclusus* as elaborated in *Ep.* 69.2). We can equally see in operation his pyramidal view of its structure. The church's charitable funds are firmly and unequivocally in the gift of its *praepositus,* its bishop (*episcopo dispensante*) via his deputed agents and clergy.

Though some of those clergy continue to be absent (*Ep.* 29), others are beginning to return to the posts they have deserted (as Cyprian their commander-in-chief viewed it). The church is, however, sufficiently recovered for the clergy generally to be receiving their regular stipends in monthly apportionment (*Ep.* 34). And even special salary arrangements can be made. Celer-inus and Aurelius are much too young for the presbyterate, destined though they are for that rank one day in the future. They are, however, to receive increased perquisites and appor-tionment appropriate not for their own junior level of reader but for that top, senior grade of presbyter (*Ep.* 39). Ecclesiastical grades come with different salary levels in this hierarchically structured church.

And with lapse (*Ep.* 41; cf. *Ep.* 14.1.1), as well as desertion (*Epp.* 29 and 34), having wrought such havoc amongst the Car-thaginian clergy, the bishop, even from his place of conceal-ment, initiates the procedures to review possible fresh recruits for those clerical ranks (*Ep.* 41). We have a tantalising glimpse of the pre-clerical testing and training such recruits might undergo (*Ep.* 29), being attached to the entourage of their bishop (Saturus and Optatus, *Ep.* 29; cf. *Ep.* 16.4.1), much in the same way as young and hopeful trainee orators might be attached to the following and household of an established forensic leader. Indeed, new clergy are actually being appointed, blessed as these candidates are with singular virtues and the distinguishing honours of public confession (Aurelius, *Ep.* 38; Celerinus, *Ep.* 39; Numidicus, *Ep.* 40; cf. Optatus, *Ep.* 29). They can by-pass, therefore, under these special circumstances, the normal procedures of community review, inquiry, and consultation that pertained under peacetime conditions (*Epp.* 29, 38).

Above all, one gets a sense of the *grand seigneur* prospect from which Cyprian viewed his clerics. They were *ministri*, that is to say, *his* servants, recipients of the *sportulae* which he dispensed. It was not merely desirable, it was altogether necessary that he should have such clerics at his disposal, for the despatch of his letters (*Ep.* 29), even for supervising the taking of transcripts of ecclesiastical documents he wished distributed (*Ep.* 32), and this at a time when the depleted clerical force in Carthage scarcely sufficed for the daily work of the church (*Ep.* 29). As answerable directly to him, they had no right to absent themselves from their clerical duties in Carthage even in the face of the perils of persecution; such absentees are to undergo a full inquiry, solemnly confronting a court of bishops and the assembled laity (*Ep.* 34). And Cyprian's rebellious presbyter Novatus offended deeply—and Cornelius the bishop was expected to register immediate horror and outrage—by appropriating the Carthaginian Felicissimus to be his own deacon "with neither my permission nor knowledge" (*nec permittente me nec sciente, Ep.* 52.2.3). Old clerical enemies, therefore, were not loath to search for chinks in such a carapace of ecclesiastical hauteur (*Ep.* 43). Cyprian was fully aware he was at the top; he had reached the *sacerdotii sublime fastigium* (*Ep.* 55.8.2). And he had the calm assurance that he had got there by divine election, for the choice of God's people is the choice of God (*Ep.* 43), and as such God would guide and assist him with His direct inspiration (*gubernanter inspirans ac subministrans, Ep.* 48.4.2).

But from that lofty pinnacle the view disclosed other neighbouring peaks of spiritual eminence, enjoyed by the charismatic confessors. Both in Carthage and in Rome the bishops, and their rivals, show themselves anxious to court their allegiance and friendship. These are the church's inspirited heroes, admired by the people (*Ep.* 51.2.2) and by their leaders (*Epp.* 28, 37). In Carthage Felicissimus' group could boast of such support (*Ep.* 43), and so could Novatian in Rome (*Epp.* 46, 49). Cyprian's new clerical appointments are significantly drawn from the ranks of such confessors (*Epp.* 29, 38, 39, 40). And Cornelius is carefully displaying abroad a Roman confessor as his dutiful messenger (*Ep.* 50.1.1) before he can triumphantly proclaim the return of Roman confessors to his congregation, and even to old clerical posts (*Ep.* 49). But the campaign is not yet over. It remains to vilify those confessors who continue in dissent. In Carthage they are embezzlers, rapists, adulterers (*fraudes et stupra et adulteria;* see *De unit.* 20 ff.); from Rome the confessor Nicostratus is denounced as robber and defrauder, absconding with sacred trust funds lodged with the church (*Ep.* 50)—a theme which Cyprian in Carthage proceeds to embroider with zestful alacrity (*Ep.* 52). This is a church which places the highest premium on confessor and martyr—it is imperative to cancel the claims for respect and to desecrate the image of those confessors who continue to be disloyal. There is point in revealing that letters to which confessors, as Novatianists, had given their endorsing signatures had been contrived by deception and fraud (*Ep.* 49): the documents could not command, therefore, the authority and deference that would normally be given to them (cf. *Ep.* 55.5.1 f.). Even a few years hence Cyprian can still feel heatedly angered, and challenged, by the taunts of a boastful and disrespectful confessor (*Ep.* 66).

But Rome and Carthage have more in common than their respect for and difficulties with their confessors.

The Roman deacon and confessor Nicostratus came across to Carthage as an emissary of Novatian (*Ep.* 51): the Carthaginian presbyter Novatus went across to Rome as an emissary of Felicissimus (*Epp.* 43 and 52). Both were looking for support and recognition for their cause in their sister church—just as Cyprian had been seeking with his *Epp.* 20, 27, and 35 which he addressed to Rome and which reached there with no fewer than twenty-two supporting documents altogether attached. Rome and Carthage were close, a matter of a few days' sail apart. And it is well to remember that the ecclesiastical traffic between the two great cities did not go only one way. Privatus, of Numidian Lambaesis, a veteran heretic, sent a scout over to Rome endeavouring to win recognition from the Roman presbyters and deacons, and anticipating the note of warning which Cyprian sent to Rome (*Ep.* 36.4). But equally Novatian sent two parties of delegates over to Carthage (*Epp.* 44, 50), seeking to win recognition from the African bishops, the second echelon anticipating one of two notes of warning which Cornelius sent to Carthage (*Epp.* 50, 52). The African Council sent two African bishops as their delegates to Rome to inquire into the circumstances of Cornelius' election (*Epp.* 44, 45, 48). But equally Cornelius appears to have sent two Italian bishops over to Carthage to protest at this move and to pressure for his own recognition as bishop (*Epp.* 44, 45, 48). Cyprian's letters and supporting documents, sent to Rome in order to win support and to clear his reputation there (*Epp.* 20, 27, 35), are matched by similar letters from Cornelius and from Novatian sent to Carthage in order to win support and to clear reputations there (see *Epp.* 44, 45, 49.1.3); Novatian's was a hefty despatch (*in librum missum, Ep.* 45.2.1), with supporting documents signed by confessors (*Ep.* 49.1.4).

In churches enjoying such close contact there was obvious need to inform each other on matters of gravity (cf. *Ep.* 36.4.1; *magna et metuenda, Ep.* 59.9.1), to document fully controversial decisions taken locally for the information—and persuasion—of the other party, and to work towards common policies on common problems.

The African Council of 251 took the grave step of solemnly excommunicating Felicissimus and his five Carthaginian presbyters (including Novatus who was in Rome). A formally signed conciliar document recording opinions expressed and decisions taken was sent over for dissemination in Rome (*Ep.* 45.4). The church there was expected to follow suit—which it did, eventually (*Ep.* 59.1.1). For his part in Rome Cornelius, at a diocesan synod of presbyters (strengthened by five visiting bishops), agreed on a policy to reinstate fully—and exceptionally—the

Novatianizing Roman confessors, without penance and without loss of clerical status: a document listing fully the individual views expressed by each member of that synod—over fifty *sententiae*—and the decisions taken was solemnly drawn up and sent to Carthage (*Ep.* 49.2.1). Cyprian was persuaded: he promptly wrote to the confessor Maximus now addressing him as presbyter (*Ep.* 54), a title which he had studiously avoided in his previous letter to him (*Ep.* 46).

But whilst commonly agreed policies were desirable (*Ep.* 30 from Rome provided welcome, and eagerly distributed [*Ep.* 32], support for his interim *forma*), Cyprian and his Council did not hesitate to deliberate and resolve by themselves on stormy and controversial issues in the face of their own acute domestic disorder. The African Council in 251 met ahead of its Italian counterpart (the Italian sessions being delayed by dispute and schism in Rome?). But Cyprian then proceeds, through the skills of diplomacy, to work towards unanimity and consent overseas for the policies they have themselves adopted at home—as he perceived that bishops should (*Ep.* 48.4.2). The decisions of the African Council were conveyed to Rome; and the policy arrived at in Rome agreed (*Ep.* 55.6.2). Cyprian had carried out the order of procedure he had enunciated nearly a year before in *Ep.* 20.3.2 (to Rome): restoration of peace, return to his own diocese, convening of an African Council of bishops, consultation with other churches in the interests of unity, and settlement on the rules and regulations (*disponere singula vel reformare*). And so it was to continue. The major decision to readmit to communion *all* genuinely repentant lapsed who were still loyally performing penance was taken by the African Council (probably) two years later (253) and it was made in the light of local circumstances (*Ep.* 57). The Roman church was certainly informed of this important change, but the decision was theirs to follow this compassionate course or not (*quod credimus vobis quoque paternae misericordiae contemplatione placiturum, Ep.* 57.5.1), which they eventually did (*Ep.* 68.5.1).[20] This structure of locally reached decisions (with the concomitant expectation of approval and agreement from abroad), when combined with the profound importance Cyprian placed on the concord of bishops for

Church unity, sets the scene for the "baptismal dispute" that is to emerge later in the decade.[21]

CHRONOLOGY OF THE LETTERS

The dating of each letter—and when possible a hazard at the actual calendar date—is discussed under the rubric "date and circumstances" in the notes to the individual letters. There is no need to repeat here, therefore, the detailed arguments which are there set out. But if the letters are being read continuously, then the following reading-order is recommended so as to get something approaching a coherent unfolding of events, in so far as the letters reveal them, from about August 250 down to high summer of the following year, 251.

First, *Ep.* 28 (to the Roman confessors), a companion piece of *Ep.* 27 (to the Roman clergy), written round about August/September of 250. Then, *Ep.* 33 (to an anonymous group of Carthaginian lapsed), followed by the pair *Ep.* 29 (to the Carthaginian clergy, enclosing a copy of *Ep.* 33) and *Ep.* 35 (to the Roman clergy, also enclosing a copy of *Ep.* 33 and, in all probability, of *Ep.* 29 as well). Then, at last, Cyprian receives his first direct replies from Rome, *Ep.* 30 (from the Roman clergy) and *Ep.* 31 (from the Roman confessors); he promptly sends copies of these two letters to his clergy in Carthage with the covering note, *Ep.* 32. Then arrives *Ep.* 36 from the Roman clergy (in reply to his *Ep.* 35, which has crossed with their *Ep.* 30). Next, there follows a run of letters *Ep.* 37 through to *Ep.* 40: *Ep.* 37, on internal evidence, appears dated to very early 251; it is to the Roman confessors and announces the arrival of Celerinus. *Ep.* 38 announces the appointment of Aurelius as lector, *Ep.* 39 that of Celerinus (after Aurelius), and *Ep.* 40, the appointment of Numidicus to the Carthaginian presbyterate. *Ep.* 34 (to the Carthaginian clergy) finds its place here in this general context of reorganization and attempts at tougher discipline shortly before Cyprian's "ecclesiastical commission" (which includes the Numidicus of *Ep.* 40) is empowered in *Ep.* 41 to excommuni-

cate the obstinately undisciplined followers of Felicissimus: *Ep.*
42 lists those so excommunicated. Then comes *Ep.* 43; it is
written to the Carthaginian flock on these turbulent events
shortly before Easter (March 23), 251. Thereafter Cyprian's
correspondence with Carthage ceases (and with that, much of
our detailed knowledge of the workings of the Carthaginian
church), for he returns to Carthage not too long after Easter. It
is not until the eve of his death some seven and a half years later
that we are to read another—and this time final—letter addressed by Cyprian to his Carthaginian flock (*Ep.* 81).

Our sights, accordingly, now turn away from Carthage
over to Rome and the dispute over the episcopal elections there
(Cornelius *versus* Novatian) which had broken out in the course
of March 251. *Epp.* 44, 45 and 48 successively disclose layers
hesitation, doubt, and delay which the African bishops experienced before the majority of them eventually recognized Cornelius as rightfully elected. *Ep.* 46 is addressed to the Roman
confessors, whilst they still favoured the side of Novatian, with
Ep. 47 as its accompanying note to Cornelius. These two should
be read along with *Ep.* 45, with which they are contemporaneous. Finally there come *Epp.* 50, 49 (both from Cornelius) and
Ep. 53 (from the Roman confessors). Cornelius and the confessors have now happily settled their differences. Cyprian's
prompt replies are respectively *Epp.* 52, 51 and 54.

By this time the African Council has been in session in
Carthage, Cyprian's tractates *De lapsis* and *De unitate* have been
publicly read and are in circulation,[22] and, as likely as not, the
Italian Council of 251 has been meeting, or is about to meet. The
second half of 251 will have not long started. In other words, we
leave off the correspondence shortly after the news of Decius'
death will have percolated as far as most corners of the Roman
world. Indeed, all the letters in this volume are connected either
with immediate consequences of Decius' orders for general sacrifice, or indirectly, with events that were themselves in some
way triggered off by those consequences (the schisms in Carthage and in Rome). But the shadow cast by Decius over Church
affairs is to stretch much further than just the short length of
the contents of this volume.

In summary, therefore, read, in order, *Ep.* 28; *Ep.* 33; *Epp.* 35

and 29; *Epp.* 30, 31, 32; *Ep.* 36; *Epp.* 37 to 40; *Ep.* 34; *Epp.* 41 and 42; *Ep.* 43; *Ep.* 44; *Epp.* 45, 46, 47; *Ep.* 48; *Epp.* 50, 49, 53; *Epp.* 52, 51, 54.

THE TRANSLATION

A word on the type of translation provided. I have maintained my conscious rejection of the allures of producing a racier and more interpretative version, electing to struggle on with my endeavors to keep as close as I can reasonably manage to Cyprian's Latin. I am only too aware that I am not producing Cyprian sentiments in the way I might have ordered and couched them myself under the circumstances—to do so is to use an intrusive method which removes the reader into a world alien from Cyprian's own. In the rendering, therefore, Cyprian still comes heavy with epithets, ponderous with adverbs, weighted with synonyms, and laden with abstractions in a way which is foreign to modern English style. But whatever the turgidity and tedium, that must be so. There must be redundance and tautology, rhetorical and even pompous vagueness, and sometimes outright obscurity, if Cyprian is to be savored in anything like the manner in which he—and his contemporaries—thought and wrote.

I translate the standard text, that of Hartel (*Corpus scriptorum ecclesiasticorum latinorum* 3.2, 1871; there is a Johnson reprint, 1965); but where I am doubtful of his version I do say so, even very occasionally feeling obliged in the interests of forestalling misunderstanding to translate an alternative reading. The notes make such rare passages quite clear. Comment on manuscript readings generally I have deliberately reduced to a scant minimum, remaining, as I have chosen to be, dependent on Hartel's (notoriously unreliable) witness to his (sometimes injudicious) selection of manuscripts. A new text of *Epp.* 30, 31, and 36 has appeared in *Corpus Christianorum (series latina)* vol. 4, 1972, edited by G. F. Diercks. I am particularly grateful to Dr. Diercks for sending to me collations he has made from the manuscripts in preparation for his new edition of the Letters (for *Corpus Christianorum*).

*   *   *

I owe thanks to many people—to the library staff of the University of Melbourne for patiently processing many requests for interlibrary loans and microfilms; to my colleagues for their amiable tolerance of a topic so far removed from interests of their own; to the University of Melbourne Arts Faculty Research Development Fund and to the Australian Research Grants Committee for financial support towards this project; to the Institute for Advanced Study, Princeton, for the generous facilities and wonderfully undemanding hospitality which made possible the concentrated work needed for completing this volume; to my family, who stubbornly but forebearingly believe I don't ever finish anything; and to my wife who still continued politely to inquire about my work when all others had wisely ceased to do so and who good-naturedly checked typescript and proofs, and cheerfully helped prepare indexes amidst the daily upheavals of family life.

LETTER 28

Cyprian sends greetings to his dearly beloved brothers, the presbyters Moyses and Maximus and the other confessors.[1]

1.1 For some time,[2] my most brave and blessed brothers, I have known by hearsay[3] of the glory of your faith and courage.[4] I have been filled with great joy and jubilation by the thought that the special favour of our Lord has prepared you, through your confession of His name, for your crown. You have been the front-line troops, the leaders into the battlefield of our day. It was you who advanced the standards of God's army. It was you who inaugurated, by your own deeds of courage, the spiritual hostilities which God has willed should now be waged. It was you who shattered the enemy's first offensives at the outbreak of war,[5] being steadfast in your strength and unshakeable in your stand. Thus resulted a fortunate beginning to the fight; thus originated the auspices of victory.

1.2 It has so happened that here as a consequence of the tortures martyrs are being brought to their fulfilment.[6] But he who has been in the vanguard of the fray and has become a model in valour for his brothers, must enjoy a share with the martyrs in their honour. You have handed over to us here the crowns which your hands have wreathed, you have passed on to your brethren here the saving cup which your lips tasted first in pledge.[7]

2.1 Not only is the glory of being the first to confess, not only are the auspices of victorious warfare due to you. You have upheld as well the Church's discipline;[8] this we perceived clearly from your vigorous letter which you recently sent to your colleagues who are united with you in confession of the Lord.[9] With anxious care you urged that the sacred precepts of the Gospel and the life-giving ordinances once entrusted to us[10]

23

should be followed with courageous and unswerving obedience.

This adds enhanced eminence to your glory; you have a further and a second claim, along with your confession, for obtaining the favour of God. For you are taking a steadfast stand, also, in this present battle which is attempting to dislodge the Gospel; with the strength of your faith you are repulsing the attacks of those who, with impious hands, seek to overthrow the precepts of the Lord. Earlier you gave the initiative in actions of bravery; now you give the lessons in right conduct.

2.2 After the resurrection, when our Lord was sending forth the Apostles, He instructed them with these words: *All power has been given me in heaven and on earth. Go, therefore, and teach all nations, baptizing them in the name of the Father and of the Son and of the Holy Spirit, teaching them to observe all things, whatsoever I have commanded you.* And the apostle John, mindful of this instruction, later asserts in his epistle: *In this we realize that we know Him, if we keep His commandments. Whoever says that he knows Him and does not observe His precepts, is a liar and the truth is not in him.*[11]

2.3 These are the commandments which you encourage others to keep; these divine and heavenly precepts you observe yourselves.[12] Indeed, to be a confessor of the Lord, to be a martyr of Christ is this: to preserve one's profession of faith under every circumstance with an unblemished and an unshakeable constancy—it is not, having become a martyr through the Lord, to endeavour to destroy the commandments of the Lord. To use against Him the graces which He has granted you, to become in a sense a rebel by means of the weapons which you have received from Him—this is to be willing to make confession of Christ and with the same breath to deny the gospel of Christ.[13]

2.4 And so, my brothers, you cause me to be filled with joy through your great fortitude and faith. I do indeed congratulate[14] the martyrs honoured here for their glorious might, but no less do I congratulate you as well for the crown which is also your due for upholding the discipline of the Lord.

The Lord has bestowed His favours with a generosity that takes many forms; He has distributed with a richness of variety spiritual glories and distinctions amongst His loyal soldiers. In your honours even we are partners;[15] your glory we reckon as our glory. Such happiness has blessed our times that we have the good fortune to see in our day servants of God tested and soldiers of Christ crowned.[16]

I wish that you, my most brave and blessed brothers, may ever fare well and be mindful of us.

LETTER 29

Cyprian sends greetings to the presbyters and deacons, his brothers.[1]

1.1 In order to keep you fully informed, my dearly beloved brothers, I am sending to you a copy of two letters, one written to me, the other my reply to it;[2] and I trust that what I have said in reply meets with your approval.

I ought to inform you by this letter of mine of another matter as well.

For urgent reasons I have written a letter to the clergy in Rome.[3] And since it was proper that I send my letter by the hands of clerics,[4] and knowing as I do that very many of our own clerics are absent[5] and that the few who are there in Carthage are scarcely enough to cope with the daily services of the church,[6] it proved necessary to appoint some new clerics who could be sent.

1.2 You should know, therefore, that I have made Saturus a reader and Optatus, the confessor, a subdeacon.[7] Some time ago[8] we all agreed together to place both of them in a rank next to the clergy.[9] In the case of Saturus, we gave him the reading several times on Easter day;[10] and as for Optatus, when we were recently putting under careful examination readers for the teacher-presbyters[11] we appointed him one of the readers for the teachers of catechumens.[12] We have therefore tested whether they possessed all the qualities which ought to be present in those being prepared for clerical rank.

I have, accordingly, in your absence, initiated on my own no new venture, but under pressure of circumstances I have advanced a process which was begun some time ago with the general agreement of us all.[13]

I wish that you, dearly beloved brothers, may ever fare well and be mindful of us. Send my greetings to all of our brothers. Farewell.

LETTER 30

The presbyters and deacons dwelling in Rome send greetings to pope Cyprian.[1]

1.1 A conscience, aware of its own right conduct and confident in the might of the Gospel teachings,[2] is usually satisfied to have God alone as its judge,[3] having become its own true witness to its fidelity to the decrees of heaven; it will neither seek the applause nor dread the censure of another. Nevertheless, they deserve to be praised twice over who, aware though they are that they need submit their conscience to the judgment of God alone,[4] yet desire that their actions should win, in addition, the approval of their own brothers as well.

1.2 And so it occasions us no wonder, Cyprian our brother, that this is your present course of action. With your customary modesty[5] and innate zeal you have wished that we should appear not so much as judges but as partners in your counsels: by giving our approval to your accomplishments we can gain applause along with you and by giving our support to your excellent counsels we can become fellow beneficiaries of them. For men will conclude[6] that we have all laboured in concert together since they will find that we are all united in complete harmony on questions of ecclesiastical censure and discipline.[7]

2.1 There can be nothing more fitting during time of peace, nothing more essential during the hostilities of persecution than adherence to the just severity of the gospel discipline. Should anybody relax this vigilance, it is inevitable that he be ever doomed to wander without any fixed course in his affairs, tossed in all directions before the changing and fickle tempests of his vicissitudes; with the helm of good counsel wrested from his hands, he will dash the vessel which bears the safety of the Church against the rocks. It is evident, therefore, that the only way to ensure that safety of the Church is to repel those who move against her like so many hostile waves and to hold securely to the ever-guarded rule of her discipline like some rudder of safety in a storm.[8]

2.2 This is no counsel of action that has only just now been devised by us, nor are these means of defence against our enemies but hasty and recent innovations for us. Rather, in them we are being true, as we read, to our ancient strictness, our ancient faith, our ancient discipline. For the Apostle would not have bestowed such praises on us when he said: *for your faith is being proclaimed throughout the world,* unless even by that time the present strength of our faith had already taken its roots in those days.[9] In truth, not to have lived up to such praise and renown would be a crime of the greatest magnitude: it is less disgraceful never to have risen to the proclamation of one's praises than to have fallen down from such a pinnacle of praise; it is less criminal not to have been honoured with favourable testimony than to have forfeited the honour of those favourable testimonies; it is less shameful[10] to have remained without fame, without praise, without judgment of one's virtues than to have lost one's legacy of faith and the praises once one's own.[11] For it is true that those things once proclaimed in order to confer renown upon another, unless upheld by careful and anxious effort, can be transformed to that person's prejudice, as grounds for grievous reproach.

3.1 That we have sound grounds for what we are saying, our earlier letter has demonstrated.[12] In it we laid out before you all very clearly our views in opposition to those who had betrayed their own loss of faith by unlawfully acknowledging to be their own sacrilegious certificates.[13] They may have thought that by this action they would elude the devil's ensnaring nets; but they were held fast, no less than if they had approached the sacrilegious altars, by that very act of witnessing to him. And we showed our opposition as well to those who had admitted to the ownership of such certificates,[14] although they had not been personally present when they were being drawn up, for they had certainly made themselves present by giving instructions that it be so written down. He is not exempt from the crime who has bidden it to be committed; he is not innocent of crime who gives his consent that the record of that crime (which admittedly he did not commit) can be publicly read out as being his.[15]

We have only to realize that the essence of the whole sacred mystery of our faith is contained in confessing the name of Christ.[16] It follows, therefore, that he who resorts to evasive stratagems in order to excuse himself has denied that faith and he who wishes to appear to have fulfilled edicts or laws promulgated contrary to the Gospel,[17] has indeed already obeyed them by the very act of wishing to give the appearance of obeying them.

3.2 What is more, we demonstrated[18] our faith, and our agreement, in opposition also to those who had defiled their own hands and lips with unlawful sacrifices, being defiled already in their own consciences, the source of the contagion which in fact defiled their hands and their lips.

3.3 God forbid that the Roman Church may ever release her hold on her old strictness by irreligious laxity; may she never let the sinews of her severity grow slack, thereby overthrowing the grandeur of her faith. Otherwise, whilst our brothers not only continue to lie where they have fallen but are even now falling to their ruin,[19] should we apply too hasty a remedy, granting them admittance to communion,[20] we are certain to provide treatment which will bring no benefit; rather, through mistaken compassion, we will impose fresh wounds upon the old wounds of their offence, with the effect both of robbing the poor wretches of repentance and of bringing them to an even greater downfall.

How is it possible that this medicine of complaisance will work, if even the doctor himself, cutting short repentance, looks with complaisant eye upon those who are dangerously ill,[21] merely concealing their wounds and not allowing the necessary remedy of time to close the scars over them? This is not to cure, but to speak the honest truth, to kill.

4. Moreover, you should have a letter from the confessors.[22] They are still here confined in prison thanks to their noble confession; in the conflict for the Gospel's sake they have indeed already received their glorious crown for the faith they have displayed in their confession.[23] This letter of theirs is in harmony with ours. They, too, advocate the strictness of the Gospel discipline; they drive away the unlawful petitions which are shaming the Church, asserting that if they readily agreed to this[24] they might not readily repair the breaches made in the Gospel discipline. And further, they point out, it is especially fitting that, above all others, they should preserve their honour untarnished by upholding the might of the Gospel teachings.[25] For the sake of that Gospel they have surrendered themselves to raving madmen to be mangled and butchered. They would rightly have forfeited their honoured rank of martyr if on the occasion of their martyrdom they had chosen to be betrayers of the Gospel. A person who, possessing something, fails to guard that possession at the very source from which he derives his possession but instead abuses that source of his possession, loses what he once possessed.[26]

5.1 And at this point it is our duty to pay you, a duty we happily render, the greatest and most abundant of thanks. By your letter[27] the darkness of their prison you have filled with light; you have visited them by the way through which you could gain entry; their hearts, stalwart in their faith and in their confession, you have refreshed by the comforting words of your letter; their triumphs you have lauded with fitting praises and you have thus enflamed them with even more ardent yearning for heavenly glory; you have driven onwards men already straining at the task; by the strength of your exhortation you have given fresh heart to those who we believe and pray will one day be victorious.

It is true that all of this may seem to depend on the faith of those who confess and on the favour of God;[28] nevertheless, as a result of your letter, they would seem to have become in some measure your debtors in their martyrdom.

5.2 But we must revert to that point in our discourse from which we seem to have digressed.

You will find attached a copy of the letter which we have also sent to Sicily.[29]

In our case it is even more imperative that we defer this question, for, since the death of Fabian of most illustrious memory,[30] owing to the difficulties of our present times and circumstances we have not had a bishop appointed who could regulate all these matters and who could, by his authority and counsel, deal with the question of those who have lapsed.

5.3 However, on this major issue we are indeed in agreement with the opinion which you yourself have argued, namely, that we must wait first, until the Church has peace,[31] and then, after bishops, presbyters, deacons, confessors and the laity who have remained steadfast[32] have exchanged views in conference together, we can deal with the question of the lapsed.

For it appears to us to be excessively invidious and oppressive to examine without the advice of many people the question of an offence which appears to have been committed by many people and not to pronounce together a united verdict[33] when it is notorious that the occurrence of a sin of such gravity has been widespread, amongst many people. Indeed it is impossible for a decree to be firm unless it shall appear to have received the consent of the great majority.

5.4 You have only to look around at the devastation which affects almost the entire globe; everywhere lie the ruins and the debris of the overthrown.[34] It is apparent that the sin is spread far and wide; the counsel we should seek must be equally extensive. The cure ought not to be smaller than the wound, the remedies fewer than the number of deaths. Those who have crashed[35] did so because they were blindly reckless and wildly impulsive; correspondingly, those who are striving to settle this problem must do so with the utmost restraint and prudence. If not, action taken otherwise than it should be may be judged by everyone as not being binding.

6.1 And so it is with one and the same purpose, with the same entreaties and tears that we should all petition and beg God in His majesty to give peace to the Church's name,[36] both we who appear so far to have escaped the calamities of these times of ours and those who appear to have plunged into these present-day disasters.

By our mutual prayers let us in turn bring to each other comfort and protection and fighting strength.

6.2 For the fallen let us pray that they may stand again, for those who still stand let us pray that they may not be assailed until they fall, for those who are reported to have lapsed let us pray that they may acknowledge the magnitude of their sin and realize that it is no instantaneous and over-hasty treatment that they need. Let us pray that the effects of pardon may follow upon the repentance of the fallen,[37] that realizing their own wickedness they may be prepared to show us patience for a time,[38] that whilst the Church is still being tossed on the waves they may refrain from rocking her still further. If not, they may appear themselves to enkindle a persecution within our own ranks and add rebellious behaviour to the already lengthy tally of their wicked deeds.

6.3 Modesty is a virtue especially fitting for those whose sins reveal a damnable immodesty of attitude. By all means let them beat at the doors but not so as to batter them down; let them approach the threshold of the Church, but not bound across it.[39] Let them keep watch at the gates of the heavenly encampment but be armed with that sense of humility by which they acknowledge that they have been deserters. Let them take up again the trumpet of their prayers—but not sound forth a battle-call. They are to be armed indeed, with the weapons of humility, and to take up again the shield of faith which by their denial they had abandoned out of fear of death. But armed as they now are, they must realize that they have been given arms against the devil, their foe, not against the Church, who mourns over their fall. They will draw much profit from a request that is modest, from respectful entreaty, from needful humility, from patience that is not inactive.[40] As the envoys for their grief they should send forth tears, their advocates should be sighs drawn from the depths of their hearts, providing proof of the sorrow and the shame that they feel for the sin they have committed.

7.1 But the truth is that if they do indeed recoil in horror at the enormity of their disgraceful conduct, if they are treating with a genuinely healing hand the far recesses of their deep-set wound and the mortal injury to their heart and conscience, they would blush even to make their request—save for the fact that it is in turn more perilous still and shameful not to have requested the aid of reconciliation. But in any case all this must be done within the sacred bounds and regulations of this kind of petition,[41] after a fitting period of time;[42] their petition should be humble, their entreaty submissive. He who is being petitioned ought to be won over, not antagonized: one ought to be heedful of God's mercy but equally one ought to be heedful of God's strict justice. It is indeed written: *I have forgiven you all your debts, for you have asked me to;* but it is also written: *Whoever has denied me before men, I will deny him before my Father and His angels.*[43]

7.2 God indeed is forgiving, but He also enforces, and zealously enforces, His own commandments. He invites to the feast, but the man who does not have a wedding garment He takes by hand and foot[44] and casts out beyond the assembly of the saints.[45] He has prepared heaven, but then He has also prepared hell, He has prepared places of refreshment,[46] but then He has also prepared places of everlasting torment; He has prepared the light that none can approach, but then He has also prepared the immense and everlasting gloom of endless night.

8. Our endeavour has been here in these matters to keep to a moderate and balanced course. We have long thought that we should make no new changes until our bishop is appointed—and we are many who are so minded, including certain bishops who live in our neighbourhood and others who have come here, being driven out by the flames of persecution from other, far distant, provinces.[47]

Rather, we have thought that we should show restrained moderation in our treatment of the lapsed. Therefore, in the meantime, as we wait until God grants us a bishop, the cases of those who can be delayed and deferred are to be held in abeyance. But in the case of those whose death is imminent and who cannot, therefore, be deferred, if they have done penance and frequently declared their detestation for their actions, if by their tears, their sighs, their sobbing they have revealed the signs of a contrite and truly penitent heart,[48] when there no longer remains, so far as man can tell, any hope of life, then and only then, with all due care and caution, should we bring them comfort.[49] God Himself knows how He should treat such cases and balance the scales of His justice;[50] but, for us, we must strive with anxious care to avoid that, on the one hand, wicked men should praise us for over-ready compliance, and that, on the other hand, the genuinely repentant should accuse us of harshness and cruelty.

We wish that you, most blessed and glorious pope,[51] may ever fare well in the Lord and be mindful of us.

LETTER 31

Moyses and Maximus, presbyters, along with Nicostratus, Rufinus and their fellow confessors send greetings to pope Cyprian.[1]

1.1 We have been plunged, dear brother, into a great many different forms of grief by the present devastation that has been suffered by so many almost the whole world over.[2] But what has brought us special consolation has been the arrival of your letter.[3] From it we have derived encouragement, and we have received comfort for the distress in our grieving hearts. We are now able to appreciate that God in His grace and providence may well have wished to keep us for so long confined in these chains of our prison[4] for the precise purpose that we might be given by this letter of yours instructions and fresh spirit for the fray, and thus be enabled to attain with a more ardent zeal the crown that is destined for us.

1.2 Your letter has dazzled us with light[5]—like clear sky in the midst of a storm, like a much desired calm in the midst of a raging sea, like repose in the midst of labours, like good health in the midst of pain and illness,[6] like bright and radiant light in the midst of pitch darkness. We have drunk it in with such thirsting hearts, we have received it with such famished longing[7] that to our delight we are by it fully fed and satisfied in readiness for our encounter with the enemy.

1.3 The Lord will pay you reward for this kindness of yours, He will render you due return for this great work of charity. For he who has given encouragement is no less deserving of being rewarded with a crown than he who has actually suffered; he who has acted is no more deserving of praise than he who has given instructions how to act; he who has provided advice is to be held in no less honour than he who has followed that advice.[8] But there is this difference: sometimes greater glory may overflow on to the teacher who has given instruction than on to the person who has offered himself as a ready pupil. For in the case of the latter, he may possibly not have known to do what he has done, unless the other had given him tuition.

2.1 And so, Cyprian, dear brother—we will say it again—we have experienced great joy, great consolation and great comfort, especially in that, with glorious and fitting words of praise, you have described, in the case of martyrs, their glorious—death I was about to say, but I mean deathlessness.[9] For their manner of leaving life deserved to have been celebrated in such language as yours, so that the events recounted might be told in words which matched the quality of their deeds. And so, as a result of your letter, we have watched the glorious triumphal processions of the martyrs; with our own eyes, as it were, we have escorted them on their journey to heaven, and we have gazed on them as they stand amidst the angels and the dominations and the powers of heaven.

2.2 Indeed, with our own ears, we might say, we have even heard the Lord giving before His Father that testimony He promised to them He would render.[10] It is this, then, which brings to our hearts daily encouragement and enkindles within us the ardour to reach such heights of honour.

3. What, we ask, could, through God's favour, befall any man which might bring him greater glory or greater bliss than this: in the very midst of his executioners, undaunted, to confess the Lord God; in the midst of the varied and refined instruments of torture, employed, in their savagery, by the powers of this world, even with body racked, mangled and butchered, to con-

fess Christ the Son of God with breath, though failing, yet free; to have left the world behind and to have journeyed to heaven; to have forsaken men and to stand among the angels; to have burst through all the shackles of this world and to take his stand, now free, in the sight of God; without a moment's delay to gain the kingdom of heaven;[11] to have become, by confessing the name of Christ, a partner with Christ in His passion; to have become, by God's favour, a judge of his own judge;[12] from the battle of confessing His name to have carried off an unsullied conscience; to have refused to comply with human and sacrilegious laws contrary to faith; with public profession to have borne witness to the truth; to have conquered, by dying, that very death which is dreaded by all; to have gained through death itself undying life; butchered and racked by every instrument of savagery, to have overcome the tortures through those very same tortures; to have wrestled by strength of spirit against all the agonies of his lacerated body; to have looked without horror upon his own blood streaming forth; to have learned to love his own tortures second only to his faith;[13] to consider as loss of life the very continuance of life?

4.1 To this battle the Lord rouses us with the trumpet call of His Gospel, in these words: *He who loves his father or his mother more than Me is not worthy of Me; and he who loves his own life more than Me is not worthy of Me; and he who does not take up his cross and follow Me, is not worthy of Me.*[14] Again: *Blessed are they who have suffered persecution for justice' sake, for theirs is the kingdom of heaven. Blessed are you when they have persecuted you and reviled you. Rejoice and be glad. For so also did they persecute the prophets who were before you.*[15] Also: *For you will stand before kings and governors, and brother will deliver up brother to death and father son; and he who has persevered right to the end will be saved.*[16]

4.2 And: *To the victor I will grant a seat upon my throne just as I too am victorious and have a seat upon the throne of my father.*[17] The Apostle also says: *Who will separate us from the love of Christ? Will trials or tribulations or persecution or hunger or nakedness or peril or the sword? As it is written: For your sake we are killed all day long; we are reckoned as sheep for the slaughter. But in all these things we are victorious through Him who has loved us.*[18]

5.1 When we read and compare these and similar passages in the Gospel and feel firebrands, as it were, set beneath us by these words of God, enflaming our faith, far from cowering back from the enemies of truth we go out and challenge them to battle. And this very act of yielding no ground to the foes of God means that we have already vanquished them, and that we have overwhelmed their impious laws against the truth.

And if we have not as yet shed our blood (but we have been ready to shed it), no-one should count as an act of clemency this delay and postponement we endure: it obstructs our progress, it impedes our glory, it postpones heaven, it thwarts the glorious sight of God. In a struggle of this nature, in a battle such as this where faith is the contestant, not to postpone martyrs by delay is true clemency.[19]

5.2 And so, dearest Cyprian, petition the Lord that each day more and more He may by His grace equip and adorn each of us more richly and more readily with armour, that He may strengthen and invigorate us with His might and power. Thus, like the perfect commander may He at long last lead forth His soldiers whom He has been training and testing, hitherto, inside the camp of our prison, onto the field for our destined battle. May He present to us heavenly arms, those weapons which know no defeat, the breastplate of justice which can never be shattered, the shield of faith which cannot be pierced, [the helmet of salvation, which cannot be broken], the sword of the spirit which is never injured.[20] Who is there more fitting to whom we ought to entrust the task of making this petition than a bishop who is covered in such glory? Those destined to be sacrificial victims thus now make their petition for help of such a high-priest.[21]

6.1 But we have further reason for rejoicing, and it is this: you have ever diligently attended to the duties of your office of bishop despite the fact that present circumstances have caused you to be separated for the time being from your brethren. By frequent letters you have given strength to the confessors,[22] you have also supplied urgently-needed funds drawn from the fruits of your own just labours,[23] in all things you have constantly made yourself present, so to speak, amongst your flock; you have never stumbled behind, like some deserter, in any aspect of your duties.[24]

6.2 But there is something else which gives us even more rousing cause for joy: in fact, we cannot fail to mention it and to laud it with all the praises we can voice. We observe that you have fittingly censured and justly reproached those who, failing to remember their own sins and taking advantage of your absence, with importunate and precipitate eagerness have wrested reconciliation from the presbyters;[25] and you have censured equally those who have given away all too freely and readily the sacred body of the Lord, casting their pearls without heed for the Gospel.[26] Whereas, indeed, so grievous a sin—one that has run riot with incredible devastation almost the whole world over—ought only to be dealt with, as you yourself write, with caution and restraint:[27] all the bishops, presbyters, deacons, confessors and faithful laity, too, must be consulted beforehand, as you declare yourself in your letters,[28] so that we can avoid occasioning further and even greater disasters by wishing unseasonably to repair those of the present.[29]

6.3 Indeed, what room will there be left for fear of God if pardon is granted to sinners so readily? Certainly the souls of sinners are to be cherished and nurtured until the right and proper season,[30] they are to be instructed from the scriptures about the gravity of the sin they have committed—in fact it is the gravest sin of all. They should not take heart from the fact that they are so many; rather, they should be restrained by the fact that they are not few. Large and shameless numbers do not usually help to extenuate a fault; rather it is shame, modesty, repentance, obedience,[31] humility, submissiveness; it is waiting for judgment from another on oneself, it is looking for a verdict from another on one's own behaviour.

6.4 This is what confirms genuine repentance; this is what draws a scar over the deep wound; this is what raises up and supports the ruins of the fallen soul; this is what quenches and brings to an end the burning and searing fever of sin.[32] The doctor will not give to the sick what is appropriate for healthy bodies for fear that unseasonable food, instead of mitigating the violence of a raging illness, may rather aggravate it. In other words, the physician must be on his guard lest a malady which could be cured the sooner by fasting and dieting, may be protracted all the longer through impatience and indigestive feeding.

7.1 And so, those hands contaminated by heinous sacrifice must be washed clean by good works, those unfortunate lips, defiled by accursed food, must be purified by expressions of genuine repentance; in the depths of their hearts there must be sown and planted a fresh spirit of faith.[33] We should hear from the penitent frequent sighs, we should see once more faithful tears streaming from their eyes.[34] In this way those very same eyes which have sinfully looked upon the heathen images may by their weeping make satisfaction to God and efface the crimes which they have unlawfully perpetrated.[35]

7.2 In the case of illness the one essential is patience.[36] Those who are ailing must struggle with their suffering; they can hope for recovery if at long last, through endurance, they have surmounted that suffering. You cannot trust a scar which a surgeon has all too hastily drawn together; the healed wound splits open at the slightest mishap unless you apply reliable remedies derived from the slow passing of time. The flame is quickly turned back again into a conflagration unless the entire fire is extinguished down to the very last spark.

Men in this situation can thus rightly appreciate that the very delay is all the more to their advantage; this essential postponement means that the remedies applied to them will be the more reliable.

8.1 Besides, for those who confess Christ, what value will there be in being shut up within the confines of their foul prison, if those who have denied Him, have in no way jeopardized their faith? What will be the value in being bound and encompassed by chains for the name of God, if those who have renounced confession of God, have not been excluded from communion? What will be the value for the imprisoned in laying down their glorious lives, if those who have forsaken their faith are not made to feel the enormity of their own sins and their own vulnerability?

8.2 But if they are excessively impatient, demanding that they be admitted to communion with intolerable speed, then whatever abuse they may cast, it is still of no avail. However outspoken and aggressive their reproaches may be, however quarrelsome and trouble-making, they are powerless against the truth. For it had certainly been within their power to retain their own right to that for which now they are compelled to beg, but the compulsion they brought upon themselves. That faith which might have confessed Christ, might have, likewise, been retained, through Christ, in communion.[37]

We wish that you, our brother,[38] may ever fare well and be mindful of us.

LETTER 32

Cyprian sends greetings to his brothers, the presbyters and deacons.

1.1 I am sending for your information, my dearest brothers, copies of several letters for you to read. They are my letter to the clergy at Rome and their reply to me;[1] also the reply to my letter by Moyses and Maximus, the presbyters, Nicostratus and Rufinus, the deacons, and the other confessors who are in prison with them.[2] With your customary zeal you should make every effort to see that what we have written as well as what they have replied should become known to our brothers.

1.2 And further, you should fully inform on these matters any bishops, my colleagues, or presbyters or deacons from other churches who may be in Carthage with you or who may come later.[3] And if they wish to make copies of these letters and take them back home, they are to be allowed to do so.

What is more, I have given instructions to the lector Satyrus, our brother, to grant permission to any individual who so desires to transcribe copies,[4] my purpose being that in our temporary and provisional settlement of the affairs of our church we may all securely keep in agreement together.[5]

1.3 But as for the remaining questions which will need to be

determined, we will treat them, as I have also indicated by letter
to large numbers of my colleagues,[6] at full length in council
together when, with God's permission, we will be able to convene.

I wish that you, my most dear and most cherished brothers,
may ever fare well. Send my greetings to all the brethren.
Farewell.

LETTER 33[1]

1.1 Our Lord, whose precepts it is our duty to fear and to
follow, regulates the dignity of His bishops and the structure of
His Church,[2] when He speaks as follows in the gospels, addressing Peter: *I say to you that you are Peter, and on this rock I will
build my church, and the gates of hell will not prevail against it. And
to you I will give the keys of the kingdom of heaven and whatsoever
you have bound on earth will be bound also in heaven, and whatsoever you have loosed on earth will be loosed also in heaven.*[3]
From this source flows the appointment of bishops and the
organization of the Church, with bishop succeeding bishop
down through the course of time,[4] so that the Church is founded
upon the bishops and every act of the Church is governed
through these same appointed leaders.[5]

1.2 This establishment has been founded, then, in this way by
law of God. I am, therefore, astounded that certain people have
had the outrageous audacity to take upon themselves to write to
me a letter "in the name of the church",[6] whereas, in fact, the
church has been established upon the bishop, the clergy and all
those who remain faithful.[7] Heaven forbid that the indomitable
might and mercy of the Lord should suffer that a band of the
lapsed should be called "the church". For it is written: *God is not
the God of the dead, but of the living.*[8]

We certainly desire that all should be brought to life, and the
prayer we make with sighing and supplication is that they may
be restored to their former condition. But if some of the fallen
will take upon themselves to be "the church", and if the church

is with them and in them,[9] then it must surely follow that we have to put our request to *them*, asking that they deign to admit *us* into the church.

Instead, they should be mindful of their sin and make satisfaction to God; they should be, accordingly, submissive, peaceable and humble in their conduct; they should not compose letters "in the name of the church", for they are well aware that it is rather they who are writing *to* the church.

2.1 I have, however, received another letter, from certain of the fallen;[10] they act with meekness and humility, in fear and trembling before God. They have never ceased to do glorious and noble works of charity in the churches;[11] and they have never considered the Lord to be in their debt for what they have done, knowing that He has said: *And when you have done all these things, say: we are unprofitable servants, we have done what it was our duty to do.*[12]

With these words in mind they have written to me, notwithstanding the fact that they have received certificates from the martyrs,[13] entreating that the satisfaction they are rendering might itself become acceptable to the Lord[14]; they state that they acknowledge their sin, that they are sincerely repentant, but that they are in no rash and importunate haste to be reconciled; they are waiting until we can be present, asserting that if they receive reconciliation in our presence[15] it will taste all the sweeter to them.

The Lord is our witness to the warm congratulations we make to them: He has vouchsafed to reveal what such servants of this kind deserve of His bounty.[16]

2.2 Having received these letters and having now read a different document which you have written,[17] what I ask is this: that you make your requests specific,[18] and whoever you are who have now sent this letter, that you add to your petition your own names and that you forward the document to me complete with your several names.[19] For it is essential to know first to whom I am to reply. Then I shall write in answer to each of the questions you raise in your letter in so far as the lowliness of our station and mode of conduct allows.[20]

I wish that you, my brothers, may fare well and live quietly

and peaceably in accordance with the discipline of the Lord.[21]
Farewell.

LETTER 34

*Cyprian sends greetings to the presbyters and deacons, his
brothers.*

1. My dearest brothers, you have acted in conformity with
propriety and discipline when you determined, upon the advice
of my colleagues who were present with you,[1] that you should
cease to be in communion with Gaius Didensis, the presbyter,
and his deacon.[2] They have been admitting the lapsed into
communion; they have been offering their oblations.[3] Though
they have frequently been detected in this erroneous and vicious
conduct of theirs and though, as you have written to me, they
have been repeatedly warned by my colleagues to desist,[4] they
have obstinately persisted in their presumptuous and defiant
behaviour.

They have thus deceived some of the brethren from among
our laity,[5] whereas it is our desire to look after their welfare by
every profitable means: we are providing measures for their
salvation not by perverted blandishments but by honest and
faithful dedication, endeavouring to ensure that they appease
God by genuine repentance,[6] by sighs and profound sorrow.
For it is written: *Remember whence you have fallen, and repent.*
And again we are told by holy Scripture: *Thus speaks the Lord:
when you have been converted and sigh, then you will be saved and
you will know where you have been.*[7]

2.1 How are they able to draw sighs and repent when their
sighs and tears are being obstructed by some of the presbyters[8]
who rashly consider they should admit them to communion?[9]
They are ignorant of the words of Scripture: *Those who call you
blessed cause you to err and overthrow the path whereon you walk.*[10]

2.2 It is not to be wondered at that we are making no head-
way at all with our health-giving and true counsels so long as

the progress of the saving truth is being blocked by pernicious allurements and flatteries.[11] The sick and wounded souls of the fallen are suffering the same experience as often befalls also those who are sick and ailing in the flesh: health-giving food and beneficial drink they reject as bitter and loathsome whilst they crave for what seems to be sweet and pleasant at the moment. But what they are doing by their heedlessness and wilfulness is bringing upon themselves death and destruction. They will make no progress towards recovering their health by means of the genuine remedies of the specialist whilst they are still under the seducing spell of deceiving blandishments.[12]

3.1 And so, as I have written to you,[13] you must take action that is in conformity with faith and conducive to salvation. These are the wiser counsels; do not withdraw from them. You should read these same letters also to any of my colleagues who may be present with you or who may come later.[14] In this way we may act in unison and harmony, adhering to the same health-giving measures for healing and curing the wounds of the fallen. Our resolve is to discuss at full length all these issues when, by the Lord's mercy, we can assemble together.

3.2 But in the meantime, if anyone—whether he be presbyter or deacon from our own or from other churches[15]—if anyone should be possessed of such headstrong and outrageous temerity as to admit the lapsed into communion before we have come to our decision, he is to be banished from communion with us; he will have to present the case for his rash conduct in the hearing of us all when, by the Lord's leave, we have assembled together.

4.1 You have also made the request that I write back to you my judgment concerning the subdeacons Philumenus and Fortunatus and the acolyte Favorinus.[16] They withdrew for a time and have now come back.[17]

I do not consider that it is proper for me to give a decision on this question by myself alone; many of the clergy are absent still and have not considered it to be their duty to resume their station even at this late date. We will have to hold an examination and inquiry into each case separately and investigate them at greater length in the presence not only of my colleagues but of the entire congregation as well.[18] This is a matter which may establish a precedent for the future concerning ministers of the church; we must, therefore, exercise mature deliberation in weighing such a question and making a pronouncement upon it.[19]

4.2 In the meantime, it would be best if they merely refrain from taking their monthly allotment.[20] The purpose is not that they should be understood to be stripped of their ecclesiastical ministry but that their case may be deferred completely without prejudice, until we can be present.

I wish that you, dearly beloved brothers, may ever fare well. Give my greetings to all of the brethren. Farewell.

LETTER 35

Cyprian sends greetings to his brothers, the presbyters and deacons dwelling in Rome.

1.1 My dearest brothers, the love we bear each other and good sense alike demand that we keep you completely informed of our affairs here.[1] In this way we can benefit our government of the church by sharing counsel together.

After I wrote to you the letter which I sent by our brothers Saturus the lector and Optatus the subdeacon,[2] a group of the fallen who refuse to do penance and make satisfaction to God had the effrontery to conspire together and write a letter to me. In this they demanded not that reconciliation should be granted to them but rather they laid claim to it as having been already granted, asserting that Paulus had granted reconciliation to everyone.[3] This you will read in their letter, of which I enclose a copy for you.[4]

1.2 I am enclosing at the same time copies of other letters for your information, both of a brief and interim reply of mine to them[5] and of a letter I wrote subsequently to my clergy.[6]

But if their effrontery has still not been held in check whether by letters from me or from you[7] and if they refuse to comply with our saving counsels, we shall act in the way the Lord has commanded in the Gospel.[8]

I wish that you, my dearest brothers, may ever fare well. Farewell.

LETTER 36

The presbyters and deacons dwelling in Rome send greetings to pope Cyprian.[1]

1.1 Twofold, our brother, was the grief and double the distress with which we were stricken and overwhelmed, after we read over your letter which you sent by Fortunatus the subdeacon.[2] For not only are you allowed no rest at all amid all the pressing exigencies of the persecution, but you are obliged as well to brand with censure the outrageous aggression of fallen brethren who have gone so far as to make such perilously rash demands.

1.2 Although the things we mention have heavily distressed our hearts, nonetheless your zeal and the strictness which you have applied according to the principles of the gospel discipline bring alleviation to the heavy burden of our grief. For rightly are you holding in check the perversity of certain people[3] and by your exhortations to penance you are indicating to them the way that leads to lawful salvation. Indeed, we are truly amazed that they have been prepared to be so precipitate as not so much to ask for reconciliation for themselves but rather to lay claim to it, indeed to assert that they actually possess it already in heaven[4]—and this, so insistently, at so premature and unseasonable a time, concerning so vast and enormous a sin and crime.

1.3 If they do possess it, why ask for what they have? But if the very fact that they ask is proof that they do not possess it, why do they not wait for the judgment of those from whom they considered they ought to ask for reconciliation (which, without a doubt, they do not possess)? Now, if they do believe that they possess from another source a special right to be admitted to communion,[5] they should endeavour to examine that claim in the light of the gospel; if there is no disharmony with the gospel law, then indeed it should prevail and stand confirmed. But how will it be possible for a decree, issued manifestly contrary to the truth of the gospel, to confer admittance to communion in accordance with the gospel? Now it is true that in every case such special claims are designed to gain privileged access to pardon, but only on the condition that there is no disagreement with the person with whom the penitent is seeking union. But if there is disagreement with the person with whom he is seeking union, it must follow inevitably that he forfeits his pardon and his privileged access to union.[6]

2.1 Accordingly, they should consider carefully what it is they are trying to achieve in this matter. For if they are saying that the gospel has laid down one decree but that the martyrs have laid down another, then, by setting the martyrs in collision with the gospel, they will be in serious danger on two counts. On the one hand, manifestly, the dignity of the gospel will already be lying prostrate and shattered if it has been possible for it to be overridden by an upstart decree that comes from another source. And on the other hand, the crown of glory for their confession will obviously have been taken away from the martyrs' heads if it is discovered that they did not gain it in preserving that gospel which enables men to become martyrs;[7] hence it is only right that the person least appropriate for issuing any decree that is contrary to the gospel is the one who is striving to gain the name of martyr through the gospel.[8]

2.2 And there is a further matter we would like to know. It would appear that martyrs become martyrs with this precise purpose in view, that by refusing to sacrifice they may preserve their peace with the church even at the expense of shedding their own blood; what they are anxious to avoid is that they may be overcome by the pain of torture and thus may lose their salvation in losing that peace. Now if this is the case, how is it that they reckon that this salvation, which they thought they would not themselves possess if they had offered sacrifice, should be granted to those who are said to have offered sacrifice, whereas, in fact, they ought to uphold the same law in the case of others which in their own case they clearly imposed upon themselves previously?

2.3 In this affair we perceive that the very action which the martyrs thought they were taking for their own advantage has brought results to their disadvantage.[9]

For if the martyrs thought that peace should be granted to the fallen, why did they not grant it themselves? Why did the martyrs judge that their cases should be sent on to the bishop, as they declare themselves?[10] If a man gives orders for something to be done, he assuredly has the ability to do himself what he orders to be done.

But, in truth, our understanding is—indeed the facts themselves shout out and declare it—that the most holy martyrs[11] considered it right that they should steer a middle course, preserving both modesty and truth.[12] Being hard pressed by large numbers, they considered that they should take measures to protect their own humility; they sent the fallen on to the bishop, thus avoiding being troubled further themselves. And they also declined themselves to admit them into communion, thereby judging that the purity of the gospel law should be preserved unimpaired.

3.1 But do you, our brother, persist in the exercise of your charity, endeavouring to hold restrained the tempers of the fallen and to supply to those in error the remedy of truth, even though the soul that is sick so frequently rejects the kind ministrations of its physicians.[13] Fresh and recent are these wounds of the fallen, their weals are still tumid and swollen. We are therefore convinced that given a longer period of time this urgency of theirs will die down and they will come to appreciate that they were delayed in order to achieve a reliable cure.[14] But this cure will be effective on condition that there are no longer those who arm them—for their peril, who give them perverse instruction, and instead of the saving remedy of delay demand for them the deadly poison of premature reconciliation.

3.2 For we do not believe that they would all have had the impudence, and so aggressively, to lay claim to reconciliation as already being theirs, had they not been goaded on by certain people. We know too well the faith of the Carthaginian church, we know her accustomed ways,[15] we know her humility. Hence our surprise to observe harsh words cast against you by letter,[16] whereas we have had frequent occasion to learn of your mutual love and of your charity and affection towards each other.

3.3 It is high time, therefore, for them to be doing penance for their sin, to give proof that they grieve for their fall, to demonstrate their shame, to manifest their humility, to display their meekness, to elicit for themselves the clemency of God by their submissive behaviour, to draw upon themselves the mercy of God by showing the honour that is due to the bishop of God. Indeed their letter would have been so much the more effective if the entreaties made on their behalf by the loyal faithful[17] had been assisted by humility on their part. A request is all the more easily obtained when the person on whose behalf the request is made is worthy of obtaining the object of the request.

4.1 As regards Privatus of Lambaesis, you have acted in your customary way in wishing to report to us a matter which might cause us concern.[18] For it does indeed befit us all to keep watchful vigil over the whole body of the church, the members of which are spread through all the various provinces. 4.2 But, as a matter of fact, even before we received your letter,[19] we had not failed to notice the perfidy of this rogue. For earlier there had come from the vicious cohort of Privatus a certain Futurus as his standard-bearer; he sought fraudulently to elicit from us a letter but he did not succeed in concealing his identity and so he failed to get the letter he was after.[20]

We wish that you may ever fare well.

LETTER 37

Cyprian sends greetings to the presbyters Moyses and Maximus and to the other confessors, his brothers.[1]

1.1 Dearest brothers, Celerinus, who has been comrade with you in your deeds of faith and valour[2] and soldier of God in your battles of glory, has made, by his arrival here, each and every one of you present to our feelings. As he approached we saw in him all of you and as he spoke tenderly and often of your affection for me, we could hear in his words your own voices. Great indeed and profound is my joy when from you such messages are conveyed by such messengers.[3]

1.2 There is a sense in which we, too, are there with you in prison. Being as we are thus joined to your hearts we believe that we are sharing with you the special distinctions which God in His goodness is bestowing upon you.[4] Your undivided love binds us to your glory: the spirit does not countenance the bonds of charity to be parted. Confession immures you there, affection me. And for our part we are certainly mindful of you, day and night; not only in the prayer we offer in the company of many during the sacrifice[5] but also in the private prayers we say in solitude, we beseech of the Lord to lend His full benison to your winning your crowns of renown.[6]

1.3 But in fact our powers are too paltry to render you adequate return; yours is the greater gift when *you* remember us in your prayers, for your hopes are now on heaven alone, you have thoughts only for God. Indeed the heights you ascend are all the loftier the longer in fact your passion[7] is delayed: by the protracted period of time you are not simply retarding, rather you are enhancing your glory.[8]

A first confession—and one only—makes a man blessed. But you make your confession every time you are invited to leave the prison, and in your faith and valour you elect to stay there.[9] Your honours are as numerous as your days in prison; as the months run their course, so your merits multiply. He conquers once who suffers at once; but the person who is constantly under torture, grappling with pain, and remains unconquered, he wins a crown every day.

2.1 Let now the magistrates parade forth, the consuls and the proconsuls; let them pride themselves in the regalia of their annual office and their twelve bundles of rods.[10] Be assured that in your own case your heavenly office has been invested with all the brilliance of a year's honours and already, by the long continuance of its victorious glory, it has traversed beyond the full revolution of the annual cycle.[11]

The rising sun and the waning moon gave light to the universe,[12] but to you in your dungeon He who made the sun and the moon proved to be a brighter light. And the resplendent radiance of Christ glowing in your hearts and souls illuminated with its dazzling and eternal light the darkness of your place of punishment, which to others appeared so dread and so deadly.

2.2 Winter passed by with the changing months; but imprisoned as you all were, you exchanged the season of winter for the winter of persecution. Winter was succeeded by the mildness of spring, glad with roses and garlanded with blossoms; but as for you, you had roses and blossoms from the delights of paradise[13] and heavenly wreaths crowned your heads. And lo! summer came, fertile with abundant harvests and the threshing-floor was filled with crops;[14] but you have sown glory and a harvest of glory you reap.[15] Stationed as you now are on the threshing-floor of the Lord you can see the chaff being burnt in unquenchable fire whilst you yourselves, already tested and stored like winnowed grains of wheat and precious corn, regard your lodgings in prison as your storehouse. In autumn, too, for discharging the seasonal tasks, spiritual grace fails you not. Outside, the vintage is being pressed, and in the vats the grape is being trodden, which afterwards will enrich the cups: whereas you, like rich clusters from the Lord's vineyard, bunches of fruit now ripe, are being trodden beneath the violence of wordly pressure. Prison is our wine-press, you can feel its crushing turns,[16] and instead of wine you pour forth blood. Courageous in the face of the sufferings you have to endure, you gladly drain the cup of martyrdom.

Such is the cycle of the year for the servants of God; such are the spiritual deserts and heavenly rewards with which the changing seasons are graced.

3.1 Truly blessed are those from your number who have travelled along these paths of glory and have now left this world; they have reached the end of their journey of valour and faith, and they have gone to receive, to the joy of the Lord Himself, the kiss and embrace of the Lord.

And yet your glory is in no way inferior; you are still engaged in the struggle; your destiny is to follow the glorious career of your comrades; you have long been waging the fight; and steadfast with unflinching and unshakeable faith, by your acts of valor you are exhibiting each day a spectacle for God to look upon. The more prolonged is your flight, the more noble is your crown. There is but one contest, but it consists of an accumulation of numerous battles. Hunger you conquer, thirst you contemn, and by your strength and vigour you spurn the filth of your dungeon and the horrors of your cell of suffering.

3.2 In your prison suffering is subjugated, cruelty is crushed. Death you do not dread, you desire it, for death is vanquished by the reward of deathlessness, so that the victor is honoured with an eternity of life. I realize the spirit that must now be within you, the nobility and generosity you must now have in your hearts, when you reflect upon such exalted goals, when the commandments of God and the rewards of Christ are the sole objects of your meditation. In your prison the only will is God's; in the flesh you may still be, but the life you are now living is not of the present world, it is the life of the world to come.

4.1 What I now must ask of you, most blessed brothers,[17] is that you be mindful of me, that, as you contemplate your great and holy thoughts, you find a place for us as well in your minds and hearts, that I figure in your prayers and supplications when your voice, ennobled and purified by confession, illustrious for the unbroken preservation of its honour, reaches as far as the ears of God. The heavens are now open to it, it passes from these regions of the universe which it has subdued to the realms above and there obtains from the bounty of God whatever it requests.

4.2 There is no petition which you may make of the Lord's favour which you do not deserve to obtain. For you have kept so faithfully the precepts of the Lord, you have adhered to the gospel discipline with all the honest vigour of your faith. With the honour of your valour unsullied, you have manfully taken your stand with the Lord's apostles and His commandments, and the wavering faith of many you have strengthened by the truth of your martyrdom. Truly you are witnesses of the gospel, truly you are martyrs of Christ.[18] Supported upon His roots, firmly founded upon the rock,[19] you have united discipline to valour, you have roused others to the fear of God, and you have made yourselves models of martyrdom.

I wish that you, my brothers most brave and most blessed, may ever fare well and that you be mindful of us.

LETTER 38

Cyprian sends greetings to the presbyters and deacons, and to all the laity.[1]

1.1 Dearest brethren, it is our custom when we make appointments to clerical office[2] to consult you beforehand, and in council together with you to weigh the character and qualities of each candidate.[3] But there is no need to wait for evidence from men when already God has cast His vote.[4]

1.2 Our brother Aurelius is a young man with a splendid record;[5] he has already received the Lord's approbation and is dear to God. Tender in years he may be, but he is far advanced in glory for his faith and courage; though junior in terms of natural age,[6] he is senior in honour.

He has striven in a double contest: twice he has made confession and twice he has covered himself with the glory of victorious confession. This occurred not only when he conquered in the race[7] and became an exile,[8] but also when he fought anew in a harder struggle and from the battle of suffering emerged triumphantly victorious. Many times it was the adversary's purpose to challenge the servants of God—but equally often he came out fighting, a soldier of exemplary keenness and valour, and equally often, he won.

It was not enough to have engaged the enemy, observed by a few only, on the earlier occasion when he was made an exile; he merited an engagement even in the forum where his valour might shine the more brightly, where, after defeating magistrates he might vanquish the proconsul as well, where, after his exile, he might overpower the tortures.[9]

1.3 I am at a loss what quality of his I should extol the more, the glory of his wounds or the humbleness of his character, the outstanding honour he has gained by his fortitude or the renown and esteem he deserves for his modesty. He is at once so elevated in dignity and so lowly in humility that he appears to have been preserved by providence in order to set an example to others for disciplined behaviour within the church,[10] demonstrating how in their confession the servants of God may be victorious by their courageous deeds and how after their confession they may be conspicuous for their personal qualities.[11]

2.1 Such a man deserved higher grades of clerical appointment and greater advancement,[12] judged as he should be not on his years but on his deserts. But it has been decided, for the time being, that he begin with the duties of reader,[13] for there is no task that more befits the voice which has confessed God with so glorious a proclamation than to resound with the formal reading of the holy scriptures: that is to say, after uttering the lofty words which declared his witness of Christ to read the Gospel of Christ whereby men become His witnesses,[14] after the pillory to approach the pulpit[15]—on the one he could be seen by crowds of pagans, on the other he can be seen by his brothers; on the one he was heard to the astonishment of the thronging bystanders, on the other he is heard to the joy of his assembled brethren.

2.2 You should therefore know, dearly beloved brothers, that I and my colleagues who were present have appointed this man to office.[16] I know that you warmly welcome this action just as you are anxious that as many men as possible of this calibre should receive appointments in our church.

If a man is joyful he is always impatient; if he is happy, he cannot stand delay. On Sunday, therefore, without waiting any longer, he read for us,[17] that is to say he has given us an omen of peace to come by inaugurating his duties as reader.[18]

You should be urgent in frequent supplication and you should support our prayers by yours that the Lord may graciously bestow His mercy upon us, and that to His people He may soon restore safe and sound their bishop and, along with the bishop, their martyr-reader.[19]

I wish that you, my dearest brothers, may ever fare well.

LETTER 39

Cyprian sends greetings to his brothers, the presbyters and deacons and all the people.[1]

1.1 My dearly beloved brothers, we ought to recognize and welcome the heavenly blessings with which the Lord has deigned to glorify and honour His church in our day. For He has granted reprieve[2] to His noble confessors and glorious martyrs, His purpose being that they who have made their confession of Christ so heroically, should subsequently bring lustre to the clergy of Christ in the service of ecclesiastical office.[3]

You ought, therefore, to rejoice and be glad with us when you read this letter of ours. By it, I and my colleagues here present[4] report to you that our brother Celerinus,[5] illustrious for his acts of bravery and for his virtues, has been joined to our clergy not by the election of man but by the favour of God.

1.2 He hesitated to consent, but by night in a vision he was admonished and encouraged by the Church herself and was thus compelled not to refuse. We tried to persuade him,[6] but She who has been given greater authority actually constrained him for the reason that it was neither right nor proper for a man to be without a place of honour in the church whom the Lord has honored with so glorious a dignity in heaven.

2.1 He was the first to go into the battle of our times, among the soldiers of Christ he marched in the van,[7] he clashed in conflict with the leader and author of the hostilities himself during the fierce onset of the persecution.[8] By indomitable steadfastness he was victorious over his adversary in the encounter and he thus opened up for others the path to victory. His was no conquest over wounds quickly gained[9] but a wonderful triumph after a protracted struggle, with sufferings long holding him in their unrelenting clasp.

2.2 For a period of nineteen days he was shut up in prison under close guard, in chains and irons.[10] But though his body was in bondage, his spirit remained unfettered and free. His flesh grew emaciated by prolonged hunger and thirst, but his soul, living by faith and courage,[11] God nourished with spiritual sustenance. He lay in the midst of sufferings, stronger than those sufferings; he was held prisoner, greater than those who imprisoned him; he lay prostrate, loftier than those who stood by him; he was in bonds, mightier than those who bound him; he was judged, nobler than those who judged him. Fettered his feet may have been, but the serpent was downtrodden, crushed and conquered.[12]

2.3 On his glorious body there gleam brightly the marks of his wounds; on his sinews and limbs, wasted by lengthy privations, you may distinguish clearly the prominent traces of his sufferings. Great indeed and wonderful are the accounts heard by the brethren of his heroic deeds of valour. And should there be some doubting Thomas reluctant to believe his ears, he certainly can rely on his eyes to see in fact what he hears. This servant of God won victory by the glory of his wounds; and that glory is preserved by his scars which recall those wounds.[13]

3.1 For our most beloved Celerinus these glorious titles of honour are no strange novelty. He is tracing the footsteps of his own kindred, and he is being made equal to his forebears and kinsmen by being similarly distinguished with God's favour. His grandmother Celerina long ago received a martyr's crown;[14] likewise his paternal and maternal uncles, Laurentinus and Egnatius, whilst once soldiering themselves also in worldly armies[15] but being true and spiritual soldiers of God, by their confession of Christ overthrew the devil and by their illustrious sufferings merited palms and crowns from the Lord. As you recall, we never fail to offer sacrifices on their behalf every time we celebrate in commemoration the anniversary dates of the sufferings of these martyrs.[16]

3.2 It was not possible for him to prove unworthy of such forebears or to be their inferior, seeing that, possessed of this aristocratic and noble lineage, he was constantly challenged by such models of courage and faith from within his own family. If, in a household of this world, to be of patrician rank is a cause for praise and esteem, it must be a cause for far greater praise and honour to become ennobled in the esteem of heaven.

3.3 I am at a loss whom I am rather to term the more

blessed—those ancestors for such illustrious posterity, or this man for such glorious origins. In this family we meet God's favours evenly distributed throughout its generations. Thus the elevation of the descendant adds lustre to the crowns of the ancestors, whilst the eminence of his forebears adds radiance to the glory this descendant.

4.1 This man comes to us, my dearly beloved brothers, thus highly favoured by the Lord; he comes illustrious with the testimony—and indeed wonderment—of his very persecutor.[17] There is no place more proper for him to be stationed than on the pulpit, that is to say on the tribunal of the church.[18] In this way, thanks to his elevated position, he may be readily seen by the whole congregation in a manner befitting the brilliance of his honour and there he may read to them those commandments and that Gospel of the Lord which he follows with such fortitude and faithfulness. My hope is that the voice which has confessed the Lord may be daily heard[19] proclaiming the words which the Lord has spoken.

4.2 There may be, to be sure, higher grades to which one can rise in the Church,[20] but the task by which a confessor can render most profit to his brethren is by reading with his own lips the Gospel. Those who hear may thereby imitate the faith of the reader.

4.3 It was only right, therefore, that he should join Aurelius as a reader,[21] being already joined with him by the common bond of divine honour, already united with him by all the decorations of virtue and commendation. Together they make a matching pair; their loftiness in glory is equalled by their lowliness in modesty; the heights they have reached through God's favour are equalled by the depths to which they humble themselves, so meek and peaceable are they. To each one of us they furnish alike models of courage and character; they are as suited for combat as for peace, in the one meriting our praises for valour, in the other for modesty.[22]

5.1 In such servants the Lord takes joy, in such confessors He takes pride. And the manner of living they pursue[23] ensures that their glory is proclaimed and that they impart thereby to others instruction in discipline. There is a reason why Christ has willed that they should long remain here in the church, why He has snatched them out of the jaws of death, and why, by performing a kind of resurrection over them, He has preserved them in safety. And that reason is this: that our community, by beholding nothing more exalted in honour, nothing more lowly in humility, may become their companions and follow in their footsteps.

5.2 You should, however, be informed that they have been appointed readers for the time being. It was fitting that their light should be placed upon the lampstand to shed illumination for all,[24] that their glorious countenances should be stationed on a more elevated position from which, visible to all who stand around, they may furnish those who see them with an incentive to glory.

But you should be further informed that we have already marked them out for the rank of presbyter on these conditions: they are to have the honour of being given their allowances along with the presbyters and at the monthly payments they are to receive a share equal to theirs;[25] they will take their seat with us when they have advanced to maturer years[26]—even though it is impossible to be found in any way deficient in years when you have already brought by honour and glory your life to its perfection.

I wish that you, my most beloved and cherished brothers, may ever fare well.

LETTER 40

Cyprian sends greetings to his dearly beloved and cherished brothers, the presbyters, deacons and all the people.[1]

1.1 It is our duty to report to you, dearly beloved brothers, a matter which brings not only joy to us all but also the greatest glory to our Church.

You ought to know that we have been advised and instructed by the grace of God[2] that the presbyter Numidicus, radiant with the brilliant light of his confession and ennobled by the dignity won by his courage and faith,[3] should be enlisted in the ranks of our Carthaginian presbyters and that he should take his seat with us amongst our clergy.[4]

It was through his own words of encouragement that Numidicus sent on ahead of him a glorious band of martyrs, to be done to death by stones and flames, and it was with joy that he beheld the wife who clung to his side burnt to ashes (or, I should rather say, preserved) along with the others. Numidicus himself was half-burnt, buried under a pile of stones and left for dead. Subsequently his loving daughter in the anxious exercise of her filial duty, searched for her father's body; he was discovered half-dead, dragged out and nursed to life, unwillingly remaining behind, separated from the comrades whom he had himself sent on in front.[5]

1.2 But, as we can see, the reason why he remained behind was this: the Lord could thus join him to our clergy and bring lustre to our ranks, which have been left forlorn by the lapse of some of our presbyters, by means of pontiffs who have been graced with glory.[6]

1.3 For, God permitting, he will undoubtedly be promoted to a more exalted ecclesiastical station when we have returned to you through the protection of the Lord.[7]

In the meantime, let us carry out what is revealed to us; let us accept with expressions of gratitude this gift from God,[8] hoping to receive many adornments of the same kind from the Lord's merciful hands. Thereby He may renew the strength of His Church and ensure that there flourish in the ranks of our clerical assembly men of like meekness and humility.[9]

I wish that you, my dearly beloved and cherished brothers, may ever fare well.

LETTER 41

Cyprian sends greetings to his colleagues Caldonius and Herculanus and to his fellow presbyters Rogatianus and Numidicus.[1]

1.1 I was profoundly distressed, my dearest brothers, to receive your letter.[2] It has been my constant goal and aspiration to keep our whole community in safety[3] and to preserve our flock without blemish, as charity demands us to do. But now you report that Felicissimus has engineered a series of evil and treacherous schemes.[4] In addition to his activities as embezzler and robber (I have been well aware of them for some time), he has now contrived actually to set a section of the people at loggerheads with their bishop,[5] that is to say, to separate the sheep from their shepherd, to divide the children from their father, and to scatter the members of Christ.

1.2 I sent you to act as deputies in my stead in order to meet the urgent needs of our brethren by the resources at your disposal; in the case of those wanting to practise their particular trade, you were to come to their assistance with such additional aid as they needed.[6] At the same time you were also to ascertain their various ages, circumstances and merits; for even under present conditions I, upon whose shoulders this duty falls, desire to be informed fully about them all and to advance everyone who is suitable, humble and meek to the duties of ecclesiastical office.[7]

And you report that when you were sent on this mission Felicissimus intervened, attempting to prevent anyone from receiving aid and making it impossible for you to ascertain by careful inquiry the matters I had requested; and you further reported that Felicissimus has actually threatened with outrageous menaces and violent intimidation those of our brothers who were the first to come forward to receive assistance, declaring that those who chose to be obedient to us should not be in communion with him at death.[8]

2.1 In addition to all this, being neither swayed by respect for my position nor cowed by your authority and presence, thanks to his goading he has driven the peace of the community into turmoil and he has come hurtling forward with a large following, wildly and madly claiming that he is the ring-leader and chief of a revolutionary faction. However, I am indeed delighted that a large number of the brethren have in fact withdrawn from his seditious schemes and have preferred to be in accord with you, remaining thereby with the Church, their mother, and enjoying her emoluments from the hands of the bishop who dispenses them.[9] In truth, I am convinced that others also will act likewise in the spirit of peace and soon withdraw from this ill-considered error.

In the meantime, in view of the fact that Felicissimus has threatened that those who have obeyed us, that is to say, those who are in communion with us, should not be in communion with him at death,[10] let him receive that sentence which he has already pronounced himself. Let him be informed that he has been excommunicated by us,[11] for in addition to his acts of embezzlement and robbery (of which we had knowledge beyond a shadow of doubt) there is now even the charge of adultery: serious-minded men from our community[12] have reported that they have discovered this and they have asserted that they will prove their claim. We will investigate all these matters when by God's leave we can meet together, along with many of my colleagues.

2.2 And, moreover, in the case of Augendus who, without a thought for bishop or for Church has become an ally and partner with Felicissimus in this conspiracy, if he persists further with Felicissimus, he is to incur the sentence which he is inviting upon himself by this foolish and divisive behaviour of his.[13] Indeed, anyone who has joined Felicissimus' conspiratorial faction should be aware that he will not be in communion with us in the Church who of his own volition has freely elected to separate himself from the Church.

2.3 You are to read this letter of mine to our brothers and to pass it on to the clergy in Carthage, attaching to it the names of those who have joined Felicissimus.[14]

I wish that you, my dearly beloved brothers, may ever fare well.

LETTER 42

Caldonius with his colleagues Herculanus and Victor along with the presbyters Rogatianus and Numidicus.[1]

We have excluded from communion Felicissimus and Augendus,[2] likewise Repostus one of the exiles,[3] Irene of the Rutili[4] and Paula the seamstress, as this note of mine should make clear to you.[5] Likewise we have excluded Sophronius and Soliassus the mat-maker,[6] also one of the exiles.[7]

LETTER 43

Cyprian sends greetings to the whole people.[1]

1.1 My dearly beloved brothers, I am well aware that Virtius is a presbyter of the greatest loyalty and integrity, that Rogatianus and Numidicus are presbyters and confessors both, radiant in the glory they have received from the Lord's favour,[2] that the deacons are honest men dedicated to the services of the church in all dutifulness; and I am well aware that they, together with all the other ministers,[3] are there in person to lavish upon you their unstinted devotion. I am also aware that they are unflagging in their efforts not only to give heart to individual brethren by their zealous words of encouragement, but also to guide and amend the souls of the fallen by their salutary words of counsel.

Nevertheless, I am proffering advice to you myself, insofar as I can, and I am visiting you in the way that I can, by this letter of mine.[4]

1.2 I speak of a letter, my dear brothers. For the spite and treachery of certain presbyters has made it impossible for me to reach you before Easter-day.[5] They have not forgotten the plots they laid, they have not lost all their old venom against my episcopate, or rather against the votes you cast and the judgement of God.[6] Accordingly, they are renewing their former attacks upon us, they are starting up afresh with all their habitual craftiness their sacrilegious schemings.

1.3 In point of fact they have now received the punishment which they had so deserved—but through the providence of God, not by any wish or desire on our part; rather, we were forgiving and held our peace.[7] Consequently, without being cast out by us they have voluntarily cast themselves out from the Church; from their own consciences they have actually passed sentence on themselves. Just as your divinely inspired votes indicated,[8] these evil schemers have expelled themselves, on their own initiative, from the Church.

2.1 It has now become clear what is the source and origin of the rebel party of Felicissimus, what is the strength which has been supporting it.

These were the men who, previously, gave encouragement and incitement to certain confessors. They were trying to prevent them from being in harmony with their own bishop, from adhering to the Church's discipline in meekness and faith according to the Lord's precepts, and from preserving the glory of their confession by blameless and unblemished conduct.[9]

2.2 As if it were not enough to have corrupted the minds of certain confessors and to have sought to shatter our community and set a part of it up in arms against the holy episcopate established by God,[10] they are now deploying their envenomed brand of deception in order to destroy even those who have fallen. They seek to lure away from the remedy which will heal their wound those who are sick and ill and who are in fact less sturdy and ready, having fallen calamitously, for taking stronger counsels; they urge them to leave off their prayers and supplications (whereas the Lord is to be appeased by prolonged and persevering satisfaction) and they are inveigling them by a delusive and fallacious reconciliation into precipitate action that spells their doom.

3.1 I beg of you, my brothers, to be vigilant against the snares of the devil and in defense of your salvation to keep anxious and jealous watch against his pernicious stratagems.

This is in effect another persecution, this is another trial.[11]

And these five presbyters are identical with those five leaders who recently were joined by edict to the magistrates in order to undermine our faith,[12] in order to entice the frail hearts of our brethren into the deadly nets by a perversion of the truth.

3.2 It is the same plan now: through these five presbyters, joined to Felicissimus, the same process of destruction is once again being staged for the overthrow of souls. They are not to beseech God: he who has denied Christ is not to appeal for mercy from the same Christ whom he denied; despite all the guilt of his sin that is with him, he is to be deprived even of repentance; no satisfaction is to be rendered to God through the bishops and priests;[13] rather, God's own priests are to be abandoned and in opposition to the discipline laid down in the Gospel there is to arise a brand-new tradition, a sacrilegious establishment.

And this, in spite of the fact that it had been firmly decided not only by us but also by the confessors and clergy of Rome,[14] and indeed by all of the bishops both within our province and overseas,[15] that no change should be introduced concerning the fate of the fallen until we should all have met together. Then, after sharing our views, we would lay down a decision which was tempered alike with strictness and with compassion. But against this decision of ours they now revolt and all the authority of the office of bishop is being annihilated by these traitors and rebels.[16]

4.1 Severe indeed is the torment which I am now made to suffer, my dearest brothers, in being unable to come to you in person at this time,[17] in being unable to approach in person each one of you, and to address in person to you words of exhortation in the way in which the Lord and His gospel instructs me to do. An exile, now in its second year, has not been enough,[18]—nor to have been miserably separated for all that time from the sight of your faces; not enough has been the continuous sorrow and distress that racks me still in my loneliness without you, a grief that does not cease, tears which flow forth night and day; the bishop whom you appointed with such love and zeal has not yet had the good fortune to greet you nor yet to be clasped in your embrace.

4.2 But our heart, ailing as it is, is now beset with sorrow even more profound: it is that at a time of such anxiety and crisis I cannot hasten to you myself. For we have to stay on our guard lest, through the menaces and plots of these traitors, our arrival might give rise in Carthage to serious disorders, lest, whilst it is a bishop's duty to ensure peace and tranquillity for all, he might appear to have been the cause for rioting and to have sparked off persecution once more.[19]

4.3 That is precisely why, dearly beloved brothers, I am sending to you from here warning as well as counsel. Do not rashly put your trust in pernicious words, do not easily give your assent to guileful phrases, do not exchange darkness for light, night for day, hunger for food, thirst for drink, poison for medicine, death for life.[20] You should let neither their years nor their authority deceive you. In their hoary wickedness they resemble the two elders: just as these elders sought to defile and violate the virtuous Susannah, so do these church elders seek by their adulterous teachings to defile the virtue of the Church and to violate the truth of the Gospel.[21]

5.1 There is the proclamation which God has spoken: *Heed not the talk of false prophets, for the dreams in their own hearts deceive them. They speak, but not out of the mouth of the Lord. They say to those who reject the word of the Lord: peace shall be yours.*[22]

So, too, they are now offering peace, whilst they have no peace themselves; they will not let the Church call back and lead back the fallen, whilst they have forsaken the Church themselves.[23]

5.2 God is one and Christ is one: there is one Church and one chair founded, by the Lord's authority, upon Peter.[24] It is not possible that another altar can be set up, or that a new priesthood can be appointed, over and above this one altar and this one priesthood. Whoever gathers elsewhere, scatters.[25] Whatever is so established by man in his madness that it violates what has been appointed by God is an obscene outrage, it is sacrilege. Flee the contagion of such men, shun their words like a canker,[26] like the plague, as you were forewarned to do by the Lord, in these words: *They are blind leaders of the blind. But if a blind man leads another blind man, they will both fall into the ditch together.*[27]

5.3 They obstruct our prayers, which you pour forth with us night and day to God in order that you may appease Him with due satisfaction; they obstruct our tears, with which you wash away the guilt of the sin that has been committed; they obstruct that peace for which in sincerity and faith, you beg of the Lord's mercy. They do not know the words of scripture: *And that prophet and dreamer of dreams who by his words has made you wander away from the Lord your God [shall perish].*[28]

5.4 Let no man, my brothers, make you wander away from the pathways of the Lord; let no man snatch you, who are followers of Christ,[29] away from the gospel of Christ; let no man drag sons of the church away from the church. To perish is what they have sought; let them perish, then, but alone, by themselves. They have forsaken the church; let them remain, alone, outside the church. They have revolted against their bishops; let them be, alone, without bishops. Let them suffer, alone, the punishment for their treachery; they have deserved to be so sentenced for their malice and treachery, as previously your votes indicated and as now God's judgment confirms.[30]

6.1 In His Gospel the Lord alerts us with these words: *You cast out what has been laid down by God, so that you can set up a tradition of your own.*[31] Those who cast out what has been laid down by God and seek to set up instead a tradition of their own, you must reject, resolutely and unequivocally. Let one fall be enough for those who have lapsed. No one should trip up by any deception on his part those who are now trying to get up again; no one should knock down and crush even more utterly those who are already lying prostrate, those on whose behalf we, for our part, beg that they may be lifted up by the hand and strong arm of God. No one should turn away from all hope of recovery those who are now half-dead and who entreat that they may recover their former health; no one should extinguish all light along the road to recovery for those who now stumble in the darkness created by their own fall.

6.2 Furthermore, we are given instruction by the Apostle

with these words: *If any man teaches otherwise and does not give his assent to the sound words and teachings of our Lord Jesus Christ, being carried away by his own foolishness, you should avoid such a man.*[32] And he also says: *Let no man deceive you with empty words; for these things the wrath of God visits the children who are stubborn and disobedient. Do not therefore be partners with them.*[33] There is no reason why you should start now to be partners in their wickedness, being deceived by their empty words. Avoid such company, I urge you, and give your assent to our counsels: we pour out daily for you to the Lord prayers without ceasing, we yearn that you should be recalled to the church through the Lord's loving-kindness, we pray for perfect peace from God first of all for the mother and then, too, for her children.[34]

6.3 And so, to our prayers and entreaties unite your prayers and entreaties also, to our weeping join your tears. Avoid the wolves who separate the sheep from the shepherd, avoid the envenomed tongue of the devil who, ever deceitful and lying since the beginning of the world, lies that he may deceive, cajoles that he may injure, pledges good that he may give evil, promises life that he may destroy it.

But now his words are made clear, his venom plain to see. He promises reconciliation, so that it should be impossible to gain it. He pledges salvation, so that the transgressor should not reach it. He guarantees a Church, whereas his design is that whosoever believes in him should perish utterly, being parted from the Church.

7.1 Now is the time, my dearly beloved brothers, for those of you who still remain standing, to display courageous perseverance; now is the time for you to preserve with unfailing tenacity the glorious constancy which you maintained during the persecution. For those of you who fell through the wiles of the adversary, now is the time, during this second trial, for you, in all faith, to look to your hope and your peace:[35] in order that the Lord may pardon you, you must not abandon His priests, since it is written: *And whatever man acts with such arrogance that he does not heed the priest or the judge, whoever he may be in those days, that man shall die.*[36]

7.2 This is the latest and the last trial of this persecution;

under the Lord's protection even it will soon pass and then we shall be there with you in person after Easter-day, along with my colleagues.[37] In the presence of these colleagues we will be able to arrange and determine whatever needs to be done, acting in accordance with your views as well as with the common counsel of us all, just as we have firmly decided to do. But whoever is scornful of doing penance and making satisfaction to God and has gone over to the party of Felicissimus and his henchmen, allying himself to that heretical faction,[38] he must realize that he will not be able, afterwards, to return to the Church and be in communion with the bishop and people of Christ.

I wish that you, my dearest brothers, may ever fare well and persist in imploring the mercy of the Lord in constant and earnest prayers with us.[39]

LETTER 44

Cyprian sends greetings to Cornelius his brother.[1]

1.1 My dearest brother, the presbyter Maximus, the deacon Augendus, a certain Machaeus, and Longinus have come to us, sent by Novatian.[2] From the letter they brought with them and from what they themselves have said and claimed, we discovered that Novatian had been made a bishop.[3] We were dismayed to learn of such a wicked and illegal appointment, made in opposition to the Catholic Church;[4] we judged, accordingly, that they must forthwith be excluded from communion with us.

1.2 Although we had meantime[5] refuted and rebutted what they, with such stubborn persistence, kept attempting to assert, I and the many colleagues who had gathered around me[6] waited, all the same, for the arrival of our colleagues Caldonius and Fortunatus. We had recently sent them off, as our envoys, to you and to our fellow bishops who had been present at your appointment;[7] on their return and after receiving their report on the truth of the matter,[8] we would be able to stamp out, with all the greater authority and with the clear proof established through them, this evil, this enemy faction.

1.3 But there arrived before them, our colleagues Pompeius and Stephanus: they, being men of integrity and honour, have also themselves provided for our information here[9] clear testimony and evidence of the situation. Consequently there was no need to pay any further heed to those who had come as agents of Novatian.[10]

2.1 But they came bursting into our assembly,[11] shouting scandalous abuse and causing an uproar; they demanded that we and the people should publicly investigate the charges which they kept saying they were laying and could prove. We refused. It ill-became our dignity to allow the good character of our colleague, already chosen, appointed and approved by many with their favouring support, to be questioned further by the malicious tongues of jealous rivals.[12]

2.2 It would take far too long to compile in a letter all their anarchic schemings, in which they have been confounded, checked, and exposed for creating heresy. You will hear full details of all of this from our fellow-presbyter Primitivus when he reaches you.[13]

3.1 But they are doing their best to ensure that there should be no end to their wild and outrageous folly: here, too, they are trying to drag asunder the members of Christ into schismatic factions and to split apart and tear to pieces His body, the Catholic Church.[14] They are running in all directions—going from door to door, calling on many in their homes, and moving from town to town in a number of districts.[15] They are on the look out for people to join them in their obstinacy, in this schismatic error of theirs.[16]

3.2 We have already given them our reply once and for all; but we are also constantly warning them to lay aside their pernicious squabbling and strife. They must realize that it is an act of impiety to abandon their mother; they must acknowledge and understand that once a bishop has been made and approved by the testimony and judgment of his colleagues and people, it is just not possible for another to be appointed. And so, if they profess to have acted in the interests of their own faith and peace of mind, if they claim to be the champions of Christ and the gospel,[17] the first thing they must do is to return to the Church.

I wish that you, my dearest brother, may ever fare well.

LETTER 45

Cyprian sends greetings to Cornelius his brother.[1]

1.1 In sending recently our colleagues Caldonius and Fortunatus, we were only doing, my very dear brother, what is incumbent upon the servants of God and especially upon His bishops who espouse justice and peace.[2] The body of the Church had been severed. They were to strive and labour to their utmost to join back together the limbs of that divided body, restoring the unity of the Catholic Church and recoupling the bond of Christian charity. They had letters from us to help them in their task of persuasion,[3] they were present in person to lend their assistance and to join in counsel with you all.[4]

1.2 Instead, the opposing faction acted with perverse and self-willed obstinacy. They rejected the welcoming embrace of their mother, they cut themselves off from their source of life.[5] Not only that. As the disaccord spread, breaking out afresh and even more violently,[6] they appointed their own bishop: they set up outside the church and in opposition to it an illicit head,[7] in defiance of the sacred ordinance firmly laid down and instituted by God concerning Catholic unity.[8]

This being so, after receiving letters not only from you but also from our colleagues,[9] and after the arrival of our colleagues Pompeius and Stephanus, men of integrity who are very dear to us,[10] we directed our letter to you,[11] acting in conformity with sacred and divine tradition and hallowed ecclesiastical practice—and as the truth demanded.[12] For they had reported to us on all these matters with firm authority and proof, and to the delight of us all.[13]

1.3 Moreover, these same matters we have in turn brought to

the notice of each of our colleagues throughout our province, directing that they too should send back brethren with letters for you.[14]

2.1 All the same, we would have already made our feelings and inclination perfectly plain to our brethren and to all the laity here in Carthage[15] at the time when, upon receiving recently letters from both parties, it was your letter only that we read out; we made it known in the hearing of everyone that you had been appointed bishop.[16]

2.2 But those bitter and abusive allegations which had been heaped up in the document forwarded by the opposing side we rejected, out of regard for the respect we owe each other and out of concern for the dignity and sanctity of the episcopate.[17] In making this judgment, we also bore in mind what was proper to be read out and heard before a solemn assembly of so many of our brothers, at which God's bishops were seated together and where His altar had been placed.[18] Besides, we ought not readily to produce nor inadvisedly and unwisely to make public matter which might be a cause for scandal to those who hear it by reason of its acrimonious tone and which might be a cause for perplexity to brethren who live at a great distance and across the sea[19] by creating uncertainty in their minds.

2.3 It is their affair if they are enslaved to their own wild and demented follies, if they do not heed God's holy law, if they take delight in broadcasting claims which they cannot substantiate, if, even though in the end they prove to be unable to destroy and ruin a man's innocence,[20] they continue satisfied to besmirch and bespatter that reputation by false rumour and lying reports. Whereas it is the manifest duty of us bishops, God's appointed leaders, to make every effort to repudiate such insinuations whenever they are written.

2.4 Otherwise what would become of that precept which we learn and teach has been written thus: *Restrain your tongue from evil and let not your lips speak guile?* Likewise it has elsewhere been written: *Your mouth abounded in malice and your tongue embraced deceit. Seated, you slandered your brother and against your own mother's son you laid scandal.* Similarly there are the words of the Apostle: *Let no evil speech proceed out of your mouth but only good, for the building up of faith, that it may give grace to those who hear it.*[21]

But, as it is, we in effect are demonstrating that we should indulge in such evil talk if we allow to be read out in our hearing any such wild and defamatory invectives that others have written.[22]

2.5 That is why, my very dear brother, when there reached me such documents written against you even from your fellow-presbyter who had his seat with you,[23] I directed that there be read to the clergy and laity only those writings which rang out with the tone of religious simplicity but not those writings which barked and howled with execrations and abuse.[24]

3.1 Now you object that we sought written testimonials from our colleagues who had been present there at your consecration.[25] But in doing so we were not seeking after some radical novelty, we were not forgetful of ancient usage. Normally, it would have been enough for you to announce by letter that you were bishop. But there stood in confrontation an opposing faction which by its foul fabrications and vilifying slanders was disturbing the hearts and confusing the minds of colleagues and brethren alike, and in great numbers. We considered it essential, therefore, in order to allay this distress, to obtain the support of unequivocal and authoritative statements written to us from Italy by our colleagues.[26]

When they attested, in their correspondence, to your strict and virtuous way of life[27] with generous testimonials, they cleared away even for your rivals and those who take pleasure in the anarchy and perversity of their actions[28] the very last scruple of indecision and doubt. And so it was on our advice reached after careful and salutary calculation that our brothers whose hearts had been tossed about on this tide of uncertainty gave their whole-hearted and unhesitating approval to your election as bishop.

3.2 Above all other goals, my brother, we strive, and ought to strive, to achieve this, to maintain to the limits of our ability that unity which was laid down by the Lord and handed on through the apostles to us their successors. We must do all we can to gather within the Church the bleating and wandering sheep[29] who are being separated from their mother through the attacks made by members of a wilful and heretical faction. Let them alone remain outside who through their stubbornness or folly will not move and refuse to return to us: they will have to render an account to the Lord themselves for deserting the Church and for this division and separation that they have caused.

4.1 To inform you what action has been taken here concerning the case of Felicissimus and the group of presbyters, our colleagues have sent to you a letter which they have personally signed.[30] From their letter you will learn what opinions and what decisions they came to after these cases were heard.[31]

4.2 But may I suggest, my brother, that it would be better if you gave instructions for there to be read also to our brothers there with you the copies of the two letters which I sent to you most recently to be read out. I sent them in the spirit of mutual charity through our colleagues Caldonius and Fortunatus. As I had written these letters about this same Felicissimus and these same presbyters addressed to our clergy here as well as to our laity,[32] they explain both the sequence and the cause of the events.[33] Our purpose is that our brothers there as well as here may be fully informed through us.

4.3 I am now sending over further copies of these same documents by Mettius the subdeacon whom I have despatched and Nicephorus the acolyte.[34]

I wish that you, my very dear brother, may ever fare well.

LETTER 46

Cyprian sends greetings to Maximus, Nicostratus and the other confessors.[1]

1.1 My dearest friends, you will have perceived many times from my letters[2] the high esteem I have professed for your confession and the love I have expressed for brothers who are united to us.[3] And so I ask of you now to give your trust and acceptance to this present letter of mine also. In what I am writing I am expressing to you my heartfelt and honest concerns about your conduct and that splendid reputation of yours.

1.2 I am weighed down with grief, I am overwhelmed with unendurable distress, I am stricken and almost prostrate with sadness:[4] I have learnt that you in Rome have given your consent to the appointment of another bishop—contrary to the ordinance of God, contrary to the law of the gospel, contrary to the unity established for the Catholic Church.[5] You have allowed a second church to be established—that is sacrilege, that is forbidden; you have agreed that Christ's members should be wrenched apart, that the Lord's flock, which has but one body and soul, should be torn into pieces by lacerating rivalry.[6]

1.3 I do beg of you that, at least so far as you are concerned, this unlawful rending of our brotherhood should not persist:[7] rather, we beg that, being mindful of your confession and of God's teachings handed down to us, you should return to your mother from whom you have departed, from whom you went forth to win the glory of your confession, bringing such jubilation to your same mother.

2.1 Nor should you suppose that you are acting as champions of the gospel of Christ[8] whilst you cut yourselves off from the flock of Christ and from the peace and concord which He established. What you ought to be doing instead, as soldiers of proven bravery and renown, is taking your stand within your own proper encampment and, there positioned, attending to and making provision for what needs to be done for the common good.[9]

2.2 With us unanimity and concord should not on any account be broken. For our part we are unable to forsake the Church, to go outside it and come over to you; therefore, it is rather up to you to return to the Church, your mother, and to your brothers. And we exhort, urge and beg you to do so with all our might.

I wish that you, my very dear brothers, may ever fare well.

LETTER 47

Cyprian sends greetings to Cornelius his brother.

1.1 My dearest brother, I have judged it to be an obligation upon me and my religious duty towards you all[1] to write a brief letter to the confessors over there in Rome[2] who have forsaken the Church, seduced through the viciousness and perversity of Novatian and Novatus.[3] My purpose is to induce them out of fraternal affection to return to their own true mother, that is, to the Catholic Church.[4]

1.2 I have given instructions that this letter should be read to you beforehand by the subdeacon Mettius[5] as a precaution against any false claim being made that I have written something that is not contained in my letter. I have, moreover, given instructions to this same Mettius (whom I am sending over to you) that he is to act in this matter according to your discretion: he is to deliver this letter to the confessors only if you have considered that it should be handed over to them.

I wish that you, my dearest brother, may ever fare well.

LETTER 48

Cyprian sends greetings to Cornelius his brother.

1. My dearest brother, I have read your letter which you sent by the hands of our fellow presbyter, Primitivus.[1] From it I gather that you are disturbed by the fact that, whereas letters were being directed to you personally from the colony of Hadrumetum[2] in the name of Polycarp,[3] yet after Liberalis and I had gone there,[4] letters started being directed to Rome addressed to the presbyters and deacons.[5]

2.1 On this matter we are concerned that you realize and are convinced that this action was taken neither lightly nor with any intention of slighting you.[6] What happened was this: we had resolved after convening together in a large gathering of bishops[7] to send as our envoys to you our brethren in Rome, our fellow bishops Caldonius and Fortunatus,[8] and meantime to leave this entire issue undetermined until these same colleagues of ours should return to us, either with affairs in Rome peacefully settled or having ascertained what was the truth of the matter.[9]

But, meanwhile, in the absence of our fellow bishop Polycarp,[10] the presbyters and deacons who dwell at Hadrumetum were unaware of this decision which we had jointly taken.

1.2 However, after our visit to them there[11] and after they had been apprised of our resolution, they proceeded themselves also to follow the line of conduct which the others had taken. Consequently, at no point has there been any breach in the harmonious agreement amongst the churches over here.[12]

3.1 Despite these precautions there are always people who at times upset men's minds and hearts by their talk, falsely reporting how the truth stands.[13] We are clear what we have been doing about this.

To all who were sailing away we explained to them the situation individually so that they should not be scandalized on their travels, exhorting them to discern the womb and root of the Catholic Church and to cleave to it.[14]

3.2 Unfortunately, our province is unusually widespread, including the adjoining areas of Numidia and Mauretania.[15] It was, accordingly, the resolution of the bishops to prevent any perplexity being created in the minds of our far-distant brethren through uncertain information about a schism in Rome.[16] We should therefore hold back the full truth of the matter[17] and the time for us to express our assent to your appointment was when the authority for so doing had been made the stronger; then, when individual consciences had been cleared of every last scruple, letters should be sent by every one of us over here, without exception (as is now being done).[18] Thus, all our colleagues should together unequivocally express their approval of, and attach themselves to, you and your communion, that is to say, abide by the unity and, along with that, the charity of the Catholic Church.

By God's grace this has all happened; by His providence our plan has succeeded. And in this we take joy.

4.1 As things are now, the bright light of truth has confirmed your legitimacy and dignity as bishop, you have been supported by the most explicit and enthusiastic testimonials. From the replies of our colleagues who have written to us from Italy[19] as well as from the reports and evidence provided by our fellow bishops Pompeius, Stephanus,[20] Caldonius, and Fortunatus, we now are all fully aware of your lawful claims to your appointment, both as regards its origins and the propriety of its procedures, as well as of your own resplendent integrity of character.[21]

4.2 God our protector will ensure that we, along with all our other colleagues, will administer our office of bishop with firmness and resolve, and keep it in the harmonious unanimity of the Catholic Church. Thus the Lord who is pleased to choose and appoint for Himself the bishops in His own Church may also shelter them when so chosen and appointed by His will and assistance, inspiring them in their government and furnishing them with the vigour required for curbing the insolence of the wicked and with the gentleness needed for encouraging penitence among the fallen.[22]

I wish that you, my dearly beloved brother, may ever fare well.

LETTER 49

Cornelius sends greetings to Cyprian his brother.

1.1 We have been gravely troubled and distressed over those confessors who were so inveigled by the evil guile and treacherous cunning of that practised imposter that they were all but taken in and estranged from the Church. This has made the rejoicing we now feel all the greater, and likewise the thanks we give to almighty God and Christ our Lord. They have realized their error, they have perceived how like a viper's is the sly poison of that spiteful man. And so, they have returned to the Church from which they had departed, coming back "with innocent hearts", as they themselves sincerely declare.[1]

1.2 First of all, brothers of ours, men of staunch faith,[2] lovers of peace, and seekers after unity, started bringing reports to us that whilst the others continued in their arrogance these confessors had become gentle in spirit.[3] But we still did not have adequate evidence for us readily to believe that they had undergone so sudden a transformation.[4]

1.3 Subsequently the confessors Urbanus and Sidonius presented themselves before our fellow presbyters and declared that Maximus, the confessor and presbyter, was anxious to join with them in returning to the Church.[5] But all the same, many things had happened by then for which they bore responsibility; you will know of them from our fellow bishops and from my correspondence.[6] It was not possible, therefore, lightly to give them our trust, but we decided that we should hear from their own lips and profession the message they had delivered through their spokesmen.

1.4 And so they came forward. The presbyters plied them with questions over their actions.[7] In particular they were concerned that numerous letters had been sent out in their name, filled with calumnies and insults; they had been distributed to all of the churches and had created havoc in practically every one of them.[8] In reply, they declared that they had been deceived; they had been unaware of the contents of those letters and had merely put their signatures to them.[9] Being so misled by his duplicity, they had even been guilty of becoming adherents of a schism and founders of a heresy in that they had allowed hands to be laid upon him as on a bishop.[10] After they had been reproached with these and their other failings, the confessors begged that these might be obliterated and the memory of them effaced.

2.1 When word was brought to me of all these proceedings, I decided to call together a meeting of the presbyters. Also attending were five bishops who happened to be in Rome that day.[11] The purpose of the meeting was to form a clear proposal of the manner in which we ought to treat their cases and to ratify it by unanimous agreement. It was also decided to convey to you for your information the minutes of our meeting, so that you would know what everyone felt and what each advised; you will find them attached below.[12]

2.2 After these transactions there appeared before the assembled presbyters Maximus, Urbanus, Sidonius, and a number of other brethren who had allied themselves to them. They beseeched and prayed most earnestly that they would cast into oblivion all their past actions, that henceforth no mention should be made of them just as if nothing whatever had been said or done. Then, after forgiving each other all their faults, they might present to God a clean and a pure heart, following the words of the gospel: *Blessed are the pure of heart, for they shall see God.*[13]

2.3 Naturally the faithful had to be notified of all these proceedings so that they might see installed in their church the very people whom they had seen, to their grief, wandering and straying away from it for so long.[14] When their feelings on the matter had been ascertained, a great number of our congregation assembled together. With one voice they all gave thanks to God, expressing in tears the joy in their hearts as they welcomed them just as if they had come freed on this very day from the confines of their prison.[15]

2.4 I quote their own words: "We acknowledge that Cornelius has been elected bishop of the most holy Catholic Church by God the Almighty and by Christ our Lord.[16] We confess our error. We have been victims of imposture. We were taken in by treacherous words and smooth talk. We may appear to have been in some sort of communion with a schismatic and a heretic, but our hearts have always remained in the Church. We are fully aware that there is one God, that there is one Christ, the Lord whom we confessed, that there is one Holy Spirit, and that there ought to be in a catholic church one bishop."[17]

2.5 Who would not have been moved by this declaration of theirs? Who would not have wished them to be installed in church, there bearing witness to the faith which they had confessed before the powers of this world? Accordingly, we gave directions that Maximus was to resume his former position as presbyter.[18] As for the others, amid wildly enthusiastic acclamation from the people, we remitted all their past actions, reserving judgment for God the Almighty to whose power all things are finally subject.[19]

3.1 To you, my dearly beloved brother, we are sending over news of these events written down the very same hour, the very same minute that they have occurred;[20] and we are sending over at once to you the acolyte Niceforus who is rushing off down to the port to embark straight from the meeting.[21] There having been no delay, you will then be able to join with us in giving thanks to God the Almighty and to Christ our Lord, present, with us, as it were, amongst our clergy here and this assembly of our people.[22]

3.2 We believe, indeed we are now fully confident, that the others who are still in this error are promptly going to return to the Church once they have seen their own leaders dealing with us. I think it is right, my dearly beloved brother, that you should send this letter to the other churches also[23] that all may learn that the treachery and fraudulence of this schismatic and heretic is being reduced to nothing as each day goes by.

Farewell, my dearly beloved brother.[24]

LETTER 50

Cornelius sends greetings to Cyprian his brother.

1.1 That felon[1] is making sure that there will be nothing lacking in his future punishment. Though struck down by the might of God with the explusion from Africa of Maximus, Longinus, and Machaeus,[2] he is nevertheless now back on his feet again.

As I indicated to you in my earlier letter which I sent by Augendus the confessor,[3] I should imagine that by now Nicostratus, Novatus, Evaristus, Primus, and Dionysius have arrived over there.[4]

You will need to take watchful care, therefore, that all our fellow bishops and brothers are alerted to the following facts:

1.2 Nicostratus is guilty of many crimes. Not only has he robbed and defrauded his secular patroness whose accounts he managed,[5] but, worse than that, he has embezzled a considerable sum of trust funds lodged with the church:[6] that has stored up for him everlasting punishment.

As for Evaristus, he has been closely associated with the leader of the schism.[7] Zetus has been appointed bishop as successor in his place, in charge of his former flock.[8]

And Novatus has perpetrated here just the same sorts of criminal activity he has always practised over there with you, so malicious is his character, so inexhaustible his greed.[9]

Now you know what they are like, these captains and bodyguards[10] which this heretic and schismatic[11] keeps constantly close by his side.

Farewell, dearly beloved brother.[12]

LETTER 51

Cyprian sends greetings to Cornelius his brother.

1.1 Dearly beloved brother, we have paid, we do assure you, and we are continuing to pay without ceasing the most profound thanks to God the Father the Almighty and to His Christ the Lord, our God and Saviour.[1] For the Church is so protected by divine favour that her unity and holiness are not allowed to be continually nor totally despoiled by the depravity and perfidy of obdurate heresy.

When we read your letter we were filled with unbounded exultation and jubilation: the prayers in the hearts of us all had been answered—the confessors Maximus, the presbyter, and Urbanus, along with Sidonius and Macarius, had returned to the Catholic Church.[2] They had cast aside their folly; they had rejected their schismatic—or should I rather say, their heretical—madness;[3] having recovered the sanity of faith, they had sought to regain the home of unity and truth. Hence they were able to return, radiant in glory, to the place from which they had marched forth to win that glory. It could not therefore be said that those who had confessed Christ had afterwards deserted the camp of Christ, or that those who had remained undefeated in the test of their courage and strength, had afterwards succumbed in the trial of their loyalty to unity and charity.[4]

1.2 Their honour truly remains unimpaired, undiminished and untarnished, their dignity as confessors remains unshaken and unspoilt.[5] For they have retreated from the company of fugitives and deserters, they have forsaken the betrayers of the faith, the assailants of the Catholic Church. Well might there be triumphant rejoicing (as you describe it) amongst your entire congregation, amongst your clergy and laity alike,[6] as they welcomed them back on their return: for on seeing confessors return to unity whilst preserving intact the glory they have won, everyone must calculate that he now gains some share and partnership in their glory.

2.1 We can get a sense of the excitement of that day from our own feelings. Here the letter itself which you sent about their declaration caused our entire community to rejoice,[7] and they eagerly welcomed with open arms the news of universal joy which it contained. How much greater must have been the excitement there where the joyful events were actually taking place and everyone could see the happiness before their very eyes.

The Lord declares in His gospel that there is the greatest rejoicing in heaven over a sinner who does penance.[8] How much greater is the rejoicing on earth no less than in heaven over confessors who return to the church of God bringing with them their glory and honour, and who prepare the way by which others may return trusting in the laudable example they have set.

2.2 Here some of our brethren had been led astray into error, wishing, by following them, to remain in communion with the confessors.[9] Now this error of theirs has been removed, light has flooded into all their hearts and illuminated the truth that the Catholic Church is one, incapable of being split or divided. Henceforth no one will be readily taken in by the torrent of words that pours forth from this raving heretic, since it has been so clearly demonstrated that the gallant and glorious soldiers of Christ could not for long be detained outside the church by his sacrilegious trickery and treachery.[10]

I wish that you, my dearly beloved brother, may ever fare well.

LETTER 52

Cyprian sends greetings to Cornelius his brother.

1.1 You have acted, my dearly beloved brother, with kindness and with zeal in despatching to us with all speed the acolyte Niceforus.[1] For he has brought us the wonderful and joyful news of the return of the confessors; and he has also brought us very full information to help combat the new and deadly devices being engineered by Novatian and Novatus[2] in their assault upon the Church of Christ.

1.2 On the one day, that gang of criminals arrived here from that iniquitous heresy[3] (itself already in ruins and doomed to bring ruin to all others who shall join it), whereas on the very next day Niceforus turned up with your letter. By it we have ourselves been informed, and we have started to inform and alert others, of the following facts.[4]

Evaristus has no longer remained even a layman from his former position as bishop. He has become an outcast from his see and his people, an exile from the Church of Christ; he now roams through far distant provinces abroad, and having become himself a castaway from the truth and faith, he seeks to cause similar wrecks amongst others of his own ilk.

As for Nicostratus, he has been stripped of the administration of his holy office of deacon, having sacrilegiously embezzled moneys belonging to the church and having refused to return deposits lodged by widows and orphans.[5] His purpose, therefore, is not so much to come to Africa as to get away from Rome over there where he is reminded of his atrocious crimes and robberies. And now, though a fugitive and deserter from the Church, he actually comes boasting and proclaiming that he is a confessor (as if changing one's country changes one's character)[6]—whereas a man can no longer be or be said to be a confessor of Christ once he has denied the church of Christ.[7]

1.3 Now the Apostle Paul says: *For this reason a man shall leave father and mother, and they will be two in one flesh. This is a great mystery: but I speak concerning Christ and the Church.*[8] These are the words of the blessed Apostle: with his own holy voice he testifies to the unity between Christ and His Church, bound together as they are by indissoluble bonds. How then can a man abide with Christ who does not abide with the bride of Christ and within His Church? How can he take upon himself the responsibility of ruling and governing the Church when he has already plundered and pillaged that Church of Christ?

2.1 And finally, Novatus. There was no need for any report to be sent from Rome to us: rather, the reverse. We ought ourselves to be disclosing to you the character of Novatus. He has always been an agitator and a trouble-maker;[9] his avarice is inexhaustible and drives him frantic with greed;[10] he is puffed up with pride and swollen with insensate arrogance; he has always been of evil repute here among the bishops; they have all always damned him as a traitorous heretic;[11] he is always on the look-out for an opportunity to betray; he is a flatterer, so that he can have the opportunity to deceive; he can never love, for he is never faithful; he is a firebrand and torch for igniting the conflagration of rebellion; he is a tornado and tempest for causing shipwrecks of the faith; he is the foe of quiet, the adversary of tranquillity, the enemy of peace.

2.2 That explains why, when Novatus departed from among you in Rome, that is to say when that hurricane and tornado departed, then there followed for you a period of some calm; and the gallant and glorious confessors who had withdrawn from the Church at his instigation, after he had withdrawn from Rome, came back to the Church.[12]

This is the same Novatus who amongst us here sowed the first flames of discord;[13] he separated some of the brethren here from their bishop; in the very midst of the persecution he was to us a sort of second persecution,[14] causing the overthrow of the souls of our brethren.

2.3 He is the one who appointed his henchman Felicissimus to be his own deacon without my permission or knowledge, such is his zest for strife and intrigue.[15] And then he sailed off to Rome taking along his hurricane to overthrow the Church there also. There he wrought similar and like havoc, tearing away part of the people from their clergy and splitting the harmony within a brotherhood which is mutually loving and closely united together. To be sure, Carthage must yield place to Rome in size: accordingly his crimes there have been graver and more serious.[16] Here he had made a deacon contrary to the Church; there he has made a bishop.[17]

2.4 In such men these actions should not occasion surprise. The wicked are constantly being carried along by the impulse of their own demented frenzy; once they have committed crimes, they are driven on by the remorse in their criminal hearts. They cannot remain in the Church of God if they have failed to be obedient to the teachings of God and the Church, whether in their actions and deeds or in the peaceableness of their characters.

2.5 In the case of Novatus, he has robbed the orphans, he has defrauded the widows, he has absconded with money deposited with the church:[18] they all cry out for him to be dealt this punishment which we can see already inflicted upon him in his raving madness. Moreover, his father died of hunger in the streets, and after his death he did not even see to his burial. His wife's womb he kicked with his heel, causing a premature and abortive birth, and the murder of his child.[19] And yet he now dares to damn the hands of those who sacrifice, even though his own feet are in fact more criminal, for by them his own son soon to be born was done to death.[20]

3. Awareness of these atrocities long tortured him with fear;[21] for this reason he was convinced that he was going to be not only expelled from the college of presbyters but even excluded from communion. Indeed, at the insistence of our brethren, the day for holding an inquiry, at which his case was to be deliberated before us, was drawing near when the outbreak of

persecution intervened. This persecution he welcomed as offering hopes of evading and avoiding condemnation. Accordingly,
he proceeded on this rampage of crime and anarchy, calculating
that, as he was to be thrown out and shut out from the church[22]
in any case, he might at least anticipate the verdict of the
bishops[23] by leaving of his own accord—as though to forestall a
sentence is to escape from punishment!

4.1 But for the rest of our brethren who have been deceived
by this impostor and who cause us such distress, we are striving
with all our might that they may escape from the dangerous
companionship of that hardened campaigner,[24] that they may
elude the deadly nets of his enticements, that they may seek
again the Church from which he himself has deserved to be
expelled by the might of God. With the Lord's assistance and
through His compassion we do indeed trust that they will
certainly be able to come back.

4.2 For it is not possible for a man to perish unless it is
plainly evident that perish he must,[25] since the Lord says in His
own Gospel: *Every planting which My heavenly father has not
planted will be rooted out.*[26] Accordingly, whoever has not been
planted in the precepts and counsels of God the Father, will
alone be able to depart from the Church and he alone will be
able to forsake the bishops and continue in the demented company of schismatics and heretics.[27] But all the others, through
the mercy of God the Father, the compassion of Christ our Lord
and our own patience, will be reunited with us.

I wish that you, my dearly beloved brother, may ever fare
well.

LETTER 53

Maximus, Urbanus, Sidonius, and Macarius send greetings to Cyprian their brother.[1]

Dearly beloved brother, we feel confident that you too are filled with great joy at our news, just as much as we are. For after mature deliberation and putting highest priority on the peace and well-being of the Church, we have set aside all the past, leaving it to the judgment of God,[2] and we have made our peace with Cornelius our bishop and likewise with all of the clergy.[3]

This letter of ours should give you the fullest assurance that these events have been greeted with rejoicing by the entire Church and indeed with demonstrations of warm affection from all of our brothers.[4]

We pray that you, dearly beloved brother, may fare well for many years.[5]

LETTER 54

Cyprian sends greetings to his brothers Maximus, the presbyter, and to Urbanus, Sidonius, and Macarius.[1]

1.1 I have read, dearly beloved brothers, your letter which you wrote to me bringing news of your return to the Church, of the peace you have made with her as well as of your reunion with your brethren.[2] I must confess that my delight on reading this letter of yours was as great as it had been previously when I first learned of your glorious confession and received the joyful news of the heavenly and spiritual honours you had won in battle.[3]

1.2 For this is truly a further confession of faith, and it brings you further honour, namely, to confess that the Church is one, to refuse to have any part in unholy error or, I should rather say, degeneracy,[4] to turn back to the encampment from which you marched out, from which you did indeed charge forth with might and main to do battle and to subdue the enemy. It was only proper that from the field of battle you should bring back your trophies[5] to the place where you had received your arms for that battle. Otherwise those whom Christ had prepared for glory might not be found within the Church of Christ after they had won their glory.

1.3 But as it is you have properly maintained your unyielding grasp on your faith; by upholding the peace the Lord has given us you have also upheld the law of indivisible charity and concord; and by the steps you have taken you have set an example for others in brotherly love and desire for peace. Thus the true Church and the sacred bonds of unity established for it by the Gospel,[6] which we continued to support, might be further strengthened and more securely linked by your allegiance; hence, too, confessors of Christ might not become guides into error who had themselves so honourably led the way to bravery and to glory.

2.1 Others indeed may wish you congratulations and from your actions derive a personal sense of triumph, but in my own case I do know I can truthfully say that on this return of yours to peace and charity I wish you profound congratulations and from this action of yours I derive a far greater sense of triumph than anyone else. For in all honesty I must tell you what I have been feeling in my heart: I felt grievous pain and deep distress that I was unable to be in communion with those whom I had once come to love.

2.2 Instead, schismatic and heretical error was there to welcome you as you stepped forth from your prison. It was thereafter as if your glory had remained behind inside that prison. There, the honour of your name seemed to have taken up its abode, for the soldiers of Christ did not return to the Church from their prison, into which they had earlier entered to the praises and plaudits of that Church.[7]

3.1 It may be true that there appear to be tares within the Church, but that ought not create any obstacle for our faith and charity. There is no reason for us to depart from the Church ourselves simply because we perceive tares to be within it. All we must do is to strive to become wheat ourselves, so that when the wheat comes to be stored in the Lord's granaries, we may reap the harvest of our labour and toil.[8]

The Apostle declares in his epistle: *In a great household there are not only vessels of gold and silver, there are also vessels of wood and clay: and some are vessels for noble use, others for ignoble.*[9] It is up to us to struggle and strive to become vessels of gold and silver, but it is the prerogative of the Lord alone to smash the vessels of clay. It is into His hands that the rod of iron has been placed.[10]

3.2 The servant cannot be greater than his master,[11] nor can a man claim as his own a task which the father has assigned to the son alone. It is ridiculous for him to imagine that he is now fit to take up the fan for winnowing and purging the threshing-floor,[12] and that he can separate all of the tares from the wheat by using human judgment. That is a sacrilegious presumption, an insolent and arrogant pretention characteristic of evil and raving madmen.

3.3 Indeed there are some who arrogate to themselves authority to make more stringent demands than what gentle justice requires, whereas, being outside the Church, they are perishing themselves. Whilst they insufferably set themselves up on a pinnacle, they blind themselves by their own overblown superiority and lose the light of truth.

That is why we have kept to a temperate course: having our eyes fixed on the Lord's scales of justice and with our thoughts set on the compassion and mercy[13] of God the Father, we long deliberated and discussed amongst ourselves and we weighed what measures we should take in the scales of justice and moderation.[14]

3.4 You can get a complete view of all our thinking by reading those pamphlets which I have read out recently here and which out of fraternal affection I have already sent to you also for your perusal.[15] In them you will find for the benefit of the fallen both the censure which reproves and the physic which cures. And, moreover, we have tried to describe as far as our modest talents allowed the unity of the Catholic Church. I am confident that this latter pamphlet will now more than ever prove acceptable to you, because you will now read it approving and loving what it says. For what we have written out in words you are now realizing in deeds: it is because of the unity of charity and peace that you are now making your return to the Church.

I wish that you, dearly beloved brothers, may ever fare well.

NOTES

The typescript of this volume was submitted for publication in April, 1979 and I very much regret that it has not proved possible to make full note of the material that has appeared in print, or which has come to my attention, since that date. An asterisk in the margin refers to one of the few additional notes.

LIST OF ABBREVIATIONS

AC	Antike und Christentum
ANRW	*Aufstieg und Niedergang der römischen Welt*, ed H. Temporini
Bayard	L. Bayard, *Le latin de saint Cyprien* (Paris 1902)
Benson	E. W. Benson, *Cyprian, His Life, His Times, His Work* (London 1897)
Blaise	A. Blaise, *Dictionnaire latin-français des auteurs chrétiens* (rev. ed., Turnhout 1967)
CCL	Corpus christianorum, series latina
CIL	Corpus inscriptionum latinarum
DACL	Dictionnaire d'archéologie chrétienne et de liturgie
Duquenne	L. Duquenne, *Chronologie des lettres de s. Cyprien. Le dossier de la persécution de Dèce* (Brussels 1972)
Fahey	M. A. Fahey, *Cyprian and the Bible: A Study in Third-Century Exegesis* (Tübingen 1971)
Gülzow	H. Gülzow, *Cyprian und Novatian: Der Briefwechsel zwischen den Gemeinden in Rom und Karthago zur Zeit der Verfolgung des Kaisers Decius* (Tübingen 1975)
Hefele-Leclercq	C. J. Hefele and H. Leclercq, *Histoire des Conciles* (Paris vol. 1 1907, vol. 2 1908)
HTR	Harvard Theological Review
JAC	Jahrbuch für Antike und Christentum
JEH	Journal of Ecclesiastical History
JTS	Journal of Theological Studies
Melin	B. Melin, *Studia in Corpus Cyprianeum* (Uppsala 1946)
MGH	Monumenta Germaniae Historica

Monceaux, *Histoire*	P. Monceaux, *Histoire littéraire de l'Afrique chrétienne depuis les origines jusqu'à l'invasion arabe*, vol. 2: *Saint Cyprien et son temps* (Paris 1902)
Nelke	L. Nelke, *Die Chronologie der Korrespondenz Cyprians und der pseudocyprianischen Schriften ad Novatianum und Liber de Rebaptismate* (diss. Thorn 1902)
PSI	Papiri greci e latini
PWK	A. Pauly-G. Wissowa-W. Kroll, *Realencyclopädie der classischen Altertumswissenschaft*
RAC	Reallexikon für Antike und Christentum
REA	Revue des études anciennes
Ritschl, *Cyprian*	O. Ritschl, *Cyprian von Karthago und die Verfassung der Kirche* (Göttingen 1885)
Ritschl, *De epist.*	O. Ritschl, *De epistulis Cyprianicis* (diss. Halle a. S. 1885)
SC	Sources chrétiennes
SCA	Studies in Christian Antiquity
TAPA	Transactions and Proceedings of the American Philological Association
Thaninayagam	X. S. Thaninayagam, *The Carthaginian Clergy during the Episcopate of Saint Cyprian* (Colombo 1947)
TLL	Thesaurus linguae latinae
TU	Texte und Untersuchungen zur Geschichte der altchristlichen Literatur
VC	Vigiliae christianae
Watson	E. W. Watson, "The style and language of St. Cyprian," *Studia biblica* 4 (1896) 189 ff.
ZfKG	Zeitschrift für Kirchengeschichte
ZfKT	Zeitschrift für katholische Theologie
ZNTW	Zeitschrift für die neutestamentliche Wissenschaft und die Kunde der älteren Kirche

Introduction

1. For bibliography on Decius and his reign, see ACW 43, n. 109 to the Introduction. For dates and bibliography on Decius' rise to power, see X. Loriot in *Aufstieg und Niedergang der römischen Welt* 2.2 (1975) 794 ff. On Uranius, see n. 40 to Ep. 55.

2. For Carpi see Lactantius, *De mort. persec.* 4.3: *nam profectus adversus Carpos qui tum Daciam Moesiamque occupaverant.* Is this the time of the flight of the mother of Maximinianus? See Lactantius, *De mort. persec.* 9.2: *Transdanuviana infestantibus Carpis in Daciam novam transiecto amne confugerat.* For a convenient tabulation of ancient sources on these events and full modern bibliography, see B. Scardigli in *Aufstieg und Niedergang der römischen Welt* 2.5.1 (1976) 225 ff. Needless to say, the precise chronology and sequence of events is open to debate.

3. According to Ammianus Marcellinus, 31.5.17, one hundred thousand were massacred, *nisi fingunt annales.* For a succinct account of this revolt of T. Julius Priscus, see G. Walser in *Bucknell Review* 13.2 (1965) 5 f. Eutrop. 9.4 seems to have garbled matters, presenting Decius with an otherwise unattested Gallic revolt.

4. That is, of Julius Valens Licinianus. He is not to be confused with the Valens who was a pretender in the time of Gallienus; cf. T. D. Barnes in *Phoenix* 26 (1972) 175; L. Homo in *Revue historique* 137 (1921) 193 ff.

5. For Nicopolis, see F. Jacoby, *Die Fragmente der griechischen Historiker,* vol. 11A (Berlin 1926) no. 100. For the titles, C.I.L. 3.1176 = I.L.S. 514 (Apulum); C.I.L. 2.4949 (near Carthago Nova in Tarraconensis), cf. C.I.L. 2.4957, 4958.

6. On the petering out of the persecution, see ACW 43, Introduction p. 30 f. Decius was able to attend to such matters as a dispute over an intestate estate and the legal powers of procurators in the course of November and the beginning of December 250. See *Cod. Iust.* 6.58.3 (*ii non Dec.*) and 3.22.2 (*K. Dec.*).

7. The remarks of Cyprian, *Ep.* 55.9.1, have been often

taken as a direct reflection of Decius' own sentiments (Cornelius fearlessly took on the Roman pontificate at a period when Decius, hostile to bishops, would more calmly learn of the revolt against him by a rival emperor than of the appointment in Rome of a bishop of God). But the observation is more realistically to be attributed to Cyprian's imaginative rhetoric in defence of Cornelius' character (elected bishop under a persecuting emperor who was also harassed by revolts).

8. See further my article in *Latomus* 30 (1971) 1141 ff.

9. But the unanimity of this stand may be only apparent. The confessor Celerinus had after all sought *libelli martyrum* for his two sisters, and in putting his request he said he was supported by other confessors in Rome (? all African). See *Ep.* 21, esp. §4.

10. See *Ep.* 56.1.1. The *civitas* is Capsa. Seven bishops are mentioned, one of whom is presumably the newly appointed bishop of Capsa—*Donatulus a Capse*. See *Sent. Episc.* LXXXVII 69. On the fourth-century evidence, see P. Zmire in *Recherches augustiniennes* 7 (1971) 15 ff; Hefele-Leclercq 1.1.539 ff.; C. Pietri, *Roma Christiana* (Rome 1976) 680 ff.

11. See Eusebius, H.E. 6.44.1; 6.46.3; 7.4 f. See also H. J. Vogt, *Coetus Sanctorum* (Bonn 1968) 53 ff.

12. *Apud* Eusebius, H.E. 6.43.5 ff. But Fabius did receive from Cornelius other documents which condemned Novatian's doctrine; see *op. cit.* 6.43.3 f; 6.43.21 f.

13. At the Council of Antioch, Fabius of Antioch was now dead (replaced by Demetrian) and Thelymidres of Syrian Laodicea (alive to receive a letter from Dionysius of Alexandria on penitence in the post-Decian debate, Eusebius, *H.E.* 6.46.2) had been replaced by Heliodorus. If, as H. J. Lawlor and J. E. L. Oulton, *Eusebius, Bishop of Caesarea. The Ecclesiastical History and the Martyrs of Palestine* (vol. 2, repr. London 1954) suppose in their commentary on Eusebius, *H.E.* 7.4, Dionysius of Alexandria is referring to the period *after* the persecution of Gallus in his extract quoted by Eusebius in *H.E.* 7.5, then the Council should be meeting after the death of Cornelius (himself a victim under Gallus).

Cyprian's assertion to Antonianus that Cornelius had won universal approval among the world's bishops without exception was, therefore, more wishful than truthful. See *Ep.* 55.8.1.

Pontius, *Vit. Cypriani* 8.4, prudently refrains from detailed reference to these scandalous quarrels and divisions; he pays general tribute instead to the skilful navigation of Cyprian, the "spiritually temperate" steersman as he successfully guides the church between the clashing waves of schisms.

14. It is, however, a trifle uncertain whether Dionysius' "unexpected arrival of peace" (in which the bishops of the East rejoice) refers to the persecution of Decius or to that of Gallus or even to the new-found peace amongst the formerly divided bishops.

15. In the rhetorical and unreliable panegyric on Gregory Thaumaturgus.

16. For a recent review of the evidence, see R. M. Grant in *Forma Futuri: Festschrift Pellegrino* (Turin 1975) 647 ff.

17. For literature and varied opinion on these *Acta*, see ACW 43, n. 218 to the Introduction.

18. According to Jerome, *De viris illust.* 69, the letter to the Armenians discerned degrees of sinfulness (*de paenitentia et de ordine delictorum*); is this independent information or merely garbled extracting from Eusebius, *H.E.* 6.46.1 f? In any case, if the Armenians were debating such an issue, should we not deduce that Decius' orders extended into their area, presumably the province of Armenia Minor, and that we have, therefore, evidence that this province was securely under Roman control at the time? Armenia Minor was retained—or regained—by the Romans after the settlement with Persia struck by Philip. For discussion, see A. T. Olmstead in *Classical Philology* 37 (1942) 256 f. This is our first information on the Armenian church.

For fragments of Dionysius of Alexandria on repentance, see C. L. Feltoe, ΔΙΟΝΥΣΙΟΥ ΛΕΙΨΑΝΑ. *The Letter and Other Remains of Dionysius of Alexandria* (Cambridge 1904) 59 ff.

19. The Canonic Epistle attributed to Gregory Thaumaturgus (MG 10.1019 ff.)—it regulates problems left in the aftermath of the barbarian raids—lays down in *Canon* XI various stages of

reconciliation for the penitent. It may well reflect processes of reconciliation that applied also to problems left in the aftermath of the Decian persecution.

20. This is more fully examined in my article, "Persecution under Gallus: Correspondence of Cyprian during the Principate of Gallus," appearing in *Aufstieg und Niedergang der römischen Welt* 2.27.

21. Most recently analysed by M. Bévenot in *Heythrop Journal* 19 (1978(123 ff.

22. Attempts to date the treatise *De zelo et livore* to this period (made, for example, by H. Koch, *Cyprianische Untersuchungen* [Bonn 1926] 132 ff.) are not compelling, though the setting of 251 is appropriate enough. Pontius, *Vit. Cypriani* 7, lists it as a companion piece of *De bono patientiae,* and on this showing it would appear to belong rather to an equally appropriate context of c.256 (*Ep.* 73.26). Certainty is not obtainable.

LETTER 28

Contents: Cyprian writes to the Roman confessors. Before, they led the van on the battleground of persecution; now, they fight on with equal tenacity and honour in the battle to uphold the Gospel teachings. On both fronts they have shown themselves models of courage and faith. The powerful letter they have sent to the Carthaginian confessors, their colleagues, on the question of Church discipline has won for them in Rome honours no less glorious than the martyrs' crowns which have in fact already been won in Carthage. The glory of both Roman confessors and Carthaginian martyrs sheds glory upon the whole Church.

Date and circumstances: Manifestly this letter is contemporaneous with *Ep.* 27 and it was therefore sent, at a rough estimate, in "mid- to late summer 250" (see introductory note to *Ep.* 27). In *Ep.* 27.4 Cyprian mentions the reception of two letters, one from the Roman clergy (addressed to the Carthaginian clergy), the other from the Roman confessors (addressed to the Carthaginian confessors). *Ep.* 27 is Cyprian's response to the Roman clergy; this letter, *Ep.* 28, is the matching response to the Roman confessors. *Ep.* 31 is the reply from the confessors to this letter.

The letter betrays careful balance and composition. It opens with elaborate and intricate flattery for the Roman confessors; they took the initial stand in confession and they must share, therefore, in the honour which the Carthaginian martyrs have gained, for they were their model in confession. The letter closes, by careful contrivance, with clear echoes of and variations on that opening theme. But firmly focussed in the centre is praise for the Roman confessors' letter, for its rigorous tenor and for its emphatic message. They continue to be a model in upholding church discipline. In this they are obedient to the missionary precepts of the Gospel. Theirs is the true witness to Christ. Thus there is praise for the confessors in Rome, praise for the martyred dead (under torture) in Carthage. Eloquently, there is no word of praise for Carthaginian confessors. Cyprian's unstated criticisms are aimed with careful accuracy.

It has been argued that Cyprian now sends copies of *Ep.* 28 and the (non-extant) letter from the Roman confessors to his Carthaginian clergy, accompanied by *Ep.* 29. If so (and I find this hypothesis very doubtful), that was before he had waited to receive any replies from Rome (*Epp.* 30 and 31). The strictness and the authority of the Roman *confessors* (along with his own carefully worded reply to them) provided Cyprian with weapons too nicely calculated for him to lay aside in his dispute with his local confessors. But, this argument would continue, it is not until he has received from the Roman clergy their highly reassuring *Ep.* 30 that he is prepared to distribute to Carthage copies of that letter along with his much less circumspectly composed *Ep.* 27, adding *Ep.* 31, the letter by then received from the Roman confessors in reply to this (see *Ep.* 32.1.1). That scenario would explain the sustained reticence of this letter and the contrasting outspokenness of the contemporaneous *Ep.* 27. But not necessarily. Deferential respect for confessors, and the importance of maintaining the invaluable support of such honoured heroes, provide an equally satisfying and less complicated explanation for the tone and tactic of this letter.

For our knowledge of the history of the persecution there are some interesting features: persecution (and arrests) came to Africa perceptibly later than in Rome (§ 1). (Cyprian should have had, therefore, fair warning to effect his retreat.) But even in Rome over all these many months two presbyters only (out of a tally of some fifty or thereabouts; see n. 1 below) have been caught; most presbyters clearly have gone underground or fallen away. But even those imprisoned have not so far been tortured (§1.2) and certainly Cyprian has had no word of unusually distressing privations or sufferings for them; there is nothing to lead him to anticipate martyrdoms amongst their number. That there is no suggestion of such miseries, nor any immediate expectation of them, in the confessors' reply, *Ep.* 31, goes some way to confirm this impression of the general circumstances of the Roman confessors (note esp. §5.1 of that letter). It appears that some of them may even still be waiting formal trial. By the time of *Ep.* 37 (winter 250/251), however, Cyprian had intelligence (*via* Celerinus) of repeated interrogations (§§1.3, 3.1) and some deaths endured by these confessors. And, later, Cyprian eulogistically conjured up for them battle trophies (scars?) in *Ep.* 54.1.2: *illuc enim erant de acie tropaea referenda unde ad aciem fuerant arma suscepta.* (On the interpretation of *tropaea* there, see n. 5 to *Ep.* 54.) Does Optatus deliver especially *Ep.* 28 (see *Epp.* 29.1.2, 35.1.1), a Carthaginian confessor to the Roman confessors, demonstrating in person that not all Carthaginian confessors were of like mind with Lucianus and his followers? Cf. n. 3 to *Ep.* 50. *Ep.* 28 is further discussed by Gülzow 79 ff.

1. A remarkable group; Cyprian mentions by name the two presbyters in their ranks as the senior clerics amongst them. There were also two deacons, Nicostratus and Rufinus (see, e.g., *Ep.* 27.4, *Ep.* 31 *init., Ep.* 32.1.1); and four other names are known to us—Celerinus (see, e.g., *Ep.* 37.1.1f.), Macarius, Urbanus, and Sidonius (see, e.g., *Ep.* 49.1.3). On the possibility of a second Celerinus, see n. 1 to *Ep.* 21. There were clearly others (see *Ep.* 37.1.3, 3.1), some perhaps included in the *plerique fratres qui eis se adiunxerant* of *Ep.* 49.2.2. Cyprian's varying combinations of names seem partly due to the formulations on the headings of the letters emanating from the group: thus *Ep.* 27.4 is matched by *Ep.* 28 [*salutatio*]; *Ep.* 31 [*salutatio*] is matched by *Ep.* 32.1.1 (in some mss); *Ep.* 53 [*salutatio*] is matched by *Ep.* 54 [*salutatio*].

Moyses disappears from the correspondence after *Ep.* 37 (i.e., he does not figure in *Epp.* 46, 49, 53, 54 in the post-persecution history of the group). The *Liber Pontificalis* puts his death in prison after a period there of eleven months: *Moyses in carcere defunctus est qui fuit ibi menses XI,* (ed. Mommsen, p. 27); the Chronog. 354 has, more precisely, *menses XI dies XI* (ed. Mommsen, MGH 9.75). He will have died, therefore, not long after the composition of *Ep.* 37 (winter 250/251), nor very long before his companions emerged into daylight, released from their internment (? Feb. 251). Cyprian and Cornelius both regarded him unequivocally as a martyr; see *Ep.* 55.5.2 and *apud* Eusebius, *H.E.* 6.43.20. Before his death in prison, according to Cornelius, he broke off communion with Novatian (ἀκοινώνητον ἐποίησεν)as well as with the five presbyters who had separated from the Church with him; see *apud* Eusebius, *H.E.* 6.43.20; cf. n. 32 to *Ep.* 14. This somewhat doubtfully puts the formal Novatianist schism very early in the year 251. Is Cornelius conveniently extrapolating, for his apologetic purposes, from the subsequent behaviour of the temporarily Novatianizing Roman confessors (see *ap.* Eusebius, *H.E.* 6.43.6) to the previous attitude expected of their companion and senior, the now martyred and honoured Moyses himself (Moyses clearly having been once associated with Novatian, being a signatory to *Ep.* 30; see *Ep.* 55.5.2)? That certainly gave the climax of Cornelius' letter to Fabius of Antioch a powerful concluding thrust, and made Cornelius' church unequivocally the church of the confessors and the martyred. But Cyrprian seems to put the timing differently for the actual schism: *posteaquam vos de carcere prodeuntes schismaticus et haereticus error excepit* (*Ep.* 54.2.2), and for that matter so do the Calendars: e.g., *Novatus . . . separavit de ecclesia Novatianum et quosdam confessores postquam Moyses in carcere defunctus est* (*Liber Pontificalis*, ed. Mommsen, p. 27). Is some (informal) death-bed renunciation by Moyses of the rigorist penitential line later to be espoused by Novatian and his party the basis for Cornelius' assertion? Cf. Nelke 69 f., n. 7, for similar hesitations. To judge from our records, Moyses was not accorded a cult in Rome, which was behind Africa in developing a regular cult of its martyrs. Cf. H. Delehaye, *Les origines du culte des martyrs* (2nd ed., Brussels 1933) 263.

Maximus survived Moyses as the leader of the group. Their period of sympathy with the Novatianist schism is revealed in *Epp.* 46 ff. (there is already "another bishop" in *Ep.* 46.1.2). According to Cornelius, (see *ap.* Eusebius, *H.E.* 6.43.6) the period was of but brief duration, and Maximus leads them back into communion with Cornelius and his *presbyterium* in *Ep.* 49, exceptionally retaining himself his clerical rank. They thus became *confessores fideles* (*Liber Pontificalis*, ed. Mommsen, p. 28). For a possibly third-century Roman tombstone of a Maximus, presbyter, in Greek lettering, see ILCV 1128 adn. (*in Callisti*); cf. L. Hertling and E. Kirschbaum, *The Roman Catacombs and their Martyrs* (tr. by M. J. Costelloe; London 1960) 59.

In 251 Cornelius could claim 46 Roman presbyters as orthodox followers (see *ap.* Eusebius, *H.E.* 6.43.11). Do we add the deceased Moyses, the schismatic Novatian, and the five Novatianist presbyters mentioned in Eusebius to get a tally for the presbyterate of Rome of well over 50 for the pre-persecution conditions?

Nicostratus was Rufinus' senior in the diaconate (*Epp.* 31 and 32) and he remained a staunch Novatianist supporter, even becoming apparently (according to the dubious and unsupported testimony of the *Liber Pontificalis,* ed. Mommsen, p. 28) a Novatianist bishop in Africa: *Novatus Novatianum extra ecclesiam ordinavit et < in > Africa Nicostratum;* cf. Chronog. 354: *Novatus extra ecclesiam ordinavit Novatianum in urbe Roma et Nicostratum in Africa* (ed. Mommsen, MGH 9.75). He certainly went across to Africa as an apostle of the Novatianist cause (*Epp.* 50, 52.1.2), and he came over to the Novatianists bringing with him Church funds (a deacon's natural preserve; cf. n. 17 to *Ep.* 3)— *ecclesiae deposita non modica,* says Cornelius in *Ep.* 50, where see n. 6—which rouses Cyprian to a spirited and memorable piece of indignation (*Ep.* 52.1.2). L. Bayard (ed.), *Saint Cyprien. Correspondance* (2nd ed.) vol. 2.333, separates in his *index des noms propres* the Nicostratus (Roman confessor deacon) of *Epp.* 27.4, 32.1.1., and 46, from the Nicostratus (Novatianist Roman deacon) of *Epp.* 50 and 52.1.2 who boasted that he was a confessor. There is no need for the separation. H. Leclercq in DACL 8 (1928) *s.v.* Laurent (saint) 1919 asserts that Nicostratus was the "archdeacon" under Fabian. That is without warrant.

Rufinus appears as a deacon in *Epp.* 31 and 32, but he disappears thereafter. Clearly there were no other loyalist clerics in this group (apart from Maximus) by the time of the reconciliation with Cornelius. Might we possibly list him, therefore, as one of the victims recorded anonymously in *Ep.* 37 among the Roman confessors, for no Rufinus figures as a Novatianist schismatic?

In 251 Cornelius could claim seven deacons (the full number) to be amongst his clergy in Rome (see *ap.* Eusebius, *H.E.* 6.43.11); there have been apparently some prompt promotions (cf. the episcopal replacement announced in *Ep.* 50.1.2).

For further reading on this group see K. Müller in ZfKG 16

(1896) 216 ff.; H. J. Lawlor and J. E. L. Oulton, *Eusebius, Bishop of Caesarea. The Ecclesiastical History and the Martyrs of Palestine*, vol. 2 (commentary), (repr. London 1954) at Eusebius, *H.E.* 6.43.5; H. J. Vogt, *Coetus sanctorum* (Bonn 1968) 41 ff.; Gülzow 71 ff.

2. *iam pridem.* On this elastic, and therefore not very informative, temporal expression, see n. 7 to *Ep.* 1.

3. *de opinione cognoveram.* That is to say, as opposed to the certain communication imparted by the letter of §2.1. Note Cyprian's intelligence service; cf. *Ep.* 9.1.1 (on Fabian's death).

4. *gloriam fidei et virtutis vestrae.* On possible resonances of the phrase *fides et virtus* in contexts of martyrdom, cf. n. 3 to *Ep.* 10.

5. *vos surgentis belli inpetus primos ... fregistis.* Cyprian is unequivocal that the Romans led the confessional stand in this persecution. It is very curious that Fabian (see n. 4 to *Ep.* 9) goes unmentioned here. If one can place reliance on the phrasing of the *Liber Pontificalis*—which is asking a bit much of those redactors' literary finesse—these Roman confessors were in fact not arrested until after Fabian's death: *Et post passionem eius Moyses et Maximus presbiteri et Nicostratus diaconus comprehensi sunt et in carcere missi sunt* (ed. Mommsen, p. 27; cf. Chronog. 354, MGH 9.75). Did Cyprian perceive Fabian's apprehension (and death) as being separable from the general perils of the persecution—a special initial arrest, perhaps? (Compare n. 2 to *Ep.* 5 on the possibility of special imperial orders against bishops in advance of the general onslaught of the persecution.)

6. *contigit hic per tormenta consummari (v.l.: consummare) martyria.* Cyprian is referring to the advent of tortures, and consequently perfected witnesses, in Carthage. He is thinking of Mappalicus, Paulus, and the other martyrs of *Epp.* 10 and 22. On the tortures, see nn. 5 and 6 to *Ep.* 10. By implication is Cyprian suggesting there are not severe tortures yet in Rome? And should we deduce that Cyprian would not be prepared to express himself thus if he regarded Fabian's death in Rome as being ascribable to tortures?

7. *de poculo salutari fratribus propinastis.* Pacian may be imitating this phrase in his *Ep.* 2.7: *novissime salutari calice propina-*

tus est; but cf. Cyprian's *Ep.* 63.7.2: *calicem prior biberet quo credentibus propinaret,* and *De bono pat. 7: salutari poculo propinavit.*

8. *disciplinae tenor.* On *disciplina,* see n. 9 to *Ep.* 11. Cyprian now sounds the dominant note of this message.

9. *ad collegas vestros in confessione vobiscum Domini copulatos.* The variant reading *Domino* yields attractive sense ("who are united to the Lord with you in confession"). On the use of *collegae* for fellow confessors, cf. *Ep.* 10 n. 25.

10. *tradita nobis semel mandata vitalia.* The *nobis* is generalizing, as opposed to the first person singular used in this letter by Cyprian of himself individually (*cognoveram, laetatus [sum], gratulatus [sum], laetor, gratulor, opto*).

11. Matt. 28.18 ff. and John 2.3 f. See Fahey 328 ff., 527. Cyprian has already alluded to the Matthew text in the companion letter, *Ep.* 27.3.3, where see n. 24.

12. *haec praecepta custodienda suggeritis, divina et caelestia mandata servatis.* With his usual technique, Cyprian picks up words from his quotations to reinforce verbally the application of the texts to the instance he is citing. *Praecepta custodienda* echoes *quaecumque praecepi* and *praecepta . . . custodiamus; mandata servatis* echoes *mandata . . . servat;* in the following sentence *servare* and *praecepta* are deliberately reused.

13. Note Cyprian's special difficulty: the widely accepted status of the martyrs made easy the way for them to mislead others, and Cyprian has few precise texts he can invoke for the actual penitential discipline which he has inherited to administer.

14. *laetor . . . gratulor.* Cyprian is now picking up in his concluding greetings phrases with which he opened his letter (*laetatus satis et plurimum gratulatus*), reinforcing the honour he acknowledges for the Roman confessors. The effect has been carefully calculated.

15. *honoris vestri participes et nos sumus.* There is a passing hint that, just as the Roman confessors have partners in the Carthaginian confessors, in confessional honours, so, with equal distinction, they have partners in Cyprian and his colleagues, in disciplinary honours.

16. *probatos servos Dei et Christi milites coronatos.* The first phrase applies essentially to the Roman confessors, the second to the Carthaginian martyrs.

LETTER 29

Contents: To his clergy, for their information, Cyprian sends copies of recent correspondence he has had. He also informs them of two clerical appointments he has made; clerical messengers were needed for the despatch of correspondence he was sending to Rome. The two men so appointed had already passed general scrutiny as prospective candidates for clerical office.

Date and circumstances: The place of *Ep.* 29 in the correspondence would be explained by the identification of the letters referred to in §1.1.

The most reasonable candidate for the letter *mihi scriptum* is the document referred to in *Ep.* 33.1.2 directed to Cyprian personally and composed anonymously, and provocatively, *ecclesiae nomine;* its general, insolent, contents are disclosed by *Ep.* 35.1.1. Hence, contrary to his habit, Cyprian does not say who wrote the message and to whom he sent his reply (contrast, for example, *Ep.* 26.1.3 or *Ep.* 27.3.2). The acephalous *Ep.* 33 appears to be the reply of Cyprian's referred to, covering altogether two or three (non-extant) pieces of correspondence directed to him by anonymous *lapsi* (addressed simply as *fratres* in *Ep.* 33.2.2).

If this is so, the exchange of letters (*Ep.* 33 *et al.*) will have occurred shortly before this letter, but after Cyprian had sent Saturus and Optatus off to Rome bearing *Epp.* 27 and 28. For when he writes to Rome next (*Ep.* 35)—perhaps even before *Epp.* 30 and 31 have come from Rome—Cyprian proceeds to send to the Roman clergy a copy of *Ep.* 33 and the offending document which provoked it, asserting specifically that this correspondence had taken place after he had last written to them. We can accordingly discern a brisk flurry of letters, promptly dealt with by Cyprian at this critical stage as he endeavours not to let the dispute over the lapsed get totally out of his episcopal control.

With such a placing for *Ep.* 29—after *Epp.* 27 and 28, but certainly before the replies to *Epp.* 27 and 28 viz. *Epp.* 30 and 31—we are in the vicinity of latish summer 250. For further reading, see among others C. H. Turner, *Studies in Early Church History* (Oxford 1912) 115 n. 3; H. von Soden in TU 25.3 (1904) 29; Duquenne 138 f.; Gülzow 14; Nelke 43.

A notable feature of the letter is Cyprian's insistence that he must have messengers of clerical status for delivering his correspondence. This tellingly reveals the mentality of a Church that has become very much a society within a society; the extent of the "clericalization" of its activities is indeed startlingly revealed. In assuming the dignity of bishop, Cyprian expected the existence of a well-developed bureau of clerical ministers, to be at his episcopal service. The measure—Cyprian assumes agreement as to its propriety—was no doubt felt to be the best safeguard against corruption of a letter's contents for the benefit of internal enemies in the Church (hence the pointed indignation of *Ep.* 9.2.2: *perquam ... grave est si epistulae clericae veritas mendacio aliquo et fraude corrupta est*) as well as a safeguard against the betrayal of a letter's content to external enemies of the Church (cf. *Ep.* 80.1.1; there had been a delay in getting word to Successus as all the clergy had been in mortal peril and none could therefore safely travel). Such messengers would not merely deliver documents; they were important contacts for the gathering of information and for the verbal exchange of news and views; they needed to be reliable witnesses and as clerics, they were answerable to their bishop (cf. the activities, for example, of Primitivus, and of Mettius and Niceforus in Rome, *Epp.* 44.2.2, 45.4.3, 47.1.2, 49.3.1, 52.1.1).

Another notable feature of the letter is the anxiety which Cyprian discloses: he takes trouble not to cause any offence with his already offended clergy. He is at pains to underline the fact that of the two men appointed clerics one was a confessor and both had been already approved collectively, by Cyprian and his clergy, as probationary clerics. Cyprian is not therefore acting, as might appear, on his own. His defensively written and cautiously worded phrases to his clergy are sensitive indicators of Cyprian's care to avoid action that his clergy might find abrasive; relations are clearly very delicate. But the fact was rather hard to disguise all the same that Cyprian was starting to build up the depleted ranks of his clergy, appointing candidates whom he found personally sympathetic and amenable, Saturus and Optatus (here), Aurelius, Celerinus, and Numidicus (*Epp.* 38, 39, 40). Presumably Saturus and Optatus, being on hand, had formed part of his own entourage in hiding (see n. 17 to *Ep.* 5; cf. *Ep.* 16.4.1 and n. 28 thereto). Cyprian's custom was to be surrounded by such companionship. Cf. the remarks of his deacon Pontius on Cyprian's last night: *eum ... continuit custodia delicata, ita ut convivae eius et cari in contubernio ex more fuerimus* (*Vita Cypriani* 15.5).

1. On this curt and colorless form of *salutatio,* see n. 1 to *Ep.* 5.

2. See introductory note to this letter. On the possibility that Cyprian may be referring to the epistle from the Roman confessors (see *Ep.* 27.4) and his reply (*Ep.* 28), see introductory note to *Ep.* 28. Cyprian's phrasing here (*quid mihi scriptum sit*), whilst the letter from the confessors was not actually addressed to him, is pretty decisive against that possibility.

3. This appears to be *Ep.* 27; see introductory note to this letter. Cyprian begins his defensive note—he acted with promptness and without prior consultation of his clergy *urguente causa.* He does not, however, venture at this stage to specify the nature of the *causa* or to send to his clergy a copy of that outspoken letter, *Ep.* 27. He does that only when he has been reassured of widespread and vigorous support for his stand from Rome in *Epp.* 30 and 31 (cf. *Ep.* 32.1.1). What he is prepared to send now is a copy of the blander and more generalized *Ep.* 33 which repeats points already made about his general stance and policy towards the *lapsi,* as contained in *Epp.* 15–20.

4. *oportuit me per clericos scribere.* Cyprian is prepared to use a strong verb to designate obligation and necessity (*oportuit*); clearly, the practice was well established and unquestioned. *Ep.*

80.1.1 reveals that Cyprian is not referring only to the delivery of important episcopal messages overseas; Successus, to whom *Ep.* 80 is addressed, is a local African bishop established at no great distance from Carthage in the Proconsular province (see J.-L. Maier, *L'épiscopat de l'afrique romaine, vandale et byzantine* [Neuchâtel 1973] 96) and messages to him also needed to be delivered *per clericos.* See generally on the subject H. Leclercq in DACL 14 (1948) *s.vv.* poste publique et privée 1631 ff.; D. Gorce, *Les voyages, l'hospitalité et le port des lettres dans le monde chrétien des IV et Ve siècles* (Paris 1925) esp. 205 ff.

5. *nostros plurimos absentes esse.* Of the steadfast clergy some may indeed be among the exiled (e.g. Rogatianus), but Cyprian is clearly referring to the many Carthaginian clergy who had simply made themselves scarce—*recesserunt* (cf. *Ep.* 34.4.1: *multi adhuc de clero absentes sint*)— and who had not yet resumed their posts (three who had recently returned are named in *Ep.* 34.4.1). With his clerical officers so deserting their posts, as Cyprian viewed it, and for so long and in such number, it is little wonder Cyprian has had such difficulties in maintaining *disciplina ecclesiastica.*

6. *paucos vero qui illic sunt vix ad ministerium cotidianum operis sufficere. Illic,* by Cyprianic usage, refers to the place to which he is writing, viz. Carthage, cf. n. 4 to *Ep.* 5; n. 36 to *Ep.* 21. R. Gryson in *Revue d'histoire ecclésiastique* 68 (1973) 361, mistakenly interprets Cyprian to be talking about clerics in his own hideaway: "un petit nombre autour de lui qui pouvaient à peine suffire aux tâches de tous les jours."—The phrasing *ministerium cotidianum operis* is a typical piece of rich Cyprianic ambiguity, *operis* being suggestive above all of works of mercy and charity (but it could be broader in application), whilst *ministerium* brings with it overtones of (subordinate) administrative duties as well as of strictly liturgical functions.

7. On readers (the lowest clerical rank in Carthage), see n. 6 to *Ep.* 23; on subdeacons, see n. 1 to *Ep.* 8. Why is Optatus given higher status (bypassing in fact the ranks of exorcist and acolyte)? He may indeed be older than Saturus or more tried as a *lector doctorum audientium* (see n. 12 below), and besides, as Cyprian's own case shows, all clerics need not necessarily go through

all the minor grades of office: *mora denique circa gratiam Dei nulla, nulla dilatio . . . presbyterium vel sacerdotium statim accepit* (Pontius, *Vit. Cyp.* 3). But his special status as confessor is probably the basic explanation for such rapid advancement in clerical office (for a good commentary, see *Ep.* 38.2.1: *merebatur talis clericae ordinationis ulteriores gradus et incrementa maiora . . .*). But Cyprian does not elaborate on the confessional honours, as he does in the cases of Celerinus, Aurelius, and Numidicus; he has, rather, the irrefutable fact of *commune consilium* to exploit. Note the presence of a released confessor with Cyprian; he is free to travel about, even to Rome (cf. nn. 6 and 36 to *Ep.* 21). On such releases in this persecution, see Introduction in ACW 43.35 and n. 209.

8. *iam pridem*. Unfortunately from this phrase we cannot tell precisely how long ago. See n. 7 to *Ep.* 1; n. 35 to *Ep.* 13. Precision might have helped in dating Cyprian's appointment as bishop.

9. *communi consilio clero proximos feceramus*. Cyprian now deliberately changes from the first person singular which he has been using hitherto (e.g. *rescripserim, misi, rescripsi, scio*) to the first person plural (*feceramus*, with *dedimus, probaremus, constituimus* to follow). Clergy and bishop had acted in concert (cf. n. 45 to *Ep.* 4; n. 34 to *Ep.* 16; n. 3 to *Ep.* 20), and the pluperfect tense used here has the effect of making the action decisive and firmly placed back in the past. Observe that Cyprian is saying distinctly that Saturus and Optatus had not been made clerics, but that they had been put on probation for appointment as such (see n. 12 below). *Proximus* may indeed bear some of its technical bureaucratic sense of "assistant to"—see n. 4 to *Ep.* 24; Watson 261. Cyprian is not saying that lectors as a class are only "next to the clergy" (*contra* J. G. Davies in JEH 14 [1963] 11); Celerinus, as a lector, is *clero nostro coniunctum* in *Ep.* 39.1.1.

10. *Saturo die Paschae semel atque iterum lectionem dedimus*. Of the clerical appointments made by Cyprian *tout seul* during his period in hiding, Saturus was the only one who was not a confessor. But, Cyprian insists, he had already been tried publicly in the basic function of his office, the lowest clerical rank of all. He reappears in *Ep.* 35.1.1. Need he be distinguished from the Satyrus (variant reading, Saturus), lector, of *Ep.* 32.1.2 whom

Cyprian appointed as official supervisor for transcribing copies
of *Epp.* 30 and 31, the replies to *Epp.* 27 and 28 which Saturus
and Optatus presumably brought back with them from Rome?
He may also be identical with the cleric, now an acolyte, who,
once again, had been in Rome, in *Ep.* 59.1.1 (Saturus; variant
reading, Satyrus).

   die Paschae. What day is being referred to? Is it the day of
Christ's suffering and death? Cf. Tertullian, *Adv. Iud.* 10.18:
pascha esse domini, id est passionem Christi; etc. That was perhaps
based on the popular derivation of *Pascha* from πάσχειν. Or
does Cyprian's usage include the day of Christ's triumph over
suffering and death as well, as suggested by *Ep.* 56.3: *inter Paschae
prima sollemnia,* and as implied unequivocally by Celerinus, a
contemporary Carthaginian, in *Ep.* 21.2.1: *in die laetitiae Paschae
flens? Pascha* by itself could also refer to the preceding Lenten
fast; see, e.g., Tertullian, *De ieiun.* 14.3: *numquam nisi in pascha
ieiunandum;* cf. Dionysius of Alexandria, *Ep. ad Basilid., init.* For
further discussion, see H. Koch in *Zeitschrift für wiss. Theol.* 55
(1914) 289 ff.; V. Saxer, *Vie liturgique et quotidienne à Carthage
vers le milieu du troisième siècle* (Vatican City 1969) 51 f.

   semel atque iterum. I cannot tell for certain whether this phrase
makes the reference to more than one Easter celebration or
merely to different times on the one Easter. In either case, by
the use of the plural *dedimus* in this context, Cyprian must be
referring to pre-persecution conditions. He was doubtless bishop, therefore, by at least Easter, April 15, 249 (see Introduction
in ACW 43.16, and cf. S. Colombo in *Didaskaleion* 6 [1928]
12—though his view that Cyprian's condition as fugitive at
Easter of 250 *must* put the readings back to 249 does not fully
convince). There may be some slight hope of pushing Saturus'
readings back to the Easter of 248—the *modo,* used next of
Optatus, is intended to stand in contrast; but it could well refer
to the period between Easter 249 and the end of that year.

   Thaninayagam 53 unconvincingly adduces this passage for
the general assertion: "The promotion, in the case of those
destined for higher orders, took place at Easter."

   11. *modo cum presbyteris doctoribus lectores diligenter probaremus.*
The construing is by no means beyond dispute. Cyprian has

switched from the indicative mood after *quando* (*dedimus*) to the subjunctive (*probaremus*). That has the effect of suggesting *cum* ought to be here construed as a conjunction, governing *probaremus*, whereas the overall framework, *quando aut . . . dedimus aut modo . . . probaremus*, suggests that *cum* ought rather to be taken as a preposition, governing *presbyteris doctoribus*. In favour of the former interpretation—here translated—are, for example, Ritschl, *Cyprian* 171 f.; R. Gryson in *Revue d'histoire ecclésiastique* 68 (1973) 362 n. 2; O. Bulhart in TLL 5.1.1776.69. The latter interpretation is made, for example, by L. Bayard (ed.), *Saint Cyprien. Correspondance* (2nd ed., 2 vols.; Paris 1961–1962) *ad loc.*; L. Bayard, *Le latin de saint Cyprien* (Paris 1902) 226; A. Vilela, *La condition collégiale des prêtres au troisième siècle* (Paris 1971) 270, 296; J. G. Davies in JEH 14 (1963) 11; Thaninayagam 53.

In either case we seem to have a class of priest designated as *presbyter doctor*. Such presbyters were obviously involved in the task of instruction. They would appear to be teachers of potential clerics, in the case of the latter interpretation, or would be most naturally teachers of catechumens, in the case of the former interpretation (see next n.); they may indeed have been both. The rare phrase occurs already in *Act. Perp.* 13.1: *Aspasium presbyterum doctorem*, and reoccurs in the later (304 A.D.) *Act. Saturnin., Dativi et soc.* 10: *o admiranda satis ac praedicandi presbyteri doctoris divina responsio.* Was the aged presbyter Caecilian, who instructed Cyprian, one such *presbyter doctor* (Pontius, *Vit. Cyp.* 4)? There may also be a reference in Ps. Clement, *Hom.* 3.71: πρεσβυτέρους κατηκητάς (unless there is to be a comma * placed between the two words).

12. *Optatum inter lectores doctorum audientium constituimus.* Though Optatus had been appointed a reader, his was a specialized task and he was still not yet a cleric. The catechists for whom he worked may well have included laymen; cf. *Ep.* 73.3.2: *doctori* without qualification; Tertullian, *De praes. heret.* 3.5: *si episcopus, si diaconus, si vidua, si virgo, si doctor, si etiam martyr . . .*; *Act. Perp.* 4.5: the Saturus who appears to have been the instructor of Perpetua is given no clerical rank; Hippolytus, *Apost. Trad.* 19: *sive clericus est qui dat* (*doctrinam*) *sive laicus.* Were the *presbyteri doctores* the leaders of the general class of catechists

(*doctores audientium*), clerical and lay, and hence the two different expressions? The tasks of the catechists (*doctores*) are outlined in Hippolytus, *Apost. Trad.* 15, 18, 19, 20; Optatus must have helped with Scripture readings; the *Catecheses* of Cyril of Jerusalem in the next century are each preceded by a Lesson. On the catechumenate generally, see n. 28 to *Ep.* 8.

Note that in the Arsinoite nome Dionysius of Alexandria summons not only the presbyters but also the "teachers of the brethren of the villages" (= catechists?) to a three-day conference in order to correct erroneous interpretations of the Scriptures current in the locality. See *ap.* Eusebius, *H.E.* 7.24.6.

There is a later and detailed picture of a developed system of young clerics undergoing their probationary period in Basil, *Ep.* 54, the beginnings of which we here see glimpsed in these pre-persecution activities of Cyprian:

"The practice that has long been followed in God's churches was to accept subdeacons for the service of the Church only after a very careful investigation. Their conduct was inquired into in every detail, to learn if they were not railers, or drunkards, or quick to quarrel, and whether they so controlled their youthful spirits as to be able to achieve that 'holiness without which no man shall see God.' Now while this examination was conducted by priests and deacons living with the candidates, these would then refer the matter to the chorepiscopi, who, after receiving the votes of those who were in the strict sense of the word witnesses and giving notice to their bishop, then enrolled the subdeacon as a member of the sacred orders." (trans. R. J. Deferrari, Loeb, vol. 1, 343 f.)

13. With careful emphasis Cyprian repeats his main points in these concluding remarks: the two appointments were envisaged long ago (*nihil ... novum, iam pridem*), were universally approved by the clergy (*communi consilio omnium nostrum*) and were now concluded only because of the special circumstances (*necessitate urguente*). This is calculated diplomacy at work. Not that we should conclude that Cyprian could not so act on his own (*contra* Dix in *Laudate* 15 [1937] 117) or against the expressed wishes of his clergy (cf., the case of Fabian and Novatian, Cornelius *ap.* Eusebius, *H.E.* 6.43.17), but that it was manifestly

impolitic not to enlist the support and agreement of the clergy for additions to their number. And that the candidates were worthy of their office (however humble) needed to be demonstrated to them. Cyprian wasn't just stacking the Carthaginian clergy with creatures of his own. Only too recently had the Carthaginian clergy suffered an appointment of which many still did not approve (Cyprian himself). *Commune consilium* was clearly the general method for selecting clerics, however, as the process for screening Saturus and Optatus demonstrates.

On clerical elections generally in Cyprian, there is recent discussion in R. Gryson in *Revue d'histoire ecclésiastique* 68 (1973) 353 ff.; P. Granfield in *Theological Studies* 37 (1976) 41 ff.; J. Speigl, in *Römische Quartalschrift* 69 (1974) 30 ff. On "collegiality" in Cyprian's administration generally, see G. H. Luttenberger in *Recherches de théologie ancienne et médiévale* 43 (1976) 49 ff.

LETTER 30

Contents: Cyprian is assured by the Roman clergy of the rightness of his own conduct both in upholding the Gospel discipline and in inviting others to share in the wisdom of his counsels. The Roman church, too, with its pedigree of ancient faith, has lived up to its own traditions in the Gospel faith: they, too, have opposed those who have acquired certificates of sacrifice whether by their own actions or through the agency of others—these lapsed have polluted their consciences no less than if they had actually committed idolatry. For so grievous a sin there can be no quick remedy, and the glorious Roman confessors concur with this view, strictly adhering to the Gospel discipline and refusing to issue certificates of forgiveness. Cyprian's letter to them has given them fresh spirit for their martyrdom. Being without their bishop, the Roman clergy must wait for a final decision on these issues until the coming of peace and until the holding of a widely based council can make possible a widely accepted solution, just as Cyprian himself advises. All must pray together for peace and for the strength to hold on until that peace comes. With the advice of neighbouring and overseas bishops the numerous Roman clergy have long been of the moderate opinion that no changes should be made until they have their new bishop. Only the most urgent cases which cannot be deferred, those of the dying, are meanwhile to be reconciled, but strictly on the condition that they have shown themselves to be truly repentant.

Date and circumstances: This letter is the Roman clergy's response, to Cyprian personally, to both his *Ep.* 20 and *Ep.* 27; it contains specific reference to *Ep.* 28, a letter contemporaneous with *Ep.* 27. It is to be dated, therefore, after the receipt of *Epp.* 27 and 28 in Rome, that is to say, after the "August/September" assigned to that pair. Furthermore, Cyprian appears to have written off to Rome *Ep.* 35 (with its enclosures) before he has received back from Rome this *Ep.* 30. There is no mention of his having received *Ep.* 30 in *Ep.* 35 and this letter from Rome makes no allusion to that correspondence and its problems. *Ep.* 35 will have crossed with *Ep.* 30. Should we allow, therefore, some little delay for the developments recorded in *Ep.* 35 and its enclosures to have taken place, before *Ep.* 30 was despatched to Cyprian, and place its composition, accordingly but vaguely, in the late summer of 250 A.D.? See, for example, Duquenne 139 n. 3 and Nelke 43 ff.

As *Ep.* 28 (to the Roman confessors) will have accompanied *Ep.* 27, so *Ep.* 31 (from the Roman confessors) will have accompanied this *Ep.* 30. *Ep.* 31 contains more manifest allusions to the enclosures of *Ep.* 20 in §6.1.

For about nine months of this year Cyprian has had little but silence from Rome. He has been aware, however, of misrepresentations of his conduct and actions made at Rome (*Ep.* 20.1.1), he has seen correspondence from Rome directed not to himself but to others, to the clergy in Carthage (the stinging *Ep.* 8, the letter mentioned in *Ep.* 27.4) as well as to the confessors of Carthage (*Ep.* 27.4). All he has received personally is a copy of the *testimonium* composed on the glorious and exemplary death of the Roman bishop, Fabian (*Ep.* 9.1); this was no doubt but one of many copies disseminated—and in the context Cyprian may well have sensed ambivalent intentions behind his being sent such a document. No reply had come from Rome to his *Ep.* 20, though letters had come to others.

Now, at long last, this humiliating silence is broken. This reply shows itself conscious of the slights and insults that have been made to Cyprian and about his conduct, and which Cyprian unmistakably had registered. It constitutes an elaborate apology for the previous attitude shown towards Cyprian and it provides deliberate and handsome vindication of the correctness both of his own personal actions and of his ecclesiastical policies.

The volte-face adopts several forms.

It ranges from the involuted arabesques of courtesy and politesse in its opening paragraphs—Cyprian has rather honoured Rome in allowing them to share in the faith and discipline to which he has borne witness—through the grandiloquent praises accorded his *Ep.* 28 (interpreted as a triumphant exhortation to martyrdom) in §5.1, to the contrived and downright flattery—Cyprian as confessor-bishop—with which the letter concludes (*beatissime et gloriosissime papa*).

But, more importantly, it deliberately aligns itself with the main points of Cyprian's disciplinary policies as they have evolved. The two grades of apostates, *libellatici* as well as *sacrificati*, are both seriously culpable (§§3.1 and 2), the abuse of *libelli martyrum* is not to be countenanced (§4), reconciliation is to be granted at this stage only to the repentant lapsed who are *in articulo mortis* (§8), final resolution of the problems must await a time when common counsel can be taken together by bishop, clergy and laity (§5.3). The key phrases for this interim policy are *temporamenti moderamen, nihil innovandum, caute et sollicite* (all in §8). Cyprian agreed.

Moreover, it is pointedly asserted that these are views long held by the majority of the Roman clergy (§8)—the counsels of *Ep.* 8.3 are, delicately, not referred to—and bishops from Italy and abroad have also concurred with them. Cyprian is made to feel that he is not struggling on alone against local and isolated problems, the universality of the devastation being stressed (§5.4). He will now be emboldened to act more confidently, given the assurance that he has allies such as these; he promptly proceeds to make careful arrangements to facilitate the wide dissemination of accurate copies of this letter. In fact, by the time of *Ep.* 55, he can boldly assert that copies of this letter have been distributed *per totum mundum* and have been conveyed to all churches and all the brethren (*Ep.* 55.5.2).

Some interesting features of the Roman church are revealed.

The refugee movement has brought into the anonymity of crowded Rome even bishops from far distant provinces. Though the persecution continues—*ruinae* are still occurring (§3.3)—it has nevertheless been possible (some time ago) to consult with these and other bishops neighbouring to Rome. Church organization here has not been hopelessly demolished.

The cases of the imprisoned confessors of Rome remain unresolved—and these confessors are firmly opposed to the issuing of "illicit petitions" (§4) or *libelli martyrum;* indeed, they are made to sound as if they have resolutely issued no such *libelli* whatsoever. That will have simplified problems considerably in Rome. Their disciplinarian attitude will, however, incline them to rigorist ("Novatianizing") sympathies.

Rome shares unequivocally Cyprian's condemnatory attitude towards *libellatici* (the far greater prominence given to them over *sacrificati* in §§3.1 f. indicates that they have been the major source of contention and discontent). As it happens, this is our first firm evidence for the issuing of certificates of sacrifice (*libelli*) in Rome, but *Ep.* 21.3.2 very probably implies their existence at a much earlier date. The run of the letter suggests that the Sicilian church has been facing parallel problems, and that they are getting similar advice.

Despite the liberal exchange of counsels between churches, resolution is still considered ultimately a local affair directed by the local bishop (§§5.2 f., 8), but sharing views as widely as possible is part of the process of satisfactorily reaching such a resolution, especially for a widespread set of problems (§§5.3 f.). Cyprian holds much the same view, evinced clearly in *Ep.* 20.3.2.

Notoriously, Novatian was the *scriptor* of this letter (*Ep.* 55.5.2: *Novatiano tunc scribente et quod scripserat sua voce recitante*), that is to say, he composed at the least the wording for his fellow presbyters and deacons. (Can Novatian in his ordination as presbyter have really enjoyed, therefore, the opposition of "all the clergy and many of the laity," as Cornelius claims *apud* Eusebius, *H.E.* 6.43.17?) But we simply cannot tell how far the sentiments of the letter itself are Novatian's own personal expressions or how far his own views were here tempered in order to find general acceptance; indeed, it is feasible that the opinions in this letter may have been generally shared by the clergy, Novatian being left the task merely of clothing them in suitable literary dress. (Compare the remarks by M. Bévenot in JTS 20 [1969] 632.) Certainly there was at least one confirmatory *subscriptio* penned to Cyprian's copy by one of Rome's priests, and imprisoned confessors, Moyses: *Moyse tunc adhuc confessore ... subscribente ut lapsis infirmis et in exitu constitutis pax daretur* (*Ep.* 55.5.2). One imagines that the letter to Cyprian came in fact with a collection of such *subscriptiones* or confirmatory signatures and messages, gathered from as many presbyters and deacons as could be located. By contrast with the unfortunate *Ep.* 8, the senders were this time identifiable as well as its writer (cf. *Ep.* 9.2).

Cyprian's copy thus came with concluding annotations such as we find appended in fact to *Ep.* 79. We can conjecture that something like the words *Novatianus scripsi et mea voce recitavi*, and *Moyses presbyter et confessor subscripsi. Lapsis infirmis et in exitu constitutis pax detur*, appeared at the conclusion of Cyprian's copy. Does Pacian of Barcelona, late in the fourth century, allude to these circumstances and this letter in *Ep. ad Sympron.* 3.3: ... *libellum de negatoribus vel lapsis recipiendis Novatianus vester, cum adhuc in Ecclesia degeret, et scripsit et suasit et legit?* Another allusion to this epistle may appear in the pseudo-Cyprianic tractate *Ad Novat.* 13.8: *iste Novatianus ... qui semper in domo una id est Christi ecclesia proximorum delicta ut propria fleverit, onera fratrum ... sustinuerit, lubricos in fide caelesti adlocutione corroboraverit.*

We might compare Eusebius, *H.E.* 5.19.3 f. Eusebius claims to have sighted the autograph signatures and brief messages of various bishops subscribing to a letter on Montanism, composed in fact by Serapion of Antioch. For further on this aspect of *Ep.*

30, see H. Koch in ZNTW 34 (1935) 303 ff.; Gülzow 90 ff. (with abundant discussion); nn. 10 and 16 to *Ep.* 9.

The style of the letter is unmistakable—floridity strained to the point of turgidity. It comes replete with many rhetorical effects and figures (choice *clausulae*, abundant anaphora, etc.); there is a notable striving to conclude sections with arresting *sententiae*, and metaphors (especially medical) are elaborated to the point of overkill; there is an inclination, even greater than Cyprian's, to abstraction and indirectness of expression (the frequency of the passive verb is outstanding). It is in fact not far removed from the high chancellery style we have well illustrated in imperial documents of the early Dominate. I note a number of resultant uncertainties and obscurities in the commentary. But it is also a well-planned and an intelligent piece of work, effective, as it appears, in its results. (The Roman confessors later complain that they were deceived *perfidia et loquacitate captiosa* [*Ep.* 49.2.4], that is, by Novatian's skill in rhetorical eloquence.) For a detailed analysis of the style, see B. Melin, *Studia in Corpus Cyprianeum* (1946).

Ep. 36 is beyond reasonable doubt by the same hand, and it is fair to conclude that Novatian helped to draft *Ep.* 31 as well; consult B. Melin, *op. cit.*, for full comparisons. Some of the lost letters may well also have been of his composition. The three extant letters are most recently edited by G. F. Diercks in CCL 4 (1972). They are all that remain to us of what must have been an extensive correspondence (note, for example, *Epp.* 44.1.1, 45.2.2 ff., 55.2.1; Eusebius, *H.E.* 6.45.1 to Dionysius of Alexandria; Jerome, *Ep.* 10.3, requesting a copy of *epistulas Novatiani*; Pacian, *Ep. ad Sympron.* 2.7; Socrates, *H.E.* 4.28; A. Harnack, *Geschichte der altchristlichen Literatur* [2 vols. Leipzig 1893–1904; repr. 1958] 1.2.654 ff).

There are ample studies on Novatian, among them being by A. d'Alès, *Novatien. Étude sur la théologie romaine au milieu du troisième siècle* (Paris 1925); R. J. DeSimone, *The Treatise of Novatian the Roman Presbyter on the Trinity. A Study of the Text and the Doctrine* (Rome 1970); Gülzow (Tübingen 1975). Novatian scores a major first for the Roman church: its first educated writer in Latin on theology. Cornelius *ap.* Eusebius, *H.E.* 6.43.14 ff., provides a grossly exaggerated and satirical version of what we know of his previous career (illness and clinical baptism, ordination to presbyterate against opposition, evasion and retirement during this persecution, etc.). Jerome, *De viris illus.* 70, lists some of the many works (now very largely lost) that came from his prolific pen. For what has come down to us (often falsely ascribed to more respectable names, especially Cyprian's) and is commonly assigned to him by modern scholarship, see now the edition of Diercks.

Most probably this letter (and *Ep.* 31) will have been delivered back from Rome to Cyprian (in hiding) by Saturus, who, along with Optatus, had been the courier for *Epp.* 27 and 28 from Cyprian to Rome. On his visit to Cyprian he was entrusted with the authority to allow transcripts to be taken of this letter and *Ep.* 31; see *Ep.* 32.1.2 and n. 4 thereto.

1. *Cypriano papae presbyteri et diaconi Romae consistentes s.* On *papa*, see n. 3 to *Ep.* 8, and cf. n. 51 below; on *consistentes*, see n. 1 to *Ep.* 1. We are still during the interregnum of the Roman presbyters and deacons between popes Fabian and Cornelius (January 250 to March 251), for which see n. 9 to *Ep.* 8.

2. *evangelicae disciplinae vigore subnixus.* Novatian sounds a thematic phrase of this letter—the rigorous maintenance of *disciplina.* Variants occur in §§1.2 (*censurae et disciplinae*), 2.1 (*debitam severitatem divini vigoris; disciplinae ipsius semper custodita ratio*), 2.2 (*antiqua ... severitas, antiqua fides, disciplina ... antiqua; vigor iste*), 3.3 (*vigorem suum*), 4 (*severitatem evangelicae disciplinae; tenore evangelici vigoris*), with such opposites as *profana facilitate* (3.3), *disciplinae evangelicae ruinas* (4), *praevaricatores evangelii* (4), *desertores* (6.3), *pronam ... facilitatem* (8) for contrast. For literature on the multivalent word *disciplina*, see n. 9 to *Ep.* 11; on *vigor* (equally wide-ranging in significance), see Melin 61 f.; Watson 275 f., n. 3.

3. *soleat se solo Deo iudice esse contentus.* Cyprian was impressed by these opening words (they were designed in part to mollify him for the attacks that had been made on his withdrawal from Carthage by his Roman critics in *Ep.* 8); he echoes this phrase unmistakably in *De laps.* 3, referring to the honourable grade of private confessors who exercised prudent withdrawal:

hic contentus Deo suo iudice consientiam puram. In this letter it is noticeable how much emphasis Novatian places on the role of conscience. He stresses pollution of conscience rather than physical pollution at the pagan altars (see §§3.1 f.). It is too fanciful to see here the influence of Stoic thinking on the model *Sapiens* (e.g., Seneca, *Ep.* 9.1: *sapientem se ipso contentum esse*)? See *Ep.* 55.16.1, 24.1 for the connexion between Novatian and Stoicism.

For a discussion of the influence which this passage may have had on the development of Cyprian's own thoughts on Church government, see M. Bévenot, *Recherches de science religieuse* 39/40 (1951/52) 397 ff. [But, *contra* Bévenot, the decision, in a previous generation, of a synod of African bishops to differ amongst themselves *in practice* over the reconciliation (or otherwise) of adulterers—*Ep.* 55.21.1 f.—surely demonstrates that the notion that "bishops are responsible to God alone" was in the background of Cyprian's own African tradition. And Cyprian's contemporary, Dionysius of Alexandria, shows that this was a kind of view not confined to Cyprian's own local area: "And in regard to causes and affairs about matters which concern individual men—how it is right to receive him who approaches from without and how him who comes from within—we counsel to obey those who stand at the head of every place who by divine election are put into this ministration—leaving to our Lord the judgment of all things which they do" (trans. from Syriac by C. L. Feltoe).]

4. *cum conscientiam sciant Deo soli debere se iudici.* This rather odd clause is discussed at some length by Melin 73 ff., but its significance is clear.

5. *pro tua verecundia.* Perhaps a consciously flattering re-use of Cyprian's own phrase about himself in *Ep.* 27.3.2 (*verecundiae nostrae*), where see n. 23.

6. *omnes credemur.* I translate Hartel's text, but Diercks' reading, *crederemur*, has good warrant.

7. Observe the effect of these contrived opening paragraphs. Any charges that have been levelled against Cyprian are eschewed, and deliberately so. Rome is carefully cast into a subsidiary role. She is far from having caused Cyprian to write in his

defence; rather, Cyprian is given the initiative for inviting Rome (by writing to the Roman church *Epp.* 20 and 27) to share in the wisdom of, and credit for, both his actions and his policies. *Epp.* 20 and 27 are metamorphosed from being apologetic defences to Rome into praiseworthy exercises in fraternal harmony and unity in the interests of upholding Church discipline. Indeed Novatian has skilfully concluded this section with a winning point about unity (*disciplinae consensione sociati*), a notion so dear to Cyprian. Cf. n. 29 to *Ep.* 20. That unhappy interchange of letters, *Epp.* 8 and 9, is passed over in remarkable silence.

8. The nautical imagery is common (see n. 13 to *Ep.* 17; n. 17 to *Ep.* 21) but the heavy elaboration of it is characteristic of Novatian's manner. In this section Novatian seems to waver between *salus ecclesiastica* meaning "the salvation which the Church provides" and meaning "the Church's own safety."

9. The quotation is from Rom. 1.8. The Church was proud of this primitive testimony to their ancient faith; Cyprian registered this pride and he exploits this text with calculated flattery back to Rome in *Ep.* 59.14.1 (*Romanos quorum fides Apostolo praedicante laudata est*) and *Ep.* 60.2.1 (*fides quam de vobis beatus Apostolus praedicavit*). For further reading on the *fides Romana* in early patristic writings, see C. Pietri, *Roma Christiana* (Rome 1976) 298 ff. One might compare the Acts of Agape, Irene and Chione, Thessalonican martyrs: the opening chapter proudly and pointedly quotes from 1 Thessalonians 1.8 and 4.9 on the world-famous faith and the fraternal charity of the primitive Thessalonican church.

Diercks suggests bracketing the somewhat awkward phrase *disciplina legitur antiqua* (originally *disciplina intellegitur antiqua;* a marginal gloss?) but the rhetorical triplet (*severitas . . . fides . . . disciplina*) and the passive verb, however ungainly (for which Novatian had an almost irresistible penchant; see Melin 207 f., cf. 59 f.), are consonant with Novatian's style.

10. *minus est sine praeiudicio virtutum. . . .* I translate Hartel's emendation. Others (Melin, Diercks) suggest *minus est < praeiudicii > sine praedicatione,* which preserves the parallelism with the two preceding sentences (*minus . . . dedecoris, minus . . . crimi-*

nis, minus . . . praeiudicii) and explicates the garbled reading of F (Hartel XXVII f.), *sine praeiudicione,* by scribal haplography.

11. An overdone series of variations on the Rome cliché "the higher your rise, the harder your fall." Cf. A. Otto, *Die Sprich-wörter . . . der Römer* (Leipzig 1890); repr. Hildesheim 1965) 17.

12. The Roman clergy are referring to the (lost) letter they addressed to the clergy in Carthage (*ad clerum factas*) which Cyprian has seen (*Ep.* 27.4). Novatian proceeds diplomatically to slip over the fact that the letter had not been addressed to Cyprian personally by using the second person plural (*vobis sententiam nostram . . . protulimus*), although he uses elsewhere throughout this letter the second person singular in addressing Cyprian (as in §§ 1.2, 4, 5.1, 8).

13. *se ipsos infideles inlicita nefariorum libellorum professione prodiderant.* From the sequel it is plain that the major controversial issue dealt with by this letter was the question of the *libellatici* (those who had not sacrificed but who had obtained, nonetheless, a certificate declaring that they had sacrificed). The letter was firm in its opposition to those who had not considered this sin of theirs seriously and to those who had sought to readmit these *lapsi* readily to communion, with or without supporting certificates from the martyrs. The argument put forward clearly was that *libellatici* merely form a variety of *sacrificati,* for both are equally guilty of apostasy, of having polluted their consciences. In this the Romans are consciously confirming the stand enunciated by Cyprian in *Ep.* 20.2.2: *qui . . . nefandis libellis nihilominus conscientiam polluissent.*

The Roman letter appears to have distinguished two classes of *libellaticus.* The second (to follow) are those who kept themselves remote, using the services of others to obtain their *libelli* (see next n.). Here, in the first group, figure those who had been more personally involved in the drawing up of their *libelli.* They had themselves got the declaration (*professio*) contained in their certificates formally authenticated, but without their actually performing the required rites. See ACW 43.31 ff. for the *professio* involved in the issuing of the *libelli,* and on bribery as a means of evading the orders to sacrifice.

We have here firm evidence that *libelli* were issued in Rome (they do not figure in *Ep.* 8); and *Ep.* 21.3.2 (the lady in Rome who did not sacrifice but who was still guilty of a sin to be reserved for the judgment of the bishop when he should eventually be appointed) suggests strongly that they date there from at least before Easter (beginning of April) of this year, 250.

14. *sed etiam adversus illos qui accepta fecissent.* On this legal phrase (*accepta facio*) and its variants, see A. Beck, *Römisches Recht bei Tertullian und Cyprian. Eine Studie zur frühen Kirchenrechtsgeschichte* (Halle 1930) 167. For the use of deputies in obtaining certificates, see *Ep.* 55.13.2 ff.—and perhaps exemplified by J. R. Knipfing in HTR 16 (1923) no. 33.

15. *crimen tamen publice legitur.* Does this refer to the reading-out of the declaration before it is signed by the official, or, rather and perhaps more probably, that a public record, solemnly asseverating idolatry on the sinner's part, can now be read in the official archives? But, in spite of probability, the general use of the adverb *publice* favours rather the former interpretation (= before the people); cf. *Ep.* 67.6.2: *actis etiam publice habitis apud procuratorem ducenarium obtemperasse se idolatriae . . . contestatus est* (of a *libellaticus* bishop).

16. *totum fidei sacramentum in confessione Christi nominis . . . digestum.* It is very probable that in this legal context of affidavits, denials, edicts, avowals of ownership, etc. *sacramentum* is meant to bear something of its technical "binding" sense of "pledge," "obligation" (cf. Tertullian, *De pudic.* 18.17: *sacramentum didicerint fidei*). For discussion of this passage, see F. J. Dölger in AC 2 (1930) 139; H. Koch, *Cyprianische Untersuchungen* (Bonn 1926) 351 f., n. 3; J. B. Poukens in J. de Ghellinck *et al.*, *Pour l'histoire du mot "sacramentum"* (Louvain-Paris, 1924) 168 f; and for studies on the word generally, see, among many others, H. von Soden in ZNTW 12 (1911) 188 ff.; J. C. Navickas, *The Doctrine of St. Cyprian on the Sacraments* (diss. Würzburg 1924) part one; C. Mohrmann, *Études sur le latin des chrétiens* (3 vols., Rome 1961–1965) 1.233 ff., and *idem* in W. den Boer *et al.*, *Romanitas et Christianitas* (Amsterdam-London 1973) 233 ff.

17. *videri propositis adversus evangelium vel edictis vel legibus satisfecisse.* Some mss read *praepositis*, which might render the

sense "to appear to the authorities to have fulfilled edicts or laws contrary to the Gospel."

18. That is, in the letter already referred to. To judge from the brief observation that follows, the problem of the *sacrificati* did not constitute the onus of their message, but the pollution of *mentes*, especially by *libellatici*, did. Cf. n. 3 above.

19. *sed et cadant eversorum fratrum ruinae.* Observe that persecution, and apostasy, continue still. This letter itself reveals the existence in Rome of loyal bishops, clergy and laity (see esp. §§8, 5.3), any one of whom might be required, if detected and reported, to account for himself before the authorities.

20. *properata nimis remedia communicationum.* The turn of phrase here does not suggest that in Rome any such reconciliations (save *in articulo mortis*) had been effected, whereas in Carthage Cyprian's position had been rendered almost untenable by some of his clergy granting in fact premature and unauthorized re-admission to communion. See esp. *Epp.* 15–17 and *De laps.* 15 ff. Cyprian would relish this pointed support to his cause. His was a policy consonant with that church which professed the faith praised by St. Paul. On the word *communicatio*, see n. 24a to *Ep.* 8; n. 18 to *Ep.* 16.

21. *indulgentiae medicina ... indulget periculis.* There is contrived play on words, with *periculis* used presumably in the medical sense of "dangerous illnesses" (cf. Minucius Felix, *Octavius* 12.3 with n. 154 in ACW 39.235). Overly elaborate medical language is noticeable in this letter as well as in *Epp.* 31 and 36; for an analysis, see Melin 50 ff., 76 f. Cyprian himself much favoured such language; for an assemblage of passages, see D. D. Sullivan, *The Life of the North Africans as Revealed in the Works of St. Cyprian* (Washington 1933) 13 ff.

22. *quamquam confessorum quoque ... litteras habeas.* The round-about expression is circumspectly skirting the fact that the letter had not been directed to Cyprian, but to fellow confessors in Carthage. Cyprian notes that he has a copy in *Ep.* 27.4 and the Romans have received *Ep.* 27 by now; they record the confessors' receipt of its companion piece, *Ep.* 28, in the very next section, §5.1.

On *quamquam* here, see J. Schrijnen and C. Mohrmann, *Studien zur Syntax der Briefe des hl. Cyprians* (2 vols., Nijmegen 1936–1937) 2.109 f.; cf. Bayard 227.

23. *quos . . . fides in confessione iam gloriose semel coronavit.* Why *semel?* Does it mean "once and for all" (= "without a doubt")? Or rather, have they appeared already but once on trial (a preliminary hearing?) to be returned to prison awaiting a further hearing? Repeated hearings are in fact recorded for them, specifically, later, in *Ep.* 37.1.3, 3.1. Cf. my article in *Historia* 22 (1973) 654 f. In either case, the credentials of these confessors are being established; they have genuinely confessed and they are persevering, and hence the value of their testimony that follows is to be appreciated accordingly.

24. *inlicitas petitiones ab ecclesiae pudore revocarunt ne si hoc facile fecissent. . . .* What are *inlicitas petitiones* and with what should we identify *hoc?* The most likely explanation is that the Roman martyrs have been petitioned to provide *libelli martyrum* of the sort issued by Lucianus *et al.* They have firmly rejected such petitions (*inlicitas*), and *Ep.* 21 (from Celerinus in Rome to Carthage) demonstrates that such favours could not be obtained locally. Cyprian's positive attitude to these confessors' (lost) letter in *Ep.* 27, and in his reply, *Ep.* 28, puts such an interpretation beyond reasonable doubt. Presumably, therefore, *hoc* vaguely refers to "this activity." This reading is consistent with the confessors' own message that comes in *Ep.* 31.6. The problems of the Roman church, with no such traffic in *libelli martyrum* as in Carthage and no rebellious presbyters reconciling the fallen, are—at this stage, before the Novatianist schism—far different from those in Cyprian's diocese. See also O. D. Watkins, *A History of Penance: Being a Study of the Authorities* (2 vols., London 1920; repr. New York 1961) 1.202 f.

25. Hartel reads, *cum nulli magis tam congruens esset tenore evangelici vigoris inlibatam dignitatem servare,* which I translate. But the emphasis of the paragraph suggests that Diercks' text is to be preferred (*tenorem . . . inlibata dignitate*), viz. "to maintain a firm hold on the might of the Gospel teachings, preserving their honour untarnished." There is much ms confusion at this juncture. On the theme here see n. 2 above.

26. In this rather turgid attempt at a pointed aphorism (several topics in the letter are concluded by like sallies), the origins of the possession are to be identified as the Gospel and its teachings, the possession itself is the dignity of martyrdom. Cyprian had more successfully turned a similar sentiment in his letter to the Romans, *Ep.* 27.3.3: *non martyres evangelium faciant sed per evangelium martyres fiant.*

27. The reference is to *Ep.* 28.

28. *quamquam hoc totum de fide confitentium et de divina indulgentia venire videatur.* For somewhat similar notions, compare Cyprian, *Ep.* 69.12.2: *ubi plena et tota fide et dantis et sumentis accipitur,* and Minucius Felix, *Oct.* 27.7: *prout fides patientis adiuvat aut gratia curantis adspirat.* Here we probably have a simple variation on Cyprian's *dans credentibus tantum quantum se credit capere qui sumit,* as expressed in *Ep.* 10.3 (and see n. 18 there for parallels). The phrase *venire videatur* does not betoken a tentative uncertainty; it is simply a stylistic mannerism of Novatian's to gain a favoured rhythmic effect (instead of a plain *veniat*). See Melin 59 ff., 207 f.

29. *quales litteras in Siciliam quoque miserimus subiectas habebis.* A. Pincherle in *Kokalos* 10/11 (1964–1965) 551 f. wants this sentence to mean that the letter for Sicily is being sent first to Cyprian (for his supporting subscription) before it is delivered in Sicily. That is highly unlikely and the word *quales* provides strong confirmation of that unlikelihood. Cyprian is receiving only a copy. Cf. *Ep.* 71.4.1: *quales super hac re litteras fecerimus ut scires, exemplum earum . . . transmisimus.* It is conceivable that for Sicily the original was in Greek? It would be natural for a ship to have come *via* Sicily. For Sicily as the trade-link between Italy and Africa, cf. G. Ch. Picard, in *Kokalos* 18/19 (1972/1973) 108 ff.; O. Perler, *Les voyages de saint Augustin* (Paris 1969) 65 f.

This is valuable testimony for the history of the church in Sicily; apart from the (fortuitous) fact that St. Paul's ship put in to Sicily on its way to Puteoli (Acts 28.12 f.), the only notice we have which might conceivably indicate the presence of Christianity in Sicily prior to this witness is Clement of Alexandria's teacher who came from Magna Graecia along with Pantaenus, "the Sicilian bee." See Clement, *Strom.* 1.1.11; cf. Eusebius, *H.E.*

5.11.4. Hierarchy are firmly recorded for the early fourth century (cf. Eusebius, *H.E.* 10.5.21 ff.) as is the Church generally (cf. Eusebius, *Mart. Pal.* 13.12). I doubt whether the fact that Porphyry composed his work against the Christians whilst established in Sicily (cf. Eusebius, *H.E.* 6.19.2) need tell us anything.

The rhythm of the letter suggests that what follows—prudent deferral of the question of reconciling the lapsed until wider counsels can be taken—constituted their major message to the Church in Sicily. That tells us that the persecution was active in this area. Legend (but legend only) attaches the martyrdom of a S. Agatha (popular name) to this time of Decius; see O. Garana, *Le catacombe siciliane e i loro martiri* (Palermo 1961) 208 ff. But I am dubious whether we can safely deduce, with H. Leclercq, that this passage adequately demonstrates "la dépendance de ceux-ci [supposed bishops of Sicily] à l'égard du pape de Rome, et l'intervention de ses prédécesseurs dans l'organisation ecclésiastique sicilienne dès ses commencements" (DACL 15.1 (1950) 1416.)

For the early history of the Church in Sicily generally see A. Pincherle, *art. cit.*; DACL 15.1 (1950) 1415 ff; O. Garana, *op. cit.*, 197 ff.; H. Delehaye, *Les origines du culte des martyrs* (2nd ed., Brussels 1933) 310 ff.

30. *post excessum nobilissimae memoriae viri Fabiani.* It is curious that Fabian is not here given specifically martyr status and terminology—just as Cyprian does not in *Ep.* 28 (see n. 5 there)—despite the notorious partiality which presumably Fabian had shown to Novatian (Cornelius *ap.* Euseb. *H.E.* 6.43.17).

Was his perhaps a death by natural causes (after making his confessional stand) but before he had time to endure the hardships of imprisonment (contrast *Ep.* 12.1.2)? See n. 4 to *Ep.* 9.

31. The Romans have such letters as *Epp.* 15, 16, 17, 20, 26, where Cyprian insists on this prior condition for reaching a solution. Cyprian quotes verbatim this first paragraph of §5.3 in *Ep.* 55.5.1.

32. *confessoribus pariter et stantibus laicis.* Observe the qualification applied to the laity only. This is not so much a betrayal of clerical prejudice but is rather due to the fact that any lapse would have automatically deprived a cleric of his office. See n.

33 to *Ep.* 14 on Cyprian's formulations for the membership of the post-persecution Council which he envisages at Carthage. Note the contrast in the order of precedence given in *Ep.* 8.3.3.

33. *et in unum sententiam dicere.* The reading, commonly found in mss and adopted by editors, *et unum* ..., renders the sense "and that one man should pronounce the verdict when ...," but the run of the argument favours the more difficult reading chosen by Hartel (and Diercks).

34. *deiectorum.* On the verb *deicio,* see n. 10 to *Ep.* 10.

35. *qui ruerunt.* Though Cyprian uses the noun *ruina* freely, he seldom uses this verb of the fallen. The verb was also used by the Roman writers of *Ep.* 8. Cf. H. A. M. Hoppenbrouwers, *Recherches sur la terminologie du martyre de Tertullien à Lactance* (Nijmegen 1961) 140.

36. *pacem ecclesiastico nomini postulemus.* I assume that *ecclesiastico nomini* is merely an attempt at an elegance of style (for the simple *ecclesiae*).

37. *ut effectus indulgentiae lapsorum subsequatur et paenitentiam.* H. Karpp, *La pénitence. Textes et commentaires des origines de l'ordre pénitentiel de l'église ancienne* (Neuchâtel 1970) 229 annotates: "c'est-à-dire que le pardon ne doit pas être donné avant l'achèvement de la pénitence"—but is the *indulgentia* God's rather than the Church's? God, "who knows how He should treat such cases" (§8), must be begged to be merciful towards these repentant sinners. The text is, however, uncertain. Diercks reads here *paenitentia* (= "that the true repentance of the fallen may accompany their being granted pardon"?).

38. *interim.* That is to say, until a conference (*conlatio consiliorum*) can be held and policy (*ratio*) formed. On the word, see *Ep.* 4 n. 30.

39. *adeant ad limen ecclesiae sed non utique transiliant.* Though the context is undoubtedly metaphorical, there lies literal meaning behind this expression. In reality, penitents might keep vigil at the vestibule outside the liturgical gathering, begging the faithful as they entered for readmission and demonstrating the urgency of their appeal by knocking at the door which excluded them: Cf. Tertullian, *De paenit.* 7.10: *conlocavit in vestibulo paeni-*

tentiam secundam quae pulsantibus patefaciat; Gregory Thamaturgus, *Ep. can.* 11; and for discussion and many other examples in Tertullian and Cyprian see H. H. Janssen, *Kultur and Sprache. Zur Geschichte der alten Kirche im Spiegel der Sprachentwicklung von Tertullian bis Cyprian* (Nijmegen 1938) 30 ff.; A. d'Alès in *Revue d'histoire ecclésiastique* 7 (1906) 16 ff.; *idem, L'édit de Calliste. Étude sur les origines de la pénitence chrétienne* (Paris 1914) 400 ff.; F. E. Brightman in H. B. Swete (ed.), *Essays on the Early History of the Church and the Ministry* (London 1918) 367 f.; W. P. Le Saint in ACW 28 (1959) 165 ff.

40. *patientia non otiosa:* that is to say, employed in the activities of repentance, good works, almsgiving, etc.

41. *sed hoc totum in sacramento, sed in ipsius postulationis lege.* I merely paraphrase, being unsure of the precise import of the Latin. On *sacramentum* here (= precept, disposition?), see the sources cited in n. 16 above.

42. *temporis facto temperamento.* On *temperamentum* here, see A. d'Alès in *Revue des questions historiques* 91 (1912) 347 n. 3. Novatian has already insisted in §3.3 on the *necessaria temporis remedia:* the need for penitents patiently to wait for the *iustum tempus* (see nn. 33 and 34 to *Ep.* 4) is being repeated.

43. Matt. 18.32 (Cyprian's text read *dimisi* for *donavi*) and a conflation of Matt. 10.33 with Luke 12.9. Cf. Fahey 300 f. Matt. 10.33 became a favourite of the schismatic Novatian. See Pseudo-Cyprian, *Ad Novat.* 7.1, 8.1, 12.1.

44. *manibus et pedibus.* Many mss add *ligatis,* no doubt under the influence of Matt. 22.13 ("binding His hands and His feet").

45. For the allusion, see Matt. 22.11 ff.

46. *refrigeria.* On this word, see n. 26 to *Ep.* 6.

47. *diu et quidem multi et quidem cum quibusdam episcopis vicinis nobis et adpropinquantibus et quos . . . nihil innovandum putavimus.* Some uncertainties are raised by this text. What word does *diu* qualify, the preceding *quaerentes* ("for a long time our endeavour has been") or the following *putavimus* (as I translate—we see this decision in operation already by the time of *Ep.* 21.3.2)? Does the word *multi* imply that there is a divergent minority view? What sort of consultation is implied; is it realistic and too formal to call it a council ("avant l'élection de Corneille un concile s'était

tenu à Rome," G. Bardy in SC 41.158 f., n. 19)? Were the foreign refugees consulted bishops only? Are we to conclude that death-bed reconciliation of repentant idolaters is no innovation for all the foreign churchmen who helped to reach this conclusion of *nihil innovandum* (see nn. 23 and 25 to *Ep.* 8)?

At all events we have a good example of the refugee movement which this persecution set in motion, the anonymity of the large and crowded city providing welcome shelter for Christian fugitives, particularly for known Church leaders likely to have been singled out for special attack (see n. 2 to *Ep.* 5; n. 5 to *Ep.* 10). And it will be noticed in what way these refugee bishops are marked out for attention and praise: the contrast with the criticism levelled at the deserting leader of the flock in that other letter from Rome, *Ep.* 8, is sharp, clear, and deliberate. Cyprian was meant to register the implications of the change in attitude.

We have no idea of the number of bishops involved in this consultation. Sixteen were present later at Cornelius' consecration (*Ep.* 55.24.2); five were at hand at Rome in *Ep.* 49.2.1. On the habit of holding such consultation with neighbouring or visiting clerics, cf. nn. 2 and 3 to *Ep.* 1.

But it is well worth noting that the policy decided upon was avowedly interim only and not innovative at that. The Romans were going to wait for decision to be made with their own bishop before their final policy was arrived at. On the phrase *nihil innovandum,* see F. J. Dölger in AC 1 (1929) 79 f.

48. Hartel reads, *dolentes ac vere paenitentes animi signa prodiderunt,* whereas good sense and mss would seem to suggest *dolentis ac vere paenitentis animi signa* is the preferable text.

49. *ita demum caute et sollicite subveniri.* Though the policy does not differ in essentials from that outlined in *Ep.* 8.3.1, the tone has significantly changed from the brusque and unhesitant *utique subveniri eis debet* in that letter (where see n. 25) to the present reserved and prudent caution in the granting of reconciliation. This *moderamen* is consistent with Cyprian's own attitude (he is making a restricted *concession*) in *Ep.* 18.1.2 and it aroused dissatisfaction and opposition (*Ep.* 19.2.1); the Roman church has now triumphantly confirmed harmony with Cypri-

an's policy as finally formulated in *Ep.* 20.3.2 (where see esp. n. 28).

50. *Deo ipso sciente quid de talibus faciat* etc. Ecclesiastical absolution has been given high premium—it might be granted by the Church after the very minimum of compensatory *paenitentia* and *opera*. But now its absolute value is severely undercut. Cornelius can voice similar reservations later, *ceteris . . . omnia ante gesta remisimus Deo omnipotenti in cuius potestate sunt omnia reservata* (*Ep.* 49.2.5). Similarly for Cyprian, e.g., *Ep.* 55.18.1 and 19.2: *Deus . . . de his quae nos minus perspeximus iudicet et servorum sententiam Dominus emendet . . . hunc* (= *vulneratum*) *curatum Deo iudici reservamus.* For a discussion, see H. J. Vogt, *Coetus sanctorum* (Bonn 1968) 118 ff. From this position it was not too distant a step (but it was nonetheless a momentous one) for later Novatianists to deny altogether the Church's ability to remit the sin of idolatry, reserving pardon for the judgment of God alone; cf. C. B. Daly in *Irish Theological Quarterly* 19 (1952) 38 f., and see Pseudo-Cyprian, *Ad Novat.* 14, for an indignant commentary on the change in policy.

51. *beatissime ac gloriosissime papa.* The "confessional" flattery in this concluding greeting is telling—Cyprian is granted epithets normally reserved for the martyred: he has suffered honourably and gloriously in his exile. The stinging criticisms of cowardice and desertion in *Ep.* 8 are now richly repudiated. For discussion, see n. 4 to *Ep.* 9; n. 2 to *Ep.* 10; A. A. R. Bastiaensen, *Le cérémonial épistolaire des chrétiens latins* (Nijmegen 1964) 26 f.; A. J. Vermeulen, *The Semantic Development of Gloria in Early-Christian Latin* (Nijmegen 1956) 69, 104 ff.; H. U. Instinsky, *Bischofsstuhl und Kaiserthron* (Munich 1955) 83 ff., esp. 91 ff.

LETTER 31

Contents: By the receipt of Cyprian's welcome letter the Roman confessors have been both comforted for the sad losses the Church has universally suffered and encouraged to face their destined martyrdom. Cyprian's reward will indeed be great in heaven and they ask accordingly that he pray they may be granted in fact the glory of shedding their own blood in witness for their faith. They have been comforted, too, by the witness Cyprian has himself given of his own zeal for the duties of his office—exhortation, charitable alms, and above all censure for the impatient, both lapsed and reconciling clergy. To heal the grievous sin of the fallen, prudence and penitence are essential; wild and importunate demands do not gainsay the fact that the lapsed might have remained, through Christ, in communion.

Date and circumstances: This letter is undoubtedly the reply to *Ep.* 28. As *Ep.* 28 accompanied *Ep.* 27, so this letter will have accompanied *Ep.* 30—Cyprian proceeds to distribute copies of both *Epp.* 30 and 31 together (*Ep.* 32.1.1). Its date is, therefore, contemporary with *Ep.* 30 ("late summer of 250 A.D.").

The letter reveals most clearly that the dossier Cyprian had sent along with *Ep.* 20 in order to clear his reputation in Rome has now been circulated and studied with care, and has been effective in its results. There are manifest references in §6 to more than half of the letters he had enclosed. The elaborations of praise and gratitude not only for the contents but even for the style (§2.1) of his correspondence demonstrate that his *apologia* has been read with appreciation. The overall tone towards Cyprian contrived by this letter is one of admiration combined with a certain deference, approval of his actions concerning the lapsed being given heavy stress towards the close of the letter. Even the lengthy, earlier section of the letter, taken up with rhetorical exultation over the glories of martyrdom, is made to depend on the stimulus of Cyprian's own words (*Ep.* 28). *Ep.* 30, from the Roman clergy, had been very much concerned with ecclesiastical policies; *Ep.* 31 is much more personal in its message. That is only proper, given the very different character of the two letters (*Epp.* 27 and 28) to which *Epp.* 30 and 31 are responses, and the different composition of the two groups involved.

The clerics at least, among these confessors, should have heard *Ep.* 30 read to them by Novatian. *Ep.* 31 has many unmistakable echoes of that letter. But the relationship between the two letters seems stronger than merely vivid verbal reminiscence and imitation; the close ressemblances in phraseology and metaphor, style and cadence, are remarkable and suggest that the writer of *Ep.* 30, Novatian, on his visit to the confessors, in fact helped them to draft their own reply to Cyprian. The parallels in *Ep.* 31 to Novatian's works are elaborately detailed by Melin, 43 ff. *Ep.* 31 is edited most recently by Diercks in CCL 4.227 ff.

1. On these four named Roman clerics and on their companions in prison, see *Ep.* 28 n. 1 (in some mss Nicostratus and Rufinus are given their rank of deacon, as in Cyprian's reference to this letter at *Ep.* 32.1.1).

2. *per totum paene orbem ruinas.* The phrase is repeated for good measure in §6.2 and has occurred already in *Ep.* 30.5.4 (*totum orbem paene vastatum*). It echoes language Cyprian had used himself in *Ep.* 19.2.1 (*totius orbis haec causa est*).

3. The reference is to *Ep.* 28.

4. *tam diu clausos vinculis carceris.* For how long? *Ep.* 37 is written to these same confessors, in winter, at the turn of 250/251; Cyprian congratulates them on a year of glorious imprisonment which had itself started in winter-time (§2.1 f.). At the time Moyses is understood to be still alive (*Ep.* 37 *init.*); he died in fact after an internment of 11 months and 11 days (see n. 1 to *Ep.* 28). Should we, therefore, compute the start of their imprisonment from the course of February of this year? If so, they will have been left languishing there now for nearly 8 months. Further discussion on the starting-time for their confinement is in Introduction in ACW 43.25 ff.

As likely as not, such a lengthy period in prison was no official *poena* or legal punishment (*contra* M. M. Sage, *Cyprian* [Cambridge 1975] 187) but a prolonged *mora* or adjournment, clemently vouchsafed to the prisoners, pending full trial or final sentence—they would have ample time to reflect and to recant. Their own words at §5.1 (*nemo hanc dilationis nostrae moram clementiam iudicet*) could reflect the sort of thing which a presiding magistrate might have said to them. For such a *mora*, cf. *Act.*

Scill. 13, and for further discussion, see my article in *Historia* 22 (1973) 654 f.

5. *inluxerunt enim nobis litterae tuae.* Compare *Ep.* 30.5.1 on the effects of this same letter—*illorum carceris tenebras litteris tuis inluminasti.* They are alluding, of course, to the frightful darkness of Roman dungeons; cf. *Ep.* 6.1.2 and *Ep.* 22.2.1.

6. *in periculis et doloribus. Periculum* with this significance of "dangerous illness" was used also in *Ep.* 30.3.3, where see n. 21.

7. *animo sitiente perbibimus et voto esuriente suscepimus.* At first sight the metaphor seems to be plainly Eucharistic, appropriately coming after what reads like a series of intercessory prayer formulae, but in the light of the remainder of the sentence there may well be reference also to the final ceremonial meal eaten on the eve of going into gladiatorial combat. Cf. Tertullian, *Apol.* 42.5: *non in publico Liberalibus discumbo, quod bestiariis supremam cenantibus mos est; Act. Perp.* 17: *cum illam cenam ultimam quam liberam vocant . . . non cenam liberam sed agapem cenarent;* Apuleius, *Met.* 4.13: *gladiatores isti famosae manus . . . noxii perdita securitate suis epulis bestiarum saginas instruentes.*

8. There are problems with the text of this sentence.

In the second clause Hartel reads, *non magis laude condignus est qui fecit quam qui et docuit,* but most mss in fact read *minus* (for *magis*), and many interchange the placing of *fecit* and *docuit*— hence Diercks' reading is: *non minus laude condignus est qui docuit quam qui et fecit.* Three consecutive clauses, each beginning with *non minus* and with the first verb in each case referring to *verbal* action, is, rhetorically, the most likely format. As usual, I translate Hartel's text.

In the third clause Hartel conjectures, *quam qui et exhortatori paruit;* Diercks, *et exoptavit;* Bayard, *et exercuit;* Melin 55, *et exercitavit;* etc., but despite the garbled ms tradition, the sense is recoverable. I suspect the cause may have been an original *quam qui et exhortatus est*—which is found—where it was not appreciated that the verb was employed, unusually, in a passive sense. Cf. Aulus Gellius, *N.A.* 15.13.1: *'utor' et 'vereor' et 'hortor' et 'consolor' communia verba sunt ac dici utroqueversus possunt . . . 'hortor te' et 'hortor abs te,' id est 'tu me hortaris';* Petronius, *Sat.*

76: *nolentem me negotium meum agere exhortavit mathematicus.*
There is discussion of both passages in Melin 54 ff.

In any case, the flattery is overpowering. That words should be valued at least the equal of deeds is a startling reversal of proverbial—and biblical—wisdom; it creates an arresting repudiation of the criticism voiced in *Ep.* 8, especially coming from those who have themselves endured eight months under Roman prison conditions.

9. *gloriosas martyrum non dicam .mortes sed immortalitates.* I doubt whether it is right to deduce (as some have done, e.g., Benson 119 n. 1) from the phrase *non dicam* (singular verb) that this reveals that the supposedly joint letter had in fact but one composer. The expression is a standard one.

10. The allusion is to the celebrated martyrdom text Matt. 10.32 (cf. Luke 12.8) which Cyprian has used himself in *Epp.* 12.1.3 and 16.2.2. The confessors are not referring to their own companions, who have not yet shed their blood (§5.1); they refer rather to the martyrs of Carthage who were mentioned in *Ep.* 28.1.2, the letter to which the confessors have specifically alluded in §1.1. In that letter much stress had been given to communion between the two churches of Rome and Carthage in the *honos* and *gloria* of their confessors and martyrs (esp. §§1.2, 2.4). They now write as if those Carthaginian martyrs were of their own number. Naturally they will have paid particular attention also to such documents as the lyrical *Ep.* 10, a copy of which had accompanied *Ep.* 20; Cyprian had himself played in that letter on the words *mors* and *immortalitas* in §2.3: *pretiosa mors haec est quae emit immortalitatem. . . .*

11. *caeleste regnum sine ulla cunctatione retinere.* There was a widespread belief that prior to the Last Judgment only the martyrs' souls were in heaven with Christ, and they were there immediately upon death; the souls of other virtuous Christians had to await, apparently, the end of time. See n. 14 to *Ep.* 6 for this notion in Cyprian. Note the use of *retineo* for the simple *teneo*—here *metri gratia?* This is discussed by Melin 162 f.

12. *collegam passionis cum Christo . . . factum fuisse . . . iudicis sui divina dignatione iudicem factum fuisse.* For the theme of the martyr as collaborator with the redemptive sufferings of Christ,

note M. Lods, *Confesseurs et martyrs. Successeurs des prophètes dans l'église des trois premiers siècles* (Neuchâtel-Paris 1958) 54 ff.; and on the word *passio*, cf. n. 13 to *Ep.* 3.

The construing of the second clause is open to doubt. As I translate it, it refers to the fact that martyrs share a seat with Christ on His tribunal and they will thus in heaven become the judge over that judge who had condemned them to death on earth. But some, a little less vindictively, construe "to have become a judge by the holy grace of his own Judge." For the notion of the martyr as heavenly judge, see n. 14 to *Ep.* 6.

13. *supplicia sua post fidem amare coepisse.* It is very possible that *post* is rather to be taken as temporal in significance and that *post fidem* should be interpreted, accordingly, as an elliptical expression for "after making confession of his faith" or the like.

14. Matt. 10.37 f., but reading *animam suam* instead of the usual *filium aut filiam*, cf. Matt. 10.39, 16.24 f.; Luke 14.26 f.

15. Matt. 5.10–12.

16. Matt. 10.18, 21 f.

17. Apoc. 3.21.

18. Rom. 8.35 ff.

19. See nn. 4 and 10 above.

20. The allusions are to Eph. 6.13 ff. There is only the flimsiest ms warrant for the bracketed clause, which should be excised. Observe Cyprian's elaboration on this text in *Ep.* 58.9.

21. ... *tam glorioso episcopo, ut hostiae destinati petant auxilium de sacerdote.* Observe the stress—Cyprian, with his higher clerical status as *sacerdos* and with his special privileges as *gloriosus episcopus* (on the martyr-overtones of *gloriosus*, cf. *Ep.* 30 n. 51), enjoys a more effective position and influence for obtaining divine favours than even the imprisoned Roman confessors. Given the acknowledged *praerogativa* and intercessory powers accorded to confessors, especially those who are destined for death, that is flattery indeed. Cyprian would appreciate particularly the support which these words gave to his position (*locus*): here are confessors respectful of and deferential towards his episcopal, his spiritual authority. He had opined at the close of *Ep.* 28: *honoris vestri participes et nos sumus, gloriam vestram*

nostram gloriam computamus; that compliment has now been nicely returned.

22. E.g. *Epp.* 6, 13, 10.

23. *sumptus necessarios de tuis laboribus iustis.* See, e.g., *Ep.* 7.2 (*de quantitate mea propria*), where see n. 11; *Ep.* 13.7 (*de sumpticulis propriis quos mecum ferebam*), where see n. 37. Benson 118 misunderstood the passage, deducing that Cyprian had sent the Roman confessors "pecuniary help from his own resources."

24. *in nulla officii tui parte quasi aliquis desertor.* This is an explicit counter to the charges of dereliction of duty and desertion contained in *Ep.* 8 (where such words as *neglegentes, deserentes, non dereliquimus, relicti,* figure prominently). Cyprian's despatch of *Ep.* 20 and its enclosures has scored—eventually—a marked success in exonerating his reputation; cf. Duquenne 98.

25. E.g., *Ep.* 17. Cf. *Epp.* 15.3.1 and 19.2.1.

26. *sine respectu evangelii sanctum Domini et margaritas prona facilitate donassent.* I.e., the rebellious presbyters (and deacons). The allusion is, of course, to Matt. 7.6. Under the influence of that allusion *canibus* has crept into the text of some mss after *Domini* and *porcis* after *margaritas.*

Sanctum ("that which is holy") is found at Matt. 7.6 but in combination, as here, with *Domini* (cf. *De laps.* 15 and 26), or even by itself (cf. Novatian, *De spec.* 5.5) it can also be used in the sense of *hostia dominica.* See further n. 3 to *Ep.* 34. On *prona* (*v.l.: profana*) *facilitate,* see the discussion in Melin 47 f.

27. *caute moderateque tractari.* An echo of Cyprian's own words in *Ep.* 17.2.1: *caute omnia et moderate . . . observari.*

28. See, e.g., *Epp.* 16.4.2, 17.3.2, 20.3.2, and cf. n. 32 to *Ep.* 30.5.3. As in Cyprian's formulations, *confessores* (but not *martyres*) occur in the Roman lists of intended participants. The correct reading seems to be here *diaconibus,* whereas the equivalent passage in *Ep.* 30 had the form *diaconis.* The change is not significant—the same writer could vary his usage. Cyprian himself used *diaconibus* in *Ep.* 20.2.3 and in the addresses to his letters (e.g., *Epp.* 5, 7, 9, 11, etc.), whereas the form *diaconis* is his marked preference in the body of his letters (e.g., *Epp.* 5.2.1, 14.3.2, 16.3.2). On the variation, see H. H. Janssen, *Kultur und Sprache* . . . (Nijmegen 1938) 98 n. 2; E.W. Watson in *Studia*

Biblica 4 (1896) 297 f., n. 2 ("with the exception of abl. *baptisma, diaconus* is the only Greek word with the form of which Cyprian took liberties"); Bayard 56 f.; and cf. C. Mohrmann in VC 3 (1949) 80.

29. *ne dum volumus importune ruinis subvenire.* . . . There are sacramental overtones to *subvenire,* difficult to translate in a metaphorical passage. See n. 25 to *Ep.* 8 on the word.

30. *ad maturitatis suae tempus.* On the need for the penitent patiently to await the *iustum tempus* for reconciliation, cf. *Ep.* 30.3.3 and n. 42 thereto—a keynote of that letter.

31. I.e., *disciplina.* On the word cf. n. 2 to *Ep.* 30 and the references given there. Is it conceivable that here the word could mean *self*-discipline (mortification)?

32. *ardentem delictorum aestuantium morbum.* So Hartel. For *morbum,* there is the variant reading *vaporem,* which Diercks adopts.

33. *in secretis cordis fidelis novellandus et conserendus est animus.* I am unsure of the construing—many take *fidelis* with *cordis* (= "in the depths of their loyal hearts"?) which seems to render less satisfactory sense. Note the elaborate verbal motif in this chapter: *fidelis . . . animus* (here), *fideles . . . lacrimae, infidelis . . . cicatrix, fideliter . . . remedia praestantur, fideliora . . . remedia.*

34. *iterum fideles ex oculis lacrimae profundantur.* Should *iterum* be construed more closely with *fideles* to give "tears once again faithful," "tears of renewed faith"?

35. *illi ipsi oculi qui male simulacra conspexerunt, quae inlicite commiserant . . . deleant.* This is not just fanciful metaphorical language—not only might a loyal Christian sputate and exsufflate when passing by a pagan idol in order to avoid pollution and contamination (for evidence see ACW 39.211 on Minucius Felix, *Oct.* 8.4), but it might actually be considered sinful for him not to avert his eyes from such an evil sight. For examples of this notion, see Tertullian, *Ad mart.* 2.7: *non vides alienos deos, non imaginibus eorum incurris* (one of the benefits of being imprisoned); Cyprian, *Ep.* 58.9.2: *muniantur oculi ne videant detestanda simulacra; De laps.* 28: *minus plane peccaverit non videndo idola;* Eusebius, *H.E.* 6.41.4 (Quinta at Alexandria); Council of Elvira, canon 59: *prohibendum ne quis christianus . . . ad idolum*

Capitolii causa sacrificandi ascendat et videat; and compare the charge of Celsus recorded in Origen, *C. Cels.* 7.62: "they cannot bear to look upon temples and altars and statues." For further treatment of this theme, see F. J. Dölger in AC 5 (1936) 144 ff.

36. *non est ni patientia in morbis necessaria.* This is Hartel's text but it is uncertainly based. Diercks reads, *non est impatientia in morbis necessaria* ("what you don't need in the case of illness is impatience"). Cf. Melin 177 n. 3. Whatever the original said precisely, the message is clear enough.

37. *fides enim quae Christum potuit confiteri potuit et a Christo in communicatione retineri.* An impressive-sounding aphorism as a conclusion, but its very abstractness leads to some obscurity in sense.

38. I.e. *frater.* But there is strong ms support for reading instead, *beatissime ac gloriosissime papa,* as at the conclusion of *Ep.* 30. It would make an effective closing note to the message of this epistle.

LETTER 32

Contents: A cover-note to the Carthaginian clergy for copies of Cyprian's correspondence with Rome, which are enclosed. The contents of these letters are to be made known to the flock in Carthage and to any clergy from other churches who may come to Carthage. Permission is freely granted for further copies to be taken and distributed so that all may be able together to adhere to a common policy, provisional and partial though it may be.

Date and circumstances: Cyprian encloses *Epp.* 30 and 31 (and some of the letters which prompted them—certainly *Ep.* 27 and possibly *Epp.* 20 and 28 as well). He will have done so, given the most encouraging and commendatory contents of *Epp.* 30 and 31, promptly on receipt of these documents. We are, therefore, still in late summer 250, and the letter falls in the sequence of the correspondence after *Ep.* 31. Cyprian's last letter to his clergy was *Ep.* 29 (which enclosed a document Cyprian had received after sending off *Epp.* 27 and 28), dated to "latish summer 250." Cf. Duquenne 140; Nelke 47.

Cyprian's emphasis on wide dissemination of the documents he encloses is noteworthy. He is anxious for their contents to be known and copies to be distributed as far as possible. His reputation has been slandered, his policies have been impugned; much of that damage has now been repaired by these highly supportive testimonials from Rome. He will now be encouraged, after their distribution, to take more decisive action (excommunication or suspension of rebellious or deserting clergy, *Ep.* 34; appointment of replacement clergy, *Epp.* 38–40; the establishment of an ecclesiastical commission in Carthage, *Epp.* 41–42). Already he is prepared to distribute copies of *Ep.* 27 which was outspokenly and hotly critical of some of the Carthaginian confessors (especially Lucianus), of rebel clergy and of turbulent lapsed, and even of some less stalwart fellow bishops in the province.

Of course, not all of his clergy could be relied upon to disseminate this material as requested—or to provide faithful and accurate copies if they did. Cyprian is at pains, therefore, to name a specific cleric who can be approached for copies; at least he was one member of his clergy he could trust (cf. *Ep.* 29.1.2 and see n. 4 below).

1. I.e., *Epp.* 27 and 30. Can Cyprian have included *Ep.* 20 also (*quales litteras ad clerum Romae agentem fecerim*), for *Ep.* 30 was the reply to both *Epp.* 20 and 27? So far, Cyprian has not distributed copies of *Ep.* 20 in Carthage (see n. 29 to *Ep.* 20).

2. I.e., *Ep.* 31. It is curious that Cyprian appears not to include a copy of his *Ep.* 28; perhaps his phrasing is at fault here? Cyprian pointedly records the name and rank of the presbyters and deacons who are among the Roman confessors (cf. n. 1 to *Ep.* 31); how they, as clergy and as confessors, viewed Cyprian's personal actions and ecclesiastical policies was an important fulcrum for Cyprian in his efforts to regain some of his lost authority among the clergy and the confessors of Carthage. On this group of confessors at Rome, see n. 1 to *Ep.* 28.

3. *si qui de peregrinis episcopi collegae mei vel presbyteri vel*

diacones praesentes fuerint vel supervenerint. The meaning of *pere-grini* (= from outside Carthage) is clear from *Ep.* 34.3.2 (*sive de nostris presbyteris . . . sive de peregrinis*). Some of these non-Cartha-ginian clergy may well be refugees in hiding in Carthage, but Cyprian also envisages that visiting clergy might, in safety, slip in and out of Carthage; they would be strangers to the authori-ties, whereas it was still out of the question for him to make an appearance there himself, and it was to continue so for a further half year. Bishops (plural) are firmly attested at Carthage shortly after this (see n. 1 to *Ep.* 34) and it will not be so very long before Cyprian can establish his ecclesiastical "commission" in Car-thage on which three (peregrine) bishops served. Bishops will also soon be visiting Cyprian in hiding (see *Epp.* 38.2.2, 39.1.1). The intensity of the persecution is perceptibly trailing off.

On the expression *collegae mei* (not *nostri*), cf. n. 2 to *Ep.* 1.

4. *Satyro lectori . . . mandaverim ut singulis desiderantibus descri-bendi faciat potestatem.* There was a Saturus in *Ep.* 29.1.2, ap-pointed lector by Cyprian in hiding; he helped to convey *Epp.* 27 and 28 to Rome (see *Ep.* 35.1.1). He will now have returned to Cyprian's hideaway bearing the replies, *Epp.* 30 and 31. It is difficult not to believe that we are dealing with the same man here, now sent off to Carthage with this epistle and its enclo-sures. Variations in spelling (Saturus, Satyrus) occur here and elsewhere in the correspondence with this name: see n. 10 to *Ep.* 29.

Cyprian has already announced permission for visiting clergy to take copies; he now appears to be making that licence even broader to include laymen as well. If that is so, it is a most unusual step and demonstrates Cyprian's anxiety to encourage maximum distribution of these documents which both exoner-ate his name and support his disciplinary stance. Individuals would apply to Satyrus, who had in his keeping a master-copy. On the technical use of *describo,* cf. R. P. E. Arns, *La technique du livre d'après saint Jérôme* (Paris 1953) 171.

Would Satyrus check the *exempla* taken against the master-copy (cf. the formula *descriptum et recognitum* on official copies of documents, e.g., *P.S.I.* 1026 1.1 = E. M. Smallwood, *Docu-ments Illustrating the Principates of Nerva, Trajan and Hadrian*

[Cambridge 1966] 330) and authenticate the copies so taken with a *subscriptio* (cf. the ὑπογραφή on the records of court proceedings; see R. A. Coles in *Papyrologica Bruxellensia* 4 [1966] 52 ff.)? That certifying procedure would act as a precaution against corruption of the text (against which authors might fulminate at the conclusion of their works with minatory curses; see, e.g., Apoc. 22.18 f.; Irenaeus, at the end of his *Ogdoad, ap.* Eusebius, *H.E.* 5.20.2; Rufinus, *Lib. de adult. libr. Origen.* in MG 17.627 f.; and for a later example Gregory of Tours, *Hist. Franc.* 10.31; and see further J. de Ghellinck, *Patristique et moyen âge,* (3 vols., Brussels-Paris 1946–1948) 2.183 ff., and nn. 12 and 15 to *Ep.* 9.

On the slight evidence here, it seems to be going too far, however, to claim, with A. Vilela, *La condition collégiale des prêtres au troisième siècle* (Paris 1971) 268, that Satyrus "était chargé des archives ecclésiastiques" (see n. 6 to *Ep.* 23 on the offices of *lector*), but one might compare the *cursus* and functions of Damasus' father—*pater exceptor, lector, levita, sacerdos* (*Epig.* 57.1 Ihm = ILCV 970): had he been once an official "copyist" too, in younger days, before or whilst he was *lector*? There is the variant reading *puer,* for *pater,* on which see P. Künzle in *Rivista di stor. della chiesa in Ital.* 7 (1953) 1 ff.; A. Ferrua in *Rivista di archeologia cristiana* 29 (1953) 231 ff.; V. Peri in *Rendiconti della pontificia accademia di archeologia* 41 (1968–69) 192 ff.

5. *in ecclesiarum statu quoquo modo interim componendo servetur ab omnibus una fida consensio.* Observe the emphasis both on the partial and temporary nature of the policy of the churches—*interim* as well as *quoquo modo* ("in whatever degree")—and on the need for uniformity in that interim policy (*ad omnibus una fida consensio*). Can *fida* be intended to mean here "in conformity with the faith"?

6. See *Ep.* 25.1.2 (*epistulae . . . plurimis collegis nostris missae*), and cf. *Ep.* 26.1.2 (*exemplum collegis . . . multis . . . misi*).

LETTER 33

Contents: After establishing the fundamental and apostolic role which bishops are divinely ordained to play in the functioning of the Church, Cyprian records the receipt of two documents. One is from a group of lapsed who arrogantly term themselves "the Church" in making their requests of their bishop. By contrast, the other is from a group of the fallen who humbly and properly do penance and good works, asserting that they patiently await the return of their bishop before they anticipate reconciliation.

He is returning to its senders the anonymous document, which he has received, for clarification and signatures before he can consider replying to its contents.

Date and circumstances: The place of this letter in the sequence of the correspondence is reasonably established. Cyprian sends *Ep.* 35 to Rome with a copy of this letter along with one of the documents he mentions in this letter. And in *Ep.* 35 he notes that this correspondence had occurred after he had sent off to Rome *Epp.* 27 and 28 ("August/September"; see introductory note to *Ep.* 27). It sounds very much as if we should place this letter of Cyprian's shortly after that date; it appears that he sent a copy of the correspondence also to Carthage, and that *Ep.* 29 should be dated after *Ep.* 33. Cyprian will be, in all likelihood, writing this letter before he has yet received *Epp.* 30 and 31 from Rome. Discussion is in Duquenne 139 and Nelke 43. In other words, we arrive at the sequence *Epp.* 27 and 28, this *Ep.* 33, then *Epp.* 29 and 35, followed by *Epp.* 30, 31 and 32.

Cyprian last communicated with Carthage in *Ep.* 26. There, obviously against vigorous pressure, he firmly stalls against deciding any cases of reconciliation until he should return. For this stand he relies heavily on the authority of fellow bishops who agree with this policy; see *Ep.* 26.1.2 ff. That letter has provoked reaction: Some write in agreement and submission, while others defiantly demand action, disregarding episcopal opinion. After his preliminary sermon on the centrality of the office of the bishop in Church government, Cyprian pointedly marshalls his material on the importunate lapsed, now become more than ever stridently urgent in their demands, around a section (§2.1) which sets out the model behaviour and attitudes of certain humble and God-fearing *lapsi*.

The next manoeuvre is to start excommunicating the presbyters and deacons who rebelliously communicate with the lapsed "before we pass our verdict," *ante sententiam nostram* (*Ep.* 34).

1. There is no introductory salutation; Cyprian does not know to whom he should direct this letter precisely. He is addressing the anonymous authors of the document mentioned in §2.2 whom he calls *fratres*. The authors of the other two documents alluded to in this letter (in §§1.2 and 2.1) are referred to, not in the second, but in the third person. Presumably Cyprian sends this acephalous reply back with the messenger who delivered the *libellus* from these *fratres*. On their possible identity, see nn. 6 and 7 below.

2. *episcopi honorem et ecclesiae suae rationem disponens.* Cyprian is firmly of the belief that bishops have the full powers of the apostles whose successors they are. See n. 16 to *Ep.* 3 on that view. It is important in reading this celebrated passage to realize the context of Cyprian's remarks. His dignity has been impugned, his authority slighted; he has been treated as a mere cipher in the Church's *disciplina,* required to endorse automatically the reconciliation proffered by the martyrs (see n. 6 below). His reaction is to emphasize the authoritarian leadership of the bishop. The bishop is the essential pivot in the Church's structure; the Church cannot be a Church without him. But even here his monarchy is not quite described as absolute— clergy and faithful also are constituents of the Church (see n. 7 below), and at the conclusion of the letter (see n. 20 below) he undercuts slightly some of the potential arrogance of this opening section.

3. Matt. 16.18 f. See Fahey 309 f. for Cyprian's other direct uses of and numerous allusions to this text, and for a discussion of this text in Tertullian and Augustine as well as in Cyprian, see G. Haendler in *Theol. Literaturzeitung* 81 (1956) 361 ff. It is

worth noting that Cyprian's basic view of this text is as a lesson
in the oneness of the Church's organization, symbolized by
Peter, rather than as a source for overriding authority reserved
for Peter's chair. Here, however, Cyprian is more concerned
with the central place which bishops as a class have been divinely given in the constitution and government of the Church.

4. *inde per temporum et successionum vices episcoporum ordinatio
et ecclesiae ratio decurrit.* A famous enunciation of the succession
principle of episcopal powers. For Cyprian this was not so
much a charismatic succession as an institutional, empirical,
"horizontal" succession, an unbroken chain linking bishops
back in time to the apostles whose prerogatives and powers (to
absolve, etc.) have been transmitted along that continuous chain.
The consecration ceremony, requiring the presence of fellow
bishops, mirrored that view of episcopal succession (see *Ep.*
67.5.1: *episcopi eiusdem provinciae proximi quique conveniant*). We
see the converse in *Ep.* 69.3.2: Novatian cannot be counted a
bishop for in scorn of apostolic tradition he is *nemini succedens,*
whereas it could legitimately be claimed of Cornelius *Fabiano
episcopo legitima ordinatione successit.* Priority was a key defence
in Cornelius' claim to the chair of Peter—he was consecrated
cum nemo ante se factus esset (*episcopus*), *cum Fabiani locus . . .
vacaret* (*Ep.* 55.8.4).

For a classic statement of the succession principle, see Irenaeus, *Adv. Haer.* 3.2.2 ff.; and for other earlier formulations, see
Hegesippus *ap.* Eusebius, *H.E.* 4.22.2 f.; cf. Polycarp and Anice-
tus in Irenaeus *ap.* Eusebius, *H.E.* 5.24.16; Tertullian, *De praes.
heret.* 20.4 ff. and 32.1ff.; and for Cyprian's contemporaries, see
Ep. 75.16.1 ff. (Firmilian); *Sent. Episc.* 79 (Clarus of Mascula); and
for some other passages in the correspondence that reflect Cyprian's views, see *Epp.* 45.1.2, 45.3.2, 55.24.2, 66.4.2, 66.8.3, 71.3.1
f., etc. The notion is prominent in Eusebius' view of the Church.

Among the many discussions of this topic are B. Poschmann,
*Ecclesia principalis, ein kritischer Beitrag zur Frage des Primats bei
Cyprian* (Breslau 1933) 16 ff., 29 ff.; W. Telfer, *The Office of a
Bishop* (London 1962) 125 ff.; J. Daniélou, *Message évangélique et
culture hellénistique aux deuxième et troisième siècles* (Paris 1961) 131
ff.; E. Flessemann-van Leer, *Tradition and Scripture in the Early*

Church (Assen 1954) 108 ff.; R. P. C. Hanson, *Tradition in the Early Church* (Philadelphia 1962) 159; J. E. Stam, *Episcopacy in the Apostolic Tradition of Hippolytus* (Basel 1969) 101 f.; A.-M. Javierre in *Unam Sanctam* 39 (1962) 207 ff.; U. Wickert, *Sacramentum unitatis. Ein Beitrag zum Verständnis der Kirche bei Cyprian* (Berlin 1971) 40 ff.

The term *ordinatio* is difficult of analysis; it is to be doubted that it means here strictly "election." See the discussion by P. van Beneden in VC 23 (1969) 173 f., and *idem, Aux origines d'une terminologie sacramentelle* (Louvain 1974) 94 ff.

5. *omnis actus ecclesiae per eosdem praepositos gubernetur.* Note the use of *per:* the bishop is the essential executive agent in the management of Church affairs. He will act on behalf of *clerus* and *stantes fideles* (who, with him, make up the *ecclesia*), as required by his commission as divinely appointed *praepositus.* That does not necessarily make him an autocrat (cf. *Ep.* 14.4: *nihil sine consilio vestro et sine consensu plebis mea privatim sententia gerere*); it does not rule out consultation with his *clerus* and cooperation with his *fideles.* But (Cyprian's argument is here tending), if anyone is to write in the name of the Church (*ecclesiae nomine*), it must be the appointed bishop: conversely, if anyone is to write to Cyprian, the appointed bishop, he must be writing to the *ecclesia* (§1.2 *ad fin.*).

On the word *praepositus* in Cyprian, see n. 7 to *Ep.* 3. For the language here compare *Sent. Episc. praef.*: . . . *Iesu Christi qui unus et solus habet potestatem et praeponendi nos* (*episcopos*) *in ecclesiae suae gubernatione et de actu nostro iudicandi.*

6. From the remainder of this section (and, indirectly, from the points made for contrast in §2.1) we can discern something of the contents and style of this lost letter. It was written in an arrogant and peremptory tone by a group of lapsed who were demanding prompt admission to communion, there being no need for them to do penance and to make satisfaction.

Ep. 35 enclosed a copy of a letter Cyprian had received from a group of lapsed and his own brief and interim reply to it. That letter appears to be the anonymous document mentioned in §2.2 below to which this letter is the brief and interim reply. In *Ep.* 35 we find that in that enclosed, anonymous, letter the group of lapsed were not so much demanding the granting of *pax* as laying claim to it, and the grounds they gave were that they had indeed received *pax* already by virtue of the universal grant issued by the martyred Paulus; there was no need, therefore, for penitence and satisfaction on their part. *Ep.* 36, in turn, expostulates on the letter from this group of *lapsi*, which had been enclosed with *Ep.* 35. We learn further that they talked of the *praerogativa communicationis* which they had obtained from the martyrs, and that they were demanding, accordingly, immediate admission to communion (*Ep.* 36.1.1 ff.). Their letter was arrogantly abusive of Cyprian (*Ep.* 36.3.2).

Cyprian's language gives us the impression that he may have received *two* documents from presumptuous and importunate lapsed. For in this §1.2 he refers to the writers throughout, remotely, in the third person plural (*quosdam ... voluisse ... facerent ... quidam lapsi ... volunt ... oportet eos*), whereas in §2.2 throughout he addresses the writers, directly, in the second person plural (*vos ... discernatis ... estis ... misistis*, etc.).

Technically, Cyprian does not know the identity of the authors of the anonymous document of §2.2; he is sending it back for signatures and clarification. But it would be economical to believe, given what we know of the contents of what appear to be two communications, that we are here dealing with the same group of *lapsi* who followed up their initial and unsatisfied request (§1.2) with another letter (*cum ... aliud scripsisse vos legerim*) making further *desideria* (§2.2). Two similarly minded but independent groups of *lapsi* must remain, of course, a possibility, or, even more confusingly, that Cyprian is not referring to a different letter at all in §2.2 but to the same document as here (see n. 17 below).

In his last letter to his clergy, *Ep.* 26, Cyprian had urged—and many of his colleagues concurred—that all lapsed must wait until their individual cases could be examined by the bishop and his assembled faithful, and even the general letter of *pax* from the confessors required this sort of process to take place. The reaction of some of the *lapsi* to that firmly procrastinating letter appears to have been to make this demand for instant settlement.

For Cyprian the essential provocation of the letter referred to here was that it failed absolutely to recognize the spiritual authority that had come to him automatically with his appointment to episcopal office; he is being treated as an ecclesiastical nonentity.

See, for further discussion, A. von Harnack in TU 23.2a (1902) 31 f.

7. *quando ecclesia in episcopo et clero et in omnibus stantibus sit constituta.* There is point in Cyprian's elaboration here. *Lapsi* would be *ipso facto* demoted from the *clerus* and, by definition, they cannot be *stantes.* The writers of this letter, being *lapsi,* cannot be part of the divine establishment of the *ecclesia.*

8. Luke 20.38.

9. *si apud illos et in illis est ecclesia.* With heavy-handed irony Cyprian is using phrases appropriate for God's bishops, not for shipwrecked apostates. He might have said, *apud episcopos et in episcopis est ecclesia.*

10. *scripserunt autem mihi quidam de lapsis.* In some mss *nuper* ("recently") appears before *quidam.* It is instructive to observe the points which Cyprian singles out for praise in this second document. Their tone is modest (as the preceding group were not); though they, too, have got *libelli martyrum,* they (unlike the other group) are continuously doing penance and good works; they beg (not demand) of their *episcopus* that the satisfaction they continue to make may be acceptable before God; they are in no wild hurry for readmission, but will contentedly wait for their bishop's return (as the previous group would not).

There is stress above all that they recognize the appointed role of Cyprian, as bishop, in the administration of the penitential *disciplina.*

11. *qui in ecclesiis (v.l.: ecclesia) semper gloriose et granditer operati sunt.* When is *semper* to date from? Ever since their fall (i.e., they were penitent at once)? Or ever since they joined the church (i.e., they have never really ceased to be true Christians in spirit)? *Gloriose* is generously eulogistic: it bears special overtones of the supreme sacrifice of martyrdom. The great charity of these Christians (it is hinted) is as efficacious in cancelling sin as the sufferings of confessors and martyrs. On *gloriose,* cf. A. J.

Vermeulen, *The Semantic Development of Gloria in Early-Christian Latin* (Nijmegen 1956).

The plural *ecclesiis* (if it is correct) is unusual. Are we to suppose that these lapsed include some *peregrini* who had come from elsewhere than Carthage? On the plural use of *ecclesia*, see Watson 257.

12. Luke 17.10.

13. It appears that the traffic in *libelli martyrum* has been so heavy (see esp. *Ep.* 27.1.1) that practically all *lapsi* in Carthage could now claim to have received a certificate of forgiveness whether by personal issue or by bloc grant. No wonder that such certificates soon cease to be a significant feature in the debate; after *Ep.* 36, which comments on this letter, they fade from our sight, and they did not figure at all in the eventual settlement (*Ep.* 55). They were hopelessly devalued by inflation.

14. *ut tamen ad Dominum satisfactio ipsa admitti possit, orantes scripserunt mihi.* Some (e.g., Fahey 357) translate "in order that their satisfaction might be acceptable to God, they have addressed to me a request," but put this way it rather unsatisfactorily leaves their request unstated. What they appear to be asking is for Cyprian's intercession before God as their *praepositus,* so that the *satisfactio* they are now making may become effective in making amends and therefore in earning reconciliation for them. Put in more institutional terms (not theirs), they want their bishop Cyprian formally to admit them as penitents so that their *paenitentia* and *opera* can contribute officially towards the satisfaction they owe. From Cyprian's point of view what is important is that they acknowledge his God-given *honos* as bishop and they respect the *disciplina* which it is his episcopal duty to administer. (For *ipsa* here, the correct reading could be *sua.*)

15. *expectare praesentiam nostram . . . nobis praesentibus.* The first-person *plural* could well have here the flavour, as so often in Cyprian, of himself along with his clergy. Elsewhere in the letter Cyprian uses the first person *singular* eight times, clearly with reference to himself alone.

Observe that even these submissive *lapsi* appear confident of their ultimate reconciliation; Cyprian is certainly under pressure.

16. *Dominus . . . dignatus est ostendere quid eiusmodi et tales servi de eius bonitate mereantur.* Some interpret this to allude to a *personal* revelation (e.g., Watson 250: "it is safe to assume that a vision is implied"). That is not at all necessary. More likely, Cyprian is referring to *biblical* revelation, to such passages as, for example, Matt. 25.31 ff. or even Luke 19.21 ff. Has Cyprian replied to these penitents in a separate, now lost, epistle?

17. *quas cum litteras acceperim et nunc aliud scripsisse vos legerim: Aliud* could well imply that its contents are at variance with those of the letter just mentioned with such commendation. From the remainder of this section we can glimpse that its tone was not submissive (Cyprian stresses the restrictions imposed by his own *mediocritas*), that its requests were trouble-making and disruptive of *disciplina* (they are urged, in the concluding greetings, to live *secundum Domini disciplinam quiete et tranquille*). Its further messages are revealed by *Epp.* 35 and 36 and are listed in n. 6 above.

It seems quite unclear to me whether the words *quas . . . litteras* refer only to the letter from the commended *lapsi*, just mentioned, or to that letter along with the letter sent by the censured *lapsi*. If the first alternative is right, then we are not dealing here with a second document from the turbulent lapsed, but Cyprian is reverting to the offensive letter whose tenor he has already described in §1.2. Translators appear to be equally divided in their interpretations. In some mss (notably Hartel's Z; see Hartel XLVIff.) *nuper* appears before *acceperim* here just as it did in the initial reference to the letter from the approved *lapsi* (see n. 10). If that reading is correct, it would identify the reference here in *quas . . . litteras* to the immediately previous letter only. I incline to this view myself.

18. *peto discernatis desideria vestra.* Have they simply asked, for example, that all of them, having received *libelli martyrum*, should now be reconciled (or the like)? Cyprian is demanding a list of names, special circumstances of each case, whether *libellaticus* or *sacrificatus*, etc. Cf. *Ep.* 15.4: *peto ut . . . designetis nominatim et sic ad nos fidei ac disciplinae congruentes litteras dirigatis.*

19. *nomina vestra libello subiciatis et libellum cum singulorum nominibus ad me transmittatis.* There are some obscurities in

interpretation. Some believe Cyprian is wanting a new document sent to him, a memorandum bearing the names of the
senders of the letter. But the verb *subiciatis* suggests he is sending back the original *libellus* to which they are to append their
names. Others believe that the second phrase, *cum singulorum
nominibus*, refers to the names of the individuals concerned in
the requests rather than to the authors of the petition itself.
What follows is against this: Cyprian is being emphatically
repetitious that he will not deal with anonymous correspondence (*ante est enim scire quibus rescribere habeam*).

20. *pro loci et actus nostri mediocritate.* Cyprian is pointedly
exploiting a cliché of epistolary politesse. The writers have
failed to exhibit *mediocritas* in *their* behaviour and in *their* place
in the Church. Furthermore, he began this letter establishing
the high *honos* of the bishop and demonstrating that every *actus*
of the Church is governed by the bishop. Now, with a neat, self-
deprecating touch, he indicates that as bishop he can go only so
far—constrained by his own *mediocritas*—in the exercise of that
honos and those governing powers. For the turn of phrase, cf. *Ep.*
20.1.2 and n. 23 to *Ep.* 27.

21. *secundum Domini disciplinam quiete et tranquille agere.* This
is a most unusual concluding greeting. Manifestly their behaviour is otherwise, not respecting the Lord's *disciplina* and not
tranquilly peaceful. See C. D. Lanham, *Salutatio Formulas in
Latin Letters to 1200: Syntax, Style and Theory* (Munich 1975) 77.

LETTER 34

Contents: Cyprian expresses his approval for the action of his
clergy in excommunicating the presbyter Gaius Didensis and
his deacon, who have persisted, despite frequent warnings, in
admitting the lapsed to communion. A similar penalty awaits
any other presbyter or deacon, whether from Carthage or elsewhere, who thus thwarts the true repentance of the fallen in the
Carthaginian flock. The cases of the three clerics who temporar-

ily deserted their posts will have to await a full hearing before bishops and the assembled congregation; they are to be deferred, without prejudice, until such an inquiry can be held.

Date and circumstances: There are unfortunately only tenuous indications for dating this letter.

After Cyprian wrote *Ep.* 33 he sent a copy of that letter to his clergy, along with *Ep.* 29; and, as on previous occasions, he also sent a copy to Rome, along with *Ep.* 35. *Ep.* 35 should be dated, therefore, not too long after *Ep.* 33. When this *Ep.* 35 went off to Rome, it included a second document, viz, a copy of a letter which Cyprian had sent to his clergy sometime after writing *Ep.* 33 (*quales postea ad clerum litteras fecerim*). That enclosure could possibly be the note to his clergy, *Ep.* 29 (although its somewhat domestic contents may have been of no great interest to Rome). The document enclosed, it has been argued, could equally well have been this letter, *Ep.* 34 (and its contents would have been of considerable interest to Rome). *If* it is *Ep.* 34, that would date our letter very conveniently to, say, late summer 250, and give it a secure place in the sequence of the surviving correspondence (putting it after *Epp.* 33 and 29 but before *Ep.* 35 and *Ep.* 36, the Romans' reply to *Ep.* 35).

The argument normally advanced against identifying *Ep.* 34 with the second document included with *Ep.* 35 is that the circumstances in Carthage indicated by *Ep.* 34 suggest a date later than summer 250: visiting bishops and Carthaginian clergy can now freely confer together (see, e.g., Duquenne 143 f.; Nelke 49). This is not decisive. *Ep.* 32, for example, firmly datable to the summer of 250, reveals circumstances that are quite parallel—visiting bishops and presbyters are in Carthage, and communications between clergy are being freely exchanged. A more telling argument against the identification is that in *Ep.* 36, the Romans' response to *Ep.* 35 concerns the contents of *Ep.* 33; there is nothing about the decisive action which *Ep.* 34 announces, which ought to have elicited from them encouraging comment, if it had been included with *Ep.* 35.

We are now entering a period when we no longer have full records of the correspondence; there is missing, for example, a memorandum from Cyprian to Rome mentioned in *Ep.* 36.4. It is possible, therefore, that a copy of *Ep.* 34 was sent to the Roman clergy (along with a now lost covering note) by the same courier who bore *Ep.* 37 to the Roman confessors in the winter of 250/251, and that *Ep.* 34 should be placed accordingly as late as the early weeks of the year 251. We simply do not know.

What we do know is that attitudes are now hardening and positions are polarizing. A notorious "laxist" presbyter Gaius Didensis (an outsider?) has been singled out for excommunication; that stands as fair warning to other presbyters should they persist in opposition to Cyprian's penitential policies. Even the advice given by Cyprian concerning the clergy who had temporarily absented themselves is relatively uncompromising in tone: a full inquiry before assembled bishops and *plebs universa* will have to be held into each case. It looks as if now the presence of other bishops who uphold his views, a group of his clergy who are openly showing that they are loyal, and, at long last, the letters from Rome which rehabilitate his reputation and reinforce his policies have all combined to encourage more determined steps against rebellion and disobedience. Positive moves are also being taken to help refill the depleted ranks of the Carthaginian clergy. This somewhat firmer and confident attitude more than other considerations suggests that a later dating—roughly, end of 250 or thereabouts—is more likely than not to be correct, but precision is not possible.

1. *ex consilio collegarum meorum.* These are bishops who are able to be present in Carthage (cf. *Ep.* 32.1.2, where their presence is at least anticipated; see n. 14 below). On *collega*, cf. n. 2 to *Ep.* 1 and n. 2 to *Ep.* 9.

We are left to speculate several things. Had these bishops visited Cyprian before proffering their counsel? Would the clergy have so determined without any episcopal persuasion and support (perhaps not; in §4 they write for Cyprian's guidance before taking any action over three clerics of minor grade who have offended much less seriously)? How far are these bishops to be identified with his "ecclesiastical commission" on which two or three bishops sat (*Epp.* 41 and 42)?

The loyal clergy have already written concerning the question (*secundum quod mihi scripsistis*); the bishops present have already warned the offenders repeatedly; it is hard to believe that the final break has now come without the prior sanction of Cyprian (*via* these bishops?). He has become strengthened in his resolve by the actual presence of like-minded colleagues locally, as well as by his awareness of sympathetic clergy and confessors across the seas. It is sheer guesswork by A. Vilela, *La condition collégiale des prêtres au troisième siècle* (Paris 1971) 299, to claim that "la plupart des prêtres et des diacres" have acted together on the advice of the bishops; we do not know what proportion of the clergy was involved.

2. *Gaio Didensi presbytero et diacono eius censuistis non communicandum.* Many questions are raised by this passage. *Didensis* ought to indicate some place-name. It is almost unparalleled in the correspondence for Cyprian to provide double nomenclature of this kind; what is the significance?

The answer may be innocent. It may be simply to avoid confusion with an unknown, homonymous Gaius presbyter in Carthage; *Didensis* merely marks the man's distinguishing place of origin. Cf. n. 4 to *Ep.* 1, where the two Geminii involved are distinguished by the addition of one of their other names.

Others suggest that *Didensis* indicates not the man's place of origin but his place of ecclesiastical operation, at some rural centre within the (extensive) *territorium* of the *civitas* of Carthage. He could be engaged, as it were, in "parish" work there, assisted by a deacon assigned to him (hence *diacono eius*). That would be an interesting piece of evidence—our first testimony for a rural priest in Africa—and some support for it might be sought in Cyprian's *Acta*. There, Cyprian is asked by the proconsul to reveal the whereabouts of the presbyters *in hac civitate* and he responds: *in civitatibus autem suis inveniuntur* (*Act. Cyp.* 1.5). Is the plural *civitatibus* significant (= "communities")? There is some evidence for incipient parish development in the large diocese of Carthage, not least the fact that some Carthaginian presbyters admit, whilst others do not, the lapsed to communion. See n. 13 to *Ep.* 5 and cf. n. 8 to *Ep.* 41. (Is Callistus' appointment to Antium under Pope Victor in any way comparable? Cf. Hippolytus, *Philos.* 9.12.13; see H. Gülzow in ZNTW 58 [1967] 111 ff.)

In this case Gaius becomes one of the five breakaway Carthaginian presbyters (*Ep.* 43.3.1), on which see n. 32 to *Ep.* 14, and we also have a rare instance of a laxist Carthaginian deacon, on which see n. 3 to *Ep.* 16.

For discussion of this view, see Ritschl, *Cyprian* 49 n. 1, 51 n. 2; cf. K. Müller in ZfKG 18 (1896) 214 ff.; DACL 12 (1936) *s.vv.* Organisation de l'église anténicéenne, 2602.

Either of these hypotheses still leaves unallayed, however, the suspicion that Gaius Didensis may in fact be a *peregrinus* presbyter who is currently in Carthage accompanied by his deacon; the presbyter Numidicus *might* be another example (see *Ep.* 40). Further on in this section, Cyprian tells his own clergy that Gaius has deceived *quosdam fratres ex plebe nostra.* That turn of phrase leaves the distinctly possible flavour that Gaius may be an interfering outsider amongst the Carthaginian *plebs* (hence *ex plebe nostra*), and I incline to this view, but there is, nevertheless, no compulsion that this should be so.

Some of one's choice depends on the identification of *Didensis,* and that raises further unprovable hypotheses. The most favoured of the interpretations canvassed is that of the adjective of
* modern Djedeida, and that ought to put Gaius as coming not from the Carthaginian diocese but from the nearby diocese of episcopal Thuburbo Minus (cf. V. Saxer in *Vetera Christianorum* 9 [1972] 114), Djedeida being some 40 km. west from Carthage, and 10 km. from Thuburbo Minus.

Note the deacon who accompanied Gaius; he appears to be attached to him. Not all presbyters could be so serviced—seven deacons would be in all likelihood the upper limit even in Carthage (see Introduction in ACW 43.40). For the deacon's functions (he will have presented the *calix* to the lapsed), see n. 17 to *Ep.* 3.

Excommunication essentially meant what is said—exclusion from communion. That was possible, therefore, even if a cleric belonged to another diocese and another's jurisdiction. Cyprian shows no qualms about threatening outside clerics with excommunication in §3.2. On this topic, consult K. Hein, *Eucharist and*

NOTES 157

Excommunication. A Study in Early Christian Doctrine and Discipline (Bern-Frankfurt am Main 1973) esp. 365 ff.; cf. n. 4 to *Ep.* 3.
3. *offerendo oblationes eorum.* Earlier epistles (*Epp.* 15, 16, 17) suggested that penitents were commemorated individually by name at the eucharistic celebration which followed their reconciliation. Does *oblatio* here refer to such sacrificial prayers offered in their honour (for other examples of being "named at the altar," see *Ep.* 15 n. 14)? Or, rather, do we take *oblatio* here more literally—the penitent provided himself the bread and wine for the eucharist which especially celebrated his reconciliation? For the provision by the faithful of the matter for the sacrifice in the African tradition, see, for Cyprian's own day, *de op. et eleem.* 15: . . . *quae in dominicum sine sacrificio venis, quae partem de sacrificio quod pauper obtulit sumis,* and, for later times, Victor Vit., *Hist. Persec.* 2.51: *procedit ad altare cum Eugenio, sicut moris est, qui fuerat caecus, suae salutis oblationem domino redditurus: quem episcopus accipiens altari imposuit.* Compare Council of Elvira, canon 28; Council of Hippo 393, canon 7; Council of Carthage 397, canon 93; and for this interpretation see also G. Philips in *XXXᵉ Congrès eucharistique international (Carthage, 1930)* (Tunis 1931) 127 n. 47 ("les fidèles, en effet, offraient à l'évêque la matière du sacrifice"). See F. J. Dölger in AC 4 (1934) 111.
4. Note the implications. There has been a lost letter to Cyprian from his loyal clergy; they also asked about the standing of clergy who had temporarily absented themselves (§4). If Gaius and his deacon had desisted, it appears that their past errors may have been overlooked as having been simply misguided: obstinate persistence in the face of Cyprian's letters and those of others (e.g., the letter from Rome referred to in *Ep.* 27.4., and if delivered by now, *Epp.* 30 and 31), as well as blatant recalcitrance before the open warnings of the bishops, have made the formal break inevitable (cf. the threat in *Ep.* 35.1.2). Cyprian's episcopal colleagues have been actively present in Carthage for some time—whether intervening on their own initiative or that of others (e.g., of Cyprian?).
5. *decipientes quosdam fratres ex plebe nostra.* On what may be the emphasis here, see n. 2 above. Cyprian is indignant—as he was before—that clergy are failing in their special duty of

instructing and guiding the *plebs* (a marked emphasis of *Epp.* 15–17).

6. *vera paenitentia et gemitu ac dolore*. There is a variant reading, *veram paenitentiam habeant et. . .*, which Bayard adopts.

7. Apoc. 2.5 and Isaiah 30.15. Observe Cyprian's characteristic technique of anticipating linguistically (*paenitentia . . . gemitu*) the texts he is about to quote (*age paenitentiam . . . gemueris*) and then of pursuing these motifs subsequently (*agere paenitentiam . . . gemitibus*).

8. *quidam de presbyteris*. Are they prudently left anonymous in case they might relent and desist? Gaius Didensis on the other hand had *publicly* proved himself to be a hopelessly obstinate offender.

9. *ut communicandum cum illis temere existiment, nescientes. . .* Who is the subject of *existiment? Cum illis* (not *secum*) suggests that it should be the laxist presbyters. In that case the *nescientes* which follows must refer, a little awkwardly, back to the subject of the main verb, *possunt*, that is to say, the lapsed (for what they are ignorant of is relevant to penitents not to presbyters). It is indeed consistent with Cyprian's view that the onus of error is basically the clergy's.

10. Isaiah 3.12.

11. *palpatione perniciosa*. Cyprian uses an unusual vulgar Latin word (traceable back to an instance in Plautus); on *palpatio* see Mohrmann, VC 2 (1948), 96. For a close parallel, cf. *De laps.* 14: *blandimentis adulantibus palpat* (where the same theme and quotation from Isaiah are discussed).

12. The dominant medical language elicits the metaphor latent (as so often for Cyprian) in *salus:* cf. *salubria . . . consilia, salutaris veritas, salubres cibos* also in this section and *salubriter, consilium salubre* in the following. See also n. 37 to *Ep.* 4.

13. *secundum litteras meas*. This could refer to such documents as *Epp.* 16, 18, 19, 26.

14. *si qui aut praesentes fuerint aut supervenerint.* Compare the similar language (*vel . . . praesentes fuerint vel supervenerint*) in *Ep.* 32.1.2. Cyprian has certain knowledge of the presence of bishops in Carthage now; did he have so already at the time of *Ep.* 32 also? Observe Cyprian's characteristic and overriding concern

for unity of policy and action amongst the episcopate; that is his churchman's instinct.

15. *sive de nostris presbyteris vel diaconis sive de peregrinis.* For the language, compare *Ep.* 32.1.2 (and n. 3 thereto). Cyprian leaves it as unthinkable that visiting bishops might be involved in any such premature reconciliations in Carthage, though he does know that this has been occurring elsewhere in the province (see *Ep.* 27.3.1). Cyprian had threatened his rebellious clergy with suspension only in *Ep.* 16.4.2 (*interim prohibeantur offerre*); now he feels secure—or determined—enough to recommend provisory excommunication: see n. 33 to *Ep.* 16. He refers to this policy in *Ep.* 55.4.3: *si quis . . . lapsis temere communicare voluisset, ipse a communicatione abstineretur.*

16. On the functions of subdeacons, see n. 1 to *Ep.* 8; on acolytes, see n. 13 to *Ep.* 7. Philumenus and Favorinus are otherwise unknown. A subdeacon Fortunatus occurs in *Ep.* 36.1.1; he has been entrusted with delivering *Ep.* 35 and its enclosures to Rome. Is it likely that the erstwhile fugitive Fortunatus would be entrusted with so important a mission; hence we have two subdeacons named Fortunatus? On the other hand, such clerical personnel are in short supply (cf. *Ep.* 29.1.1) and Fortunatus may be anxious to rehabilitate his reputation by undertaking this mission, and hence we may have evidence for but one Fortunatus.

As the balance of the evidence weighs against the likelihood that *Ep.* 34 is earlier than *Ep.* 36 we ought, in the end, to keep two subdeacons named Fortunatus for the Carthaginian church.

17. *medio tempore recesserunt et nunc venerunt.* On the idiomatic use of *medius,* see n. 21 to *Ep.* 22. We hear generally of the absence of clergy also in *Ep.* 29 (where see n. 5). We are clearly now at a stage when the perils of persecution are perceptibly easing off—local clergy can begin to emerge from their places of concealment, and outside clergy (bishops, presbyters, deacons) are revealing their presence in Carthage and are actively, and safely, involving themselves in its church's affairs. But it does mean that the Carthaginian church has been without *multi . . . de clero* for almost a year.

18. It is an astonishing revelation of Cyprian's thorough-going hierarchical attitude that he can, without any apparent embarrassment, accept flight for himself as being fully sanc-tioned and justified, but he can calmly require, at the same time, that his subordinate clergy should remain at their posts, con-tinuing their ministries under the persecution. See further G. Pell, *The Exercise of Authority in Early Christianity from about 170 to about 270* (diss. Oxford 1971) 343 ff.; Thaninayagam 25; and on Cyprian's *fuga*, see n. 2 to *Ep.* 5.

Observe the presence of fellow bishops at the future court of inquiry. If the *plebs universa* is also to be present at the proceed-ings, Cyprian may intend that the *cognitiones* will be held at a plenary African Council meeting (such as took place after Easter in the year following, 251): at such meetings the Carthaginian *plebs* were present in full (see *Ep.* 45.2.1 f) or in large part (256 A.D., *Sent. Episc. praef.*). But we might have envisaged instead a meeting of the local church in council, assisted in its delibera-tions by the corroborative authority of visiting bishops, especial-ly from the surrounding locality, or perhaps even convened in conjunction with a synodal meeting of proconsular bishops; its conclusions however, could set precedents for the future (see next n.), so it was not an unimportant gathering.

19. Note Cyprian's Roman cast of mind. He thinks according to the legal model of precedent-creating judgments and deci-sions. Cf. *Sent. Episc.* 4: Novatus *a Thamogade* (= Thamugadi/ Timgad) appealing to "the decree of our colleagues of most holy memory," and see further *Ep.* 1.1 (and n. 22 on that letter).

20. *se a divisione mensurna tantum contineant.* On the payment of Cyprian's clerics, see n. 21 to *Ep.* 1 and *Ep.* 39.5.2. The church is organized enough to distribute such monthly stipends to the clergy even whilst the persecution continues; see *Epp.* 5.1.2 (and n. 9), 7.2 (and n. 11), 13.7 (and n. 38) for evidence of other financial arrangements earlier in this year, and *Ep.* 41.1.2 (and n. 6) for later provisions. Note the monthly allotment. Tertullian, *Apol.* 39.5, shows that contributions came in from the brethren on a monthly basis (*menstrua die*).

LETTER 35

Contents: For the information and benefit of the Roman clergy Cyprian is enclosing three documents. One comes from a group of the fallen who are laying claim to the reconciliation which, they assert, they have already received. The second is his reply to them. The third is a letter of his to his clergy.

Date and circumstances: The dating is dependent on the identification of the enclosures; and the description of the letter from the lapsed and of Cyprian's reply to it leaves us in little doubt that he is referring to his *Ep.* 33 and the document which provoked it (see nn. 4 and 5 below). And, as Cyprian tells us here, *Ep.* 33 was written *after Epp.* 27 and 28 were sent off to Rome. We should be now, accordingly, towards the end of summer, 250, or thereabouts. Moreover, the impersonal way in which Cyprian talks to the Roman clergy about the despatch of his *Ep.* 27 to Rome—without any word of the lengthy, splendid and glowing reply it gratefully provoked—strongly suggests that Saturus and Optatus are still to arrive back from Rome bearing *Epp.* 30 and 31. In all likelihood this letter crossed with those letters coming from Rome. That makes the probable sequence of letters *Epp.* 27 and 28 (to Rome), *Ep.* 33 (to the lapsed), *Ep.* 29 (to the clergy) and this *Ep.* 35 (to Rome), and then, *Epp.* 30, 31 and 32. See further Gülzow 14 and n. 64; H. von Soden in TU 25.3 (1904) 26, 36 f.; Duquenne 139; A. von Harnack, *Geschichte der altchristlichen Literatur* (2 vols., Leipzig 1893–1904; repr. 1958) 2.344 f.; Nelke 43.

Despite the continued—and, for Cyprian, galling—silence from Rome, Cyprian's tone is assured. The Roman clergy have already declared their firm and consistent attitude on this question of reconciliation for the lapsed in the lost letter they sent to the Carthaginian clergy. Indeed, just as in *Ep.* 27 Cyprian allowed himself a more outspoken expression of his true sentiments than, diplomatically, he was prepared to voice at the same time to his clergy (*Ep.* 26), so here he can exasperatedly threaten the turbulent lapsed with excommunication (see n. 8 below), whereas he wisely withholds such threats and frankness from his *Ep.* 33 which is addressed to those lapsed. Cyprian, we can discern, is still trying to win the approving support of colleagues in Rome whilst at the same time he wishes to avoid irretrievably alienating dissident groups in his own flock in Carthage.

1. *dilectio communis et ratio exposcit . . . nihil conscientiae vestrae subtrahere de his quae apud nos geruntur.* There is no need to read into these remarks any sense of dependence on the part of Carthage upon Rome; rather, Cyprian's sense of the interdependence of the churches demanded the charity of helpfully sharing information and counsel. But by this letter Cyprian will not only be advising his colleagues in Rome of the further problems he is encountering and of his policy towards them; he will also be revealing, incidentally, his robust maintenance of church discipline. It is entirely likely that Cyprian has not yet received from Rome *Ep.* 30. From Cyprian's perception he has had to write to Rome not only *Ep.* 9 but also *Ep.* 20 (with its 13 enclosures), *Ep.* 27 (with its 6 enclosures), and send off this letter (with its 3 enclosures)—4 letters in all with 22 supporting documents—before at long last a suitable personal reply eventually reached him from Rome.

2. That is, *Ep.* 27. Cyprian writes as if he has as yet received no reply back from Rome to that letter. On Saturus and Optatus, see *Ep.* 29.1.2 (and nn. 7, 10, 12).

3. On Paulus, see *Epp.* 22.2.1 (and n. 10) and 27.1.2 (and n. 4).

4. This refers to the document mentioned in *Ep.* 33.1.2 and to which *Ep.* 33 itself is a rejoinder (see further *Ep.* 33 nn. 6 and 7).

5. *quid eis ego breviter interim rescripserim.* This description fits *Ep.* 33 admirably—*eis* are importunate lapsed, the letter is short (*breviter*), and it is a provisional reply (*interim*), until further clarification and details are forthcoming.

6. *quales postea ad clerum litteras fecerim.* There is no certainty about identification, but the possibilities are threefold. The most likely candidate is *Ep.* 29. With that epistle Cyprian encloses (*Ep.* 29.1.1) copies of a letter he has received and of his reply to it; he does not, most unusually, say from whom he received the letter or to whom he directed this reply. That makes the anonymous

Ep. 33 almost certainly one of the two documents enclosed along with the letter from the unidentified *lapsi.* Cyprian would have kept his clergy informed of such a development.

Less likely is *Ep.* 34. That letter does not concern directly disobedient lapsed but disobedient clergy. If *Ep.* 34 was the letter enclosed, it is odd that Cyprian does not proceed here to expatiate even a little on the new theme introduced by that letter, as is his custom; rather, he goes on to make further remarks which apparently still concern disobedient *lapsed.* Contra, for example, Pearson and Fell, and Bayard, *ad loc., Ep.* 34 is, therefore, unlikely to be the letter enclosed, especially as the reply to this letter (*Ep.* 36) fails to reflect any of the important contents of *Ep.* 34. It is much less surprising if the (uncontroversial and less serious) contents of *Ep.* 29 are passed over in silence by the Roman clergy in that reply of theirs.

A third possibility is that Cyprian is referring to a letter which we no longer possess. But when we do have a candidate which appears to fit the requirements (*Ep.* 29), this must remain the least satisfying hypothesis. The evidence which is in its favour is provided by *Ep.* 36.4—the Roman clergy have been informed about Privatus of Lambaesis; could that possibly have been a topic in the (hypothetically lost) letter to the Carthaginian clergy, a copy of which is here enclosed?

7. *si temeritas eorum . . . nec vestris litteris compressa fuerit.* This does not supply secure evidence that *Ep.* 30 has yet reached Carthage: for there has already been one (lost) letter from the Roman clergy to the Carthaginian clergy which vigorously campaigned against *properata nimis remedia communicationum* (*Ep.* 30.3.3). See *Ep.* 27.4 (and n. 27) and *Ep.* 30.3 (and n. 20) for its contents.

8. *agemus ea quae secundum evangelium Dominus agere praecepit.* I am unsure of the precise allusion. In *Epp.* 59.20 and 69.1 Cyprian quotes Matt. 18.17 about the need to shun those who refuse to listen to the Church; he may be thinking of that passage here ("If your brother commits a sin, go and take the matter up with him, strictly between yourselves, and if he listens to you, you have won your brother over. If he will not listen, take one or two others with you, so that all the facts may be duly established on the evidence of two or three witnesses. If

he refuses to listen to them, report the matter to the congregation; and if he will not listen even to the congregation, you must
then treat him as you would a pagan or a tax-gatherer"—Matt.
18.15 ff. N.E.B.). This seems to be the first real threat by
Cyprian of *excommunication* (in the more formal sense) for recal-
citrant *lapsed;* (the later?) *Ep.* 34 openly discloses excommunication for persistently rebellious clergy.

LETTER 36

Contents: The letter delivered by Fortunatus has brought distress to the Roman clergy by its news of Cyprian's continued
troubles. These have been caused by lapsed who are demanding
immediate reconciliation on the grounds that the martyrs so
decreed. They cannot indeed be martyrs if they have acted
contrary to the Gospel, but in fact the martyrs merely passed
the cases of the lapsed on to the bishop, thereby gaining for
themselves respite from the importunities of the fallen. For so
serious a wound the cure for the lapsed will have to be slow in
order to be effective; penance and humility they need to demonstrate, not impatience and abuse of their bishop.

True to his custom, Cyprian has sought to warn Rome of an
emissary from Privatus of Lambaesis, but they saw through his
deceptions even before Cyprian's warning reached them.

Date and circumstances: The Roman clergy are responding to *Ep.*
35 and its enclosures (§1.1, where see n. 2 below) as well as to an
additional memorandum from Cyprian concerning Privatus
(§4.1, where see n. 19). We should now be at the end of summer
250, given the date ascribed to *Ep.* 35. The Romans will have
recently sent off *Ep.* 30 which, we have seen, appears to have
crossed with *Ep.* 35. Cf. Nelke 47 f.

In their response the Roman clergy reiterate their firm stand
concerning the lapsed. Moreover, they are well aware of the

presence of trouble-stirring clergy who are provoking the lapsed to their extremes (§3.2); copies of earlier correspondence (e.g., *Epp.* 15 ff.) will have disclosed their machinations, not necessarily a copy of *Ep.* 34 which may well be of later date. This reply will helpfully lend further strength to Cyprian's hand in his negotiations with these clergy and lapsed; in the end he feels in sufficiently consolidated a position to deal with the source of trouble, the rebellious presbyters and deacons, by means of excommunication *via* his own clergy.

In this letter the Romans regard the motivations of the martyrs who have proffered *pax*, with marked beneficence (§2.3). Such a kindly construing would be of some diplomatic value in what would be in essence a public document (and it has, in fact, some of the ring of truth about it); it helps to bridge the unfortunate breach that has opened between martyrs and bishop in Carthage.

We also catch a glimpse of a church that is slowly returning to a more normal life; Privatus' mission from Numidia to Rome suggests that circumstances for the churches are now becoming more settled by contrast with the turmoil and confusion which prevailed at the height of the persecution.

The letter shows all the stylistic signs that make composition by Novatian highly plausible. See for a detailed analysis Melin 61 ff.; also A. von Harnack in *Theologische Abhandlungen: Carl von Weizsäcker zu seinem siebzigsten Geburtstage* (Freiburg 1892) 17 ff. For the most recent text see G. F. Diercks, CCL 4.247 ff., and for recent discussion of the letter see Gülzow 106 ff., 145 ff.

1. For this salutation, cf. *Ep.* 30 and n. 1 thereto.

2. *litteras tuas quas per Fortunatum hypodiaconum miseras.* To judge from the contents which follow, the Romans have clearly received *Ep.* 35, along with its enclosures (which included *Ep.* 33). This Fortunatus is unlikely to be the same subdeacon Fortunatus of (the later?) *Ep.* 34.4.1 (see n. 16 thereto). In *Ep.* 8 the Roman writers used the hybrid formation *subdiaconus;* see n. 1 to *Ep.* 8.

3. *quorundam improbitatem iuste coerces.* From what follows it

is clear that the *quorundam* does not refer to rebellious clergy (as the word does in §3.2 below) but to turbulent lapsed (the subject of *Ep.* 33).

4. *immo iam et in caelis habere se dicerent.* This appears to be an echo of their own phraseology—the martyred Paulus (*Ep.* 35.1.1) who, on his death-bed, had granted them *pax* (*Ep.* 22.2) is now seated, with efficacious authority, at the throne of judgment. For a commentary on the thinking behind this claim, see *Ep.* 21.1.3 ff. with introductory note to that letter.

5. *praerogativam communicationis habere.* Again, this appears to reflect words actually used by the lapsed in urging their claim. On this use of *praerogativa*, see *Ep.* 18.1.2 (and n. 5 there). The Roman writers of *Ep.* 8 used the formation *communio* instead of *communicatio;* see n. 24a to *Ep.* 8.

6. It is generally assumed that the "person" involved (*ab eo cui sociari quaerit*) is Christ, and that is the reasonable interpretation. But the focus of the argument of the letter is on the unnecessary breach between the lapsed and their bishop (*cur non iudicium eorum sustinent a quibus petendam pacem . . . putaverunt?*); could the person, therefore, conceivably be rather the bishop into whose company the lapsed are endeavouring to be readmitted by insisting so vehemently on the *privilegia* they claim to have gained *via* the martyrs?

7. *de evangelii conservatione . . . unde martyres fiunt.* For this notion in Cyprian, cf. *Ep.* 27.3.3: *per evangelium martyres fiant; Ep.* 38.2.1: *evangelium Christi . . . unde martyres fiunt;* and see also n. 26 to *Ep.* 30. Relevant, too, is *De unit.* 19, denying the *praemia* of the church to those who are outside it, and *De unit.* 14 on the allied theme *esse martyr non potest qui in ecclesia non est.*

8. The argument is sophistic but its essence is simple. The authority of the Gospel would be shattered were it to be overridden by the authority of the martyrs—but the martyrs would no longer have the authority of martyrs were they to seek to override the Gospel.

For the use here of *merito* (*ut merito* being translated by "hence it is only right"), see Melin 79 ff.

9. The train of thought (as this section later reveals) is that

the intentions of the martyrs have been misunderstood by the lapsed. The martyrs sought peace from the importunities of the lapsed by referring their cases to their bishop, but that innocent act of referral is now being misused and misinterpreted by the lapsed. The Romans suggest a noticeably kindlier view of the motivations of the martyrs than Cyprian has been prepared to voice (contrast his indignant commentary in *Ep.* 27.2.2).

10. *illos ad episcopum, ut ipsi dicunt, remittendos censuerunt.* The clause *ut ipsi dicunt* is somewhat ambiguous. Does it refer to the lapsed ("as the lapsed admit themselves") or to the martyrs ("to quote the martyrs' own words")? The change in tense (*dicunt . . . censuerunt*) makes the former interpretation the more probable, but the latter is still possible, especially in the light of the process of referral before the bishop clearly envisaged by the martyrs (*Epp.* 22.2.2, 23).

11. *sanctissimi martyres.* Cyprian's habitual epithet would have *beatissimi* with *martyres;* see n. 2 to *Ep.* 10. But observe in the Cyprianic fragment l.20, *sanctissimas sorores nostras,* and in l.2 (as a marginal addition), *dominis meis fratribus (sanctissimis)*; see M. Bévenot in the *Bulletin of the John Rylands Library* 28 (1944) 77 f. = M. Supp. 1, 41 f. Discussion of these epithets is in H. A. M. Hoppenbrouwers, *Recherches sur la terminologie du matryre de Tertullien à Lactance* (Nijmegen 1961) 68 ff., 147 ff.

12. *temperamentum et pudoris et veritatis.* The right reading for the first *et* could well be *ut* (in the sense of *veluti?*), for which there is good ms warrant (Hartel even suspecting an original *ut pudoris sic et veritatis*). The word *temperamentum* has already appeared twice in *Ep.* 30.

13. For the elaborate medical language, cf., for example, *Ep.* 30.3.3, *Ep.* 31.6.4 f. There may be an echo of this sentiment in *Ep.* 34.2.2; but the parallelism in language is too slight to make it the basis for determining the relative dating of *Epp.* 34 and 36.

14. *ad fidelem se dilatos esse medicinam.* For a parallel in thought and language, cf. *Ep.* 31.7.2: *fideliora de necessariis dilationibus remedia praestari.*

15. *novimus institutionem. Institutio* could well signify not so much the church's *mores* as her instruction in doctrine, her

training in the faith, etc. The emphasis of the passage is, however, on the church's *practice* in charity rather than on her education.

16. Hartel conjectures *quod quaedam inter vos per epistulam iniecta durius notaremus* ("hence our surprise to observe harsh words hurled by you against each other by letter"). This reading is unsatisfactory: the implicit rebuke against Cyprian (included in *vos*) is most unlikely in view of the general tone of this letter, and it is rendered even more improbable by the specific gloss which follows in §3.3—it is high time for the lapsed to do penance that they may "draw upon themselves the mercy of God by showing the honour that is due to the bishop of God (*de honore debito in Dei sacerdotem*)": they have not been respectful of their bishop. I translate, with most editors, the reading *in te per* (for Hartel's *inter vos per*) which keeps closer to the (garbled) mss readings, *interpetere, in te petere, interprete*, etc. (which corruptions are explicable through haplography).

The reference is to the letter from the lapsed written *ecclesiae nomine*, which was enclosed with *Ep. 35*.

17. *pro ipsis preces stantium.* These words could imply that the lapsed reported in their lost letter that *stantes* gave their support to their cause. But so specific a reference is not necessary. *Stantes* will have prayed (*preces*) as a matter of course for their lapsed brethren.

18. *pro tuo more fecisti qui rem nobis tamquam sollicitam nuntiare voluisti.* It is important to appreciate the context of this remark. Cyprian, for his part, has shown the customary charity of the Carthaginian church in wanting to forewarn the Romans on a matter that would be of special concern to them. One cannot here deduce that Cyprian is expected dutifully to report on all such serious matters out of deference to or dependence upon Rome. All the same, Rome was but a few days' sail away, and in Rome was, so far as we know, the biggest as well as the senior church (*ecclesia principalis*)—and the most accessible major church out of North Africa. For someone who had met with disapproval in Carthage, the next obvious step for him to take was to seek to win approval for his cause in Rome. Felicissimus' mission to Rome in 252 was aimed precisely at such side-step-

ping of a local condemnation. Carthage needed to keep Rome regularly informed on such matters in the general interests of the Church. (In *Ep.* 59 Cyprian's mission to forewarn Rome gets there too late, with embarrassing consequences.) Rome sends similar advice to Carthage, e.g., *Ep.* 50. For further discussion, see M. Bévenot in *Dublin Review* 228 (1954) ii, 313 f.; A. Demoustier in *Recherches de science religieuse* 52 (1964) 337 ff., 555 ff.; E. Caspar, *Geschichte des Papsttums* (2 vols., Tübingen 1930–1933) 1.72 ff.; etc.

Privatus, bishop of Lambaesis in Numidia, had been condemned in the previous decade, during the bishopric of Donatus of Carthage (d. 248/9) and the pontificate of Fabian (236–250), and probably early within that period (in *Ep.* 59 in 252 Cyprian dates the condemnation *ante multos fere annos*). We do not know the grounds for the condemnation, doctrinal or disciplinary; perhaps the latter to judge by Cyprian's phrase in *Ep.* 59.10.1: *ob multa et gravia delicta ... condemnatum,* though he is liberally termed *haereticus* at the same time. He was condemned by the verdict of 90 bishops in a synod held much more probably at Carthage rather than at Lambaesis (the wording of *Ep.* 59 is misleadingly ambiguous on this point). The unprecedentedly large number of bishops who mustered for this condemnation suggests that this had been a *cause célèbre;* Rome lent her supporting vote to the condemnation. After his condemnation Privatus had proceeded to set up a breakaway church (Felix was one of his early *pseudepiscopi*), by 252 claiming to have the support of 25 bishops—though Cyprian avers that there were in reality only five of them, whose names he provides (*Ep.* 59.10.1 ff.)

Privatus appears now to be seeking to take advantage of the undisciplined confusion in the church of this period; he is on the move for reinstatement. He may indeed have heard word that Cyprian is *persona non grata* in Rome and is seeking to exploit that rumored disagreement. At the Carthaginian synod of 251 it was found necessary to excommunicate for the second time Privatus and his followers. The subsequent story of Privatus' church is picked up in *Ep.* 59.10 f.

For further reading, see DACL 8 (1928) *s.v.* Lambèse, 1068;

DACL 14 (1948) *s.v.* Rome, 2570; Hefele-Leclercq, *Histoire* 1.162; Monceaux, *Histoire* 2.32; P. Hinchliff, *Cyprian of Carthage* (London 1974) 81 f.

19. *ante litteras tuas.* We know of no such letter. We have to presume that Cyprian sent off to Rome a letter of warning soon after Fortunatus had left bearing *Ep.* 35; in his hideaway he had just received, tardily, word of this attempt by Privatus to deceive Rome. For the first time in the surviving correspondence we have an indubitable example of a lost letter of Cyprian's own. See W. Sanday in *Studia biblica et ecclesiastica* 3 (1891) 321 f.; A. von Harnack in TU 23.2a (1902) 20; H. von Soden in TU 25.3 (1904) 19 f.; Gülzow 104 f.

20. I presume Futurus was seeking from Rome a letter of support and goodwill; was he hoping that with Fabian dead and the church in Rome without a bishop he might the more readily obtain such a document? He failed, fatally, to keep suppressed his connexion with the notorious Privatus. Other named supporters of Privatus are given in *Ep.* 59.10.2. There may be a special touch of irony intended in the use of the military language here (*ex ipsius nequitiae cohorte . . . vexillarius*): Privatus and Futurus come from a famous military centre, Lambaesis, the military headquarters of the one legion normally stationed in Africa, the *Legio III Augusta.*

LETTER 37

Contents: Cyprian can see vividly the Roman confessors in the person of Celerinus, their former comrade, who has now arrived. In fact Cyprian might be said to be over there in prison with them, being present in spirit through the unbroken ties of mutual love and affection, for they figure constantly in his prayers. Their honours grow with each day that they continue to be there. Indeed they are now entering on the second year of their spiritual office; the four seasons may have gone by outside, but within they have garnered spiritual crops of glory. Some of their number have completed their glorious journey whilst they who remain, despite their material distress, already live the life of the world to come. Their courageous stand for their faith as for the Gospel discipline has made them exemplars of martyrdom.

Date and circumstances: The martyrs have lived through an annual cycle from one winter to the next (§2.2: *sic apud servos Dei annus evolvitur*); indeed, to be more precise, they have passed beyond "the revolution of the now returning year" (§2.1: *iam revertentis anni . . . circulum . . . transgressa*). That ought to put us in the winter of 250/251 and, more exactly, in the early weeks of the new year, 251. See further Duquenne 140 ff. and nn. 10 and 11 below, as well as Nelke 48 f.

Cyprian appears stimulated to compose the letter by the arrival of the confessor Celerinus. He has brought verbal messages from the Roman confessors and fresh news—we hear, for the first time, of deaths in their ranks (§3.1). Their circumstances are not described with any specificity, but hunger, thirst, and squalor figure rather than lurid depictions of torture-sessions and horror stories of mangling. But we can see that after all these long months they are still under pressure to recant (§1.3), probably awaiting a final sentence (see n. 9 below), which, in all likelihood, was never passed. They are to be released not too many weeks later.

Cyprian's preoccupation with his own undisciplined confessors is very apparent, especially in §4. The Roman confessors are made to figure (sc. by contrast with some local counterparts) as true witnesses to the Gospel as much as they are to their faith. The dead from their number, now to be considered hallowed martyrs, are, remarkably, given but one short sentence in §3.1. The focus of the letter is rather on the veritable glories that come from patient steadfastness, long-suffering perseverance and unswerving loyalty to the Gospel precepts. Copies of the letter would have a local circulation as well. For further discussion of the letter, see Gülzow 108 f., 147 f.

The letter is composed with manifest artifice, it is florid with imagery and rhetoric. Its extravagant praises were meant to be relished by its recipients in their squalid dungeons, its colorful phrases to be savoured during their dreary ordeal. Penning such a lyrical composition was itself an act of charity; it would help keep their long-tested spirits uplifted, encouraging ultimate perseverance to their glorious goal. We ought to remember that it would be read out to men and women who could see each other slowly dying, from disease and their long-endured privations.

Celerinus presumably travelled over to Carthage at the very end of the sailing season (it officially closed in early November; see Vegetius, *De re mil.* 4.39); he may have taken a little time to reach Cyprian in his place of hiding. This letter of Cyprian's, in turn, probably had to wait some time before it could catch one of the scarce ships that ventured into the risky winter seas. (Observe the tone of Augustine, *Ep.* 97.2 on a mid-winter voyage from Africa to Italy: *qui urgenti necessitate pro salute civis sui etiam media hieme quomodocumque ad illas partes venire compulsus est.*) On the evidence for winter shipping, see J. Rougé in REA 54 (1952) 316 ff.; O. Perler, *Les voyages de saint Augustin* (Paris 1969) 68 ff.; and see D. Gorce, *Les voyages, l'hospitalité et le port des lettres dans le monde chrétien des IV et Vᵉ siècles* (Paris 1925) 205 ff. on the general topic of letter-carrying and delivery.

1. For Moyses, Maximus, and their companions, see n. 28 to *Ep.* 27, n. 1 to *Ep.* 28.

2. *fidei ac virtutis vestrae comes.* The combination *fides ac virtus* is to recur in the letter (§§1.3 and 3.1), this emphatic repetition stressing the twin virtues essential for martyrdom. On the combination of words, see n. 3 to *Ep.* 10.

3. *quando a vobis per tales talia perferuntur.* Even if we had no other evidence it would be clear from this paragraph that Celerinus has been in Rome, that he has made his confession there, and that he has now come to Cyprian in his African hideaway. As he comes with tidings of goodwill from the Roman martyrs, he cannot have left Rome, at the very earliest, until after the exchange of letters, *Epp.* 28 and 31, had established favourable relations between the two parties (i.e., late summer 250). Indeed, he is likely to have left Rome more recently than that, bringing Cyprian messages and relatively fresh news of affairs there (e.g., §3.1, deaths among these confessors—but no word yet of Moyses' martyrdom). We are still left, however, to speculate on

the length of time for which Celerinus may have been out of prison in Rome itself before his departure (on this see n. 1 to *Ep.* 21) and on what grounds he had been so released. Celerinus is discussed generally in the introductory note and n. 1 to *Ep.* 21.

4. *divinae dignationis ornamenta vobiscum sentire nos credimus.* Note the heavy elaboration on the theme of partaking in, through the links of charity, the glories, and merits of the martyrs; it is not an uncommon *topos* (cf. *Epp.* 10.5.2 and 28.1.2 ff.). Cyprian shows himself now fully confident of his reinstated reputation. (There is reported a variant reading—*hortamenta* for *ornamenta*—but its attractions are superficial.)

5. *quando in sacrificiis precem cum pluribus facimus.* Observe the technical use of *prex* (singular) in the sense of the "eucharistic oblation"; see n. 26 to *Ep.* 1. By contrast, Cyprian employs the plural of the word when he refers to his own personal prayers in the clause that follows (*privatis precibus*). On Cyprian's sacrificial view of the eucharistic celebration (*in sacrificiis*), see n. 12 to *Ep.* 1.

By this time Cyprian appears to enjoy considerably freer communications: his company can now be described as *plures.* On Cyprian's entourage generally, see n. 17 to *Ep.* 5.

6. *coronis ac laudibus vestris plenam Domini faventiam postulamus.* Consonant with his high-flown tone Cyprian chooses a suitably recherché word (*faventia*) with its sacral and augural connotations. For a similar heightened effect he chooses in the next section the unusual verb *praelegere* in the portentously rare sense of "select" ("you elect to stay there"). See Watson 312.

7. *mora ipsa passionis.* On the Christian use of the word *passio,* see n. 13 to *Ep.* 3.

8. *longoque temporum ductu glorias vestras non trahitis sed augetis.* In the context I am a little unsure of the precise significance of *trahitis.* Could it mean here "attenuate" rather than "protract"?

9. *vos totiens confitemini quotiens rogati* etc. The passage implies that attempts are being made to induce the martyrs to apostatize, and go free. And that, in turn, rather suggests that they have not been committed to imprisonment as a legal penalty (*contra* M. M. Sage, *Cyprian* [Cambridge 1975] 187) but are still

technically in the course of their trial before final sentence has been passed. See the introductory note to *Ep.* 22 on the use of imprisonment for adjourned cases (a softening-up treatment to encourage recantation), with further discussion in my article in *Historia* 22 (1973) 654 f.

10. *annuae dignitatis insignibus et duodecim fascibus glorientur.* Consuls and proconsuls (of consular rank) were technically entitled to an entourage of twelve lictors each. The lictors carried a bound bundle of rods (*virgae*) symbolic of the magistrates' power to beat and to coerce. Outside Rome that *fasces* might be bound along with an axe, symbolic of the magistrates' *ius gladii.* See PWK 6.2 (1909) *s.v. fasces,* 2002 ff.; E. S. Staveley in *Historia* 12 (1963) 458 ff. Some time-indication may be intended—the eponymous consuls, like many magistrates, entered office at the beginning of the calendar year; but on the other hand, proconsuls did not take up their duties in their provinces until later in the year, though by what month precisely is not entirely clear— see *Latomus* 31 (1972) 1053 f.; T. D. Barnes, *Tertullian. A Historical and Literary Study* (Oxford 1971) 260 f. Perhaps Cyprian is stimulated to elaborate his analogy by being now at the season, early in the new year of 251 A.D. (see next n.), when as a general rule incoming magistrates, the supreme temporal authorities, preened themselves in the resplendent finery and accoutrements of their new offices.

11. *dignitas caelestis ... honoris annui claritate signata est ... iam revertentis anni volubilem circulum ... transgressa est.* Characteristically, secular magistracies expired with the end of the calendar year, but the spiritual elite of the martyrs have now entered into a second calendar year of their office. Cyprian's arithmetic may well be imprecise for rhetorical convenience and exploitation, but we should deduce (i) with certainty that the martyrs have been imprisoned at least from one winter (249/250) to the next (250/251) and (ii) in all probability that we have now entered into the new year 251 A.D. The literary inexactitude of Cyprian's computations is disclosed by the chance information we have that Moyses' imprisonment lasted in fact just short of twelve full months (eleven months and eleven days, to be precise; see n. 1 to *Ep.* 28); Cyprian does not

yet know of the death of Moyses (an addressee). If it is a correct inference that these Roman confessors were not arrested until after Fabian's death (see n. 5 to *Ep.* 28), which occurred in late January 250, then it is a fair guess that Moyses will have died just about the time Cyprian is composing this letter.

A. J. Vermeulen, *The Semantic Development of Gloria in Early-Christian Latin* (Nijmegen 1956) 143 f., is concerned with the distinction that should be drawn between *claritas* and *claritudo* in Cyprian. ("The probable reason is that *claritudo* was more suitable to express the meaning of light. This confirms our impression that St. Cyprian understood *claritas* primarily as renown"—p. 144.) Artistic variation is an equally probable explanation for Cyprianic usage, both words being used in this same section (*honoris annui claritate* here, and *Christi claritudo* below).

12. *inluminabat mundum sol oriens et luna decurrens.* Commentators have contrived to see indications here of specific dates. *Sol oriens* dates the time to after the winter solstice, i.e., December 21, 249 (so A. Bludau in *Römische Quartalschrift* 27 [1931] 29); *luna decurrens* dates the time between December 8 and December 20, 249, there being a new moon on December 21, 249 (so J. Moreau, in SC 39 [1954] vol. 2, 214 f.). Neither interpretation carries conviction in such a lyrical context as this. In the darkness of the dungeon shone light eternal, brighter and more reliable than the world's illumination provided by its transient heavenly bodies. Cyprian is not supplying precise astronomical data but a rhetorically effective contrast. See also Introduction in ACW 43.26.

13. *rosae et flores de paradisi deliciis.* Roses are the one flower specifically mentioned as they are associated with the crimson colour of martyrdom. For an explication and parallels, see n. 34 to *Ep.* 10. For a full analysis of the images and literary arrangement of this flamboyant paragraph, see J. Fontaine, *Aspects et problèmes de la prose d'art latine au troisième siècle. La genèse des styles latins chrétiens* (Torino 1968) 172 ff.

14. *aestas ecce messium fertilitate fecunda est et area frugibus plena est.* Some have concluded that 250 was a good year for harvests (e.g., G. Mercati in *Opere Minori*, vol. 2 = *Studi e Testi* 77 [1937] 186, "Consta da S. Cipriano che l'annata del 250 fu assai

abbondante"; A. d'Alès in *Recherches de science religieuse* 8 [1918] 336 n. 1, "Nous savons par Cyprien que l'année 250 fut une année d'abondance"), but such a literal reference is quite out of keeping with this imaginatively poetical passage.

Cyprian can use the image of the threshing-floor with other interpretations (e.g., *Ep.* 54.3.2, of penitent apostates and see Fahey 266 f. for his other allusions to Matt. 3.12). For the varied history of the parable, see J. S. Alexander in JTS 14 (1973) 512 ff.

15. *gloriam seminastis frugem gloriae metitis.* An echo of Gal. 6.8.

16. *pressurae saecularis infestatione calcati torcular nostrum carcere torquente sentitis.* Cyprian boldly and characteristically plays on the literal and figurative use of his words: *pressura* can be used both to refer to wine and oil pressing and, in Christian usage, to persecution (cf. n. 15 to *Ep.* 22); likewise *torqueo* is used for the turning of a wine press and for torture. For such play on words in Cyprian, see C. Mohrmann, *Études sur le latin des chrétiens* (3 vols., Rome 1961–1965) 1.289 ff. For illustrations of the Roman *vindemia* see K. D. White, *Roman Farming* (London 1970) plates 53 ff., and on the *torcular*, A. G. Drachman, *Ancient oil mills and presses* (Copenhagen 1932) 50 ff.

17. *fratres beatissimi.* On the epithet (picked up again in the concluding greetings), characteristic of the martyr in Cyprianic usage, see n. 2 to *Ep.* 10. On the efficacy of the prayers of the martyrs (still living), a theme which Cyprian now introduces, see M. Pellegrino in *Revue des sciences religieuses* 35 (1961) 159 ff., and for other parallels E. L. Hummel in SCA (1946) 156 ff.

18. *martyrii vestri veritate . . . vere evangelii testes et vere martyres Christi.* As in his previous letter to these confessors (*Ep.* 28) Cyprian is heavy-handed in his stress on the genuineness and sincerity of their witness (*sincero fidei vigore . . . incorrupto honore virtutis . . . martyrii vestri veritate . . . vere martyres . . . martyria vestra exempla*) as being demonstrated and established by their faithful adherence to the Gospel (*Domini mandata servastis . . . evangelicam disciplinam tenuistis . . . cum praeceptis Domini stantes . . . vere evangelii testes . . . disciplinam cum virtute iunxistis*). He manifestly has in mind confessors who have proved not to be equally witnesses of Christ *and* of His Gospel (cf. n. 26 to *Ep.* 30,

and n. 7 to *Ep.* 36). For the play on the words *testis—martyr*, see n. 29 to *Ep.* 21; E. L. Hummel, *op. cit.* in preceding note, 28 f.

19. *radicibus eius innixi, super petram robusta mole fundati.* The bold images have presumably biblical resonances, e.g., John 15.1 ff. (vine and branches), Matt. 7.24 ff. (house built upon rock: Cyprian's text read at verse 25: *fundata enim super petram* [*Test.* 3.96]; Fahey 289 omits the allusion). Would Roman martyrs see an allusive touch also in *super petram ... fundati* to their Church's founder, the martyred Peter?

LETTER 38

Contents: Cyprian, along with episcopal colleagues, has appointed the confessor Aurelius to the post of reader. The customary formalities of scrutiny and approval, normally carried out by the bishop and his flock together, can be dispensed with in this special case. God has passed judgment already on his character: his deserts are apparent in his brilliant confessional honours, his personal qualities in his model humility. To start with, it will be suitable for him to be a reader, proclaiming the Gospel of God which makes men into martyrs.

Date and circumstances: Indications are weak but we must be, at the least, in the later stages of Cyprian's sojourn in hiding. Certainly the confessor Aurelius has been released from custody and bishops (plural) can now visit Cyprian in hiding together. The heavy emphasis on submissiveness and obedience as the qualities most desirable in the clergy suggests the same climate as *Ep.* 34, that is to say, around the end of 250 or thereabouts. This letter certainly comes before *Ep.* 39 (Celerinus to join Aurelius in the lectorate, *Ep.* 39.4.2), and there are already hints in this letter that such additional appointments are to follow (§2.2). This letter would thus fit nicely after *Ep.* 37 (which announces Celerinus' arrival), dated to very early 251, but that attractive placing cannot be established definitely. Beyond that we cannot go. Cf. Nelke 49 f.

Cyprian is now not only restoring the depleted ranks of his clergy. He is drawing into his clerical following what has proved to be a source of potential rivalry and rebellion—those blessed with the special graces and spiritual prerogatives of confessors. He goes about his task with circumspection. He relies, in this instance, on a lavish and elaborate description of the *divina suffragia;* in the next example (*Ep.* 39) his case is further bolstered by a compelling vision (*hortatu in visione per noctem compulsus est ne negaret,* §1.1) as well as by the exceptional *merita* (§2) and family credentials (§3) of the candidate; and in the third instance, *Ep.* 40, Cyprian has been supported by divine monitions (*admonitos nos et instructos . . . dignatione divina,* §1.1, *quod ostenditur fiat,* §1.3) after the confessor has been wondrously preserved (§1.1). Cyprian is moving with studied deference.

J. Chapman in JTS 4 (1902) 108 f. identifies this letter concerning Aurelius *bis confessus et bis . . . gloriosus* with Cyprian's exhortatory composition which is described in Pontius, *Vit. Cyp.* 7.11: *quis denique tot confessores frontium notatarum secunda inscriptione signatos et ad exemplum martyrii superstites reservatos. . . .* The two *inscriptiones,* however, should more naturally refer to baptism as well as to "confession" rather than to the double confession of this letter. For further discussion, see H. von Soden in TU 25.3 (1904) 52 ff.

This letter is also discussed (and a text produced) by D. Balboni in *Miscellanea liturgica in onore di sua eminenza il Cardinale Giacomo Lercaro* (vol. 1, Vatican City 1966) 441 ff.

1. *presbyteris et diaconibus item plebi universae s.* Cyprian has not, hitherto, included the *plebs universa* in his epistolary addresses, save in *Ep.* 17 which, for special reasons, is directed to the laity alone. It is clear from the opening remarks of this letter that the *plebs* formed part of the electorate which appointed holders of clerical office; they appear, therefore, here as well as among the addressees of *Epp.* 39 and 40. On the whole, the function of the *plebs* in such elections appears to have been rather acclamatory or confirmatory—we are not involved in what could be described as "popular elections." Elections are held, literally, *plebe praesente,* with the laity standing by as the

(generally passive) witnesses of the spirit-bearing church. For such evidence in Cyprian on episcopal appointments, see, e.g., *Epp.* 55.8.4: *de plebis quae tunc adfuit suffragio,* of Cornelius in Rome; 59.5.2: *post populi suffragium;* 68.2.1: *plebis suffragio;* 67.3 ff.: *ipsa* [sc. *plebs*] *maxime habeat potestatem . . . eligendi dignos sacerdotes; sacerdos plebe praesente sub omnium oculis deligatur* etc. This role of the *plebs* can be traced as far back as Clement of Rome, *Ep. ad Corinth.* 44.3, and is firmly and unequivocally stated by Hippolytus, *Trad. apost.* 2. Compare also Origen, *Hom. in Levit.* 6.3: the presence of the people is required at the ordination of a bishop (*praesentia populi*), and the most eminent, learned, and virtuous man among them is to be chosen bishop— *ille eligitur ad sacerdotium et hoc astante populo.*

There are, however, some notable occasions when the laity staged more active intervention in such episcopal appointments, e.g., Eusebius, *H.E.* 6.11.2 (Alexander of Jerusalem) and 6.29.3 (Fabian of Rome); Pontius, *Vit. Cyp.* 5 (Cyprian himself); and for an unsuccessful bid by "all the clergy as well as many laity" to prevent the ordination of Novatian to the presbyterate, see Cornelius *ap.* Eusebius, *H.E.* 6.43.17.

For further discussion and examples, consult J. Straub in *Mullus. Festschrift Theodor Klauser* (Münster 1964) 336 ff.=*idem, Regeneratio Imperii* (Darmstadt 1972) 369 ff.; A. Vilela *La condition collégiale des prêtres au troisième siècle* (Paris 1971) 306 ff.; P. Granfield in *Theological Studies* 37 (1976) 41 ff.

The *plebs* did not figure in *Ep.* 29: there the candidates were already on clerical probation, having been approved *communi consilio omnium nostrum.* Does Cyprian take care now to include his *plebs* (no previous consultation having, in this case, occurred), assured that they would approve of a *martyr lector* and thus would offset any unrest that might come from his clergy?

2. *in ordinationibus clericis.* On the word *ordinatio,* see n. 18 to *Ep.* 1 and the discussion by P. van Beneden in *Aux origines d'une terminologie sacramentelle. Ordo, Ordinare, Ordinatio dans la littérature chrétienne avant 313* (Louvain 1974) 123 f., on this letter.

3. *mores ac merita singulorum communi consilio ponderare. Ep.* 29.1.2 reveals this process of sifting potential candidates, before

the Decian persecution began; and even before the persecution is fully over we see that Cyprian has his "ecclesiastical commission" register the *aetates, condiciones,* and *merita* of men who might make suitable clerics. The ranks of his clergy have been depleted both by desertion from his following and by defection from the faith.

4. *praecedunt divina suffragia.* That is to say, the special graces and signal marks of honour in being blessed with confession—and not one confession at that, but two (§1.2). Behind this statement lies the traditionally close connexion between confessor and clerical office. There are many earlier examples of confessors being taken into the ranks of the clergy, e.g., Hegesippus *ap.* Eusebius, *H.E.* 3.20.6 (Domitianic confessors); Tertullian, *Adv. Valent.* 4.1 (Valentinus passed over in episcopal preferment in favour of a confessor—*alium ex martyrii praerogativa loci potitum;* cf. Hippolytus, *Philos.* 9.11 f. with similar preferment for Callistus); Eusebius, *H.E.* 6.8.7 and 6.11.4 (confessors who become bishops of Antioch and Jerusalem); is the youthful confessor Dioscorus in Dionysius of Alexandria *ap.* Eusebius, *H.E.* 6.41.19 f. the Alexandrian presbyter of the same name eight years later, Dionysius of Alexandria *ap.* Eusebius, *H.E.* 7.11.24? And it is notorious that in the canons of Hippolytus there are recorded ecclesiastical privileges traditionally recognized for confessors—confession without torture merits presbyterate, with ordination by the bishop; confession with torture merits presbyterate, without such ordination—*immo, confessio est ordinatio eius (can.* 43 ff.). See H. Achelis in TU 6.4 (1891) 67 f., 164 f., 221 ff., 294 f.; J. E. Stam, *Episcopacy in the Apostolic Tradition of Hippolytus* (Basel 1969) 50 ff.; W. H. Frere in H. B. Swete (ed.), *Essays on the Early History of the Church and the Ministry* (London 1918) 289 ff.; E. L. Hummel in SCA 9 (1946) 147 ff.

Cyprian's action here is, therefore, within an established tradition, but he is nevertheless anxious to avoid giving offence, should he appear to be acting autocratically or unilaterally. He takes the trouble to note below (§2.2) that he has had the full support of episcopal colleagues in making this appointment, as well as to pen a *testimonium* of Aurelius' exceptional *merita* (§1.2) and *mores* (§1.3); and Aurelius' period of probation has been carried out by God Himself—by his confession he is *a Domino iam probatus* (§1.2). Though this mollifies it does not quite disguise the fact the Cyprian *can* appoint to clerical office independently of his clergy.

5. *Aurelius frater noster inlustris adulescens.* A youthful confessor named Aurelius occurs in *Ep.* 27.1.2 (where see nn. 10 and 11); he has endured tortures as has the Aurelius of this letter (§1.2 *ad fin.*). We are presumably, therefore, dealing with the same person. In *Ep.* 27.1.2 we see Lucianus issuing certificates of forgiveness in the name of the confessor Aurelius; Cyprian has now managed successfully to prise that confessor away from any adherence to the *secta* of Lucianus—just as he succeeds with the confessor Celerinus, an old friend of Lucianus'. There is no hint, however, that Numidicus may have been inclined to that party also.

6. *minor in aetatis suae indole.* The phrase is repeated in *Ep.* 39.5.2: *minor . . . aetatis indole,* meaning, I take it, "junior by the natural endowment of years."

7. *quando vicit in cursu.* This has been taken by some as literal, that his trial took place (as many public trials did) in the stadium (so J. A. F. Gregg, *The Decian Persecution* [Edinburgh-London 1897] 259). Not only is it dubious Latin to interpret *cursus* in this sense (and, besides, this first trial is said below to have taken place *sub oculis . . . paucorum*), but a metaphorical meaning, based on the Pauline analogy of the foot-race (e.g., 1 Cor. 9.24 ff., 2 Tim. 4.7 f.), is much more likely. It is so used metaphorically in the Cyprianic fragment; see M. Bévenot in *Bulletin of the John Rylands Library* 28 (1944) 78 = ML Suppl. 1, 41 f.): *in cursu et stadio sanctitatis.*

8. *factus extorris.* See *Ep.* 10.1 and n. 5 thereto. Are we to date this event, Aurelius' first trial, on the evidence of *Ep.* 10, to before mid-April of 250 A.D.? See next n. for discussion of the circumstances.

9. *post magistratus et proconsulem vinceret, post exilium tormenta superaret.* Aurelius has faced two hearings. The first was before

magistrates (plural); it was observed by few only and ended in exile. The second was before the proconsul; it took place in the forum, and it was accompanied by tortures.

At first sight this might appear unexceptional. Aurelius appeared before the local magistrates, having refused to sacrifice. He was then referred to the proconsul for major trial, the matter being capital and thus *ultra vires* for the local magistrates. But this scenario unfortunately leaves the intervening period of exile unaccounted for. Strictly speaking, local magistrates had no powers to impose so grave a penalty, neither did even the proconsul's legates. See *Dig.* 1.16.6 and 1.16.11 against C. Saumagne, in *Byzantion* 32 (1962) 4; cf. *idem, Saint Cyprien. Évêque de Carthage. "Pape" d'Afrique (248–258)* (Paris 1975) 43.

We have evidence in contemporary trials of Christians that local magistrates, in their enthusiasm, did attempt to usurp legal powers not their own (see, for example, *Act. Pionii* 15.2; cf. Pliny, *Ep.* 10.114.4, for an incidental example of local magis-
* trates exceeding their rightful powers). Did this occur in Aurelius' case and the proconsul subsequently detect the irregularity, correctly insisting on a personal hearing, with the usual tortures to induce apostasy? (C. Saumagne, *op. cit.* in preceding paragraph, 43, strangely concludes: "Aurelius n'a donc pas été torturé pour avoir refusé d'apostasier.")

An alternative hypothesis available is that local magistrates did possess some summary powers to expel trouble-makers from
* their towns. Was Aurelius merely driven out of town (*extorris*), not formally "exiled," by virtue of such powers? But (we might continue to speculate) proselytizing persistence by the ardent Aurelius caused him subsequently to be brought to trial, appearing this time before the higher magistrate, the proconsul, in the forum at Carthage.

A third possibility that has been canvassed, namely, that all exiles were formally recalled for retrial in an effort to induce apostasy, is discussed in my article in *Historia* 22 (1973) 650 ff.

Note that Aurelius has now ended up released, out of compassion for his youthful years, perhaps. Compare Optatus (*Ep.* 29), Celerinus (*Ep.* 21), Saturninus (*Ep.* 21), and see further discussion in my article in *Antichthon* 3 (1969) 67 f. He does not appear to have languished long in prison—or at least Cyprian fails to dwell on such sufferings, which is unlikely given his present purpose to highlight Aurelius' *merita*.

C. Saumagne in *Byzantion* 32 (1962) 3, considers these experiences of Aurelius to be "le cas typique" for this persecution. This is difficult to substantiate (cf. my article in *Historia* 22 [1973] 661 f.), and indeed Cyprian's purpose here seems to be to establish, in so far as he can, the special features which distinguish Aurelius' career as a confessor and, therefore, his *special* spiritual credentials.

10. *ad ecclesiasticam disciplinam ceteris esset exemplo*. See n. 8 to *Ep.* 4 on Cyprian's use of the phrase *ecclesiastica disciplina*.

11. Observe the laboured emphasis on the paragraph: *verecundia morum, pudoris admiratione laudabilis, humilitate summissus, ad ecclesiasticam disciplinam . . . exemplo*. The foremost qualities sought for the ideal cleric are not those of, say, charity or chastity, but they are those of humble reserve and disciplined obedience. The message for the presbyters and deacons of Carthage who will read this is made manifestly clear.

12. *clericae ordinationis ulteriores gradus et incrementa maiora*. In *Ep.* 39.5.2 we learn that Aurelius and Celerinus are "designated" for the honour of presbyter, and, exceptionally, already receive a monthly stipend commensurate with the rank of presbyter, although they are still too young actually to hold that office. Can *incrementa* here possibly refer to the emolument that goes with higher office? For this specialized use of *incrementum*, see TLL 7.1 *s.v. incrementum*, 1044, and cf. *De bono pat.* 13: *de divini faenoris incremento caelestes sibi thesauros recondentes*. On clerical salaries see n. 21 to *Ep.* 1, and cf. *Ep.* 34.4.2 (with n. 20 *ad loc.*).

13. *interim placuit ut ab officio lectionis incipiat*. On the clerical office of *lector* see n. 6 to *Ep.* 23. The word *interim* implies further plans for Aurelius, revealed by *Ep.* 39.5.2 (see previous n.). Cyprian employs, perhaps designedly, the impersonal and formal *placuit*, leaving it until later to be clarified, in §2.2, by the phrase *a me et a collegis qui praesentes aderant ordinatum* (on which see n. 16 below).

14. *evangelium Christi legere unde martyres fiunt*. On this theme

of the Gospel and the martyr see, for example, *Ep.* 27.3.3, *Ep.* 37.4.2 (and n. 18 for reference to other passages). There is an interesting iconographic illustration of the idea in the mosaic of Lawrence in the Galla Placidia mausoleum: on the one side figure the Books of the Gospels in a cupboard, on the other side Lawrence bearing cross and holding book, in between appear the fire and grill of his martyrdom: the Gospels and the Martyr are iconographically linked and balanced. See A. Grabar, *Martyrium—recherches sur le culte des reliques et l'art chrétien antique* (3 vols., Paris 1943–1946) Album Plate XXXVII and 2.35 f. For the effects of the needs of lectors on the larger than usual book-hands in some early Christian texts (fair sized letters being easier to read aloud from), which leads to the development of the later "biblical majuscule," see E. G. Turner, *The Typology of the Early Codex* (University of Pennsylvania 1977) 84 ff.

15. *ad pulpitum post catastam venire.* The *pulpitum* was a raised dais which made the (often youthful) lector visible to the congregation. Besides the *altare,* it is the only church furniture mentioned by Cyprian. See V. Saxer, *Vie liturgique et quotidienne à Carthage vers le milieu du troisième siècle* (Vatican City 1969) 68; Watson 270. The *catasta* was a podium upon which defendants might be placed to be visible by the *corona* during their trial; prisoners might also be tied to such a platform for undergoing punishment *ad bestias* or other *poenae.* Either sense could be intended here, though the former is the more likely—from it his voice was heard "to the astonishment of the thronging bystanders." See DACL 2 (1925) *s.v. catasta,* 2527 ff.; DACL 7 (1927) *s.v.* Iubé 2767 ff.; Th. Mommsen, *Römisches Strafrecht* (Leipzig 1889, repr. 1955) 359 ff.

16. *hunc . . . a me et a collegis qui praesentes aderant ordinatum.* Cyprian has acted with some circumspection, and he expresses himself with some care. He has not appointed unilaterally or irresponsibly, but in conjunction with fellow bishops. And, in concert, these bishops have acted as solemnly as if they were appointing to presbyteral or episcopal office: for nowhere else does Cyprian use the verb *ordino* for appointing to the *lower* clerical orders (but *facere, constituo, promoveo, clero adiungo,* etc.); See P. van Beneden, *Aux origines d'une terminologie sacramentelle.*

Ordo, ordinare, ordinatio *dans la littérature chrétienne avant 313* (Louvain 1974) 78 f. on this passage and 66 ff. for Cyprian's use elsewhere of *ordino* with *episcopus, sacerdos* and *praepositus* only.

17. *dominico legit interim nobis.* Interpreting this clause is a little hazardous. *Dominico,* as I have translated it, is an abbreviation for *dominico die;* it could, however, refer to the "Lord's sacrifice." Cf. *Ep.* 63.16.3: *numquid . . . dominicum post cenam celebrare debemus; De op. et eleem.* 15: *dominicum celebrare, in dominicum sine sacrificio venis.* Further discussion is in F. J. Dölger in AC 6 (1950) 110 ff., esp. 114 f.—Is *legit* present (e.g., Fahey 34 translates: "he reads for me on Sundays . . .") or past (as I have interpreted it, to fit in better with the run of the sentence)?— *Interim* is vague, but I take it to signify, most naturally in the context, "before we can return," "before you can give your approval," or the like.

18. *auspicatus est pacem dum dedicat lectionem.* We are apparently to understand that Aurelius is presaging a return to essentially peace-time conditions by starting up his liturgical functions; he is exchanging his war-time role of *confessor* for that of *lector.* On the phrase *dedicat lectionem,* see RAC 3 (1957) *s.v. dedicatio,* 646, with many parallels. See J. H. Strawley, *The Early History of the Liturgy* (Cambridge 1913) 132, unnecessarily sees in it evidence for "a blessing or salutation preceding the lesson."

19. *reddat . . . martyrem cum sacerdote lectorem.* Cyprian pointedly reserves the honorific title of *martyr* (not now *confessor* as applied to Aurelius elsewhere in the letter) to clinch his argument; customary formalities are rendered superfluous in such a case and Cyprian's own position is enhanced by such close association with one so honoured. On this use of *martyr* (of the living), see n. 1 to *Ep.* 10. This particular example is discussed by E. L. Hummel in SCA 9 (1946) 8 f.

LETTER 39

Contents: Cyprian, with episcopal colleagues, has appointed the confessor Celerinus to the clergy, the latter's hesitation to consent being overcome by a vision. His confession before that was notable for the courageous stand he made at the outbreak of the persecution, in the face of the adversary himself, and he has scars to bear witness to his sufferings. In all this he is living up to the traditions of the honoured and martyred dead in his own family. He should, therefore, be heard proclaiming the Gospel of the Lord where all may see his glory. He is, accordingly, to join Aurelius as a reader, being the equal to the latter in virtues as well as valour. The higher office of presbyter is destined for them both when they advance in years.

Date and circumstances: All we can tell is that this letter must be subsequent to *Ep.* 37 (in *Ep.* 37.1.1 Celerinus arrives at Cyprian's hideaway but he is not yet a reader) which is to be dated to early 251. It must also be subsequent to *Ep.* 38 (Celerinus is to join Aurelius, already a lector, *Ep.* 39.4.3). Cyprian must be writing before the end of March 251 (Easter falling on March 23, by which date Cyprian was hoping to return to Carthage, *Ep.* 43.1.2). As likely as not, we are in the month of February 251. Cf. Nelke 49 f.

The circumstances are similar to those of *Ep.* 38. In informing his congregation of the appointment of Celerinus to the lectorate, Cyprian feels equally constrained to justify his action. He does not stress the adverse circumstances which prohibit the established procedures of consultation and scrutiny nor does he plead the present shortage of clerics (contrast *Ep.* 29). His arguments are more positive: Celerinus has unique claims to clerical dignity. They include (1) his *visio* (the church herself urging him to accept office, §1.2), (2) his illustrious confession, singled out from others by its occurrence at the opening trial of the persecution, held before the persecutor himself and including 19 days of harsh sufferings (with scars to prove it), §§2.1ff., (3) a remarkable spiritual pedigree (grandmother and two uncles all martyrs) which reveals God's special favours to this family, §§3.1ff, (4) outstanding virtues—humility and meekness as well as courage and fortitude, §4.3. Cyprian is writing in the *elogia* tradition, of which our most notable sample is Augustus' *Res Gestae*. In this genre the most compelling claim to distinction and glory is to assert uniqueness or to establish priority in any achievement. See, briefly, P. A. Brunt and J. M. Moore, *Res gestae divi Augusti* (Oxford 1967) 2 ff. Cyprian's central arguments are couched in this form; the care he has taken so to formulate them discloses his anxiety to win the approval of his flock for his action. At the same time another potential supporter of Lucianus and his rebels has now been won over to Cyprian's side.

In the concluding paragraph we are afforded a fascinating glimpse of Roman attitudes translated into ecclesiastical organization—Celerinus and Aurelius are too young for higher office but they are to get some of the prerogatives of that higher office, notably its salary. They will get the actual prestige rank of *presbyter* when they have reached the appropriate age. For fuller discussion, see my article, "The Epistles of Cyprian," in *Auckland Classical Essays Presented to E. M. Blaiklock* (Auckland 1970) 208 f.

1. For this form of address cf. n. 1 to *Ep.* 38.

2. *commeatum dando.* Although Cyprian has in mind here one particular confessor, Celerinus, it must have happened often enough by now that confessors have regained their freedom so that he can make this general assertion; indeed, we have no firm knowledge that in Carthage any confessors still remain at this date in prison.

3. *clerum . . . ministeriis ecclesiasticis adornarent.* For the close link that had become traditional between confession and clerical office, see n. 4 to *Ep.* 38.

4. *ego et collegae mei qui praesentes aderant.* For Cyprian's care in noting that he has not acted on his own but with the support and concurrence of fellow bishops, cf. *Ep.* 38.2.2 and n. 16 thereto.

5. On Celerinus' previous history, see n. 1 to *Ep.* 21.

6. *compulsus est ne negaret. nobis suadentibus cui plus licuit et coegit.* . . . This is Hartel's punctuation (which has the support of some mss); other mss have the stop after *suadentibus,* thus providing the attractive sense ". . . was thus compelled not to refuse our efforts at persuasion." A. d'Alès in *Revue d'ascétique et de mystique* 2 (1921) 258, misinterprets the nature of Celerinus' *visio:* "au cours de la persécution, tel chrétien, qui déjà chancelait, reçoit la nuit, dans une vision, un avertissement de l'Église, qui le transforme et en fait un confesseur de la foi . . ." The phraseology is quite against such an interpretation, e.g., *cum consentire dubitaret* (= when he hesitated to *consent,* that is, to join our clergy), but the abrupt and elliptical way in which Cyprian introduces this topic of Celerinus' hesitation is understandably responsible for the misinterpretation.

Note the pride of place given to the vision as the persuasive influence. For that compare *Ep.* 16.4.1f. (with nn. 27ff.) and *Ep.* 11.3.1, 5.1 (with nn. 21 and 32). Celerinus is therefore being given clerical rank not by the wish of ecclesiastical *praepositi* but rather by the will of God and of His Church. He has been doubly singled out by divine favour (the grace of confession as well as his *visio*), and he has also manifested, in this episode of his hesitation, that modesty combined with holy obedience which Cyprian wishes to underline as ideal virtues for those who hold clerical office (cf. §4.3 below and *Ep.* 38.1.3 with n. 11 thereto).

7. *hic inter Christi milites antesignanus.* The precise significance of *antesignanus,* at various periods, in its literal sense, is matter for dispute; but the metaphorical meaning is clear—a front-line skirmisher. See J. D. Denniston (ed.), *M. Tulli Ciceronis in M. Antonium orationes Philippicae prima et secunda* (Oxford 1926; repr. 1970) 139 f.; PWK 1 (1894) 2355 f. On this evidence Celerinus must take his place among those Roman confessors who made their stand before even the persecution became effective in Carthage (cf. *Ep.* 28.1.1 f.: *vos enim primores et duces ad nostri temporis proelium facti,* etc.) and indeed as the very first confessor among them (*hic ad temporis nostri proelium primus*).

8. *hic inter persecutionis initia ferventia cum ipso infestationis*

principe et auctore congressus. In *Ep.* 22.1.1 Lucianus recalls Celerinus' triumphant victory (*vicisti*), achieved by inspired and terrifying words of defiance, over *ipsam anguem maiorem, metatorem antichristi.* Cyprian appears to be alluding here to that same episode in Celerinus' trial. Did that trial in fact include an outspoken *apologia* for the Christian faith, delivered by Celerinus (cf. §4.1 below), as we have represented in many of the *Acta?* See n. 5 to *Ep.* 22 where it is argued that here *ipso infestationis principe et auctore,* on the accumulated evidence, refers in all likelihood rather to the Emperor Decius than to the arch-enemy Satan. Celerinus was thus, most unusually, tried before the Emperor himself, to emphasize this unusual feature being germane to Cyprian's present purpose (whereas in fact all confessors everywhere could be said to have wrestled with Satan at their trials: see n. 35 to *Ep.* 21). Celerinus' trial occurred at the least before Easter of 250 A.D. (see n. 1 to *Ep.* 21). For further discussion see my article in *Antichthon* 3 (1969) 63 ff.; F. Millar, *The Emperor in the Roman World (31 B.C.–A.D. 337)* (London 1977) 568; E. L. Hummel in SCA 9 (1946) 86 f.

9. *non brevi conpendio vulnerum victor.* The meaning seems a little elusive. Others interpret variously, "he was not victorious over wounds that were hastily inflicted", or, "he was not victorious with a small number of wounds", and even (misleadingly), "not victorious through any absence of wounds" (so Hummel, *op. cit.* in preceding note, 87).

10. *per decem novem dies ... in nervo ac ferro fuit.* Celerinus' "scars" and "wounds" are presumably traceable to this period of his confinement and to this precise treatment. These 19 days in fact constitute his "protracted period of suffering." With no further details vouchsafed (would Cyprian have omitted them, Celerinus being present to disclose full particulars?), we are forced to conclude that Celerinus' release promptly followed this harsh form of detention which, it was discovered, had been inflicted on him to no avail.

11. *animam fide et virtute viventem.* On the motif of these twin virtues of *fides et virtus,* see n. 3 to *Ep.* 10 and n. 2 to *Ep.* 37; the combination is used again in §3.2 below.

12. *galeatus serpens et obtritus et victus est.* This is Hartel's

text—which I do not translate—whereas the overwhelming consensus of the mss is to read *calcatus* (=crushed) for *galeatus*
(= helmeted, or, by extension, crested). *Calcatus* has the virtues
of rendering adequate sense, providing a rhetorical triplet with
obtritus and *victus,* and making a passing biblical allusion, which
enjoyed wide currency in similar contexts. For the source of the
allusion consult Gen. 3.15 and cf. Luke 10.19 (where the Vulgate
reads, *ecce dedi vobis potestatem calcandi supra serpentes et scorpiones
et supra omnem virtutem inimici*); and for parallels (among many),
compare *Act. Perp.* 4.7 *calcavi illi caput; Act. Fruct.* 7.2: *diaboli
caput calcaverunt; Ep.* 58.9.1: *cum serpens calcari a nobis et obteri
coeperit.* I have accordingly translated *calcatus.* For further discussion of the reading see Watson 213 n. 1; J. Sajdak in *Eos* 20
(1914–15), 141; F. J. Dölger in AC 3 (1932) 180 f.; E. L. Hummel
in SCA 9 (1946) 87 n. 90.

13. *in servo Dei victoriam gloria vulnerum fecit, gloriam cicatricum memoria custodit.* The latter clause has occasioned some
difficulty, for the parallelism with the former clause can work
either way—*cicatricum* may be construed with *gloriam* (to parallel *gloria vulnerum*) or it may be construed with *memoria* (again
to parallel *gloria vulnerum*—subject noun with a dependent genitive). I have translated according to the latter construing, the
better to fit into the run of sense (*memoria* = memorial, reminder, marks left behind); the former construing yields, less satisfactorily, something like "and men's memories preserve the glory
of his scars" (*memoria* = history, living memory).

The allusion to *aliquis Thomae similis* is of course based on
John 20.27 ff. See Fahey 370 f.

14. *avia eius Celerina iam pridem martyrio coronata est.* There
was in Carthage a *basilica Celerinae.* Augustine delivered ser-
mons there (*serm.* 48; *Enarratio in Ps.* 99), and the *Passio septem
monachorum* records the martyrs' burial *in monasterio Biguae
contiguo basilicae quae dicitur Celerinae* (CSEL 7.114). Victor Vi-
tensis, *Hist.* 1.9, speaks of *basilicam maiorem* (of Perpetua and
Felicity) . . . , *Celerinae vel Scillitanorum et alias quas non destrux-
erunt* (CSEL 7.5): that could possibly mean that the *basilica
Celerinae* housed the remains of the Scillitan martyrs. See J.
Vaultrin, *Les basiliques chrétiennes de Carthage; étude d'archéologie*

et d'histoire (Algiers 1933) 163 f. Cf. P. Allard, *Histoire des persécutions pendant la première moitié du IIIème siècle* (Paris 1894) 98 f., n. 5, mistakenly reads this evidence to conclude that "on voyait encore, au cinquième siècle, le tombeau de Celerina dans une des basiliques de Carthage." But we cannot be sure that the *basilica Celerinae* was in fact dedicated to our *Celerina*, or was merely donated by some unidentified *Celerina*. The name is not recorded in the sixth-century African Calendar. (The *Mart. Hieron.* does register a Laurentius and Celerina for September 24, and the same company of martyrs, in variant form, as African martyrs for September 28; another Celerina for February 3.)

15. *patruus eius et avunculus Laurentinus et Egnatius in castris et ipsi quondam saecularibus militantes.* The expression *et ipsi* strongly suggests that Celerinus' profession, in Rome, had been that of a soldier also. If so that might account for the role which the *imperator* Decius played in Celerinus' trial (see n. 8 above); he was acting in his specific capacity as commander-in-chief. Indeed the plethora of military metaphors in this letter becomes doubly piquant if Celerinus had been serving in fact as a secular soldier.

We do not know the occasion of the martyrdom of Laurentinus and Egnatius: the *quondam* suggests a date that is reasonably remote. Barrack life and the ceremonies of Roman military parades notoriously facilitated the detection of Christian sympathies (witness *inter alia* Lactantius, *De mort. persecut.* 10.2 ff.; Tertullian, *De corona, passim;* in fact, E. W. Watson in *Essays in History Presented to R. L. Poole* (Oxford 1927) 131, favours the identification of Laurentinus and Egnatius with the hero of that tractate of Tertullian's: that is unpersuasive speculation). Again, Laurentinus and Egnatius go unregistered in the Carthaginian Calendar.

We have here casual evidence for Christians willing to adopt the profession of soldiers despite the strictures of Hippolytus, canon 13.71 ff.; cf. Tertullian, *De corona* 11; Origen, *C. Celsum* 8.73. The scattered evidence for Christian soldiers in the early church has been much discussed: see A. von Harnack, *Militia Christi: Die christliche Religion und der Soldatenstand in den ersten drei*

Jahrhunderten (Tübingen 1905; repr. 1963) 66 ff.; DACL 11 (1933) *s.v. militarisme*, 1108 ff.; C. J. Cadoux, *The Early Christian Attitude to War* (London 1919) esp. 228 ff.; M. Durry, *Les cohortes prétoriennes* (Paris 1938) 348 ff.; R. H. Bainton in HTR 39 (1946) 189 ff.; H. F. Davis in *Blackfriars* 30 (1949) 477 ff.; E. A. Ryan in *Theol. Studies* 13 (1952) 1 ff.; H. von Campenhausen, *Tradition and Life in the Church* (London 1968) 160 ff.; J. Fontaine in *Concilium* 7 (1965) 107 ff.; J. Helgeland in *Church History* 43 (1974) 154 ff.; R. Klein, *Tertullian und das römische Reich* (Heidelberg 1968) 102 ff.; W. Rordorf in VC 23 (1969) 105 ff.; R. F. Evans in *Stud. Patr.* 14 (1976) 23 ff. (the last three being more specifically on the evidence in Tertullian for Christians in military service); J.-M. Hornus in *Archiv für Papryrusforschung* 22–23 (1973–74) 223 ff. Cyprian's spiritual militancy, his lavish and elaborate employment of military imagery and metaphor in the glorification of martyrdom, is not suggestive of a notably pacifist mentality. See the study of J. Capmany-Casamitjana, *"Miles Christi" en la espiritualidad de san Cipriano* (Barcelona 1956).

16. *sacrificia pro eis semper . . . offerimus quotiens . . . dies anniversaria commemoratione celebramus.* The language (*semper, quotiens*), like the previous touches (*iam pridem, quondam*), suggests an ancestral pedigree; that could possibly be misleading. On the annual ceremonies in honour of the martyred dead, see *Ep.* 12.2.1. The language here, as there, implies some form of ecclesiastical calendar. It is salutary to be reminded that the *cultus* of martyrs, once established, could still fall into desuetude in later centuries. See H. Delehaye, *Les origines du culte des martyres* (2nd ed., Brussels 1933) 374.

17. *testimonio et miraculo eius ipsius qui se persecutus fuerat inlustrem.* See n. 8 above for explication. With some irony Cyprian employs expressions that would be appropriately used in the regular procedures for selecting clerics (and cf. *Ep.* 38.1.1 f.: *testimonia humana . . . inlustris adulescens*).

18. *super pulpitum id est super tribunal ecclesiae.* Cf. *Ep.* 38.2.1 and see n. 15 there on the ecclesiastical *pulpitum*.

19. *in his cottidie quae Dominus locutus est audiatur.* Cyprian is praying for peace-time conditions (cf. *Ep.* 38.2.2 and n. 18). Note the adverb *cottidie;* for daily (eucharistic) services at this time, see

Ep. 57.3.2: *sacerdotes qui sacrificia Dei cottidie celebramus; Ep.* 58.1.2: *se cottidie calicem sanguinis Christi bibere; De dom. orat.* 18: *eucharistiam eius cottidie . . . accipimus.* They are the likely occasion for Celerinus' anticipated readings; see further V. Saxer, *Vie liturgique et quotidienne à Carthage vers le milieu du troisième siècle* (Vatican City 1969) 218 f.

20. *viderit an sit ulterior gradus ad quem profici in ecclesia possit.* This could be less generalizing than I have translated it and more specific—"it's up to him to see if he deserves promotion to some higher order in the church".

21. For Aurelius, see *Ep.* 38.

22. Compare *Ep.* 38.1.3 (with n. 11) for the heavy stress on the ideal martyr who is, whilst courageous, also humble, submissive, lowly, obedient, modest, meek, and peaceable. Cyprian leaves his congregation in no doubt about his message.

23. *quorum secta et conversatio.* For the word *secta*, see n. 21 to *Ep.* 27; for *conversatio*, see n. 48 to *Ep.* 11.

24. On this allusion to Matt. 5.15, see Fahey 272 f.

25. *et sportulis idem cum presbyteris honorentur et divisiones mensurnas aequatis quantitatibus partiantur.* It is unclear whether the two *et* clauses repeat the same notion for the purposes of emphasis, or whether there is in fact a distinction to be drawn between the *sportulae* and the monthly apportionment (*divisiones mensurnas*) which these two confessors exceptionally are to receive along with the presbyters. If there is a difference, *sportulae* are likely enough to refer to gifts in kind contributed by the faithful, whereas *divisiones* would be the clerical stipend paid out monthly, clearly at different levels for the various grades of office. The topic of clerical stipends was raised by *Ep.* 1.1.2, where see n. 21 thereto. Tertullian, *De ieiun.* 17, may refer to graded *sportulae* (*duplex apud te praesidentibus honor binis partibus deputatur*), and note the testimony of *Didasc. Apost.* 9 in R. H. Connolly, *Didascalia Apostolorum* (Oxford 1929) 90 f.: "But let the portion of the pastor be separated and set apart for him according to rule at the suppers or the bounties (*in agapis et erogationibus*). . . . But how much (soever) is given to one of the widows, let the double be given to each of the deacons . . . (but) twice twofold to the leader (*qui praeest*) for the glory of the Almighty. But if anyone wish to

honour the presbyters also, let him give them a double (portion), as to the deacons. . . . But if there be also a lector, let him too receive with the presbyters. To every order, therefore, let everyone of the laity pay the honour which is befitting him, with gifts and presents. . . ."

26. *sessuri nobiscum provectis et corroboratis annis suis.* E. L. Hummel in SCA 9 (1946) 149 f. comments on this passage: "He also informs the community that he will permit them to be elevated to the episcopate when they have reached the proper age." That is a misunderstanding. Cyprian is foreshadowing eventual progression to the *presbyterate*, for the presbyters characteristically *sat* with their bishop enthroned in their midst, whilst minor orders and laity stood. The physical remains of later African churches regularly reveal a presbytery consisting of benches—*subsellia*—in the apse with a throne in the centre (see, for example, J. B. Ward Perkins and R. G. Goodchild in *Archaeologia* 95 [1953] 63 f. on the Tripolitanian evidence). For parallel expressions describing presbyters seated with their bishop see *Ep.* 40.1.1: *Numidicus presbyter . . . nobiscum sedeat in clero; Ep.* 40.1.3: *tam mites et humiles faciat in consessus nostri honore florere* (in connexion with Numidicus *presbyter*); *Ep.* 45.2.5: *conpresbyteri tecum considentis* (in connexion with Novatian *presbyter*). For fuller discussion, see DACL 1 (1907) *s.v.* Afrique (archéologie de l') 672 f.; W. Telfer, *The Office of a Bishop* (London 1962) 201; Watson 263; A. Vilela, *La condition collégiale des prêtres au troisième siècle* (Paris 1971) 274 ff.; F. J. Dölger in AC 2 (1930) 161 ff.; and the dissertation of H. Selhorst, *Die Platzordnung im Gläubigenraum der altchristlichen Kirche* (Münster 1931).

Cyprian does not mention intermediate grades for Celerinus and Aurelius; at this date (as later) they might be by-passed, as his own clerical career demonstrates. See Pontius, *Vit. Cyp.* 3: *presbyterium vel sacerdotium statim accepit. quis enim non omnes honoris gradus crederet tali mente credenti?*

LETTER 40

Contents: Cyprian reports that, as the Lord has indicated, he has enrolled Numidicus in the Carthaginian presbyterate. He is a candidate signally honoured by his confession, his preservation from a martyr's death allowing him to bring glory and strength to the depleted ranks of the clergy of Carthage. He is destined for a loftier dignity in the church after the return of peace.

Date and circumstances: The letter cannot be placed with precision, but it coheres with *Epp.* 38 and 39 (and belongs, therefore, to early 251). Cyprian is continuing his attempts to restore the decimated forces of the Carthaginian *clerus.* The tone makes such a placing altogether probable. Cyprian's carefully chosen final words in this letter are not concerned with the confessor's courage, valour, bravery, and fortitude; they are concerned with meekness and humility, virtues desirably to be found in clerics which received similar prominence in the testimonials for Aurelius (*Ep.* 38.1.3) and for Celerinus (*Ep.* 39.4.3). We are in the same period of turbulence and revolt which Cyprian is experiencing in his relations with his Carthaginian clergy. We cannot be, however, at a date too late in Cyprian's exile. Numidicus is involved, apparently as a *Carthaginian* presbyter, in the activities of *Epp.* 41–43. Cf. Nelke 50.

What is noticeable is the different tactic which Cyprian employs from that used in those two parallel letters. There is not the same elaborate apology for having to act unilaterally; he does not invoke the consensus of episcopal colleagues in his support. He is more curt and less circumspect in declaring what he proposes should be done. The explanation may well be that this letter comes last in the series and that, after the acceptance of the two previous appointments, Cyprian feels less obliged to wrap up his message. Even so, Cyprian still takes care to hedge around the description of Numidicus' confessional stand with indications both at the beginning (*admonitos nos et instructos . . . dignatione divina*) and at the end (*quod ostenditur fiat*) that the action being taken is under divine inspiration and sanction.

Indeed, it is the Lord, not Cyprian, who is to add him to the clergy; he is a veritable "gift from God" (*hoc Dei munus*). But the circumstances might also be different from those of *Epp.* 38 and 39, thus helping to explain the variation in tactic. On this question, unfortunately, the letter suffers in a crucial phrase from ambiguity: *Numidicus presbyter adscribatur presbyterorum Carthaginensium numero* (§1.1). Does this mean either that Numidicus (previous clerical grade unstated) is to be enrolled as a presbyter in the ranks of the Carthaginian presbyters (a case of clerical *appointment*) or that Numidicus (already a presbyter) is to be enrolled in the ranks of the Carthaginian presbyters (a case of clerical *translation*)?

If it is a case of *appointment*, we have, curiously, no apology at all for appointing Numidicus direct to the presbyterate, and yet Cyprian's own experience would have taught him what an explosive move that could be; neither do we have, as we might expect, any word of ceremonial ordination for him, merely *nobiscum sedeat in clero* (§1.1).

These notable omissions are certainly explicable if Numidicus is already a presbyter (from another diocese): his appointment to Carthage is temporary only (*interim quod ostenditur fiat*). Indeed, the broad expectation of promotion for him (*et promovebitur quidem . . . ad ampliorem locum religionis suae*) makes easier sense if he is to be advanced to a bishopric elsewhere (in his home diocese?) after peace has been restored. This gift of God, we should conclude, is but a temporary blessing for the church in Carthage; it is not a case of presbyteral ordination by Cyprian alone. Hence the changed tactic of this letter. We are still, however, left with the puzzle that if Numidicus is a temporary refugee in Carthage, if the see in his home town is currently vacant (his own bishop having died or scandalously defected), why does Cyprian not say so?

This question has been much discussed: see, among others, Thaninayagam 54, 72f.; R. Gryson in *Revue d'histoire ecclésiastique* 68 (1973) 366; C. H. Turner *Studies in Early Church History* (Oxford 1912) 117; A. Vilela, op. cit. in n. 26 to *Ep.* 39, 276 ff.; M. Bévenot in JTS 24 (1973) 257 f.; W. Telfer, *The Office of a Bishop* (London 1962) 172; H. Hess, *The Canons of the Council of Sardica,*

A. D. 343. A Landmark in the Early Development of Canon Law
(Oxford 1958) 71 ff.—I do not know by what warrant B. Kötting
in JAC 19 (1976) 18, claims Numidicus to have been a Numidian
presbyter; did he deduce it from nomenclature?
The letter is also a salutary reminder of the fitful nature of
our evidence for this persecution.
We have had—without detail—indications of popular hostility towards Christians (see *Ep.* 6.4 and n. 32 there), but here we
can now see what looks like an actual lynching with the stoning
and burning of the crowd's victims. This has all the air of a mob
pogrom; it is no official execution when a prisoner can be left
abandoned, undespatched. It is easy to underestimate the strain
on the Christian communities when such outbursts of wild and
extreme hostility might erupt at any time against them. It would
not require many similar episodes for tempers to become taut
and downright hysterical as the bleak months of apprehension
stretched on overshadowed by the threat of this unreasoned
savagery. The growing schisms and dissensions in such communities have an understandable human context. We cannot tell,
however, how far we are to imagine that such incidents occurred spasmodically through the African provinces during this
persecution—or indeed throughout the Empire. Alexandria provides, of course, our nearest picture, in the fragments of Dionysius' correspondence as preserved in Eusebius, *H.E.* 6 and 7.

1. On the form of address and its implications, see n. 1 to *Ep.*
38.
2. *admonitos nos et instructos sciatis dignatione divina.* For Cyprian's use of divine monition to guide or justify actions, cf. n. 6 to
Ep. 7, n. 30 to *Ep.* 16. Celerinus' *visio* in *Ep.* 39.1.2 is closely
parallel in this context. It is clear, therefore, that when Cyprian
uses below the expression, *quod ostenditur fiat*, this does *not*
mean, "let what I have indicated be done" (so Fahey 508), but,
rather, "let what is revealed to us be done." Cf. Watson 250. The
plural *nos*, by Cyprianic usage, ought probably to embrace others in Cyprian's flock as well as specifically Cyprian himself; the
divine message applies to the congregation generally. Cf. n. 45
to *Ep.* 4, n. 34 to *Ep.* 16, n. 3 to *Ep.* 20.

3. *virtutis ac fidei honore sublimis*. For this prevalent motif of *virtus ac fides* in Cyprian's description of confessors, cf. n. 3 to *Ep.* 10, n. 2 to *Ep.* 37, n. 11 to *Ep.* 39.

4. *nobiscum sedeat in clero:* For the privilege of presbyters to be seated with their bishop, see n. 26 to *Ep.* 39. If this is a case of translation it is not without parallel, but even when we do find other illustrations there is the same apologetic insistence on divine intervention. See, for an example, Euseb. *H.E.* 6.11.1 ff. Cyprian appears to be taking a step against which later Councils tended to be firm, especially in the West: consult H. Hess, *The Canons of the Council of Sardica, A.D. 343. A Landmark in the Early Development of Canon Law* (Oxford 1958) 71 ff., 88 f., for the evidence (notably the Council of Arles, canon 21, and the Council of Nicaea, canons 15 and 16; Hefele-Leclercq 1.1.294, 597 ff.).

5. If Numidicus was a presbyter already, then he provides an example of a married cleric. On this topic, see n. 6 to *Ep.* 1. We know neither the place nor the precise date of the incident here described. For close parallel note the stoning and burning of Christians at Alexandria in 249 A.D.; see Dionysius of Alexandria *ap.* Eusebius, *H.E.* 6.41. 3 ff. Stoning is frequently attested as a form of group violence in antiquity; cobbles, broken tiles, rocks might lie to hand in the streets as ready weapons. See R. MacMullen, *Roman Social Relations 50 B.C. to A.D. 284* (New Haven-London 1974) 66, 171 n. 30.

By the repetition (*ante se misit . . . ipse praemiserat*) at the two ends of the description of Numidicus' confession it is emphasized that Numidicus was the leader of these martyrdoms. See n. 33 to *Ep.* 6 for the special credit accorded such leadership-role in cases of confession and martyrdom.

6. *. . . desolatam per lapsum quorundam presbyterorum nostrorum copiam gloriosis sacerdotibus adornaret.* For the first time we now learn that some Carthaginian *presbyters* have apostatized; previous information has been more general on clerical lapses. Observe that there is no mention as yet of formal losses by schism; but see *Ep.* 34 (and n. 2) for a case of excommunication.

gloriosis sacerdotibus. This remark needs to be read in conjunction with the following sentence. By itself it would constitute one of the two only examples in Cyprian's writings where *sacerdos* may be used unequivocally in the sense of presbyter (as opposed to bishop). But, in fact, Cyprian is here being designed- ∗ ly honorific and proleptic—he confidently anticipates that the *clerus* of Carthage will enjoy the distinguishing honour of having a bishop elected from amongst its number. For opinions on the passage, see Watson 258; F. E. Brightman in H. B. Swete (ed.), *Essays on the Early History of the Church and the Ministry* (London 1918) 396; A. A. R. Bastiaensen, *Le cérémonial épistolaire des chrétiens latins* (Nijmegen 1964) 30 n. 1; R. Gryson in *Revue d'histoire ecclésiastique* 68 (1973) 386 n. 3; A. Vilela, *La condition collégiale des prêtres au troisième siècle* (Paris 1971) 282 f.; H. H. Janssen, *Kultur und Sprache*... (Nijmegen 1938) 87; B. Renaud in *Recherches de théologie ancienne et médiévale* 38 (1971) 37 n. 1; V. Saxer, *Vie liturgique et quotidienne à Carthage vers le milieu du troisième siècle* (Vatican City 1969) 84 ff.

7. Cyprian can hardly mean that Numidicus will be elected to the see of Carthage (he has the general view of one occupant per see). Does he rather assume that the clergy and *plebs* of Numidicus' home diocese (aided by the advice of neighbouring bishops, of which he will no doubt be one himself, see *Ep.* 67.5.1 and cf. *Ep.* 56.1.1) must choose so honoured a presbyter for their (vacant) *cathedra* when peace is restored? So A. Vilela, *op. cit.* in preceding note, 282 f. There is, in fact, the attractive, but not strongly attested, ms variant, *ad ampliorem locum regionis suae* (for *religionis suae*), which, if genuine, would confirm such an interpretation (promoted "to a more exalted station in his own district"). An alternative, but less likely, explanation is that we have here foreshadowed a case of incardination. Numidicus will be appointed to a special role of honour within the Carthaginian presbyterate itself. So R. Gryson, *art. cit.* in preceding note, 366.

8. *cum gratiarum actione suscipiamus.* Probably an echo of 1 Tim. 4.4: *nihil reiciendum, quod cum gratiarum actione percipitur* (Vulg.).

9. *tam mites et humiles faciat in consessus nostri honore florere.* *Consessus* implies that Cyprian is talking about presbyters (and bishop) rather than clerics generally. Cf. n. 4 above. On the epithets *mites et humiles* and their implications, see introductory note to this letter.

LETTER 41

Contents: Felicissimus has broken the unity of the flock. He has set about thwarting the distribution of charitable alms to the needy, threatening to deny communion to those who receive assistance through Cyprian's appointed agents. He has thus noisily drummed up a large faction but already many of those have sensibly renounced their error. Meantime Felicissimus is to incur himself his own sentence and to be excommunicated; charges of adultery laid against him as well as his financial peculation and sedition will be fully investigated in due course in council. His ally Augendus, if he persists, is to incur the same penalty, and all who act likewise. The congregation and clergy are to be apprised of the contents of this letter along with the names of Felicissimus' followers.

Date and circumstances: An ecclesiastical commission has been appointed by Cyprian (still in hiding): it includes the presbyter Numidicus and it was therefore established after *Ep.* 40 (? very early 251 A.D.; see also n. 1 below). It has gone to Carthage and duly set about its tasks. Felicissimus has taken objection to the detailed inquiries that these tasks entailed. His objections have roused a large faction of followers. Enough time has elapsed for many of those followers to have had second thoughts and to have returned to their former allegiance. A report on these events has then been sent to Cyprian. Cyprian now replies, no doubt after painful consideration of the formal schism which this letter of his will create. This timetable of events suggests we may be now close enough to March of 251; Cyprian's next letter, *Ep.* 43, comes close to Easter 251 (March 23). See further Nelke 51 f.; Duquenne 145 ff.

The letter itself makes plain the authority vested in Cyprian's commissioners, formally rehearses the tasks assigned to them, recounts the regrettable facts they have had to report and authorizes the naming by them of the persistent henchmen of Felicissimus who incur excommunication. It must dispel any doubts that might linger among some Carthaginians concerning the formal legitimacy of the commission. Its status and the authority deputed to it by the bishop are made plain. Rebellion against it is rebellion against the bishop who sent it, and is therefore rebellion against the Church, which cannot be tolerated.

Cyprian has contended with disobedient clergy since, he claims, the outbreak of persecution; some few have indeed been visited with excommunication whilst others have incurred suspension pending inquiry (*Ep.* 34). But now for the first time there has been a major and formal challenge to his episcopal standing. Not only have his deputies not been recognized but loyalty to Cyprian has been publicly declared to involve exclusion from communion. An *aliud altare* is being erected. Such open defiance of his episcopal standing could not be left to fester; but Cyprian's treatment of it is nevertheless cautious.

If he reacts overvigorously and intransigently he will be apprehensive that he may drive beyond the pale, irrevocably, the confessors, presbyters, deacons, and faithful who in large numbers incline to lend support to Felicissimus. The way is carefully left open for their return, without recriminations, whilst they are nevertheless left in no doubt of the sentence which persistent rebellion will inevitably invite.

Felicissimus' challenge clearly brought out into the open and helped to cohere, if only for a period, various groups dissatisfied with Cyprian: clergy critical of his appointment as bishop, those critical of his flight and retirement during persecution, above all confessors, clergy and laity alike critical of his penitential policies and favouring a less rigorous discipline. Even the detailed inquiries involved in registering potential recruits for the clergy (§1.2) may well have roused sentiments of rebellion among otherwise loyal members of the Carthaginian church. Its inquiries might also entail that present recipients of church benefits, without an entirely clean record, could run the risk of being excluded from the lists of beneficiaries, for Cyprian limited benefaction to the worthy and the meritorious (see n. 8 to *Ep.* 5, n. 18 to *Ep.* 12, n. 15 to *Ep.* 14). Cyprian has already been left with ample material for pondering the composition of the *De unitate,* which he will have begun to draft under the stress of these events. Note H. Koch, *Cyprianische Untersuchungen* [Bonn 1926] 100 ff., on stylistic parallels.

Cyprian has employed bishops already to act on his behalf in Carthage. His use of them now, combined with the assistance of local (and loyal) presbyters, to carry on the tasks incumbent upon the bishop is a logical continuance of that outlook. But it is also a tangible recognition that he could not reliably leave it to his clergy by themselves to distribute adequately alms to the (deserving) poor, and to advise justly and with discernment on candidates suitable for appointment to the now depleted clerical ranks. The reaction to that manifest display of mistrust was not beyond calculation but relations between Cyprian and some of his flock were now so poor (cf. *Ep.* 34) that little choice may have been left if Cyprian wished the reorganization of the church (clearly now possible) to be started before he could return himself. And at this stage he cannot yet see any immediate prospect of his being able to return. Episcopal duty simply required him to do all that was possible to restore the church services—charitable and liturgical—that had been thrown into chaos by the persecution. (A brief but spectacular glimpse is thus given in §1.2 of the extent of church social services and of the recruiting of church personnel.)

1. *Caldonius:* see *Ep.* 24 n. 1 on this senior (proconsular?) bishop; he is a confessor and has now been released from prison for quite some time. The combination of seniority as bishop and special status as confessor would no doubt increase the likelihood of respect being paid to his authority—a sage choice for the leader of the delicate task that now confronted Cyprian's "commission" in Carthage.

Herculanus: he figures as 18th (out of 31 or 32) in the list of bishops who sent *Ep.* 70: as these are as likely as not all proconsular bishops we should assume that he hails from somewhere within the neighbourhood of Carthage. That would indeed make sense of Cyprian's employment of him for the present tasks—a totally unfamiliar stranger, deputed to help organize affairs within Carthage, was more likely to meet with increased resistance and stir up unnecessary resentment. He was not present at the Council of September 256, so we do not know his precise locality. See Benson 107; J.-L. Maier, *L'épiscopat de l'afrique romaine, vandale et byzantine* (Neuchâtel 1973) 332.

Rogatianus: we first met in *Ep.* 6 a Rogatianus presbyter, who was an early confessor (see n. 1 to *Ep.* 6; cf. *Epp.* 7 and 13). In *Ep.* 43.1.1 the same Rogatianus as here figures as a *presbyter confessor;* we ought to assume identity between the Rogatianus of *Epp.* 41–43 and the Rogatianus of *Epp.* 6, 7 and 13. Like Caldonius he is a released confessor (cf. *Ep.* 13.7); he can now be expected to return to Carthage and carry out pastoral work there (§1.2 below). In *Ep.* 7, before arrest, he enjoyed a trusted role as distributor of episcopal largesse; he is now called on to resume that work. Cyprian has carefully selected one of his senior Carthaginian presbyters (he is a *gloriosum senem, Ep.* 6.4), who is also distinguished by confessional honours, to assist his "commission."

Numidicus: see *Ep.* 40. His appearance here, without any word of introduction or apology, suggests beyond reasonable doubt that he is now installed as a member of the Carthaginian *presbyterium* (we are, therefore, later than *Ep.* 40); he certainly figures as a fully established Carthaginian presbyter in *Ep.* 43.1.1. Has Cyprian chosen Numidicus in preference to, say, the presbyter Virtius (*Ep.* 43.1.1) who was also available and who would be senior to Numidicus, because of the special attractions of Numidicus' brilliant confessional honours? They would be calculated to win confidence and deference from the Carthaginian flock.

This group of four was joined in its work by another bishop, Victor (see n. 1 to *Ep.* 42). On this ecclesiastical commission, see introductory note to this letter.

2. The contents of this lost letter can be recovered from §1.2. It dealt with the cases of Felicissimus and Augendus who were attempting to thwart the accomplishment of the tasks which Cyprian had formally entrusted to these clerics. It was apparently written from Carthage. (Benson 107 n. 3 needlessly deduces from §2.3 that the members of this commission are currently away from Carthage.)

3. *universam fraternitatem nostram incolumem continere.* See n.

3 to *Ep.* 5 on the ambiguous word *incolumis.* In this context Cyprian is obviously thinking in terms of spiritual integrity.

4. *Felicissimum multa improbe et insidiose esse molitum.* From what follows, Felicissimus' crimes, besides the present sedition, included *fraudes et rapinas* committed in the past (a significant group of mss record in fact *fraudes veteres*)—could that imply, at the least, some activities as a businessman? He is termed by many "a wealthy layman" (e.g., B. Aubé, *L'église et l'état dans la seconde moitié du troisième siècle (249–284)* [Paris 1886] 246: "laïque riche et brouillon"; DACL 5 [1922] *s.v.* faillis 1074: "un laïque riche et influent"; cf. Monceaux, *Histoire,* 2.31), presumably by drawing that implication. He appears to be able himself to dispense to the needy emoluments (§2.1)—are these drawn from his own personal resources? At least Cyprian does not openly accuse him here of embezzling the church's current relief funds or of sequestrating the community's purse, as many commentators assume Felicissimus did in fact. That charge is rather left for other rebels with whom Felicissimus is soon to join forces, the Roman deacon Nicostratus and the presbyter Novatus. But the description of Felicissimus by the time of *Ep.* 59.1.2 (summer 252) is not too far dissimilar; he is there, among other things, *pecuniae commissae sibi fraudator.*

Felicissimus appears later as a deacon assisting Novatus (*Ep.* 52.2.3, where see n. 15; cf. *Ep.* 59.1 f. for his mission to Rome). It would make perfectly good sense were he now not a layman but rather a deacon, with responsibility for the care and distribution of the church funds—and possibly aggrieved by the invasion by this present commission of his traditional ecclesiastical preserve. At least he needs some clerical and spiritual authority, one would think, to be able to threaten that those who persist in their loyalty to Cyprian *"secum in morte non communicarent"* (§1.2). He appears to have the open backing of some rebel confessors and of five hostile presbyters by the time of *Ep.* 43 (see esp. §§2, 3; cf. *Ep.* 45.4.1 f.). The ultimate fate of his faction is lost in obscurity, its original forces perhaps splintering between the Novatus-Novatian nexus (with Maximus as its Carthaginian bishop) and those (? the bulk) who remained with the Fortunatus-Privatus nexus (with Fortunatus as its Carthaginian bishop); see *Ep*. 59.9.1 ff. where we also have our last glimpse of Felicissimus. Does the author of *Ad Novat*. 2.5 refer (with execrable punning) to these two groups: *quid ad ista respondeant perversissimi isti Novatiani vel nunc infelicissimi pauci?* For discussion of this passage, see A. von Harnack in TU 13.1 (1895) 23 ff.

The layman-confessor Felicissimus of *Ep*. 6.4 should be kept distinct, in all probability (see n. 31 to *Ep*. 6), though it is tempting to discern that some of his spiritual imperialism might be due to the dignity of confessor.

Further general discussion on Felicissimus is in Benson 153 f.; Ritschl, *Cyprian* 173 f.; K. Müller in ZfKG 16 (1896) 212 f.; P.A. Leder, *Die Diakonien der Bischöfe und Presbyter und ihre urchristlichen Vorläufer* (Stuttgard 1905) 241 ff.; Thaninayagam 75; Duquenne 146 n. 2; etc.

5. *cum episcopo portionem plebis inlidere*. Though the sense is not in doubt, especially given the explanatory clause which follows, there is ms uncertainty over the verb (e.g., *illudere, dividere* are also found). I cannot find a parallel for *inlido* followed by *cum*. Cf. TLL *s.v. illido* ii.

6. *si qui vellent etiam suas artes exercere additamento . . . iuvaretis*. Not only is the commission to distribute basic necessities for survival amongst the Christian poor, it appears that it has been authorized to provide as well (*etiam*) bridging-finance or setting-up grants for tradesmen. Confiscations have been common in this persecution for those who fled—or who were caught (see, e.g., n. 8 to *Ep*. 5; n. 5 to *Ep*. 10; n. 19 to *Ep*. 12); the Christian refugees into Carthage would similarly have had to leave behind the tools of their trades in their furtive haste to escape detection. In a community where so many people only just managed to attain a subsistence level of livelihood such abandonment or confiscations of even meagre goods and possessions would constitute an irreversible loss.

For the encouragement of crafts and work by one's own hands generally in Christian circles, from the New Testament period onwards, see J. Leipoldt, *Der soziale Gedanke in der altchristlichen Kirche* (Leipzig 1952) 158 f.; A. Bigelmair, *Die Beteiligung der Christen am öffentlichen Leben in vorconstantinischer Zeit* (Munich 1902) 299 f. And for fourth-century evidence of church registers of the poor, J. H. W. G. Liebeschuetz, *Antioch: City and Imperial Administration in the Later Roman Empire* (Oxford 1972) 239 f.

W. Telfer, *The Office of a Bishop* (London 1962), 172, seems seriously to misunderstand the passage; he considers the function of the commission was "to carry money to the clergy in Carthage to make up the sportulae in arrears. Cyprian notes that some clergy may have supported themselves on earnings during the emergency, and this is to be taken into account in computing the back pay now due to them."

7. Cyprian is continuing the work of finding replacement clergy as we have seen him in *Epp.* 38–40. The essential virtues here sought accord with those letters—prospective *clerici* need to be not simply *digni* but specifically *humiles et mites*. A continuing context of rebellion among the clergy is clear.

Note also Cyprian needs to know *aetates* as well as general *condiciones* and *merita*. Cf. *Ep.* 39.5.2 on the restrictions of age for church office. Part of the general agitation amongst the congregation may well be due to this census-inquiry that included *condiciones* and *merita;* that would disturb at the least all those whose conduct during the persecution had not been clearly above suspicion.

8. *secum in morte non communicarent qui nobis obtemperare voluissent.* As the text stands Felicissimus appears to be excluding all Cyprian's loyalists from communion, even at the last (though the phrase *in morte* is unusual in this sense). If Felicissimus is a deacon, he may be, in a literal sense, threatening to withhold the *viaticum* from the dying. The variant reading *in monte* (? the Byrsa) has met with some favour (e.g., adopted by Bayard); that would suggest that Felicissimus was excluding such loyalists from his own parish area or district "on the hill"—at this stage his breakaway threat was no broader than that. But Cyprian's alarmed reaction of distress and dismay suggests that his act of rebellion was more sweeping and less localized than this reading of *in monte* seems to imply. (The same ms uncertainty occurs again in §2.1 below.)

There seems to be little profit in invoking (as some have done) the fact that Roman Novatianists could (much later) be called

Montenses. For the evidence, see F. J. Dölger in AC 2 (1930) 54 f.

9. *cum ecclesia matre remanerent et stipendia eius episcopo dispensante perciperent.* The emphases are significant (receive *her* emoluments from the hands of the *bishop*): the rebellious have been receiving *stipendia* from the hands of someone else (sc. *Felicissimo dispensante?*). On the bishop as controller of church alms, see n. 10 to *Ep.* 5.

Stipendia seems to be used in a general sense—Cyprian is referring to *plurimi fratres;* they enjoy regular benefits (like pay, *stipendia*) from their bishop. Some take it to refer to clerical payments exclusively (e.g., Blaise *s.v.*); that would seem to imply that, at least temporarily, a very large proportion of the clergy had given allegiance to Felicissimus' faction. That inference is not certain. At all events Cyprian shows himself careful to leave the way still open for return to his following, whilst being firm, in exemplary fashion, with the ringleaders and blatantly persistent offenders. Are those five presbyters (*Ep.* 43) prudently left unmentioned at this stage in the (vain) hopes that any support given by them to Felicissimus might be only short-lived and quietly overlooked? In other words, we might well suspect some propaganda element in this picture of the rapidly collapsing breakaway church.

On the theme of *mater ecclesia,* see n. 3 to *Ep.* 10.

10. *non communicaturos in morte secum.* See n. 8 above on the text. The mss record *in monte[m]*.

11. *accipiat sententiam quam prior dixit, ut abstentum se a nobis sciat.* This is in effect a provisional or temporary excommunication. Cyprian wisely goes to the trouble to have his stance solemnly confirmed by the Council of 251 (action planned in *Ep.* 43.7.2 and executed in *Ep.* 45.4.1; cf. *Ep.* 59.1.1, 9.1), after the full inquiry had been held which he foreshadows at the end of this section. See n. 4 to *Ep.* 3 on the bishop's power to excommunicate alone.

12. *fratres nostri graves viri.* P. G. Caron in *Revue internationale des droits de l'antiquité* 6 (1951) 19 sees in this expression possible origins of the later *seniores laici* of the African Church, comparing Tertullian, *Apol.* 39.5: *probati quique seniores.* But Cyprian is surely not alluding to a class, rather to the sober-

minded probity of his informants. By the time of *Ep.* 59.1.2 Felicissimus has become, in lurid colours, *stuprator virginum . . . matrimoniorum multorum depopulator atque corruptor.*

13. There is an *Augendus diaconus* in *Ep.* 44.1.1 (where see n. 2); he appears to be a *Roman* follower of Novatian sent over to Carthage whose arrival Cyprian is there reporting to Cornelius (cf. *Ep.* 68.2.1: *cum ad nos in Africam legatos [Novatianus] misisset*). There is also an *Augendus confessor* in *Ep.* 50.1.1 (where see n. 3); he has acted as a letter-carrier from Cornelius in Rome to Cyprian in Carthage. These two appear to be distinguishable from the Augendus here. We cannot tell whether he enjoyed any clerical rank (cf. *Ep.* 42).

14. *Carthaginem ad clerum transmittite additis nominibus eorum quicumque se Felicissimo iunxerint.* Does the separate action of handing over a copy of the letter to the clergy suggest that they were not assembling with the loyal congregation under the presidency of the visiting bishops? That is to say, many of them were thought to be in a state of disaffection? The addendum of Felicissimus' excommunicated supporters appears to be *Ep.* 42.

LETTER 42

1. There are no epistolary greetings to Cyprian (some editors misleadingly provide *Cypriano s.*). This is not a formal, separate letter but an annotation added to the end of *Ep.* 41 when copies of it were circulated as requested. Caldonius is composing it himself (hence *annotatione mea* below) whilst reporting the collective action of the commission of five (hence the plural *abstinuimus* in the letter). Would Cyprian have received back for his information one of the copies of his original letter, so annotated, which the commission has been asked to distribute (*Ep.* 41.2.3)? We can assume, at least, that a transcript of the annotation was sent to him by messenger. Discussion in Ritschl, *Cyprian* 60 ff.; K. Müller in ZfKG 16 (1896) 213 f.; Benson 114 n. 1; Duquenne 146 f.; etc.

Observe that the commission has been joined by an additional member. Victor is a common episcopal name, the nearest see known to us to have been occupied by a bishop so named being at Gorduba, some 60 km. from Carthage. See n. 1 to *Ep.* 4 where the episcopal Victors are discussed. It is a fair guess—but certainly no more that that—that we are meeting the same bishop who was invited to share counsel with Cyprian in *Ep.* 4. Were the services of this Victor now invoked on the grounds that an additional bishop would lend further weight and authority to the serious sentence which is about to be passed?

2. For Felicissimus and Augendus, see nn. 4 and 13 to *Ep.* 41.

3. *item Repostum de extorribus.* Observe that by now open return to Carthage is possible for the banished (or for those who had taken flight as refugees; see n. 5 to *Ep.* 10 on the word *extorris*). The title of confessor seems to be here deliberately eschewed. Cyprian in fact complains in *Ep.* 43.2.1 f. that some confessors had been corrupted; they had been deceived into lending support to Felicissimus' faction.

R. B. Donna, *The Fathers of the Church* 51 (1964) 106 n. 9, suggests that this Repostus may be the African bishop who induced many of his flock to follow him into paganism and who joined the rebels against Cyprian (i.e., Repostus Sutunurcensis, *Ep.* 59.10.3). That is totally improbable. This Repostus was a banished confessor, whereas the other fell in the course of the persecution (*in persecutione ipse cecidit*).

Item (repeated below) is common in enumerations and perhaps introduced an entry started on a new line; it is used similarly to introduce new clauses in official documents. Caldonius is making a formal declaration.

4. *Irenem Rutilorum.* Does *Rutilorum* indicate a family group (*Rutilus* is a Roman surname), or even a place name? Many speculatively suggest that there was a sodality of martyr-enthusiasts who called themselves the *Rutili* ("ruddied with blood" or "the golden"; *rutilus* is an epithet for red gold). Is Caldonius likely to make such membership the distinguishing mark for Irene in this context? Cf. n. 21 to *Ep.* 21 on the *Floridii*.

5. *quod ex adnotatione mea scire debuisiti.* Does the singular verb (editions supply often the plural) address the presumed reader of the annotation, or is it rather meant primarily for

Cyprian who would have to receive a copy for his information?

6. *budinarium.* It is guesswork that the word is connected with *buda*, a sort of reed which could be used, *inter alia*, for making a sleeping-mat. See Benson 117 for other suggestions. Might the word conceivably harbour some proper name (<*et*> *Budinarium*)? The word is an *hapax legomenon.*

7. Hartel reports that the late (15th century) Codex Vindobonesis 798 records a concluding salutation (*optamus te bene valere et nostri meminisse semper et ubique venerande et percolendissime pater*). This effusive salutation savours of later centuries and could well be a scholar's composition appended when it was not appreciated that *Ep.* 42 was structurally not a separate epistle. It is unlikely (to judge from the style of address alone) to derive from any words of greetings that may have been added to the version of the annotation which Caldonius sent back to Cyprian.

LETTER 43

Contents: Although there are in Carthage loyal and dedicated clergy to advise the laity, Cyprian is sending a letter to them also, for he is prevented from coming himself. Old opponents to his appointment as bishop have renewed their attacks; just as they incited the confessors to indiscipline, so now they deceive the lapsed by proffering to them a delusive reconciliation. They are acting counter to the decision taken by the universal bishops, that is, to make no changes on the question of the lapsed until councils can be held. Despite the urgency of the situation Cyprian cannot end his lonely exile and return to Carthage for fear of stirring up tumult against his people. They must shun these hypocritical elders who, in defiance of the Gospel, set up a sacrilegious altar and prevent the due satisfaction being rendered to God that will earn His compassionate forgiveness. When this ultimate phase of the persecution is passed, Cyprian will return together with other bishops; together they will debate and come to a settlement over the lapsed, just as they have planned all along. But those who scorn penitence and join the heretical faction are cutting themselves off, irrevocably, from communion.

Date and Circumstances: Easter approaches (§§1.2, 7.2)—Easter Sunday fell on March 23 in 251. Impressions are that Cyprian is writing this letter in time for it to be read to his people in Carthage at Eastertide (see n. 5 below). Therefore, we are in the vicinity of early to mid-March 251. See Duquenne 147; Nelke 51 f.; Ritschl, *De epist.* 10 f.

The situation has deteriorated noticeably since Cyprian wrote his last letter that we have, addressed to his clerical "commission," on this same subject (*Ep.* 41). There, two rebel leaders only were mentioned—Felicissimus and Augendus—and Cyprian appeared confident that their initial following would continue to fall away. Now, there are five presbyters, of seniority and authority (§4.3), who have come out openly in support of Felicissimus' faction; they are in so strong a position that they can forestall Cyprian's projected return to Carthage in time for Easter (§§1.2, 7.2)—and Cyprian no longer has any words about the dwindling numbers of their followers. Rather, the breakaway movement appears to have gained in momentum, as old hostilities have come out publicly to lend their weight to it.

In *Ep.* 41 the formation of a schismatic group is analysed as revolt against the activities of Cyprian's commission, and hence against the episcopal standing of Cyprian. Now, in *Ep.* 43, there has emerged a clear disciplinary, if not doctrinal, issue—the reconciliation of the lapsed. The fallen keep reappearing throughout the letter. And at the heart of *that* issue Cyprian discerns, rightly, that there lay a challenge to his episcopal authority (e.g., §3.2 *ad fin.*); he is, therefore, insistent on his legitimate, divinely sanctioned, claims to sacerdotal (i.e. episcopal) leadership. He is fighting to hold that position and to keep his church together until he can return with further, episcopal, reinforcements (§7.2). He appears to be outnumbered in his local presbyteral supporters (see n. 2) and, for the moment, outmanoeuvred (§1.2).

This is a carefully laid out letter, and the initial flattery and praise for the still loyal clergy in Carthage (§1.1) leads adroitly to a contrasting picture of the morals and motivations of his old enemies, and the five presbyters, now in revolt. They appear as agents of the devil, the initiators of a sacrilegious altar and of a second persecution. By contrast again stands Cyprian, a lonely exile yearning to return to his people and his duties—but forced by his enemies' machinations to delay that return, in the interests of his people. General counsels and exhortations follow naturally from there, with the biblical citations and admonitions interwoven with some care.

Cyprian has composed a deliberate and important letter. Hopes of conciliation with those presbyters are now forlorn. He has, therefore, made a public stand, at long last, against that *presbyterium*. Even though they have been undisciplined *a primo statim persecutionis die* (*Ep.* 59.12.2), he has persisted in rebuking and instructing them, warning and threatening them (e.g., *Epp.* 15 and 34). Now they are lost. Their formal excommunication was left to the Council soon to meet (*Ep.* 59.9.1: *ex quinque presbyteris iam pridem de ecclesia profugis et sententia coepiscoporum nostrorum multorum et gravissimorum virorum nuper abstentis*).

His major bid now is to retain his influence with his *plebs*. He had been a popular choice as bishop. It was the *suffragia* of the people which had made him bishop—he reminds them so, four times, at strategic intervals—and those *suffragia* expressed the will of God (see nn. 6, 8, 30, below). He appears confident of retaining the *stantes* among them—they get but little mention (§7.1), whereas he is careful to attribute all blame for past irregularities among the *confessores* to the rebel presbyters; the confessors are still a group of some significance (§2.1, cf. n. 14 below). But, once again, it is the *lapsi* among his *plebs* who are the focus of attention; the battle is being fought over them.

The persecution is now over in Carthage (see nn. 11 and 12), and apparently so elsewhere, for the language of §7.2 would naturally imply that the Council, planned for so long, will be convening some time after Easter (see n. 37). And *pax* for the church had long been laid down as the prior condition necessary for that Council to be held. We are left to speculate how all this may have eventuated. A copy of this letter was soon to be sent on to the new bishop of Rome, Cornelius (*Ep.* 45.4.2); elections for the vacant seat were being held there about the time this letter was being composed (see C. H. Turner in JTS 17 [1915/16] 345 ff.). Soon after this letter, the Carthaginian presbyter Novatus sailed off to Rome to win support there. He arrived before Novatian's illegal consecration as bishop and the (temporary) period when the Roman confessors favoured Novatian's cause (*Epp.* 52.2.2f.): it pleased Cyprian to see cause and effect in this.

Cyprian will be drafting, in the face of these grim events, his treatises *De unitate* and *De lapsis,* later to be read in Carthage (*Ep.* 54.3.4). Many of the biblical quotations and allusions here are to be found also in one or the other of the two *libelli.* For detailed analysis of the relations between this epistle and those tractates, see H. Koch, *Cyprianische Untersuchungen* (Bonn 1926) 100 ff.

1. *Cyprianus plebi universae s.* The salutation nearest to this formula comes with *Ep.* 17. But, there, Cyprian is addressing the *stantes* only (*fratribus in plebe consistentibus*). Here, he is including very firmly not only the stalwart but in particular the lapsed who, by reason of their condition and thanks to the promises of Felicissimus' *factio,* are being tempted to abandon their bishop (see esp. §7.1). If this letter is intended to reach Carthage for Eastertide, are the lapsed expected to hear it read out at the Easter ceremonies as they stood, penitentially and symbolically, beyond the threshold of the church, *in vestibulo* (cf. n. 39 to *Ep.* 30)? Cyprian does not include in his address his presbyters and deacons as well (as he did in *Epp.* 38–40), nor apparently does he write to them separately (as he did in *Ep.* 16, when he addressed *Ep.* 17 to his *plebs*); might one surmise that he has seen those of them who are still loyal to him (§1.1) at his place of retirement, now that the dangers have eased? Certainly he has been well briefed about the mood and circumstances in Carthage (§4.2). *Ep.* 45.4.2 alludes to this letter along with a letter addressed *ad clerum* on the question of Felicissimus and the presbyters; is the second document a loose description of *Ep.* 41, or can it in fact be a missing letter written to the clergy at the same time as this epistle (see n. 32 to *Ep.* 45)?

2. Note the carefully chosen epithets and descriptive phrases for the three (loyal) presbyters who are currently in Carthage. Virtius is *fidelissimus adque integerrimus: fidelissimus* would contrast with the five presbyters who had defected (§§3.1 f.), *integerrimus* with those presbyters who had lapsed (*Ep.* 40.1.2). Virtius' place at the head of the list suggests he is senior to the other two, but Cyprian may have dislocated the normal order so as to place the other two *presbyteri confessores* together. Virtius has managed to survive the persecution in Carthage intact, having been neither a refugee nor a confessor.

On Rogatianus, see n. 1 to *Ep.* 41; on Numidicus, see *Ep.* 40 and n. 1 to *Ep.* 41. Cyprian is not loath to extol the special charismatic quality of these two presbyters who continue to support him.

The way Cyprian writes should leave us with no doubts that there are at this time only three loyal presbyters at work in Carthage, as opposed to the five dissident presbyters. There may have been other Carthaginian presbyters with Cyprian—or soon to return themselves from hiding or from exile. Is, for example, Primitivus one such (*Epp.* 44.2.2, 48.1)? But, even so, the bald numbers make plain that the present situation for Cyprian's church in Carthage can only be termed threatened, if not desperate.

3. *diaconi boni viri . . . cum ceteris ministeriis.* Cyprian refers to his deacons and lower clerical ranks as a class loyal to him—there have, however, been troublesome deacons (see n. 3 to *Ep.* 16) and less than fully obedient clerics of lower status (see, for example, *Ep.* 34.4.1), as well as lapsed clerics. We cannot conclude, therefore, with any security that the impression we gain from this passage of a lower ministry basically intact and loyal is justified. On the numbers involved, see ACW 43.39 ff.

Observe that the bishops who have been active in Carthage (*Epp.* 41 and 42) are no longer there. They would have rated a special notice otherwise. It is a fair surmise they will have gone to their home dioceses for the Easter celebrations (cf. *Ep.* 56.3).

4. *admoneo et quomodo possum visito vos litteris meis.* It is not quite clear whether Cyprian is being specific (*litteris meis* = "by this letter of mine") or generalizing (*litteris meis* = "by letters

from me"). The concluding echo in §4.3 (*hinc, tamen, fratres dilectissimi, hinc admoneo*), after the present circumstances have been fully expounded, suggests rather that he is referring specifically to this present epistle, and is not generalizing.

5. *malignitas et perfidia perfecit ne ad vos ante diem Paschae venire licuisset.* A natural reading would be that Cyprian is writing shortly before the Easter period, but it is technically possible for the sentence also to be translated, "the spite and treachery made it impossible . . ." Hence, presumably, the observation of J. Chapman in *Revue bénédictine* 20 (1903) 29 n. 4: "on ne comprend clairement si cela est écrit avant ou après Pâques". But Cyprian's remarks in §7.2 should eliminate the uncertainty: he is unlikely to have said that he would be present in Carthage after Easter-day (*ut repraesenter vobis post Paschae diem*) if it were already *post Paschae diem*.

See n. 10 to *Ep.* 29 on the meaning of *Pascha* in Cyprian. See also n. 19 below on the *minae et insidiae* of these presbyters. Easter was manifestly a time for a congregation to gather in prayer and solemn ceremony together (see esp. *Ep.* 56.3); the five presbyters' manoeuvrings have meant that Cyprian could not exploit the Easter vigil and assemblies for rallying his flock behind him and preaching to his people against the rebels. Rather, he would be conspicuously absent—still the deserting, but nevertheless, rigorous, shepherd.

6. *immo contra suffragium vestrum et Dei iudicium.* Cyprian is referring to his turbulent election to the episcopate; his candidature was openly and bitterly opposed by certain *antiquiores*, but that opposition was triumphantly overridden by an enthusiastic populace. See Pontius, *Vit. Cyp.* 5.

P. Hinchliff, *Cyprian of Carthage* (London 1974) 38, remarks on this passage: "One can only guess what he meant by 'the judgment of God,' " and speculates whether Cyprian may be referring to some revelatory dream or prophetic utterance. That speculation is unnecessary. In Cyprian's view, the voice of God's people, by their popular acclaim, recorded the judgment of God. So, too, Pontius *Vit. Cyp.* 5: *iudicio Dei et plebis favore ad officium sacerdotii et episcopatus gradum . . . electus est; in dilectionem eius et honorem totus populus inspirante Domino prosiliret.*

Consequently Cyprian will emphasize, according to context and argument, that bishops are the elect of God, or that they are the elect of God's people, or, both. See n. 1 to *Ep.* 38 on the *suffragium* of the *plebs* in episcopal elections. Hippolytus reveals a similar dualism of attitude on the election of bishops: *Trad. Apost.* 2 enjoins: *episcopus ordinetur electus ab omni populo,* whereas *Trad. Apost.* 3 records in the prayer of consecration: *hunc servum tuum quem elegisti ad episcopatum.* See, for discussion, J. E. Stam, *Episcopacy in the Apostolic Tradition of Hippolytus* (Basel 1969) 18 f. And Sulpicius Severus, *Vit. Mart.* 9, describes a similar episcopal election—popular acclaim as well as opposition from clerical and sacerdotal ranks. The election duly took place, all the same, *divino nutu;* it was not possible for the clerical opponents to obstruct *quod populus, Domino volente, cogitabat.*

7. *nobis hoc nec volentibus nec optantibus immo et ignoscentibus et tacentibus.* Pontius, *Vit. Cyp.* 5, extols Cyprian's gentleness, benevolence and clemency in pardoning those who openly resisted his election (*quam clementer ignovit, amicissimos eos postmodum et inter necessarios computans, mirantibus multis*): the fight must have indeed been a bitter one if it called for such virtuous, and astonishing, forgiveness.

8. *secundum vestra divina suffragia.* This seems to mean that the people's divinely inspired votes which were cast in favour of Cyprian were also, in effect, rejecting the opponents of Cyprian. It is tempting to emend the text logically to *secundum vestra <et> divina suffragia* = according to your, and God's votes; but the temptation should be resisted—the syncopated version is characteristic of Cyprian.

9. *ne confessionis suae gloriam incorrupta et immaculata conversatione servarent.* This does not inevitably mean that the presbyters urged some of the confessors to the misconduct for which they are rebuked in *Ep.* 13—gross moral delicts, *contentiones, aemulationes, discordiae;* rather, that they were courted and encouraged by them to issue unacceptable *libelli pacis* (*Ep.* 15.4) and to make immoderate demands, counter to Gospel and tradition, on behalf of the lapsed (explicit in *Ep.* 16.3.2). In his earlier epistles Cyprian upbraids his presbyters and deacons for failure properly to advise and counsel the confessors (e.g., *Ep.* 16.2 f.);

they are now accused of more positive incitement to sinful rebellion.

10. *adversus sacerdotium Dei.* Cyprian is inclined to use *sacerdos/sacerdotium* (in preference to *episcopus/episcopatus,* words fundamentally associated with administration) in order to exploit their sacral and hierophantic connotations—and in order to equate the New Testament bishop with the Old Testament high-priest (as in Deut. 17.12, quoted in §7.1 below). Here the sacrilege of rebellion is underscored by this choice of noun. On the word *sacerdos,* see also n. 6 to *Ep.* 40.

11. *persecutio est haec alia et alia est temptatio.* For a good exposé of Cyprian's view of persecution as a time of chastening and testing (*temptatio*), see *Ep.* 11, esp. §§5, 7. Cyprian's phrasing here should mean that he regards the previous *persecutio* and *temptatio* as now over. Compare the phrasing in *Ep.* 52.2.2: *alia quaedam persecutio nostri fuit* (of Novatus); *Ep.* 59.18.2: *ipsam pacem persecutione peiorem fratribus faciunt* (of Novatianists); *De laps.* 16: *non est pax illa sed bellum; persecutio est haec alia et alia temptatio.* This motif of heresy as persecution is a favourite of Augustine's; for some passages see H. F. von Campenhausen, *Die Idee des Martyriums in der alten Kirche* (2nd ed., Göttingen 1964) 169.

In the preceding sentence there is a passing allusion to Eph. 6.11.

12. *quinque primores illi qui edicto nuper magistratibus fuerant copulati.* The tense of this verb must mean that the association between *primores* (leading citizens) and magistrates has now ended. Cyprian's vague *nuper* does not however assist in being more precise about the chronology. The *edicto* could well refer to a proconsular edict, issued by the governor, regulating the local implementation of the imperial orders; the panel of commissioners who supervised the sacrifices varied from province to province and district to district in those instances where we possess particulars: see for details Introduction in ACW 43.30 f. Would, in Carthage, *magistratus* mean the *duoviri*—or were other local officers, such as aediles and quaestors, perhaps involved, given the heavy task of supervising the whole population of Carthage as they individually offered sacrifice? (See A.

Audollent, *Carthage romaine (146 av. J.-Ch.-698 ap. J.-Ch.)* (Paris 1901) 325 ff., on the Carthaginian magistrates.) At any rate the city "magistrates" by themselves were apparently not enough for the work.

Bayard, in ed. *ad loc.*, (unnecessarily) sees in this passage another vision of Cyprian's; cf. J. Lebreton and J. Zeiller, *The History of the Primitive Church* (tr. by E. C. Messenger, 4 vols., London 1946) 3.694 n. 2 ("the five priests whom he had previously seen in a vision as accomplices of the persecuting magistrates"). P. Keresztes in *Latomus* 34 (1975) 773, also misinterprets the passage, but differently ("some priests seem to have gone so far as to join the commission"). C. Saumagne, *Saint Cyprien. Évêque de Carthage. "Pape" d'Afrique (248–258)* (Paris 1975) 73, in a flight of fantasy, makes the *quinque primores* into Christians: "nécessairement des chrétiens (car quel crédit auraient eu des 'gentils'?)."

13. *nec per episcopos et sacerdotes* Domini *Domino satisfiat*. Observe the ecclesiastical view of penitence, the bishop being the essential channel for rendering satisfaction to God and the one who controlled the formal terms of penance (cf. n. 34 to *Ep.* 4). Hartel needlessly reads both *Domini* and *Domino*, either one word or the other being found in the mss: the confusion is unexceptional (due to abbreviated forms).

14. *placuerit . . . confessoribus et clericis urbicis*. Cyprian proceeds to refer verbally to the views expressed in *Ep.* 30 (§§8 and 5.3) by the Roman clergy; and the Roman confessors consistently upheld ecclesiastical *disciplina*. It appears deliberate that *confessores* appear before *clerici*—the Carthaginian *plebs*, it is anticipated, being more impressed by the authority of the former than of the latter. Or is it also an adroit and indirect piece of flattery to the standing of the confessors amongst the *plebs*, who are now being addressed?

15. *item universis episcopis vel in nostra provincia vel trans mare constitutis*. On *provincia nostra* in Cyprian, see n. 14 to *Ep.* 27; and see, for example, *Ep.* 25.1.2 for evidence of widespread agreement in Africa on the proposed plan of action. *Ep.* 30.8 contains our only direct evidence for Cyprian's awareness of the views of overseas bishops. But messengers delivering epistles to

and from Rome, and travellers from Rome (e.g. Celerinus), could well have brought further information. Even so, *universi episcopi* is manifestly an exaggeration, for even within Africa some bishops had been acting otherwise (*Ep.* 27.3.1).

16. Observe the *episcopal* view of the church. To object to a plan agreed upon by *universi episcopi* is to undermine the fundamental structure of the Church. By the clause *omnes in unum convenerimus* Cyprian does not mean a universal council. He envisages that local views should be formed at gatherings of local bishops, and then these are to be exchanged with opinions engendered by other groups of bishops, and ultimately universal episcopal agreement is thereby to be reached. See *Ep.* 20.3.3 for an enunciation of this (sanguine) prospectus.

17. *quod ipse ad vos inpraesentiarum venire non possum.* For good measure Cyprian repeats *ipse* ("in person") three times rhetorically to emphasize his physical absence at this season of Easter. Can he here have in mind in particular the opportunity for preaching to his people and of meeting his congregation assembled together which the Easter liturgical ceremonies would have presented?

18. *non suffecerat exilium iam bienni.* By Roman inclusive counting Cyprian means by this expression that he has been longer than one year (and not more than two full years) in "exile" (i.e., hiding). If Cyprian is now writing shortly before Easter 251 (March 23), he must have withdrawn from Carthage at least some time before the equivalent date in 250 A.D.—that is, round about February (within the range, January to very early March). See ACW 43.25 ff.

19. *per minas et per insidias perfidorum cavemus ne advenientibus nobis tumultus illic maior oriatur,* etc. How are the *minae* and *insidiae* of the presbyters to have the consequences which Cyprian fears? Cyprian echoes the arguments he has rehearsed earlier for his initial, and then continued, withdrawal from Carthage— that is, so as not to provoke *violentia gentilium*, to prevent increased *seditio*, etc. He was personally an object of popular pagan hostility, his presence would bait the already angry crowd and only serve to stir up terrorism for the Christian community generally. His language here invites us to see a

parallel. Have the presbyters threatened to set upon the loyal congregation a pagan mob (suitably apprised of Cyprian's whereabouts), should Cyprian return to Carthage for Easter? The official *persecutio* may be over but the popular violence associated with the *persecutio* (cf. *Ep.* 40) can be reawakened, readily enough.

Cyprian can, nevertheless, plan on returning after Easter (§7.2). The presbyters cannot hope to stall his return indefinitely. But to have Cyprian absent for Easter was clearly of tactical importance to them. Were there to be staged at that season massed and spectacular ceremonies of reconciliation and admission into communion for the benefit of those lapsed who had recently joined the cause, the hopes being to win even further loyalists away from Cyprian? Perhaps it was even hoped in those massed gatherings of Easter to elicit the *suffragium* of the *plebs* for a new bishop—consecrated eventually by Privatus and his following of four *pseudoepiscopi* (see *Ep.* 59.10.1 ff.).

20. That is, *mortem pro salute*. As so often in Cyprian, the primary sense of *salus* ("healthy life") has not been altogether lost.

21. The allusion is, of course, to Dan. 13.1 ff. Cyprian puns on the word *presbyteri* (= "elders," as well as "presbyters"), exploiting the fact that the five presbyters were senior in terms of years. The connexion between *presbyter* and the story of Susannah had already occured to Irenaeus, *Adv. Haer.* 4.26.2 ff. There is a charming wall painting in Praetextatus: a lamb labelled *Susanna* is flanked on either side by a wolf, labelled *Seniores*. See M.-L. Thérel, *Les symboles de l'* "*ecclesia*" *dans la création iconographique de l'art chrétien du IIIe au VIe siècle* (Rome 1973) Pl. X, fig. 16.

22. Jer. 23.16 f.

23. *nec ecclesiam lapsos reducere et revocare permittunt qui de ecclesia recesserunt.* So Hartel, but his text is open to doubt. There is ms warrant for reading *in* for *nec*, and *promittunt* is the universal reading for Hartel's conjecture *permittunt*. These alternative readings certainly produce an easier text and a sharper antithesis—"they promise to call back and lead back the fallen

into the church, whilst they have forsaken the church themselves."

24. Allusions to Eph. 4.5 and to Matt. 16.18. Cf. Fahey 309 ff., 484 ff.

25. *quisque alibi collegerit spargit.* An allusion to Matt. 12.30 or Luke 11.23. Cf. Fahey 303.

26. *sermones eorum velut cancer.* An allusion to 2 Tim. 2.17—a favourite of Cyprian's for describing heretical doctrines.

27. Matt. 15.14.

28. Deut. 13.5. The verb (in the Vulgate *interficietur*) has dropped out. Bayard prints it as a question: "Is he a prophet or visionary who . . .?"

29. That is, *Christiani*, a word in fact used with relative infrequency by Cyprian. When he does use it he is aware of its etymology (as here), its general use in *pagan* society (as in *Ep.* 55.14.1), the servile connotations of its *-ianus* ending (as in *Ep.* 58.6.3), its employment to designate a *secta* (as in *Ep.* 55.16.1). He seems to employ the term, in other words, often with some self-consciousness.

30. *olim secundum vestra suffragia nunc secundum Dei iudicia.* A variation on the theme explicated in n. 6 above. Presumably God's judgement is being currently evinced by the sentence of excommunication that the rebels are passing upon themselves (cf. §1.2 above, §7.2 below).

31. Mark 7.9.

32. Taken from 1 Tim. 6.3 f.

33. Eph. 5.6 f.

34. The care with which Cyprian has elaborated in this paragraph themes and words from his scriptural citations is notable (*decipiat inanibus verbis* ~ *decepti inanibus verbis; participes eorum* ~ *pravitatis eorum . . . participes; discede ab huiusmodi* ~ *discedite a talibus; adquiescit sanis verbis* ~ *adquiescite consiliis nostris*). This is a letter over which Cyprian has taken some pains. A copy was subsequently sent on to Rome and further copies were sent later to ensure a wide dissemination (see *Ep.* 45.4.2 f.).

With some irony Cyprian has been constantly stipulating first of all peace (from persecution) for the church, before peace (i.e., reconciliation) for the fallen can be settled (see, e.g., *Epp.* 20.3.2 and 26.1.2). Though peace (from persecution) has already come, he still has to beg now for *plenissima pax* for the church—peace from factions, dissensions and outright revolt—before peace for the brethren can be attained.

35. Cyprian continues his image of the present season of discord as a period of persecution. Just as the lapsed might win forgiveness for their fall by a courageous stand during a second trial under persecution conditions, so, too, now the fallen, by showing steadfast loyalty during this second round of severe testing, will foster their hopes of forgiveness. For passages in Cyprian on the cancellation of apostasy by a subsequent confession of faith, see n. 17 to *Ep.* 19.

36. Deut. 17.12.

37. *ut repraesenter vobis post Paschae diem cum collegis meis.* See n. 5 above. Cyprian plans to return accompanied by fellow bishops. We cannot tell whether he simply means that men like Caldonius and Herculanus, who would have special knowledge of the local problems, will be coming along with him, lending their assistance and support. The phrasing, however, suggests something less casual than that. The council of the following year (252) was meeting on the Ides of May (see *Ep.* 59.10.1), that is to say about one month away from the time of Easter. If anything like the same timetable was to apply this year (251), word of this gathering would have had to be distributed by now if the widely scattered bishops were to make their way in to Carthage by the due date after celebrating Easter with their own people (cf. *Ep.* 56.3). Cyprian may well be alluding, therefore, to the proposed council (though exactly when it did convene is difficult to establish; see Monceaux, *Histoire* 2.42 f.). The sentence which follows only goes to confirm this conjecture; it describes *conciliar* activities.

38. *se haereticae factioni coniunxerit.* Though Cyprian did at times recognize schism as orthodox dissent (*versus* heresy, doctrinal error), and although the present rebels appear to be generally orthodox, he characterizes the faction here by the more pejorative term *haeretica.* They had cut themselves off from the

Church; minor niceties were negligible before that cataclysmic fact. For discussion of "heresy" and "schism" in Cyprian, see n. 18 to *Ep.* 3, and cf. n. 10 to *Ep.* 49.

39. To judge from the contents of the letter (e.g., §§5.3, 6.1) Cyprian is not imploring the mercy of the Lord for the sin of heresy that is being committed in their community; it is for the sin of apostasy that so many have committed in the persecution. The battle between Cyprian and Felicissimus with his *presbyterium* (cf. *Ep.* 45.4.1 f.) is being waged over the *lapsed*.

LETTER 44

Contents: Envoys arrived in Carthage from Novatian bearing the dismaying news of the illegal appointment of Novatian as bishop. These envoys were promptly excluded from communion. Cyprian and his fellow bishops still awaited, however, the return of their own envoys to Rome who would bring back certain proof against this evil and schismatic faction. Their return was in fact anticipated by the arrival of the bishops Pompeius and Stephanus who brought with them trustworthy testimony on the matter. The subsequent and violent efforts of the envoys from Novatian to secure a hearing for their allegations against Cornelius were firmly resisted; but that has not stopped them from going around drumming up followers in the towns and cities about. They have been warned that if they are to be genuine champions of the Gospel, as they claim, they must first return to the Church.

Date and circumstances: It is the most reasonable calculation, on the evidence we have, that Cornelius was elected bishop of Rome in the first half of March, 251: see, among many others, A. von Harnack, *Geschichte der altchristlichen Literatur* (2 vols., Leipzig 1893–1904, repr. 1958) 2.351 n. 2; C. H. Turner in JTS 17 (1915/1916) 345 ff.; L. Reekmans, *La tombe du pape Corneille et sa région cémétériale* (Vatican City, 1964) 110 f. Notoriously, that election was disputed and Cornelius' fellow presbyter Novatian, stimulated by Novatus who had arrived in Rome from Carthage, promptly got himself consecrated also (? by end of March or early April: speed of action is played up by Cornelius *ap.* Eusebius, *H.E.* 6.43.7 ff.). In the course of the month of April—towards its end ?—the African Council was meeting (we might assume) in Carthage (see n. 37 to *Ep.* 43); it was confronted by messages from Cornelius (see *Ep.* 45.1.2, 3.1) as well as by envoys and messages from Novatian (see *Ep.* 44.1.1). Recognition of either as the rightful bishop of Rome was suspended (see *Ep.* 48.2.1), whilst two bishops Caldonius and Fortunatus were sent from the Council to Rome to collect data on the elections, in particular affidavits from the bishops present at Cornelius' consecration. By the time they had returned—it might have taken some weeks to collect this evidence—two bishops had arrived from Rome (Pompeius and Stephanus) and the Council was no longer in session (see *Epp.* 45.1.3, 48.3.2). Cyprian and bishops with him in Carthage decided firmly, on the information received, to recognize Cornelius whose character was cleared of slander and innuendo and whose temporal priority as bishop was established beyond doubt. This run of events could bring us down as far as, say, early June—even though the passage from Ostia to Carthage might take only a brisk two to three days (see L. Casson in TAPA 82 [1951] 139 and 145).

Cyprian is writing now, that is to say, about the middle of 251, a letter of explanation to Cornelius, following on his own official letter of recognition. It is intended to be a mollifying epistle. The delays in making his commitment have been embarrassingly lengthy and the presbyter Primitivus is being sent with the letter (see n. 13 below) in a special attempt to buffer the affront which Cyprian senses those delays may have occasioned; he has surmised—rightly—that trouble has been brewing.

He emphasizes (with manifest exaggeration) the rebuff given to Novatian's envoys immediately upon their arrival (*statim*)—what if their claims had proved in the end to be valid?—and he devotes a whole paragraph to their subsequent rejection (§2) and insists on his ceaseless efforts to instruct them on the wickedness of their error (§3.2). Cyprian is painfully aware that he is exposed to a charge of having harboured and heeded the *legati* of

Novatian: they have been in and around Carthage now for some time. And he plays up (with some deception) the decisive role of the bishops from Italy, Pompeius and Stephanus, in clarifying and settling the issue (see nn. 9 and 10 below). What if *they* (surely envoys from Cornelius) had been as misleading as the *legati* from Novatian? He ends his letter on moralizing notes about Mother Church, faith, peace, Gospel—and Cornelius' generous approbation by *plebs* and episcopal colleagues.

Cyprian has gone to some trouble to present as good a front as truth (partially viewed) would allow in a very awkward and indeed virtually irretrievable situation. After all, the personal worthiness of Cornelius for episcopal election had been called into serious doubt and they had gone to quite unprecedented lengths to investigate the allegations made against him. (It must be remembered that Cyprian's personal bias may well have been, at the very early stage of the dispute, in favour of Novatian, who had penned those letters [cf. *Epp.* 30 and 36] which had vindicated his honour and upheld his disciplinary policies. And Novatian had the prestigious backing of the Roman martyrs and confessors who had also exonerated and supported him. Doctrinal issues were yet to emerge clearly in this dispute.)

We are afforded an unusual and fascinating opportunity to view no fewer than three versions of these same events which Cyprian is eventually constrained to present to Cornelius—this present letter, the next letter, *Ep.* 45, in response to further protests from Cornelius, and thirdly, *Ep.* 48, in which further disclosures to Cornelius force Cyprian to come clean over the full sequence of events. Together, they present a nice picture of ecclesiastical diplomacy in action. Cyprian had striven to remain neutral and to leave options open—for the most honourable of reasons—for as long as was necessary. But he is now forced to live through the embarrassing consequences of that policy of cautious neutrality.

This tangled web is unravelled with splendid dexterity most recently by M. Bévenot in JTS 28 (1977) 346 ff.; cf. *idem, St. Cyprian's De Unitate Chap. 4 in the Light of the Manuscripts* (Rome 1937) 73 ff.; for another succinct but penetrating study, see Ritschl, *De epist.* 13 ff. (though he unconvincingly argues for the priority of *Ep.* 45 over *Ep.* 44). For a fuller analysis of these developments, see, amongst many others, Benson 129 ff.; A. von Harnack, *Geschichte der altchristlichen Literatur* (2 vols., Leipzig 1893–1904, repr. 1958) 2.350 ff.; H. Koch, *Cyprianische Untersuchungen* (Bonn 1926) 117 ff.; Monceaux, *Histoire* 2.33 ff., 220 ff.; Nelke 56 ff.; M. M. Sage, *Cyprian* (Cambridge 1975) 249 ff.; H. J. Vogt, *Coetus sanctorum* (Bonn 1968) 45 ff.

1. *Cyprianus Cornelio fratri s.* This bland and matter-of-fact form of address Cyprian maintains throughout his extant interchange of letters with Cornelius. It must be remembered that he will have addressed to Cornelius already an official communication formally acknowledging his election to the see of Rome; this was in (eventual) reply to the letter Cornelius had sent himself announcing his own election. On such letters of recognition, see also n. 12 below.

2. *missi a Novatiano Maximus presbyter et Augendus diaconus et Machaeus quidam et Longinus.* Maximus, Machaeus, and Longinus reappear in *Ep.* 50.1.1 (from Cornelius) as having been, in the end, driven out (*expulsi*) from Africa; see n. 2 to *Ep.* 50. There are five rebel Novatianizing Roman presbyters mentioned as a group by Cornelius *ap.* Eusebius, *H.E.* 6.43.20. This *Maximus presbyter* is likely to have been one of their number. (He is clearly distinguishable from the Roman confessor and presbyter, also named Maximus, whose period of Novatianizing sympathy is revealed in *Epp.* 46 ff. A. d'Alès, *La théologie de saint Cyprien* [Paris 1922] 147 n. 1, is hopelessly confused: "Ce Maxime, prêtre africain, avait sacrifié dans la persécution avant de se rallier au parti de Novatien qui en fit un évêque." He is confusing him with Maximus, supporter of Privatus-Fortunatus.) The deacon Augendus, as an emissary from Novatian, appears to be Roman; separable, therefore, from the Carthaginian follower of Felicissimus? See n. 13 to *Ep.* 41. (It is certainly conceivable that the Carthaginian Augendus accompanied Novatus on his mission to Rome, dated to before Novatian's consecration, and is now returning to Carthage.)

It is a fair assumption that Novatian would have despatched this party to Africa promptly after his own consecration as bishop. He would need to move swiftly before loyalties had firmed. They will have arrived in Carthage, therefore, on any reasonable calculation, about the end of March or early in April 251, bearing their letter from Novatian.

3. For a (satirical) version of Novatian's consecration, see Cornelius *ap.* Eusebius, *H.E.* 6.43.7 ff. Cyprian is here being disingenuous about the actual sequence of events; he seeks to give the impression that he had heard that Novatian had been made bishop only after he had personally recognized Cornelius' own election. That is far from frank.

The vituperative tone of the (lost) letter from Novatian is revealed by *Ep.* 45.2.2. In Eusebius, *H.E.* 6.45, there is preserved a portion of a letter written by Dionysius of Alexandria, apparently answering a letter sent by Novatian upon his own election; it is likely, therefore, that this fragmentary letter from Dionysius reveals some of the contents of the (lost) letter despatched by Novatian about the same time to Cyprian in Carthage. Similar documents would indeed have gone out to all the major churches at this period. (The letter from Novatian referred to in *Ep.* 55.2.1 appears to be a later document. The dispute has by then entered into its disciplinary and doctrinal stage; its contents are revealed by the refutations in §§ 10 ff., 20 of that letter.)

4. *inclicitae et contra ecclesiam catholicam factae ordinationis pravitate commoti.* On *ordinatio,* see n. 18 to *Ep.* 1. For discussion, see P. van Beneden, *Aux origines d'une terminologie sacramentelle. Ordo, ordinare, ordinatio dans la littérature chrétienne avant 313* (Louvain 1974) 96 ff. On *catholicus,* see n. 8 to *Ep.* 25 (Cyprian would be thinking of the essentially *undivided* church). For Cyprian the basic illegality (*inlicitae*) of Novatian's *ordinatio* was chronological. The see was already filled by a candidate who had won approval both from his *plebs* and from his episcopal colleagues. Cyprian suppresses any reference to the interval when that approval had been withheld by many, pending unresolved doubts about the worthiness of that prior candidate, Cornelius: was he apostate [and therefore ineligible], or not?

5. *refutatis interim ac retusis quae* . . . The meaning of *interim* becomes clear only in the sequel: it refers to the (considerable)

interval whilst Cyprian and his colleagues awaited the return of their own African envoys bearing solid information on the events surrounding the elections. *Ep.* 55.10 ff. reveals some of the claims that the Novatianists were now alleging about Cornelius.

6. *ego et collegae plurimi qui ad me convenerant.* Does this refer to the Council meeting of 251 (see *Ep.* 43 n. 37)? The personal note (*ego, ad me*) makes one hesitant to agree; Cyprian could well be referring to an *ad hoc* group of episcopal advisers called in to come to a decision on receipt of the report of the African envoys. The matter needed clear guidance and firm decision, and they were ready and waiting in Carthage prepared to act so soon as they were able to do so. They may have stayed behind after the Council with this express purpose. Certainly in the next letter (*Ep.* 45) the Council has already convened, but its session appears to be already ended. The eventual recognition of Cornelius was made by individual, not collective, episcopal letters from Africa. This could be true of the time now referred to also.

The incident is described again in *Ep.* 48.2, which makes it plain, as Cyprian does not here, that no commitment to either side had in fact been made until the return of their own African envoys (*omnia interim integra suspenderentur;* cf. *ibid.,* §3.2: *retenta a nobis rei veritate,* on which phrase see M. Bévenot in JTS 28 [1977] 346 ff.). That could well bring the formal recognition of Cornelius down into the period May–June of this year.

7. *adventum collegarum nostrorum Caldoni et Fortunati quos ad te nuper et coepiscopos nostros . . . miseramus. Nuper* in Cyprian is a vague indicator of time, on this occasion conveniently elastic (cf. n. 27 to *Ep.* 1). Caldonius and Fortunatus, it appears from the language of *Ep.* 48.2.1, had been despatched by the Council meeting of 251 as its *legati,* and the Council had resolved (*quid nobis in commune placuisset*) meanwhile to suspend judgment on the question of the rightful bishop of Rome. That resolution could have been made some time ago (in the course of April?). The episcopal *legati* were instructed to gather written affidavits in Italy from the sixteen episcopal witnesses who were present at Cornelius' consecration; their inquiry especially concerned

Cornelius' *character* (*mores, vita, disciplina*), about which the Novatianist supporters had raised serious doubts (see *Ep.* 45.3.1). These witnessing bishops may well have dispersed to their sees by the time Caldonius and Fortunatus arrived (they reconvened for an Italian synod, ? held about the middle of the year, after the African synod). To gather their testimony at this date could have taken, therefore, some considerable time. The supporting documents they did in the end produce are described in *Ep.* 55.8.4 as *litteras honorificas et laudabiles et testimonio suae praedicationis inlustres*.

The custom of having comprovincial episcopal witnesses at a bishop's consecration is generously referred to by Cyprian in *Ep.* 67.5.1 as a *traditio divina et apostolica observatio*. See P. Zmire in *Rech. aug.* 7 (1971) 15 ff. and further discussion and references on *Ep.* 56.1.1.

On Caldonius, see introductory note and n. 1 to *Ep.* 24. Fortunatus (on the evidence available to us) is most likely to be identified with the Fortunatus *a Thuccabori* who appears as 17th in *Sent. Episc. LXXXVII.* A bishop Fortunatus also occurs in 11th place in *Ep.* 57 (out of 42 present), 9th in *Ep.* 67 (out of 37), and 14th in *Ep.* 70 (out of 31 or 32 proconsular bishops). These are all as likely as not to be one and the same person, identical with this bishop Fortunatus (but it must be noted there is a bishop so named in *Ep.* 56 *init.*, a second in *Ep.* 57 *init.*, as well as the *pseudoepiscopus* of *Ep.* 59.10.3: the name is *very* common). On the evidence, therefore, a reasonably senior and conveniently proconsular bishop (Thuccabor, modern Toukabeur, being situated some 65 kilometres west of Carthage). See Benson 580; J.-L. Maier, *L'épiscopat de l'afrique romaine, vandale et byzantine* (Neuchâtel 1973) 220 ff.; H. von Soden in *Königl. preussischen historischen Institut in Rom* 12 (1909) 260; J. Mesnage, *L'Afrique chrétienne. Évêchés et ruines antiques d'après les manuscrites de Mgr. Toulotte et les découvertes archéologiques les plus récentes* (Paris 1912) 161 f.

Cyprian used the opportunity of the despatch of Caldonius and Fortunatus to entrust to them copies of *Epp.* 41 and 43 for delivery in Rome (they were to call on Cornelius also—*ad te . . . et ad coepiscopos nostros*, §1.2). From Cyprian's point of view it was also important to establish at Rome his own standing and orthodoxy in the face of counterrumour, against the allegations and misrepresentations of Felicissimus and the five Carthaginian presbyters. He would be acutely aware that Novatus had been at work in Rome even before the date of the consecration of Novatian. Caldonius and Fortunatus also had with them a (lost) letter that urged in general terms unity and peace, see *Ep.* 45.1.1 (and n. 3 thereto), and also n. 14 to *Ep.* 54.

8. *rei gestae veritatem.* This is a nicely vague turn of phrase. They were to ascertain in particular the proprieties and chronological facts of the two *ordinationes* (observe the clear statement at the end of this letter §3.2 and cf. *Ep.* 48.4.1: *ordinationis tuae et origo necessaria et ratio iusta*) as well as the personal credentials of Cornelius. Understandably, Cyprian chooses not to reveal to Cornelius that his character had been so questioned, until events forced him to do so.

9. *supervenerunt vero Pompeius ac Stephanus collegae nostri qui et ipsi quoque ad instruendos istinc nos manifesta secundum gravitatem ac fidem suam indicia . . . protulerunt.* Hartel emends the mss reading *istic* ("here") to *istinc*, whereas the unemended text makes entirely satisfactory sense. For *istic* used by Cyprian = "here in Africa," *Epp.* 45.4.2, 48.2.2, 48.3.2, 51.2.1, 52.2.1, etc. *Istinc* would have to mean (unusually for Cyprian) "from there" (=Italy, for which *inde* is his normal usage). I have translated the unemended text.

As unemended, Pompeius and Stephanus would naturally be *Italian* bishops, sent as envoys to Africa by Cornelius to clear his name (they bring *indicia ac testimonia*). That would make sense of Cyprian's careful and placatory annotation here of their qualities as informants (*gravitas, fides*), whereas he does not so annotate the African envoys Caldonius and Fortunatus. Their designation in *Ep.* 45.1.2 as *boni viri et nobis carissimi collegae nostri* also fits in with the description of visitors from abroad (addressed to the one who sent them), whilst the African episcopal envoys remain simply in that same letter plain *collegae nostri* (§§1.1, 4.2). These two bishops could have been as well the vehicle for Cornelius' complaints, to which *Ep.* 45 is the reply; these complaints they perhaps diplomatically withheld until

Cyprian and his colleagues had made their decision in favour of Cornelius quite clear. We might indeed surmise that Cornelius had been stimulated to despatch to Carthage Pompeius and Stephanus by the extraordinary inquiries being carried out in Italy by the African envoys Caldonius and Fortunatus.

On Pompeius and Stephanus see Bévenot, *JTS* 28 (1977), 349 f., (against H. Koch, *Cyprianische Untersuchungen* [Bonn 1926] 122 n. 2); see also Nelke 59 n. 8 for an anthology of views. For the record, there is a contemporary Tripolitanian bishop named Pompeius, *Sent. Episc.* 84. See P. Romanelli in *Rendiconti della Pontificia Accademia di Archeologia* 4 (1926) 157 ff.; J. B. Ward-Perkins and R. G. Goodchild in *Archaeologia* 95 (1953) 7 ff. No African bishop named Stephanus chances to be recorded for this period.

The phrase *et ipsi quoque* provides some hint that Cyprian had got *indicia ac testimonia* from the other witnessing bishops as well, *via* Caldonius and Fortunatus (cf. n. 7 above).

10. *nec necesse fuerit audiri ultra eos qui a Novatiano venerant missi.* Cyprian fails to reveal that he and his colleagues did not in fact act solely on the testimony of Pompeius and Stephanus (as he here rather implies). They continued to wait for the arrival of Caldonius and Fortunatus until they produced their *relatio ac testimonia* (this emerges clearly from *Ep.* 48.4.1). It is also implied by *Ep.* 45.1.2: Cyprian recognized Cornelius *acceptis litteris tam tuis* (= of Cornelius) *quam collegarum nostrorum* along with the arrival of reports delivered by Pompeius and Stephanus in person. There, the *litterae . . . collegarum nostrorum* can be none other than the affidavits and *testimonia* from the college of bishops who were present for the election and consecration of Cornelius. Those affidavits were brought back in the hands of the bishops Caldonius and Fortunatus.

The word *ultra* here provides a slight giveaway. It presupposes that the exclusion of the Novatianist envoys, indicated in §1.1, had not been as absolute as suggested earlier. Diplomacy would have dictated that options should remain open.

11. *in statione.* The meaning here has been much discussed—is this a Council meeting, a liturgical assembly, or a congregational gathering? The last interpretation (where bishop and

people might meet for discussion and debate) seems the most likely in this present context. The word is also restored by Hartel in *Ep.* 49.3.1 (Cornelius); cf. the *conventus* described in *Ep.* 45.2.2. Discussion is in J. Schümmer, *Die altchristliche Fasten-praxis* (Münster i. W. 1933) 116, 118; V. Saxer, *Vie liturgique et quotidienne à Carthage vers le milieu du troisième siècle* (Vatican City 1969) 45; C. Mohrmann, *Études sur le latin des chrétiens* (3 vols., Rome 1961–1965) 3.328; G. G. Willis, *Further Essays in Early Roman Liturgy* (London 1968) 9; A. Hilhorst, *Semitismes et latinismes dans la Pasteur d'Hermas* (Nijmegen 1976) 168 ff., esp. 171.

12. Cyprian employs the first person plural in this passage (*a nobis et plebe, gravitati nostrae, collegae nostri... honorem*). That could suggest that he had present other assisting bishops (the *collegae plurimi* of n. 6 above?) at this *statio* (we might have expected, for example, *collegae mei... honorem* otherwise). Note the phases of Cornelius' acceptance as bishop: not only is he *delectus* and *ordinatus*, but he is also subsequently *laudabili multorum sententia comprobatus*, i.e., he receives "letters of communion" sent from fellow bishops which acted as a sort of subsidiary guarantee of a bishop's legitimacy. These letters are sometimes called *formatae*; see Optatus of Milevis 2.3. Cyprian is even prepared to allude to this custom, with purpose aforethought, as *divinae traditionis et ecclesiasticae institutionis sanctitas* in *Ep.* 45.1.2. Further discussion of this passage is in P. van Beneden, *Aux origines d'une terminologie sacramentelle. Ordo, ordinare, ordinatio dans la littérature chrétienne avant 313* (Louvain 1974) 82 ff.

13. Primitivus is chosen as messenger. He is of unusually high rank for this purpose, but his mission was not just that of courier of *Ep.* 44. The situation was delicate. Cyprian needed support himself to help combat his local dissensions, whilst the delays in recognizing Cornelius had been embarrassingly protracted. Primitivus is to act as a diplomatic envoy orally conveying to Rome the intricacies of the situation. Instead, however, he returned from Rome bearing the angry protest of Cornelius to which *Ep.* 48 is the mollifying reply. Primitivus ought to be a Carthaginian presbyter in every likelihood; see Thaninayagam 73.

14. *catholicae ecclesiae corpus suum scindere.* For *suum* there occurs the easier reading *unum.* Given the preoccupations of the context, that *unum* could possibly be right (with the 's' acquired by haplography).

15. *ostiatim per multorum domos vel oppidatim per quasdam civitates discurrentes. Civitas* seems to be used here in the sense of administrative district (major city plus surrounding territory), but that may be needlessly precise. Verbal parallelism with the preceding phrase may have suggested this particular wording to express simply "through various towns and cities."

16. *erroris scissi sibi quaerant comites.* Doubts are legitimately entertained about the correctness of the reading *scissi* (*sui* or *schismatici* are common emendations) in the sense required here ("divisive" or "schismatic"), but *Ep.* 46.1 provides a reasonably close parallel: *corpus unum discissa aemulatione lacerari.*

17. *si pacifice sibi ac fideliter consuluisse, si se adsertores evangelii et Christi esse confitentur.* Cyprian may possibly be echoing claims being voiced by the Novatianists; on the second clause, see n. 8 to *Ep.* 46 (on *nec putetis sic vos evangelium Christi adserere*). The precise meaning of the first clause remains a little elusive. Does *pacifice . . . ac fideliter* signify "as defenders of the faith and peace", with *sibi . . . consuluisse* approximating to "following their own consciences"? The apologetic emphasis thus obtained has its attractions.

LETTER 45

Contents: Cyprian reassures Cornelius that the bishops Caldonius and Fortunatus were sent to Rome in order to assist in healing the breach that had occurred in the Church there. Instead, however, the violence worsened so that an illicit head was actually set up outside the Church. But Cyprian, apprised of the truth, was able to recognize the rightful bishop and to direct his colleagues to do likewise. Indeed, his personal feelings had already been made clear when he read out before the assembly of clergy and people in Carthage the letter from Cornelius, with its tone of religious simplicity, but refused to read publicly the abusive and disrespectful documents that came from the Novatianists. That Caldonius and Fortunatus were acting against established custom in seeking testimonials from the bishops present at Cornelius' consecration in Rome was only out of interest for the brethren and for Church unity. Authoritative documents were essential in order to counteract the calumny of the opposing faction; they could then make their recognition of Cornelius' episcopate without remaining scruple. And to uphold Church unity, recalling to the right fold the wandering sheep, is the sacred duty of all pastors. Copies of documents are forwarded, to be read out to the brethren in Rome, fully informing them of the events surrounding Felicissimus and the presbyters associated with him in Carthage.

Date and circumstances: The general circumstances are set out in the introductory note to the previous letter, *Ep.* 44.

Cyprian is on the defensive. He has now heard complaints that Cornelius is making and seeks to defend himself against those criticisms. The complaints surround the irregular procedure of sending Caldonius and Fortunatus to Rome to initiate their inquiries.

The defence is threefold:

(1) Caldonius and Fortunatus by their personal presence, assisted by a (lost) persuasive document, were to help to reconcile the divided factions within the Church, a sacred duty (§1).

(2) Caldonius and Fortunatus were to gather testimonials not in order to stir up trouble (*non . . . novum aliquid quaerebamus*) but in order to be able to set the anxious minds of the brethren, in Africa, at rest (§3).

(3) Cyprian's own personal position was above reproach. Cornelius' letter which announced his appointment as bishop—but not communications from the Novatianists—had been given a public reading before local bishops, clergy and brethren (§2).

Cornelius may have written these complaints to which Cyprian is responding but there is no word of any (missing) letter. It is easiest, therefore, to suppose that they have been conveyed to Cyprian by travellers from Rome, possibly Pompeius and Stephanus, or even Caldonius and Fortunatus themselves. Cyprian is aware that Cornelius has refused to read out letters which Caldonius and Fortunatus had brought with them to Rome.

Cyprian is thus following up *Ep.* 44 with further explanations as they appear required. Primitivus is yet to come back from Rome, after delivering *Ep.* 44, bearing the letter from Cornelius to which *Ep.* 48 is Cyprian's reply. We ought, therefore, to be at a date closely following *Ep.* 44, perhaps mid-year 251. Cyprian also sends *Ep.* 46 (to the Roman confessors) and the covering note, *Ep.* 47, at this same time.

The attempts by Ritschl, *De epistulis* 19 ff. to place *Ep.* 45 *before Ep.* 44 do not convince. They are largely based on the fragile grounds that the tenses in §§1.2 f.—*adventantibus, direximus, mandavimus*—imply that Cyprian has only just now sent off his letter of recognition to Cornelius, immediately upon the arrival of Pompeius and Stephanus. Cyprian's tenses do not, however, permit such precise constructions to be built upon them. E.g., the preterite is used of correspondence of the past in *Ep.* 55.6.2: *Romam super hac re scripsimus;* cf. *Ep.* 26.1.2: *exemplum iam misi; Ep.* 27.2.1: *sub epistula priore transmisi; Ep.* 27.4: *litterae quae vobis proxime misi.* See also, *contra* Ritschl, H. von Soden in TU 25.3 (1904) 26; C. H. Turner, *Studies in Early Church History* (Oxford 1912) 121; Nelke 60 f.

1. *Cyprianus Cornelio fratri s.* For this *salutatio,* see n. 1 to *Ep.* 44.

2. *maxime sacerdotibus iustis et pacificis.* The epithets are not idle. Cyprian is about to defend his sending off Caldonius and Fortunatus on their investigative mission to Rome. The grounds he is to urge are that (1) he was only doing his duty to help restore unity and charity in Rome (that is, the work of peacemakers) and (2) in the interests of his fellow Christians, he had to ascertain who was the rightful bishop (that is, the work of justice).

3. *persuasione litterarum nostrarum.* This appears to be a lost letter, additional to the copies of the two documents that Caldonius and Fortunatus were to deliver (§4.2). It would have served to introduce Caldonius and Fortunatus as accredited

envoys and explained their mission; it was presumably addressed, with studious neutrality, to the presbyters and deacons of Rome (cf. *Ep.* 48.1.1). If it had aimed to smooth the troubled ecclesiastical waters (as is here claimed), it can only have urged peace and unity in the most general and diplomatically poised of terms. So far as Cyprian was aware, the issue could still be decided either way. See also n. 14 to *Ep.* 54.

4. The bias of this opening paragraph has been contrived with care—duty, justice, peace, charity, Church unity, persuasion, and counsel are motives and methods to which it is difficult for a churchman to raise objections. That must undercut Cornelius' criticism of the mission of Caldonius and Fortunatus, and of its major objective, which is held back, with tactical foresight, until later (§3.1).

5. *radicis et matris sinum adque conplexum recusavit.* A clause which defies neat translation. ("Of our original mother," suggests J. C. Plumpe, *Mater Ecclesia: An Inquiry into the Concept of the Church as Mother in Early Christianity* [Washington 1943] 93 n. 32. Cyprian reuses it in *Ep.* 48.3.1 writing on this same set of incidents. There is an arresting echo in Optatus of Milevis 1.11: *a radice matris ecclesiae invidiae falcibus amputati.*

6. *gliscente et in peius recrudescente discordia.* This appears to be a general reference to the worsening and then the ultimate breakdown in relations with Novatian. But there is a chance that the allusion might be specific. In *Ep.* 52.2 f. Cyprian views, with polemical effectiveness, Novatus' arrival in Rome as marking the critical point in this breakdown—causing the defection of the Roman confessors and the pseudoepiscopate of Novatian. Does his wording here (*in peius recrudescente*) suggest some such particular incident?

7. *adulterum et contrarium caput.* Although *adulter* regularly means "counterfeit," Cyprian exploits, characteristically, the moral overtones of *adulter* in its sense of "adulterous." Cf. *Ep.* 68.2.1 on these same events: *profanum altare erigere et adulteram cathedram conlocare.* Cyprian may well have been thinking of Christ as the Pauline *sponsus* of the Church (*Ephes.* 5.32: *sacramentum istud magnum est, ego dico in Christum et ecclesiam*); cf. *Ep.* 52.1.3 and n. 8 thereto.

8. *contra sacramentum semel traditum divinae dispositionis et catholicae unitatis.* I have interpreted this somewhat opaque phrase as an hendiadys, but it is possible to take its two parts separately and view *divinae dispositionis* as referring with particularity to the appointment of bishops. In Cyprian's next letter, *Ep.* 46.1.2, the elements here are rephrased as *contra Dei dispositionem, contra evangelicam legem, contra institutionis catholicae unitatem.* No doubt Matt. 16.18 f. would be the text Cyprian has in mind for such a *divina dispositio* and *evangelica lex.* See Fahey 309 ff.

On the use of *sacramentum* here, see C. A. Kneller in ZfKT 40 (1916) 676 ff.; A. d'Alès, *La théologie de saint Cyprien* (Paris 1922) 119 f.; J. de Ghellinck *et al., Pour l'histoire du mot "sacramentum,"* vol. 1 (Louvain-Paris 1924) 191 ff., where it is urged at 192 n. 1 that *divinae dispositionis et catholicae unitatis* should be construed not with *sacramentum* but with *adulterum et contrarium caput* ("a head which adulterates the catholic unity established by God"), a possible but awkward reading.

9. *acceptis litteris . . . collegarum nostrorum.* This ought to refer to the attestations of the bishops who were present at Cornelius' elevation to the episcopate, brought back by Caldonius and Fortunatus. Cyprian pointedly mentions, in passing, this document *before* he refers with richer emphasis to the arrival of Pompeius and Stephanus. He thus continues to give the diplomatically misleading impression that it was *their* arrival from Rome that was the vital factor which decided Cyprian's recognition of Cornelius. Cf. n. 10 to *Ep.* 44.

10. *adventantibus bonis viris et nobis carissimis collegis nostris.* Note the descriptive phrases of approval—not accorded those other trusted colleagues (who are African), Caldonius and Fortunatus; see n. 9 to *Ep.* 44 for discussion of Pompeius and Stephanus (Italian bishops in all likelihood). The friendly annotation might have a further adroit objective. Pompeius and Stephanus could well have delivered the complaints made by Cornelius to which Cyprian is now making the conciliatory reply. To praise thus Cornelius' agents would forward that task of conciliation; it makes the clear impression that for Cyprian's part no offence has been taken by Cornelius' criticisms.

By using the present participle *adventantibus*, does Cyprian wish to produce the effect "immediately upon the arrival of . . ."?

11. *litteras nostras ad te direximus*. From the next section (§1.3) it is clear that Cyprian is referring to his (lost) letter in which he has recognized Cornelius as bishop of Rome.

12. *secundum quod divinae traditionis et ecclesiasticae institutionis sanctitas pariter ac veritas exigebat*. A surprisingly fulsome description for the custom of writing letters of communion to newly appointed fellow bishops. But a conscientious Cyprian could not be expected to pen such a solemn and august document idly, without meticulous inquiry and punctilious hesitation. The phrasing is further analysed by U. Wickert, *Sacramentum Unitatis. Ein Beitrag zum Verständnis der Kirche bei Cyprian* (Berlin 1971) 29 f., n. 81.

13. *cum laetitia communi*. That is to say, there was general rejoicing that it was Cornelius who emerged from the evidence produced as the rightful bishop, exonerated from the charges laid against his personal *mores*.

14. This ought to imply that the Council in Carthage was no longer in session when the question of Cornelius' legitimacy was finally resolved.

15. *quamquam . . . iam tunc fratribus et plebi istic universae manifestatum fuisset*. From the description in §2.2 (see n. 18 below) Cyprian is referring to a solemn assembly (doubtless the Council of 251) where bishops as well as laity were present. *Fratres* here will, rather oddly, refer to clergy, whether Carthaginian or visiting, bishops, presbyters, and deacons, while *plebi istic universae* is the assembled Carthaginian laity.

The clause has sometimes been misconstrued; with the meaning of *quamquam* here ('and yet'), the subjunctive expression *manifestatum fuisset* should be made to bear its full effect. Cf. J. Schrijnen and C. Mohrmann, *Studien zur Syntax der Briefe des hl. Cyprians* (2 vols., Nijmegen 1936–1937) 2.109.

16. *episcopatus tui ordinationem singulorum auribus intimavimus*. Cyprian appears to have read out publicly Cornelius' (lost) letter which announced his own election (cf. §3.1). He does not, however, tell us what covering remarks (if any) he made at such

a reading. But the phrase of *Ep.* 48.3.2 (*retenta a nobis rei veritate*), along with the circumspect advice Cyprian was giving to Christian travellers going off to Rome at this time, *Ep.* 48.3.1, suggests that the occasion was kept, prudentially, as bland as possible: *singulorum auribus intimavimus* is as far as Cyprian can squeeze the facts in his defense. See P. van Beneden, *Aux origines d'une terminologie sacramentelle. Ordo, ordinare, ordinatio dans la littérature chrétienne avant 313* (Louvain 1974) 99 f.

17. Cornelius sent Fabius of Antioch an abusive letter on Novatian (*ap.* Eusebius *H.E.* 6.43.7 ff.). We may assume that this early letter from Cornelius was not written in such a vein, or Cyprian could well have suppressed it as he did the offensive Novatianist material; this letter of Cornelius' was probably written promptly after his election before the full controversy developed, and hence its tone proved acceptable to Cyprian. This letter is, therefore, to be distinguished from the (lost) correspondence from Cornelius mentioned in *Ep.* 49.1.3 which dealt with the *later* course of the schism (the schismatic confessors). On the letter from the Novatianists, see n. 3 to *Ep.* 44.

18. *in tanto fratrum religiosoque conventu considentibus Dei sacerdotibus et altari posito.* It is difficult to resist the conclusion that this must refer to the Council of 251 where in fact the assembled bishops sat in solemn conclave together (*considentibus Dei sacerdotibus*), whilst minor clergy and the local *plebs* would remain standing. For it was this Council of 251 which decided to suspend judgment whilst their envoys investigated the matter of the rightful bishop of Rome, as the language of *Ep.* 48.2.1 implies (*cum statuissemus collegae complures qui in unum conveneramus*). They would have done so after receiving—in quick succession—precisely such conflicting letters as Cyprian here reports. This present *conventus*, it appears, ought to be distinguished from the *statio* mentioned in *Ep.* 44.2.1 (where see n. 11)—at least Cyprian gives the impression, misleadingly or not, that the rowdy incident there described occurred *after* their recognition of Cornelius as bishop (*collegae nostri iam delecti et ordinati*).

Note the *altare* (the language suggesting some temporarily placed structure—Christian altars at this stage often being tables and made of wood: see ACW 39.225 for evidence and references); and compare, for a transportable *altare*, *Ep.* 59.18.1: *recedentibus sacerdotibus ac Domini altare removentibus.* Indeed, would this large gathering of several hundreds be held in some open-air area on the outskirts of town? On the theme of the sanctity of the altar, see F. J. Dölger in AC 2 (1930) 161 ff.

Such communications, it would appear, were regularly read out to the congregation in the course of the Eucharistic service. Compare Eusebius, *H.E.* 4.23.11: "In this same letter he [Dionysius of Corinth] also quotes the letter of Clement to the Corinthians, showing that from the beginning it had been the custom to read it in the church. 'To-day we observed the holy day of the Lord, and read out your letter [from Pope Soter], which we shall continue to read from time to time . . . as we do with that which was formerly sent to us through Clement.' " This was no setting for hearing calumniating and slanderous documents.

19. *fratres longe positos et trans mare constitutos.* Cyprian repeats the idea here in *Ep.* 48.3.2, which passage makes it quite clear that he is referring to his fellow North African Christians. Indeed, it is conceivable that by *mare* Cyprian is referring not to the waters between Italy and Africa but rather the sea on the African coastline. Travel to the distant Mauretanias as well as to the less remote cities along the littoral would be most expeditiously effected, wind direction permitting, by the coastal sea routes (*trans mare*).

20. *iactitare interim gestiunt . . . cum innocentiam destruere adque expugnare non valeant.* I have added in the translation "in the end" in order to bring out the effect here of *interim.* The bias of the smear campaign (the quotations which follow all inveigh against malice and slander) is here revealed. It was to "destroy innocence," i.e., to establish the ineligibility of Cornelius for the bishopric of Rome on the grounds of gross moral delicts.

21. Ps. 33.14; Ps. 49.19 f.; Eph. 4.29.

22. *haec fieri debere ostendimus si quando talia . . . legi apud nos patimur.* There is good manuscript support for reading *non* after *nos* (which renders much easier sense: *haec* more readily refers to "these precepts" than to "these evil slanders"). Discussion is in Benson 130 n. 2.

23. *et compresbyteri tecum considentis scripta.* I.e. from Novatian. On the seating of presbyters together, see n. 26 to *Ep.* 39.

24. *clero et plebi legi praecepi quae religiosam simplicitatem sonabant.* Cyprian is rounding off his point by repeating the notion with which he opened this section (cf. n. 15), but he has effectively held in reserve flattery of Cornelius' message (*religiosam simplicitatem*) until its end. In all probability the letter was but a simple note (see n. 17 and cf. *satis erat ut te episcopum factis litteris nuntiares,* §3.1). Presumably Cyprian gives instructions to his *lector* to read out the document.

25. *quod autem scripta collegarum nostrorum. . . desideravimus.* The turn of phrase makes it clear that Cyprian is answering an objection made by Cornelius; such a demand for testimonials was contrary to established custom, *veteres mores* (and, besides, it implied doubts about the veracity of the message Cornelius had sent). We do not know whether this complaint was made by letter or by verbal message delivered, for example, by Pompeius and Stephanus; the failure to mention an epistolary source suggests the latter.

26. *scribentium nobis inde collegarum nostrorum firma et solida auctoritas.* Cyprian reverts to the argument he has already prepared with some care in his opening remarks. His actions have been guided by the demands of fraternal charity, abroad (§1) as well as at home (here); cf. nn. 2 and 4 above.

27. *moribus ac vitae et disciplinae tuae condigna . . . testimonia.* The burden of the inquiry is made clear; it was about Cornelius' *mores* (his *innocentia,* cf. n. 20 above) rather than his doctrines. See also n. 8 to *Ep.* 44. On the word *disciplina* (which can, of course, be used to refer to teachings but in the present verbal collocation is more likely to refer to strict *adherence* to teachings), see n. 9 to *Ep.* 11.

28. *aemulis . . . et rerum vel novitate vel pravitate gaudentibus.* Cyprian could be referring not only to the Roman Novatian and his followers (*aemulis*), but also to their Carthaginian counterparts, the rebel Novatus (with Felicissimus and company) who had lent support to Novatian's cause; they are the subject of the next section.

29. *balabundas et errantes oves.* The reading *balabundas* has the

ms authority, though the word is found nowhere else, whereas *palabundas* (which is elsewhere attested) has weaker ms support but is used by Cornelius in his reply to Cyprian, *Ep.* 49.2.3 (*errantes et palabundos;* see n. 34 below). Note the discussion on such -*bundus* words in Aulus Gellius, *Noc. Att.* 11.15 (it emerges that the general force is one of intensification and that recent formations were not infrequent in Gellius' day); and for the present collection of words, compare Fronto, *Ad M. Caes.* 2.13: [*oves*] *palantes balantesque oberrant.* Hartel's text, allowing Cyprian some verbal novelty within expected limits, should probably stand. For discussion, see Watson 303 f.; Bayard 26; M. T. Ball, *Nature and the Vocabulary of Nature in the Works of Saint Cyprian* (Washington 1946) 267 f.

30. *litteras ... manu sua subscriptas.* The decisions (*singula placitorum capita*) of the African Council of 251 were sent on to Rome (see *Ep.* 55.6.1 f.; cf. Eusebius, *H.E.* 6.43.2 f.). This document now forwarded appears, however, to be distinct; it concerned one specific item on that Council's agenda. Cyprian's language emphasizes that the statement comes with all the authority of a signed episcopal document, presumably containing the *sententiae* recorded in the minutes of this item (cf. *Ep.* 49.2.1 [Cornelius]: *ut motum omnium et consilium singulorum dinosceres, etiam sententias nostras placuit in novitiam vestram perferri*).

Cyprian (*via* his commission) had himself excommunicated Felicissimus and Augendus; now the Council has confirmed that action and included the five rebel presbyters hitherto not formally expelled. Although Cyprian wishes to underline by his language the synodal (and not personal) character of the decisions taken, the third-person nature of the expressions here (*manu sua, miserunt, senserint, pronuntiaverint, eorum litteris*) suggests, nevertheless, that Cyprian himself, as a party to the dispute, had no part in the proceedings, and the subsequent drafting and signing. A convenient conjecture is that he was absent on a brief, and possibly diplomatic, trip to Hadrumetum during this particular inquiry; another possibility is that there was set up an investigative subcommittee such as the *consilium* of nine bishops—Cyprian himself not a member—that was formed at this same time to investigate the conduct of followers of Privatus, but the language of *Ep.* 59.15.1 militates against this possibility (*plures tunc adfuerunt*). Altogether it is possible to overstrain the third-person expressions. In *Ep.* 72.1.3 Cyprian refers to a document in the third person, which *collegae nostri ad coepiscopos . . . fecerunt*—and in which Cyprian himself heads the list of signatories.

Cornelius has failed to inform his Roman flock on the facts of the Carthaginian rebels (see below). To emphasize the serious-ness of the situation Cyprian is now forwarding a document that may have been drawn up some time previously; it would have served for general distribution around the dioceses of North Africa as well. Importantly for Cyprian, the document authori-tatively upheld Cyprian's position against the claims of his clerical rivals. We probably ought to draw the conclusion that, as Caldonius and Fortunatus were sent off to Rome from the African Council with documentation about Felicissimus and his *factio* but not with these Council minutes, the Council had not yet completed its findings on the case of Felicissimus when they departed. Cyprian now seizes the opportunity for sending a copy of their completed deliberations (to reinforce his further copies of *Epp.* 41 and 43: see n. 34 below).

For discussion, see Ritschl, *De epistulis* 11 f.; H. von Soden in TU 25.3 (1904) 37 f.; Benson 132; O. D. Watkins, *A History of Penance: Being a Study of the Authorities* (2 vols., London 1920; repr. New York 1961) 1.197; etc.

31. *auditis eis.* An ambiguous phrase—taken by some to refer to the letter now being enclosed (= "on hearing this letter") but, given that the phrase *ex eorum litteris* closely follows, that interpretation is unlikely. Cyprian is referring, therefore, to the hearing given to the rebels before this synodal inquiry (called *iudicium et cognitio* in *Ep.* 59.15.1).

32. *quae de eodem Felicissimo et de presbyteris isdem ad clerum istic, non et ad plebem scripseram.* The ungainly repetition *legenda . . . legi . . . iubeas* is deliberately emphatic; Cyprian wants public dissemination in Rome of the condemnation of Felicissimus and his *presbyterium*. Hartel adopts the reading *presbyteris isdem* whereas *presbyterio eiusdem* (which has strong ms claims) happily renders that touch of malice characteristic of Cyprian in polemi-

cal vein ("Felicissimus and his chapter of presbyters"); cf. A Vilela, *La condition collégiale des prêtres au troisième siècle* (Paris 1971) 275. The text is discussed by Bayard 355 f.

Clearly the letter *ad plebem* on this issue would be *Ep.* 43 (where see n. 1). What is the letter addressed *ad clerum?* On the topics mentioned we have only *Ep.* 41 which is addressed to two bishops and two presbyters who are in Carthage (*istic*). We might have expected *ad clerum*, however, to refer to a letter sent generally to the presbyters and deacons there; but unless there was a letter parallel to the one addressed to his *plebs* written at the same time as *Ep.* 43—and it has left no trace—we ought to conclude that *Ep.* 41 (written, indeed, to "clergy in Carthage") is the letter to which Cyprian here refers. It was in fact to be *delivered* to the clergy of Carthage (*Has litteras meas . . . Carthaginem ad clerum transmittite, Ep.* 41.2.3). Cf. H. von Soden in TU 25.3 (1904) 37 f.; Ritschl, *De epist.* 12 f.

Were these letters really sent to Cornelius personally (*ad te . . . miseram*) at a time when Cyprian did not know for sure that Cornelius was the rightful bishop? Or were copies, more circumspectly, to be delivered to the Roman presbyters and deacons generally—and that included both Cornelius and Novatian (cf. n. 3 above)? Cf. Ritschl, *De epist.* 18 f. (the envoys from Carthage were to exercise their discrimination on the spot in Rome). Obviously word has come back to Cyprian (*via* Caldonius and Fortunatus?) that Cornelius would not read out these letters of Cyprian's which indicated Cyprian's episcopal authority (after all, Cyprian had yet to acknowledge Cornelius' episcopal authority).

33. *et ordinationem et rationem rei gestae. Ordinatio* is mistakenly interpreted by some (e.g., by R. E. Wallis in *Ante-Nicene Fathers*, vol. 5 [repr. New York 1919]) as "declaring your ordination," whereas Cyprian is referring to the events surrounding Felicissimus and his followers.

In this letter Cyprian has emphasized that he read out publicly Cornelius' letter and that he was the prime-mover in informing the North African *fraternitas* of Cornelius' vindicated claims to the episcopate. He is now, gently, remonstrating for some reciprocal services. Cyprian has ejected supporters of Novatian from Carthage; Cornelius must not harbour supporters of Felicissimus in Rome.

34. Cyprian's anxiety that Novatus should not stir up support against him in Rome is demonstrated by the unusual despatch of multiple copies (*exemplaria*) for distribution. His instincts are right; he has later qualms about the reception granted there to Felicissimus and his turbulent followers (see *Ep.* 59.2).

Mettius was also to deliver *Ep.* 46 and its cover note, *Ep.* 47. Nicephorus returned from Rome bearing *Ep.* 49 from Cornelius (*Ep.* 49.3.1 cf. *Ep.* 52.1.1). I do not know on what grounds R. B. Donna in *The Fathers of the Church* 51 (1964) 118, calls Nicephorus "a Roman acolyte."

LETTER 46

Contents: Cyprian urges the Roman confessors to return to the Church they have forsaken. They have acquiesced in the appointment of a second bishop in Rome and they have thus helped to divide the Church which should be, by divine ordinance, undivided, the Church which has so rejoiced in the glory of their confession.

Date and circumstances: The letter (together with its diplomatically-worded covering note, *Ep.* 47) was forwarded to Rome along with *Ep.* 45 (? mid-year 251) by the hands of the subdeacon Mettius. See introductory notes to *Epp.* 44 and 45. Some of the background circumstances to the composition of that *Ep.* 45 are now further revealed. Cyprian was already well aware (*via* the messengers who conveyed Cornelius' complaints if not earlier) that the prestigious group of Roman confessors continued to favour the appointment of Novatian over Cornelius, and those confessors included among them two Roman clergy as well (Maximus and Nicostratus, presbyter and deacon respectively). It is revealed by other sources that a third confessor cleric, the presbyter Moyses (now dead), had for a period been a supporter of Novatian also (Cornelius *ap.* Eusebius, *H.E.* 6.43.20; but see n. 1 to *Ep.* 28).

Cyprian is anxious not to give offense to so honoured and influential a group, a group which moreover had provided earlier its welcome and invaluable backing to his own disciplinary policies. He phrases his plea to them for a return to unity with some tact and caution, insisting on the principle of the essential unity of the Catholic Church whilst studiously avoiding altogether the particulars of the case. After all, Cyprian was himself vulnerable to the malicious charge that his own period of hesitancy and indecision over the recognition of Cornelius, from which he has only just emerged, had been not dissimilar in its divisive effects.

Other bishops are now writing to these confessors in similar vein. Eusebius, *H.E.* 6.46.5, reports the existence of a letter by Dionysius of Alexandria addressed "to the confessors there [i.e., Rome] while they were still in agreement with the opinion of Novatus (*sic*)" as well as another letter addressed to the people in Rome "On Peace." Had Cornelius' messengers solicited the despatch of such "letters of persuasion" (cf. *Ep.* 45.1.1)? To win the spiritual leadership of the confessors, models in heroic virtue, would be a major tactical victory in the propaganda warfare between the opposing sides. Novatian had already so exploited their advocacy (the universally disseminated letters to which they had given their endorsing signatures), and Cyprian claims in *Ep.* 51.2.2 the immediate and spectacular effect that the news of their return to the Church exercised on Carthaginian Novatianists.

Are these confessors still in prison (as some have suggested they may be, e.g., M. Bévenot in JTS 28 [1977] 356)? The situation is far from clear but the language of *Ep.* 54.2.2 (*posteaquam vos de carcere prodeuntes schismaticus et haereticus error excepit* ...) is most naturally—but not necessarily—interpreted to mean that they did not formally join the schismatics until they left their prison. They are in this letter clearly identified as being on the side of the schismatics; therefore, they are no longer in prison.

Moreover, it could be argued that they were physically present at the consecration ceremony of Novatian, which has already taken place (see *Ep.* 49.1.4: *ut paterentur ei manum quasi in episcopatum inponi,* where see n. 10). They must have been released from prison by the time of that event. And there is a further hint. They are never referred to hereafter, even in persuasive flattery, as *martyres,* only *confessores.* Contrast, for example, *Ep.* 38.4.2 (to these same Roman confessors when in prison): *vere martyres Christi . . . martyria vestra exempla fecisti.* The Roman confessors (we might very tentatively deduce) now no longer have any prospects of dying a martyr's death; they are out of prison. (Cf. E. L. Hummel in SCA 9 (1946) 32 f., and n. 1 to *Ep.* 15 on this distinction between *confessor* and *martyr.*) The arguments are not, of course, conclusive, and see further n. 15 to *Ep.* 49 and n. 7 to *Ep.* 54.

Cornelius *ap.* Eusebius, *H.E.* 6.43.5, describes Novatian as having the support of these confessors with him "right from the beginning" (κατ'ἀρχάς), that is to say, from late March or early April (see introductory note to *Ep.* 44). Cyprian was, therefore, probably aware of the side they favoured from the time that the mission of Maximus, Augendus, *et al.* first reached Carthage. He places the defection of the confessors after the arrival of Novatus in Rome: *qui de ecclesia illo incitante discesserant* (*Ep.* 52.2.2).

In the light of the contents of this epistle (there is already an *altera ecclesia,* an *alius episcopus* whom the confessors favour) it is strange to read by C. Saumagne, *Saint Cyprien. Évêque de Carthage. "Pape" d'Afrique (248–258)* (Paris 1975) 104 f.: "C'est leur autorité qui avait orienté le 'collège presbytéral' de Rome à porter son choix sur Cornèle (mars 251)." In fact, Moyses' is the only case Cornelius can cite for any repudiation of Novatian that can have been made by members of the group by that stage. See Cornelius *ap.* Eusebius, *H.E.* 6.43.20.

For the sequel see *Epp.* 49, 51, 53, 54.

1. *Cyprianus Maximo et Nicostrato et ceteris confessoribus s.* This group of Roman confessors was last encountered in *Ep.* 37. Since then (we can assume) the presbyter Moyses has died, to be

numbered among the martyrs (*Ep.* 55.5.2: *Moyse tunc adhuc confessore nunc iam martyre*). The deacon Rufinus (last heard of in *Ep.* 31) might also be presumed dead—at least he figures no more among the group. Cyprian here punctiliously avoids accrediting any clerical rank to his principal addressees (Maximus being a presbyter, Nicostratus a deacon), whereas he carefully includes clerical title when he next addresses Maximus, but that is after Maximus has been solemnly reinstalled in the Roman *presbyterium* (see *Ep.* 49.2.5). Nicostratus is obstinately to remain a staunch supporter of Novatian's (see n. 1 to *Ep.* 28 for assembled evidence and cf. n. 4 to *Ep.* 50).

2. *frequenter . . . ex litteris meis.* Notably *Epp.* 28 and 37.

3. *fraternitati conexae dilectionem.* Cyprian loses no time in sounding the keynote of his letter—*fraternitas conexa* is to be echoed by such expressions as *unitas, animum et corpus unum, pax, concordia, unanimitas,* in contradistinction to *discerpi, discissa, lacerari, discidium, separatis, scindi, ecclesia derelicta,* etc.

4. Cyprian indulges in a plenitude of alliteration and assonance to wring compassion for his piteous condition: *perculsi et paene prostrati pectoris maestitia praestringit.*

5. *contra Dei dispositionem, contra evangelicam legem, contra institutionis catholicae unitatem.* (*Dei* is added by Hartel; was it lost by haplography with the initial letters of the following word?) *Ep.* 45, written at the same time, has similar turns of phrase: *contra sacramentum semel traditum divinae dispositionis et catholicae unitatis,* cf. *divinae traditionis et ecclesiasticae institutionis sanctitas* (*Ep.* 45.1.2). All three phrases here are most likely designed to refer to the notion of unity as an essential feature of the Church, the dominant concept in the letter. Some, however, have interpreted the first phrase as referring to divine selection in the choice of bishops (on which see n. 9 to *Ep.* 3, and n. 6 to *Ep.* 43).

6. *discissa aemulatione lacerari.* On the unusual usage of *discissa* ("divisive"), see n. 16 to *Ep.* 44.

7. *in vobis saltem inlicitum istud fraternitatis nostrae discidium non perseveret.* Is the wording intended to suggest that Cyprian has but faint hope that other supporters of Novatian (such as the diehard Novatus and his followers) will be so readily amenable to the persuasion of dogmatic reasoning?

inlicitum ... fraternitatis ... discidium. Any verbal play intended? Overtones of sacrilegious divorce of parties who ought to remain indissolubly united?

8. *nec putetis sic vos evangelium Christi adserere.* Is Cyprian echoing a catch-cry of the Novatianists? Cf. *Ep.* 44.3.2 (of Novatianists): *si se adsertores evangelii et Christi esse confitentur.* Cornelius *ap.* Eusebius, *H.E.* 6.43.11, appears to provide a Greek equivalent, again used tauntingly, ὁ ἐκδικητής τοῦ εὐαγγελίονε—"This vindicator of the Gospel did not know that there should be one bishop in a Catholic Church...." Notoriously, the Novatianists prided themselves on their gospel reading: their watchword was *Legite et docete.* (*Ad Novat.* 8.5) and hence the jibe in *Ad Novat.* 2.8: *Novatiani apud quos scripturae caelestes leguntur potius quam intelleguntur* (? a parody in turn of Novatian's own words in *De trinit.* 25.2: *si umquam intellegerent aut intellexissent quod legunt.*)

9. *ea quae in commune tractanda sunt agere ac providere.* The terms are vague but elsewhere Cyprian can use them of mutual discussion and settlement of the vexed penitential and disciplinary issues, e.g., *Ep.* 14.4: *de his quae ... sunt ... gerenda ... in commune tractabimus.* The confessors should be lending their guiding counsel and salutary influence in helping to settle questions that are currently so agitating the Church.

LETTER 47

Contents: Cyprian advises Cornelius that he has composed a letter to the Roman confessors; Cornelius is to decide, after hearing its contents, whether it should be forwarded on to them or not.

Date and circumstances: We are manifestly dealing with a covering note which accompanied *Ep.* 46. The date is, therefore, very roughly, mid-251 (see introductory note to *Ep.* 46).

The caution with which Cyprian treads is noteworthy: Cornelius has been gravely offended already (see *Ep.* 45). Cyprian is

clearly anxious not to risk giving any further affront (that his
actions are dictated by duty has to be underlined), and he
certainly wants to avoid any possible misrepresentations of his
position (his stance had been ambiguous for an uncomfortably
long duration). The possibility of any hint of conspiracy between himself and his old allies, the Roman confessors, has to be
punctiliously eschewed.

Ritschl, *De epist.* 22 argues that *Epp.* 46 and 47 should be
placed after *Ep.* 48, claiming that Cyprian is now not on the
defensive, and that Cornelius is no longer suspicious. That is
hardly persuasive. Further discussion is in H. von Soden in TU
25.3 (1904) 26 f.

1. *Et religiosum vobis et necessarium existimavi.* There is a ms
variant *nobis* for *vobis* (confused commonly enough) which has
been adopted by some editors. But the tone of this letter is
deliberately personal; Cyprian is writing as one colleague to
another. Throughout Cyprian studiously uses the first person
singular. *Nobis* should therefore be ruled out here. The plural
vobis clearly refers generally to the Christians of Rome (as later,
in reference to Mettius: he is sent *a me ad vos*). Elsewhere in the
letter Cornelius is addressed personally, in the second person
singular.

2. *ad confessores qui illic sunt . . . litteras breves facere.* By an
aberration R. B. Donna in *The Fathers of the Church* 51 (Washington 1964) 119 n. 3, observes, "We do not have this letter." From
the description of its contents in §1.1, it must be identified as *Ep.*
46. On these confessors, see introductory note to *Ep.* 46.

3. *Novatiani ac Novati obstinatione et pravitate seducti.* For the
first time in the correspondence Cyprian specifically links Novatian with Novatus (on whom see introductory note to *Ep.* 43)
but he has been aware already of Novatus' machinations in
Rome (as implied by the anxiety revealed in *Ep.* 45.4.2, where
see n. 34). He is soon to expatiate in lurid detail on Novatus'
pravitates in *Ep.* 52.2, linking the period in which the confessors
sided with Novatian precisely to (and because of) the presence
of Novatus in Rome.

4. *ad matrem suam id est ecclesiam catholicam.* This precise turn

of phrase is unique in Cyprian, the *suam* being unusually emphatic. The phrase is discussed by J. C. Plumpe, *Mater Ecclesia. An Inquiry into the Concept of the Church as Mother in Early Christianity* (Washington 1943) 94 ff.

5. Mettius, along with Nicephorus, is the carrier of *Ep.* 45 and its enclosures (where see n. 34). It is the simple and economic hypothesis that he goes to Rome bearing *Epp.* 46 and 47 at the same time as *Ep.* 45.

LETTER 48

Contents: Cornelius has protested that as a consequence of Cyprian's visit to Hadrumetum the clergy there ceased to address him as bishop. Cyprian writes to assure Cornelius that the move was but temporary; it was taken on the solemn authority of a synodal decision and was to last only until they had received the fuller information which would enable them properly to recognize Cornelius as bishop. To their delight they are now able to do so. No insult was intended. He and Cornelius can now look forward to a future of harmony and unanimity in their government together of the Catholic Church along with all their other episcopal colleagues.

Date and circumstances: Cyprian has by now written to Rome formally recognizing Cornelius as bishop and warmly assuring him of his prompt loyalty, despite unseemly overtures from agents of Novatian (*Ep.* 44). On its way over to Rome is another letter (*Ep.* 45) in which Cyprian defensively attempts to mollify Cornelius who had taken umbrage at the presence in Rome of an investigative mission of two African bishops. See n. 1 below. Unfortunately, whilst letters of recognition are now due to arrive from all over Africa (*Ep.* 45.1.3; §3.2 below) openly welcoming Cornelius as the rightful bishop of Rome, there has turned up in Rome a letter (apparently delayed) from Hadrumetum (§1). Some time ago the church there had, in fact, jumped the gun and effectively recognized Cornelius in a letter addressed to him as bishop (in ignorance of the general decision of the African Council to hold fire), but they had been persuaded by Cyprian to withdraw that effective recognition in a second letter addressed, with studious neutrality, to the presbyters and deacons of Rome. By regrettable timing, that letter now arrives in Rome, after Cyprian might reasonably have hoped to have calmed the diplomatic waters.

Because of the affront which Cornelius had registered, Cyprian is now forced to reveal (as he has tried so far not to do) that there was indeed a stretch of time in which Cornelius' claims had formally, at a full Council of bishops, not been recognized (§2.1, with the clear implication that serious doubts were entertained about his legitimacy). Indeed (to prevent confusion among their distant flocks, §3.2) the full details of the schism were not generally disclosed, by synodal resolution (§3.2). Hitherto, Cyprian has been able to convey the impression that news of Novatian's opposition came only just as they gave their ready recognition to Cornelius and that any delay in recognition did not mean that they had not favored Cornelius and been convinced of his rights all along.

Though apologetic and embarrassed, Cyprian is still not without defensive resources. He stresses effectively the paramount value in Church government of *consensio* (§2.2), united action (*universi collegae nostri*, §3.2), *unitas* (§3.2), and *unanimitas* (§4.2). It was in obedience to *consensio* that Hadrumetum had written that second and offending letter; it was only that they might all, at the one and the same time, join in unity with Cornelius that they had all agreed to so delay their recognition; and God will see to it that in His Church the bishops He has chosen should govern together in harmonious unanimity.

In tactic, therefore, Cyprian emphasizes the positive values of the policy they have pursued and in particular its underlying principles and justifying success. There is no word of the opposition—even in heated condemnation—of Novatian who had offended so fundamentally against that basic principle of Church unity. Rather, it is towards the joy of the happy outcome that he is (tactfully) eager to rush, to the prospect of a future of harmonious Church government together. In that rush he manages to skate swiftly over some dubiously safe patches (e.g., see §3.2 and n. 17 below). All the same, the passionately held themes of the *De unitate*, a copy of which he is soon to send—or has recently sent—to Rome, emerge clearly as current preoccupations.

The date of the letter seems clear. It would follow close on *Ep.* 45, but with time for Primitivus to have journeyed to Rome, to have delivered *Ep.* 44, and to have returned with Cornelius' protest (see n. 1). The letter is to be located, therefore, in (?) mid-year 251, in close company with those two letters. See also Ritschl, *De epist.* 21 f.; Nelke 61 f.

C. Saumagne, *Saint Cyprien. Évêque de Carthage. "Pape" d'Afrique (248–258)* (Paris 1975) 165 ff. tries to date the letter much later, in the vicinity of autumn 253, because of the phraseology in §3.2: *nostra provincia habet etiam Numidiam et Mauritaniam sibi cohaerentes*, his argument being that in 253 + the three provinces were united militarily under a single *ducatus*, that of Octavianus. That is a totally implausible deduction from the phrasing, on which see n. 15 below. Saumagne goes on to propose [p. 167] that it was over the question of second baptism that the African church, and Hadrumetum, had been so disposed towards Cornelius: that is gratuitous fantasy—there is no evidence of any such dispute until the pontificate of Stephen.

Hereafter Cyprian shows himself staunchly and admirably outspoken in his loyalty to and support of Cornelius. But we are obliged to wonder whether Cornelius, after his experiences and the letters 44, 45, and 48, did not continue to harbour some suspicion and mistrust of Cyprian. Next year Cornelius was prepared to give ear to a rowdy collection of Carthaginian dissidents, old enemies of Cyprian's (see *Ep.* 59.2.1 ff.), an action which roused Cyprian to hurt, heated—and lengthy—indignation.

1. Primitivus conveyed *Ep.* 44 to Cornelius. It is the simple assumption that Cornelius sends him back on his return journey to Carthage with this (lost) letter of protest. *Epp.* 45 to 47 could still be on their way from Carthage to Rome, crossing this letter from Cornelius; Cornelius employs one of their bearers, Nice-

forus, to deliver his next letter to Cyprian, *Ep.* 49. See further n.
6 to *Ep.* 49 on this letter from Cornelius.

2. *de Hadrumetina colonia.* On Hadrumetum (modern Sousse
in Tunisia) on the coast some 120 kilometres to the SE from
Carthage, see Benson 606 f.; PWK 7 (1912) *s.v.* Hadrumetum
2178 ff. Its colonial status appears to date back a century and a
half to the period of Trajan, to judge by its official titulature of
colonia Concordia Ulpia Traiana Augusta Frugifera Hadrumetina.
For discussion (and reference to divergent opinion), see J. Gas-
cou, *La politique municipale de l'empire romain en Afrique procon-
sulaire, de Trajan à Septime-Sévère* (Rome 1972) 67 ff. On the
Christian antiquities of the town (including celebrated catacombs), see A. Leynaud, *Les catacombes africaines. Sousse-Hadru-
mète* (Sousse 1910); DACL 6 (1925) *s.v.* Hadrumète 1980 ff.; L.
Foucher, *Hadrumetum* (Paris 1964) 307 ff., 326 ff.; A. Ferrua in
Aevum 47 (1973) 189 ff. (on the inscriptions of the catacombs).
From the evidence of Tertullian, *Ad Scap.* 3.5, the Christian
community of Hadrumetum could boast of a martyr by the late
second or (more likely) early third century ("Adrumeticum
Mavilum")—see T. D. Barnes, *Tertullian. A Historical and Literary Study* (Oxford 1971) 267 ff.; A. von Harnack, *Die Mission und
Ausbreitung des Christentums in den ersten drei Jahrhunderten* (2
vols., Leipzig 1924) 2.903.

3. *Polycarpi nomine.* Bishop Polycarp had clearly been absent
from his diocese (§2.1 below). Was he at that time yet to get back
from hiding after the persecution? Or (more simply) was he still
in Carthage attending the lengthy deliberations of the Council
meeting there or even waiting behind after the Council meeting
was over to serve on any "executive committee" of bishops
formed to deal with the settlement of the Roman question on
the return of their special envoys (cf. introductory note and n. 6
to *Ep.* 44)?

Polycarp appears in third place in the *Sent. Episc.* of 256,
evincing a worthily curt *sententia* (*qui haereticorum baptismum
probat nostrum evacuat*). He appears in a similar senior position
at other meetings (third after Cyprian, *Ep.* 67; sixth after Cyprian, *Ep.* 70; can the Polycarp of *Ep.* 57 be the same—36th in a list
of 42?). See Benson 570 f.; H. von Soden in *Königl. preussischen*

historischen Institut in Rom 12 (1909) 254, 256; J.-L. Maier, *L'épis-copat de l'afrique romaine, vandale et byzantine* (Neuchâtel 1973) 383; DACL 9 (1930) *s.vv.* listes épiscopales 1284; J. Mesnage, *L'Afrique chrétienne. Évêchés et ruines antiques d'après les manu-scrites de Mgr. Toulotte et les découvertes archéologiques les plus récentes* (Paris 1912) 146 ff.

It seems quite unwarranted to conclude with A. von Harnack in TU 23.2a (1902) 33, that it was Polycarp who had caused the upset, being hesitant between Cornelius and Novatian, and supporting now one, now the other (cf. Benson 570 f.).

4. This is Cyprian's only known visit out of Carthage (disre-garding his period in hiding, and his later relegation to Curu-bis). It is tempting to surmise that the visit of Cyprian, with a very senior proconsular bishop as companion, was not acciden-tal. Had word come (perhaps *via* the Novatianists noisily lobby-ing in Carthage and vigorously proselytizing in the surrounding towns) that Hadrumetum had openly declared for Cornelius? It was necessary to bring Hadrumetum into diplomatic line (de-spite any consequential embarrassments); the conclusion of the issue could still well turn out to be in Novatian's favour. Cypri-an may have even interrupted his attendance at the Council meeting in order to make this trip—he appears to be absent from its deliberations for a period; see n. 30 to *Ep.* 45, and for further analysis, and speculation, see Benson 132 f., 570 f.

Liberalis, a very senior proconsular bishop (diocese un-known), appears first after Cyprian in the lists of *Ep.* 57 and of *Ep.* 70. He was not present at the meeting of September 256. See Benson, Appendix H, 565 ff.; H. von Soden, *art. cit.* n. 3 above, 256 ff.; J.-L. Maier, *op. cit.* in n. 3 above, 348.

5. *coepissent illuc ad presbyteros et ad diaconos litterae dirigi.* That is to say, they changed to a neutralist stand, studiously and pointedly avoiding any explicit recognition of Cornelius' claims to be bishop—or of Novatian's, for that matter. Cornelius must have learnt of the source of the change (i.e., Cyprian) either from the letter itself or from its messengers.

One might compare Eusebius, *H.E.* 7.30.3: the sixteen bishops report that when Dionysius of Alexandria wrote to Antioch he addressed his letter not to Paul of Samosata, the bishop, but to the community generally ("neither deeming the leader of the heresy worthy of being addressed nor writing to him personally, but to the whole community"): this was a diplomatic declaration of Dionysius' view of Paul as a heretic. See P. Nautin, *Lettres et écrivains chrétiens des IIe et IIIe siècles* (Paris 1961) 114 ff. The Roman clergy who composed *Ep.* 8 (addressed not to the bishop, Cyprian, but *ad clerum*) may have intended a similar sort of snub.

Coepissent could well be used with its sense of inception much attenuated, *coepi* being employed by Cyprian as an auxiliary in verbal periphrases. See Watson 240; J. Schrijnen and C. Mohrmann, *Studien zur Syntax der Briefe des hl. Cyprian* (2 vols., Nijmegen 1936–1937) 2.21 ff.; Bayard 99 f.

6. *nulla id levitate aut contumelia factum.* Cyprian proceeds to illustrate these two points. He emphasizes that they were acting on no less than the authority of a solemn episcopal resolution, agreed upon at a fully-attended gathering of bishops (*collegae conplures*): this was no idle whim. And their motives were of the highest: the search for the truth, the dictates of scrupulous consciences, the desire for unity and charity, and the importance of unanimity among the churches are to be given as factors behind the policy (esp. in §3.2 below).

7. *cum statuissemus collegae conplures qui in unum conveneramus.* This appears to be reporting action taken by the Council of 251: see *Ep.* 44 intro, and n.6, and *Ep.* 45 n.18.

8. *legatis ad vos coepiscopis nostris Caldonio et Fortunato missis.* Cyprian slips from the second person singular (e.g., *ad te litterae dirigerentur*, §1) to the second person plural; formally, the legates were despatched not to Cornelius but to the Roman community generally. Earlier, in less candid terms, he had spoken to Cornelius of their having been despatched *ad te* (*Ep.* 44.1.2); cf. *Ep.* 45.4.2: *ad te legenda. . . . miseram.*—On the mission of Caldonius and Fortunatus, see *Ep.* 44 n.7.

9. Cyprian now makes perfectly plain, as he has hitherto endeavoured not to do, that there was a formally agreed period when judgment was completely suspended on Cornelius' claims to the Roman bishopric. The envoys were to come back *rebus illic aut ad pacem redactis aut pro veritate conpertis: Ep.* 45 *init.* had

diplomatically and defensively stressed the former, peace-seeking, nature of the mission (where see n. 3).

10. See n. 3 above.

11. *ubi nos in praesentia venimus.* Hartel somewhat cryptically annotates: *in praesentia venire pro in praesens v. dictum videtur.* Apparently, therefore, he viewed *in praesentia* as temporal in reference (= for the moment, temporarily, briefly) rather than local, in which usage the phrase *in praesentia* is rather found (= on the spot). See further J. Schrijnen and C. Mohrmann, *Studien zur Syntax der Briefe des hl. Cyprian* (2 vols., Nijmegen 1936–1937) 1.142, 2.139.

12. *ut in nullo ecclesiarum istic consistentium consensio discreparet.* Should this rather be an emphatic purpose clause ("so that at no point should there be . . .")—Cyprian highlights unanimity as an overriding value to be sought and preserved in §§3.2 and 4.2 below? As I have interpreted it (a result clause), Cyprian, in his apologia, is sheltering behind concerted ecclesiastic *consensio,* at a safe estimate over a hundred bishoprics being represented by the African churches. Such a solidly united front makes a formidable line of defence.

13. *quidam tamen mentes nonnumquam et animos sermonibus suis turbant. . . .* This seems to be a generalized statement about rumour mongers rather than a specific reference to the rowdy peddlers of Novatianist propaganda who were actively touting support in Carthage (on whom, see *Ep.* 44. 1 ff.).

14. *nos enim singulis navigantibus, ne cum scandalo ullo navigarent, rationem reddentes, nos scimus hortatos esse ut ecclesiae catholicae matricem et radicem agnoscerent ac tenerent.*—As emerges from the next section (§3.2), the full confusion of the situation in Rome does not appear to have been divulged to the African Christians generally. Those who happened to be going across to Rome (*navigantibus*) at this period of uncertainty had to be alerted to the situation in more detail (*rationem reddentes*): they were so apprised individually (*singulis*), lest they suffer scandal on their arrival in Rome (or, possibly, *cause* scandal, by unwittingly espousing the wrong cause). They were discreetly warned to choose the party that represented the universal Mother Church; bland counsel to be sure—but consistent with the strongly

orthodox but nevertheless properly and cautiously neutralist stand which Cyprian is representing as the African position at the time. See A. d' Alès, *La théologie de saint Cyprien* (Paris 1922) 149 f.; M. Bévenot in JTS 28 (1977) 352 f.

On the arresting phrase *ecclesiae catholicae matricem et radicem*, see J. C. Plumpe in TAPA 70 (1939) 542 n. 13; *idem, Mater Ecclesia: An Inquiry into the Concept of the Church as Mother in Early Christianity* (Washington 1943) 96 f. (*ecclesiae catholicae* being probably an epexegetic genitive—they are to find their fostering mother, their root-church, which is the Church universal: see H. Koch in ZNTW 13 [1912] 165 ff.; *idem, Cyprianische Untersuchungen* [Bonn 1926] 76. Compare *Ep.* 71.2.2: *ad veritatem et matricem redeant*).

15. *sed quoniam latius fusa est nostra provincia, habet etiam Numidiam et Mauritaniam sibi cohaerentes.* Cyprian is not boasting: he is laying stress on the communication difficulties along the North African littoral (as he did similarly in *Ep.* 45.2.2:*fratres longe positos ac trans mare constitutos*, where see n. 19). *Provincia* here seems to mean area of episcopal authority; and it is worth noting that in this expression *nostra* could indeed include Cyprian's fellow bishops (as it does elsewhere in this epistle), Cyprian throughout stressing joint episcopal responsibility and authority for the actions taken. Nevertheless, within this area of episcopal authority and amongst these bishops, Cyprian did manifestly exercise a *de facto* form of leadership: he must have inherited such a role as a legacy from his predecessors. On Cyprian's use of the word *provincia*, see n. 14 to *Ep.* 27; and on Cyprian's nascent "metropolitan" status, see Ritschl, *Cyprian* 228 ff.; Monceaux, *Histoire* 2.11 ff.; G. Pell, *The Exercise of Authority in Early Christianity from about 170 to about 270* (diss. Oxford 1971) 333; C. H. Turner, *Studies in Early Church History* (Oxford 1912) 74 ff.; J.-L. Maier, *op.cit.* in n. 3 above, 246 ff.; etc.

On the Numidian church which was beginning to enjoy some separate corporate life of its own, see *Epp.* 62 and 70.

Mauritania here as elsewhere seems to be general for the two provinces (Caesariensis and Tingitana). There is little actual evidence for Christianity so far West, though Tertullian, *Ad*

Scap. 4.8, attests the presence of Christians there earlier in this century, and Quintus (*Ep.* 72.1.3) is a known contemporary Mauretanian bishop who has *coepiscopi* in his area. Mauretania does not figure in the earlier Council of Agrippinus (*Ep.* 71.4.1), nor in Cyprian's Council of 71 bishops in (?) spring of 256 (*Ep.* 73.1.2), but was represented in September 256 (*Sent. Episc. praef.*). It must have been particularly remote from Carthage. On early Christianity in Mauretania, see R. Thouvenot in REA 71 (1969) 354 ff.; Benson 607; Monceaux, *Histoire* 2.10 f.; O. Giordano in *Nuovo Didaskaleion* 15 (1965) 25 ff.; T. D. Barnes, *Tertullian. A Historical and Literary Study* (Oxford 1971) 280 ff.

16. *ne in urbe schisma factum absentium animos incerta opinione confunderet.* Ritschl, *De epist.* 16, strangely insists that by *urbe* Cyprian is here referring not to Rome but to Carthage: his fears were that Cornelius might favour the cause of Felicissimus and his following rather than his own. *Ep.* 45.2.2 *ad fin.* is very closely parallel in language and sentiment: *fratres longe positos ac trans mare constitutos incerta opinione confundant;* there the reference is explicitly to the *Novatianist* schism in Rome, not to Carthaginian dissensions, and should put the interpretation here beyond doubt.

17. *placuit ut per episcopos retenta a nobis rei veritate....* A frankly puzzling clause, raising a number of problems of construing and interpretation. Cyprian has just insisted on the communication difficulties of their far-flung *provincia* and the goal of avoiding needless confusion amongst the *absentium animos* in that *provincia:* any construing and interpretation must accommodate and explain that insistence.

(i) With what is *per episcopos* to be construed? It is extremely awkward if both *per episcopos* and *a nobis* depend on *retenta* (in the sense of "hold back"); for what is the distinction between the two? Many mss omit *ut*, in which case *per episcopos* might (unusually) be constructed with *placuit* to express part of the episcopally sanctioned plan. Otherwise, it would be neatest to place a comma after *per episcopos* and have that phrase picked up again and expanded later by *per omnes omnino istic positos* (sc. *episcopos*): it would thus be emphatically anticipatory.

(ii) What is the meaning of *retenta?* Its most natural meaning should be "held back," i.e., "suppressed" (as strongly argued by M. Bévenot in JTS 28 [1977] 346 ff.; cf. Ritschl, *De epist.* 15); that is to say, in the light of the problems of communication and out of charitable concern for the peace of mind of their flocks, the bishops agreed not to reveal the full story of the Roman disputes and schism until incontrovertible facts were available to them (so, too, in *Ep.* 45.2.2).

The difficulty here is that, clearly, many must have had *some* knowledge of the dispute. Cyprian had in fact divulged communications from Cornelius (*Ep.* 45.2.1), whilst Novatian's agents were actively lobbying in and around Carthage (*Ep.* 44.1 ff.). Perhaps it was intended simply to contain the area of potential confusion to where it could most readily be countered. In that case, Hadrumetum provides an example of the failure of such a plan.

An alternative possibility seems to be to take *retineo* in the rarer sense of "grasp" ("comprehend"), where the prefix *re* simply acts as an intensifier (cf. the examples of *repromitto* in Cyprian quoted in n. 26 to *Ep.* 10, and *retineo* itself in n. 11 to *Ep.* 31.) That is to say, "when the truth of the matter had been firmly grasped by us through the agency of our (envoy) bishops." For this sense see Blaise *s.v.* retineo (e.g., Augustine, *Contr. ep. Parm.* 2.2.4: *deum mentiri non potuisse fide certissima retinemus* = hold for certain). But such a construing does here appear somewhat forced and unnatural.

(iii) *rei veritate:* A studiously ambiguous turn of phrase to describe what was to be "held back." From Cornelius' perception, this might be read as innocently meaning the formal and open acknowledgment of his legitimate claims to the Roman episcopate, whereas the bishops in reality may have meant details of the scandalous schism, the poisonous bickerings, the unedifying vituperations occasioned by the dispute (cf. *Ep.* 45.2.2 and n. 17 there).

18. *per omnes omnino istic positos litterae fierent, sicuti fiunt.* Note the tense: "Letters of recognition" (on which see n. 12 to *Ep.* 44, and *Ep.* 45.1.2 f.) are only now being sent across to Rome. Little wonder Cornelius was ready to register affront on receiving that second letter from Hadrumetum (penned on Cyprian's

authority). He could still not be certain of the support of the African churches. (Benson 146 n. 2 gravely misunderstands the passage; he paraphrases: "Bishops should cause letters to be circulated among all in all directions here.")

19. On the testimonials sought from the sixteen bishops who had witnessed Cornelius' consecration, see *Ep.* 45.3.1 (and n. 25 there).

20. On Pompeius and Stephanus, see *Ep.* 44.1.3 (and n. 9 there).

21. *ordinationis tuae et origo necessaria et ratio iusta et gloriosa quoque innocentia omnibus nosceretur.* This tellingly reveals the grounds for hesitation, or complaint, about Cornelius. *Ep.* 55.8 f., 24 provides helpful glosses on the same issue.

Objection seems to have been bruited that Cornelius had himself improperly *sought* election (*nec postulavit nec voluit, Ep.* 55.8.3), forcing on his candidature (*non ut quidam vim fecit ut episcopus fieret*) when he was untrained and ill-qualified for the post (*non iste ad episcopatum subito pervenit, Ep.* 55.8.2). Not only that. It was apparently suggested that he had been elected invalidly, when the see was no longer vacant (*et factus est episcopus . . . cum nemo ante se factus esset, Ep.* 55.8.4) and that his choice had not had the proper support of clergy, laity, and comprovincial bishops. That deals with the *origo necessaria et ratio iusta* of his appointment: it did in fact originate *de Dei et Christi eius iudicio,* being confirmed in due process (*ratio*) by the enthusiastic *consensio* of His priests and people (*Ep.* 55.8.4). Compare *Ep.* 67.4.2: *sit ordinatio iusta et legitima quae omnium suffragio et iudicio fuerit examinata.*

But there was a further objection, viz., that Cornelius had a character morally unfit for the post (and was, therefore, ineligible): he was an apostate, he was *libelli . . . labe maculatus,* he was in sacrilegious communion with bishops themselves guilty of pagan sacrifices (*Ep.* 55.10.1). Now, his personal *mores, vita* and *disciplina* (*Ep.* 45.3.1), his *innocentia,* have been vindicated. With studied and compensatory flattery Cyprian employs the powerfully eulogistic epithet *gloriosus,* which he normally reserves exclusively for confessors and martyrs: soon he is in fact prepared to describe Cornelius even more positively, as *inter glorio-*

sos confessores et martyras deputandus (Ep. 55.9.2). (On *gloria* in Cyprian, see n. 6 to *Ep. 5*.)

Observe that there is no word of *doctrinal* differences and disputes between the two parties. On this evidence we ought to conclude that if these existed at this stage they cannot yet have emerged as major factors in the dissensions.

22. *ad lapsorum fovendam paenitentiam lenitatem.* The only possible hint in the three letters (*Epp.* 44, 45, 48) that there might be any disagreement between Cornelius and Novatian over penitential discipline for the lapsed. And clearly here Cyprian is thinking in general terms, of the disciplinary problems that lie ahead for all bishops, of the virtues they will need in confronting them, not of doctrinal positions in Rome particularly.

Observe that Cyprian regards bishops as not only chosen by God; they are directly inspired by Him (*Dominus . . . gubernanter inspirans*). See nn. 27 ff. to *Ep.* 16.

LETTER 49

Contents: Cornelius writes in haste to Cyprian to let him know the joyous news that the Roman confessors have seen through the imposture of Novatian and have returned to the Church. Preliminary word of their change of heart had come *via* peacemaking brethren. Then two of the confessors had themselves come forward to make known their intentions. A subsequent meeting between them and the Roman presbyters revealed the extent to which they had been duped. Accordingly, an assembly of visiting bishops and the Roman presbyters unanimously agreed upon the treatment they should receive (copy of minutes attached); the confessors then appeared before the assembly and presented their case. The people also being in agreement with the proposals, a full gathering of the Roman congregation was assembled and amid loud acclaim the confessors made their profession and resumed their places in the church, Maximus taking up his position as presbyter. Cyprian should see to it that news of these happy events should spread to all the other churches in order to reduce even further Novatian's dwindling following.

Date and circumstances: Niceforus left Carthage in (?) mid-251 bearing letters for Cornelius as well as *Ep.* 46 in which Cyprian urged the Roman confessors to cease from splitting the Catholic Church. See *Ep.* 45.4.3 and n. 34 thereto. Niceforus now returns from Rome delivering this letter, with news that the Roman confessors have indeed healed their breach with Cornelius (§3.1 below). Though Niceforus may have had to wait in Rome some time until he could report a happy outcome to the negotiations in train (cf. n. 21 below), we ought to be not too far wrong in placing these events (very roughly) in around about July or so, 251, say, towards end of July. (The opening chapter of *De lapsis*—sent over to Rome about this time, *Ep.* 54.3.4 and n. 15 thereto—could have been an allusion to the death of Decius [*ultione divina securitas nostra reparata est*], i.e., to about June of this year. That would help to clinch the timetable; but unfortunately this allusion could be a later literary embellishment added to the final version, or it may not be an allusion to Decius' death at all.)

This calculation assumes that Niceforus is on the *same* round trip, and on our information that seems a perfectly reasonable assumption. However, for all we know it could be a later trip, but there is nothing which compels us to think so. It is worth noting that up to this point the dispute between Cornelius and Novatian—so far as our evidence goes—has been about chronology, procedures of appointment, suitability for office. But when Cyprian writes back to the confessors on hearing of these events, it is obvious that there is now dispute between the two parties over penitential policy and that Cyprian is aware of the position Cornelius has taken on the issue. Cornelius would have made his stand clear by the Roman Council of 251, at which sixty bishops attended and many more presbyters and deacons (see Eusebius, *H.E.* 6.43.2); it took place *after* the African Council this same year (see *Ep.* 55.6.2). Cornelius must have held back the convening of his Council until his own position was reasonably settled and accepted: Novatian and his followers were condemned by it. It is possible, though idle speculation, that the confessors were in fact stimulated to seek reconciliation as a consequence of this Council meeting, after so resounding a defeat for the Novatianist cause by such an impressive gathering of the local clergy and hierarchy. This is not a logically compelling timetable, but it is feasible for these events to have all occurred in Rome by the "July or so" assigned to this letter, but we do not have the controls to be able to fix them more precisely. They should not be pulled down too late in the year, however (as some have placed them, e.g., B. Aubé, *L'église et l'état dans la seconde moitié du troisième siècle (249–284)* [Paris 1886] 74; cf. Monceaux, *Histoire* 2.35, 292: "vers la fin de la même année"); it is still the sailing season, with traffic freely coming and going across the seas (e.g. the new echelon of Novatianist emissaries to Africa announced in *Ep.* 50). *Epp.* 50 (also from Cornelius) and 53 (from the confessors) could well have come by the same bearer.

Discussion on this timing is in Nelke 68 ff.; Benson 159 ff.; H. J. Lawlor and J. E. L. Oulton, *Eusebius, Bishop of Caesarea. The Ecclesiastical History and the Martyrs of Palestine* (vol. 2, 1928; repr. London 1954) 230 f.; Ritschl, *De epist.* 22 f.; Duquenne 31 f.; A. von Harnack, *Geschichte der altchristlichen Literatur* (2 vols., Leipzig 1893–1904, repr. 1958) 2.352; H. Koch, *Cyprianishe Untersuchungen* (Bonn 1926) 110 ff.

Immediately noticeable in this letter is the score of expressions to designate the guile and deception perpetrated by Novatian (matched by the collection in Cornelius' fragments preserved by Eusebius, *H.E.* 6.43.5 f.). Such richness of abuse is not just gratuitous; the language helps considerably to exonerate the honest but simple confessors hoodwinked by such reserves of duplicity. For there is defensive tactic in the letter.

Cornelius is anticipating adverse reactions to his news. He prepares against those who would object to the conclusion of the proceedings, viz., the full readmission to communion of the erstwhile schismatics (§2.5). Not only is it made laboriously plain that this was no hasty and ill-advised decision, it was widely discussed, unanimously adopted, and enthusiastically executed by the whole Christian community, clergy and laity alike (§§2.1ff). But the confessors also—from their own courageous lips—themselves declared that their hearts had never left the Church (§2.4); there was no taint of heresy in them—they were merely the naive and innocent victims of Novatian's smart talk.

On the other hand, there could still lurk the undermining suspicion that the confessors had been overborne by Cornelius and steam-rollered by him into submission. Cornelius anticipates such subversion of the hoped-for effect of his news (§3.2) by making it abundantly clear that the initiative and enthusiasm all came from others, from honest Christians (§1.2), the confessors themselves (§1.3), the Roman clergy (§1.4). His own role is studiously hesitant (§§1.2 f.) and impartial (§2.1) and it is kept clear of the politics of the situation and the debates (§2.1). The proposals adopted are not his own, they are formed by unanimous consent (§§2.1, 2.3) and there are the marshalled *sententiae* to prove it (§2.1).

Cyprian's own letter to the confessors (*Ep.* 46) and any part it may have played in the reconciliation is ignored. The complicated and delicate negotiations that led up to that reconciliation may indeed have been in train well before it arrived in Rome and there were clearly many other letters coming in to the confessors in similar vein from around the world. This letter could be a sample of the type of reply that was hastily being despatched to the writers of those letters and to the leading churches round the world on these events. Cornelius is now triumphant enough not to feel the need to be particularly tactful towards Cyprian individually.

The procedures in the negotiations are of interest and bear some analogies to the process of submitting a petition or *libellus* to the Emperor. First of all, a preliminary and informal sounding of reactions (§1.2), then presentation of the *libellus* itself in person (Urbanus and Sidonius), to be conveyed *via* an agent or patron (*presbyteri*, §1.3). This is followed by a preliminary examination by lesser officials (§1.4), before it is examined by the Emperor/Bishop and his *consilium* (§2.1) prior to calling in the actual petitioners (§2.2). Compare F. Millar, *The Emperor in the Roman World (31 B.C.–A.D. 337)* (London 1977) 230 ff., 537 ff.; and see for further analysis P. Batiffol, *Études de liturgie et d'archéologie chrétienne* (Paris 1919) 121 ff.

Cornelius seems to have exploited to the maximum the publicity value of his prize: the actual reconciliation of the confessors is effected at a specially convened public congregational meeting which gives the appearance of having been skilfully stage-managed.

Cornelius has another and abbreviated version of these same events, addressed to Fabius of Antioch and preserved in Eusebius, *H.E.* 6.43.6 (and see n. 14 below).

The text of *Ep.* 49 is discussed by G. Mercati in *Opere Minori* vol. 2 (Vatican City 1937) 2.226 ff.

1. *sicuti ipsi ex suo corde profitentur, simplici voluntate venerunt.* Cornelius appears to be quoting or paraphrasing words used by the confessors themselves. In the verbatim report given in §2.4 they declare that their hearts have always remained with the church. Cornelius, in this short opening paragraph, is carefully providing a preliminary view of his basic line of argument: the Roman confessors were merely hoodwinked by Novatian's fast talk (cf. *loquacitas,* §2.4) into being absent from the church for a time. They were the innocent victims of *dolus, malitia, calliditas, malignitas, astutia venenata,* the object of verbs such as *circumvenio, decipio.* As such their *voluntas* was never contaminated, they were never polluted by the contagion of heresy. This will all lead naturally, and effectively, after elaboration, to the final section of the letter where they are received back fully into their communion, extraordinarily, without penitence or loss of status (see n. 18 below).

2. *fratres nostri probatae fidei.* It is possible, in the context, that *fidei* should be interpreted more generally—men of undoubted credit (one meaning for *fidei*), men on whose testimony one could rely. But men possessed of proven orthodoxy (another meaning for *fidei*), as well as of charitable concern for the church's peace and harmony, make more impressive mediators. The defensive touch in the letter is already beginning to emerge clearly. Despite agents of such sterling virtues, Cornelius still acts with sensitive and hesitant circumspection. His was no

hasty and ill-considered decision. Nor were the confessors brow-beaten into submission; all the initiative is left to them, and these virtuous men of good-will merely act as messengers of their change of heart.

3. *tumorem illorum horum mollitiam nuntiabant.* So Hartel's text (which I translate). With this reading it is an awkward, but not impossible, consequence that the confessors referred to here by *horum* become *illos* a line later in the same sentence. The emendation *tumorem illum* [attested variant] *horum mollitum iam* ("their old pride has now been mollified") holds attractions, therefore, and is textually explicable (*mollitiam* readily corrupted from *molit[um] iam*): it emphasizes the all-important change in the attitudes of the confessors. For discussion of the text, see G. Mercati, *art cit.* above, 2.232 f.

4. *illos repente esse mutatos.* For *repente* there is found the ms variant *penitus* ("so thorough a transformation"), a nice reading but with only weak textual support. See G. Mercati, *art. cit.* above, 2.233.

5. *adfirmantes Maximum confessorem et presbyterum * * secum pariter cupere in ecclesiam redire.* Hartel's indication of a lacuna seems unwarranted, equally the suggestion in his *apparatus* that an otherwise totally unattested *presbyterum Secundum* might replace the putative gap. Some editors insert after *presbyterum* the words *et Macarium* (derived from *Ep.* 51.1.1). This is not a necessity, the messenger (Niceforus) could verbally produce such an additional detail on delivery of this letter. Further discussion on the text here is in H. Koch, *Cyprianische Untersuchungen* (Bonn 1926) 112 f.

Note that with some anticipatory subtlety Cornelius is already prepared to designate Maximus *et presbyterum* (even allowing that this is reported speech). By contrast, Cyprian was careful to avoid any such reference to clerical rank in his *Ep.* 46 (where see n. 1).

6. *multa praecesserant ab eis designata, quae tu quoque a coepiscopis nostris et ex litteris meis cognovisti.* Note the unusual sense of *designata* (= perpetrate) which Cornelius reemploys in his next letter. It is not a Cyprianic usage. The main charges are rehearsed in the next section.

coepiscopis nostris. The *coepiscopi* should include the (Roman) envoys Pompeius and Stephanus, if not the African bishops Caldonius and Fortunatus (see nn. 7 and 9 to *Ep.* 44). That dates Cyprian's knowledge of the stance of the Roman confessors to at least the advent of Pompeius and Stephanus in Carthage (cf. introductory note to *Ep.* 46); but before then the Novatianist envoys (see *Ep.* 44.1 f.) can be expected to have vaunted the fact that they had such overwhelmingly prestigious adherents on their earlier arrival in Carthage. Little wonder, therefore, that the African bishops hesitated to give their allegiance to Cornelius.

ex litteris meis. The letter of protest brought by Primitivus could well have included indignant remarks about the disgraceful behaviour of the Roman confessors, with warnings to disregard the abusive and misleading letters to which they had lent their signatures. And there is a lost letter from Cornelius, delivered by Augendus, which alerted Cyprian to an impending second invasion of Novatianist emissaries. They could well have come armed with supporting credentials from the confessors—and Cornelius cautioned Cyprian, therefore, about their treachery. A less likely candidate is the letter from Cornelius referred to in *Ep.* 45.2.1 (where see n. 17).

*   For discussion, see A. von Harnack in TU 23.2a (1902) 8 f.

7. *a presbyteris quae gesserant exigerentur.* Hartel's suggestion of *eis ingererentur* ("reproaches for their performance were heaped upon them") for ms T's *eis ingrederentur* would relieve the difficulties here of *exigerentur* (are we to understand [*rationes eorum*] *quae gesserant exigerentur:* "an account of their actions was demanded. . . ."?). Observe how Cornelius studiously keeps himself above personal involvement in any exchange of reproaches or castigations: the meeting with the presbyters was an informal one. It acted as a preliminary hearing (before lesser magistrates, as it were) before a formally convened "diocesan synod" was summoned.

8. *per omnes ecclesias litterae calumniis et maledictis plenae eorum nomine frequentes missae fuissent....* The opprobrious flavour of Novatianist documents and their potential for disruption are described by Cyprian in *Ep.* 45.2.2 (Cyprian tactfully

avoiding there any reference to supporting confessors); *Ep.* 55.2.1 also bears witness to the effectiveness of Novatian's letters. Does Pacian possibly refer to one such letter when he talks of *Novatianus quem absentem epistola episcopum finxit, quem consecrante nullo linteata sedes accepit (Ep.* 2.3)? On such letters from Novatian generally, see n. 3 to *Ep.* 44, and see A. von Harnack, *op. cit.* in n. 6 above, 12 f. (adding Socrates, *H.E.* 4.28, on his circulating calumniating documents). Novatian (like Cornelius) clearly felt strongly the need to win wide and general recognition: this in turn suggests that he perceived for the Roman see a central role, as the *ecclesia principalis,* in the communion of bishops. Cf. J. Colson, *L'épiscopat catholique. Collégialité et primauté dans les trois premiers siècles de l'église* (Paris 1963) 95.

9. *tantummodo subscripsisse.* On *subscriptiones* to documents, see n. 16 to *Ep.* 9. Cornelius has chosen with care the example he reports. It illustrates nicely the honest simplicity of the confessors outwitted by the wiles of the scheming Novatian. The importance of these confessors' signatures is revealed by *Ep.* 55.5.1 f.: even after this disclosure Cyprian can cite the fact that Moyses (then confessor) gave his supporting signature to *Ep.* 30 as a knock-down argument for accepting the contents of *Ep.* 30.

10. *se commisisse quoque schismati et haeresis auctores fuisse ut paterentur ei manum quasi in episcopatum inponi.* I translate the first four words as Hartel prints them, but it would make better sense in the rhythm of the passage if we had here not an admission by the confessors but rather a further reproach levelled against them by the presbyters. Read, therefore: . . . *se commisisse: quodque schismatis* . . . ? For discussion, see G. Mercati, *art. cit.* above, 2.237 f.

Observe the rhetorically cumulative use of *schisma* and *haeresis.* On Cyprian's usage see *Ep.* 3 n.18, *Ep.* 43 n.38. It is unwise, therefore, to deduce simply and solely from the presence of the word *haeresis* here (*contra* M. J. Routh, *Reliquiae Sacrae* [2nd ed., 4 vols., Oxford 1846] 3.42) that a *doctrinal* rift over penitence had now opened up between the opposing parties. But see *Ep.* 52.2.5, *Ep.* 54.3 f. for evidence that disciplinary questions are in fact now emergent.

manum quasi in episcopatum inponi: on the imposition of hands in the ceremony of episcopal consecration see Hippolytus, *Apost. Trad.* 2. It is the attendant bishops who lay on their hands; and one of them, at the request of the witnessing clergy and faithful, lays on his hand, pronouncing the prayer of consecration. See V. Saxer, *Vie liturgique et quotidienne à Carthage vers le milieu du troisième siècle* (Vatican City 1969) 101; J. E. Stam, *Episcopacy in the Apostolic Tradition of Hippolytus* (Basel 1969) 19 ff.

Cornelius is careful to assign to the confessors a minimal and passive role at these liturgical proceedings; they simply failed to stage any resistance at the ceremony which is described with such satirical relish and verve by Cornelius to Fabius and is preserved in Eusebius, *H.E.* 6.43.8 ff. (the attendant bishops were three drunken rustics who, hung-over and befuddled, "were compelled by force to give him a bishop's office by a counterfeit and vain laying on of hands"). Further on these bishops in n. 7 to *Ep.* 50.1.1.

11. *placuit contrahi presbyterium. adfuerant etiam episcopi quinque, qui et eo die praesentes fuerunt, ut consilio firmato . . . statueretur.* This is a clear example of a "diocesan synod" strengthened by the presence of prelates who happened to be visiting Rome. (I suspect *firmato consilio* means here "with the council strengthened [sc. by their presence]" rather than, as it is usually interpreted, "with clear proposals formed.") Unlike the description of the earlier and informal hearing, the language now becomes more technical and formal. Would the meeting take place in the church-building around the benches of the *presbyterium?* Note that the laity become involved, but only by way of assent (not deliberation) and at the very conclusion of the process. Further discussion is in A. Vilela, *La condition collégiale des prêtres au troisième siècle* (Paris 1971) 383 ff.

Cornelius shows himself careful to underline the broad assent given the proposals about to be adopted and the punctilious caution and propriety with which they were formed. He does not figure himself as their prime-mover; he appears rather as the instrument of the enthusiastic *consensus* of others, his clergy and his people. The famous formulation of Cyprian to his clergy in *Ep.* 14.4 is pertinent for the role in which Cornelius is casting himself: "It has been a resolve of mine, right from the beginning of my episcopate, to do nothing on my own private judgment without your counsel and the consent of the people." Does the change in tense *adfuerant . . . qui et eo die . . . fuerunt* indicate that the five bishops had also attended the preceding meeting ("there had been in attendance . . . who were also present on that day")?

12. . . . *sententias nostras placuit in notitiam vestram perferri, quas et subiectas leges.* This appendix has, of course, not come down to us (similarly the *addendum* to *Ep.* 62). The concern to have Cyprian (and, therefore, the African churches, §3.3) so fully informed and in such detail is arresting. To parade thus the recorded *sententiae* of the ranks of the (forty-five) Roman presbyters, harmonious in their unanimity, would have powerful propaganda value: where Cornelius was, there also was the Roman church (cf. Cornelius *ap.* Eusebius, *H.E.* 6.43.11 f., for the same line of argument and the statistic of 46 presbyters, which would include the now reconciled Maximus). The document would also allay any lingering doubts about the genuineness of the reconciliation of the confessors, the adherence of the confessors being a key weapon in this battle (cf. *Ep.* 51.2.2 on the immediate effects in Carthage of their switch in allegiance). And anyone who might disagree with the Roman decision to reinstate the confessors, without reserve, in their communion would have before him this intimidating list of some fifty-one fully recorded views to the contrary.

The *Sent. Episc. LXXXVII* provide an immediate parallel for the procedures, for the type of document enclosed, and for the ulterior motives in having it drawn up and distributed. Cornelius *ap.* Eusebius, *H.E.* 6.43.21 f., provided Fabius of Antioch with a similarly impressive appendix: "At the close of the letter he made a catalogue of the bishops present at Rome who condemned the stupidity of Novatus (*sic*), indicating at once both their names and the name of the community over which each one presided; and of those who were not present, indeed, at Rome, but who signified in writing their assent to the judgment of the aforesaid, he mentions the names and, as well, the city where each lived and from which each wrote" (tr. J. E. L.

Oulton). There is further discussion in A. von Harnack, *op.cit.* in n. 6 above, 10 f.

13. An allusion to Matt. 5.8. This is the only biblical quotation in the letter; we can suspect that its quotation was not offhand. The Novatianists were now arguing that *they* were the pure wheat of the church, remaining uncontaminated by the tares of the penitents; see, for example, Cyprian's closely contemporary letter to these confessors on their reconciliation, *Ep.* 54.3.1 f. The confessors are now lending their spiritual authority to establish the counterclaim that the pure of heart are demonstrably to be found inside the communion of Cornelius.

14. *quos errantes et palabundos tam diu viderant et dolebant.* Are we to suppose a time-shift between the negotiations with the bishops and presbyters, and the subsequent convocation of this general congregational assembly? Cornelius writes of the former as occurring more remotely in time than the latter.

On the language here (*errantes et palabundos*), see n. 29 to *Ep.* 45. By this language Cornelius cleverly presumes the deep pastoral concerns that motivate the wishes of his people; we are made instinctively to approve of the *ingens populi suffragium* (§2.5) which puts an end to such pastoral distress. For pathetic effect the erring confessors have been lost "for so long" (*tam diu*). But in the description of these same events which Cornelius *ap.* Eusebius, *H.E.* 6.43.6, sends to Fabius of Antioch, the chronology—and desired effect—is otherwise: "[Novatian's tricks] they made known in the presence both of a number of bishops and also of very many presbyters and laymen, bewailing and repenting the fact that for a brief time (ὀλίγον χρόνον) they had left the Church under the persuasion of this treacherous and malicious wild beast." In that letter Cornelius is concerned to show that Novatian's trickery was never effective for long ("Know that now he has become bare and desolate, for everyday the brethren desert him and go back to the Church"). Manifestly, we are dealing with tendentious documents.

15. *quasi hoc die poena carceris fuissent liberati.* Cyprian exploits with heavy hand this sort of imagery in his letter to the reconciled confessors, *Ep.* 54, giving the same impression as this turn of phrase does here, that the Roman confessors were not clearly

identified as Novatianists whilst they were in prison but only upon their release See e.g., *Ep.* 54.2.2: *posteaquam vos de carcere prodeuntes schismaticus et haereticus error excepit. . . . illic enim resedisse vestri nominis dignitas videbatur quando milites Christi non ad ecclesiam de carcere redirent. . . .* See introductory note to *Ep.* 46.

16. *Cornelium episcopum sanctissimae catholicae ecclesiae electum a Deo omnipotente et Christo Domino nostro scimus.* Somewhat disingenuously, Cornelius allows the impression that this is a spontaneously generated statement; we are permitted to surmise, however, that at the least Cornelius approved of its wording. The phrasing leaves no room for overlooking the all-important divine basis of Cornelius' election as bishop. And the epithets attributed to the Church to which they avow Cornelius has been so elected do not appear to be idle. The confessors are identifying where the *ecclesia catholica* is to be found (i.e., with Cornelius), and by the superlative *sanctissima* they are now emphatically locating Holiness within Cornelius' (and not Novatian's) *coetus*. The word *sanctissimus* is exploited with similar effects in the *Sent. Episc. LXXXVII* (e.g., *sententia* 4: *secundum decretum collegarum nostrorum sanctissimae memoriae; s.* 8: *tanto coetu sanctissimorum consacerdotum;* etc.), and by Cyprian in *Ep.* 59.19.1: *florentissimo illic clero tecum praesidenti et sanctissimae adque amplissimae plebi.* A. A. R. Bastiaensen, *Le cérémonial épistolaire des chrétiens latins* (Nijmegen 1964) 28 is in error, therefore, when he claims "*Sanctus (sanctissimus)* n'est pas du vocabulaire de Cyprien."

17. *unum episcopum in catholica esse debere.* The language used by Cornelius *ap.* Eusebius, *H.E.* 6.43.11, is remarkably close: ". . . there should be one bishop in a catholic church" (ἕνα ἐπίσκοπον δεῖν εἶναι 'εν καθολικῇ ἐκκλησία).

18. *Maximum presbyterum locum suum agnoscere iussimus.* At this point in the ceremony, the above statement having been recited, Maximus may have—dramatically—at Cornelius' bidding resumed his actual seat in the *presbyterium.*

The elaborate procedures have all been leading up to this remarkable and exceptional conclusion. For in similar cases the contemporary rule was firm: if a cleric returns to the catholic fold after a period with an heretical or schismatic group, he can be admitted back only as a layman, losing his clerical status and then, normally, after a period of penitence. The African Council of *Ep.* 72.2.1 ff. spells this out in no uncertain terms (*cum revertuntur ut communicent laici,* §2.1). One of the bishops who assisted at Novatian's consecration was so treated by Cornelius himself (see *ap.* Eusebius, *H.E.* 6.43.10); the case of bishop Trofimus, also decided by Cornelius, is closely similar (see *Ep.* 55.2.1, 11.1f.)—his fault being described in terms of schism rather than apostasy. Lapsed clerics were treated with similar conditions of laicization (see e.g., *Epp.* 64.1.1, 65.1.1, 67.6.2 f.)

Cornelius has been preparing us all along for this unexpected outcome: fellow-presbyters, five bishops, the assembled laity, it is emphasized, were all of one mind on the matter. And the faith and hearts of those who had confessed Christ before men had not changed. They had been merely duped by an imposter (*"imposturam passi sumus"*); they brought no contagion of heresy with them. The episode bears eloquent witness to the strength of the following commanded by Maximus and his companions; such respected figures needed special handling.

The Council of Nicaea (can. 8) followed this precedent: the Pure (καθαροί) were granted similarly favourable terms of reconciliation (but including the laying-on of hands). See Hefele-Leclercq 1.1.576 ff. (with lengthy discussion).

And, for a later parallel, at the Conference of Carthage in 411 Catholics made the undertaking to Donatist bishops that *si . . . in sua communione potius veritas ostenderetur ecclesiae, honores episcopales eis non se negaturos, Brev. Coll.* 1.5. Further discussion is in Benson 165 f.; J. H. Bernard in H. B. Swete (ed.), *Essays on the Early History of the Church and the Ministry* (London 1918) 232 f.; R. C. Mortimer, *The Origins of Private Penance in the Western Church* (Oxford 1939) 39 ff.; S. L. Greenslade, *Schism in the Early Church* (London 1953) 149 ff.; M. M. Sage, *Cyprian* (Cambridge 1975) 255 ff.; etc.

19. *ceteris cum ingenti populi suffragio omnia ante gesta remisimus deo omnipotenti in cuius potestate sunt omnia reservata.* Note the *suffragium* of the people: that is to say, acclamation, shouts of approval. They could indicate, but bluntly, assent—or dissent. Compare Cornelius *ap.* Eusebius, *H.E.* 6.43.10 on the successful

intercession of the laity to allow reconciliation to a Novatianist bishop. Earlier, the schismatic Natalius rolled at the feet of the laity as well as of the bishop (Zephyrinus) and the clergy in his efforts to win readmission; see *ap.* Eusebius, *H.E.* 5.28.12.

The text as Hartel produces it raises some difficulties: most unusually *remitto* appears to have two dependent datives (*ceteris. . . . deo omnipotenti*). Not surprisingly, therefore, textual variants are to be found, most notably *ceteros cum ingenti populi suffragio recepimus* (or *recipimus*), *omnia ante* etc., which renders the easy sense: "The rest we welcomed back amidst thunderous applause from the people, entrusting all their past actions to the judgment of God."

Whatever the precise text, the implications are still tolerably clear. The rest were fully restored to membership of the community, but whilst the language is penitential in flavour no actual penitential ceremony seems to have taken place. After all, they had not *deliberately* sinned. The reservation of final judgment for God is not exceptional. Compare *Ep.* 30.8: *caute et sollicite subveniri, Deo ipso sciente quid de talibus faciat,* etc., where see n. 50 for other references. Discussed by H. Koch, *Cyprianische Untersuchungen* (Bonn 1926) 211 ff.; A. d'Alès, *La théologie de saint Cyprien* (Paris 1922) 285 f., n. 1; H. J. Vogt, *Coetus Sanctorum* (Bonn, 1968) 52 f., 118 ff.

20. *haec. . . . eadem hora eodem momento ad te per scripta transmisimus.* There is something to be said for reading *perscripta* ("written out", on which *eadem hora,* etc., depend) rather than *per scripta* ("we are sending, in written form," etc.). The fact that Cornelius interrupts the joyful celebrations to write out his account serves to demonstrate his eagerness to share the good news with Cyprian as promptly as possible.

21. *Niceforum acoluthum descendere ad navigandum festinantem de statione.* On Niceforus, see *Ep.* 45.4.3 and n. 34 thereto. How long has he been waiting in Rome, if he is still on the same round trip in which he delivered to Rome *Epp.* 45–47 and enclosures? *Ep.* 59.9.4 suggests a Roman messenger-acolyte might be delayed in Carthage for some time, awaiting further despatches (*accipiendis aliis epistulis a nobis detinetur*). On the epistolary convention of concluding with an allusion to the

waiting messenger and the adverse circumstances of composition, compare *Ep.* 75.5.1, 13.1 and see K. Thraede, *Grundzüge griechisch-römischer Brieftopik* (Munich 1970) 117; H. Koskenniemi, *Studien zur Idee und Phraseologie des griechischen Briefes bis auf 400 n. Chr.* (Helsinki 1956) 78 ff.

The text at *festinantem de statione* is most uncertain, *de statione* being a restoration of Hartel's from the *destinatione* of many mss. It is unwise, therefore, to see here with E. Dekkers in *Miscellanea liturgica in honorem L. Cuniberti Mohlberg* (vol. 1, Rome 1948) 241, clear evidence for early morning eucharistic services. On *statio* (if it is here correctly restored), see n. 11 to *Ep.* 44. The text is discussed by G. Mercati, *art. cit.* above, 2.234 f., who reads *adnavigandi destinatione,* but in favour of retaining some form of *festino* note Cyprian, *Ep.* 51.1.1: *festinato ad nos mittendo Niceforum acoluthum.*

22. *in isto populi coetu.* On the word *coetus,* compare Novatian's *extra sanctorum coetum* (*Ep.* 30.7.2) and *Sent. Episc. LXXXVII* 8 (Crescens of Cirta): *tanto coetu sanctissimorum consacerdotum.* Cyprian is inclined to use *plebs* instead of *populus.* * *Populus* by itself is not so commonly met in Cyprian, whereas it occurs three times in this letter; in Cyprian it means "God's collective people," not just, as here, the laity.

23. *has litteras puto te debere . . . et ad ceteras ecclesias mittere.* Cornelius is well aware of the potential for his cause in the news he is sending. He has won over the persuasive backing of the *sanctissimi* confessors, and Carthage stands at the communication centre for all the North African churches. The *debere* is a touch strong: he reveals himself anxious to ensure full dissemination.

24. *bene vale, frater carissime.* Cyprian does not employ this abbreviated and unceremonial formula of farewell. See A. A. R. Bastiaensen, *Le cérémonial épistolaire des chrétiens latins* (Nijmegen 1964) 19.

LETTER 50

Contents: Cornelius repeats his warning to Cyprian that five Novatianists are due to arrive in Carthage. Fellow Christians there should be alerted to their crimes and vicious characters.

Date and circumstances: This is a formal note, meant to be copied and distributed widely. It lists the names of heretical and undesirable characters African Christians should be on the look-out against. The note arrived by the same carrier as *Ep.* 49. If we are to believe the last-minute circumstances in which Cornelius describes his hastily writing *Ep.* 49 (see §3.1 of that letter), then this note ought to have been already in the letter-carrier's pouch before *Ep.* 49 was added to it and the messenger sped off.

Cyprian meticulously responds to both *Epp.* 49 and 50 separately, his replies (*Epp.* 51 and 52) carefully reflecting the tone and contents of the two different letters.

We have here a neat sample of ecclesiastical polemic in the swift character-assassinations of Nicostratus and Novatus. It was important for Cornelius' cause to discredit these Novatianist messengers, for they were coming to represent a church which claimed to be the haven for the pure and the holy. Cyprian picks up that disparaging theme with some relish in *Epp.* 52 and 55 adding cruelty, violence, and unnatural impiety to their (elaborated) depravities.

The text is discussed by G. Mercati, art. cit. in introductory note to *Ep.* 49, 2.231 ff. Pacian (*Ep.* iii) certainly had *Ep.* 52 and possibly this letter also before him (see ML 13.1064, 1065, 1076).

1. *huius scelerati hominis.* I.e., Novatian. Cornelius seems to affect horror at pronouncing the foul name of the heresiarch; he fastidiously eschews mentioning his name in all his extant letters. The forensic technique of "no-naming" in order to register hostility is Ciceronian, e.g., in *Pro Sest.* 15 ff. Cicero attacks three enemies at very great length, Clodius, Gabinius, and Piso in succession, without ever actually naming any of them. Cf. J. N. Adams in *Classical Quarterly* 28 (1978) 163 f.

2. *cum Maximus et Longinus et Machaeus inde fuissent expulsi.*
These three characters were encountered in *Ep.* 44.1.1 as Novatianist envoys sent to Carthage along with a certain Augendus
diaconus (who disappears from our view). Cornelius pointedly
omits Maximus' clerical rank of presbyter. In *Epp.* 44 and 45,
though Cyprian valiantly defends his dealings with these envoys, it is clear that their presence was still being actively felt in
and around Carthage at the time of writing those letters. Cyprian could, however, assert that on their arrival *a communicatione
eos nostra statim cohibendos esse censuimus* (*Ep.* 44.1.1). Is their
expulsion here anything more than such exclusion rigidly maintained? In *Ep.* 59.9.2 (on the same incidents) Cyprian himself
registers no further special action on his part: *Maximum presbyterum nuper ad nos a Novatiano legatum missum adque a nostra
communicatione reiectum.* Ultimately they withdrew, their mission unaccomplished, with Cyprian and most of his episcopal
colleagues having openly declared for Cornelius. Maximus was
later to return to Carthage, however, there to be found in the
following year (252 A.D.) as Novatianist bishop (see *Ep.* 59.9.2).

3. *sicut prioribus litteris tibi per Augendum confessorem tibi
significavi.* On this (lost) letter from Cornelius, see n. 6 to *Ep.* 49.
Observe Augendus *confessor.* Is he so designated in order to
distinguish him from the Augendus *diaconus* associated with
Maximus, Longinus, and Machaeus (*Ep.* 44.1.1), or is it simply in
order to register his special title of distinction? Probably the
latter. If he is *Roman,* as he appears to be, we have a rare
example of a Roman confessor and one who is on Cornelius' side
before the group led by Maximus *confessor et presbyter* has re-
joined the church (his journey having been in advance of *Ep.* 49
which hastily announced that news). He is being used in the
church's employ—but apparently not with clerical appointment—perhaps in much the same way as Cyprian took pains to
draw into the ranks of his clergy appropriate confessors (Optatus, *Ep.* 29; Aurelius, *Ep.* 38; Celerinus, *Ep.* 39; Numidicus, *Ep.*
40). There would be no little propaganda value for Cornelius in
being able to display the fact that he can command the respect
and loyal service of such a man of heroic faith, a confessor.

4. *putem Nicostratum et Novatum et Evaristum et Primum et*

Dionysium illo iam pervenisse. Primus and Dionysius are other-wise unknown; Nicostratus, Novatus and Evaristus are about to have their distinguishing crimes enumerated—and elaborated further by Cyprian where he can, in *Ep.* 52. We learn from *Ep.* 52.1.2 that this *Ep.* 50 reached Cyprian the day after this second invasion of Novatianist missionaries in fact landed in Carthage. We also learn (*Ep.* 52.2.2) that they started on their journey to Carthage before Maximus, Sidonius, *et al.* were so ceremonious-ly reunited with Cornelius' church. Did they leave Rome aware of the impending reconciliation (the culmination of long and delicate negotiations), being anxious to forestall, if they could, any damaging effects that the news might have on their cause when it got to Carthage (cf. *Ep.* 51.2.2)? Cyprian, with character-istic verve, puts it more dramatically, and metaphorically: the storm of Novatus having passed from Rome, the Roman confes-sors were then free to return to the haven of the church; see *Ep.* 52.2.2.

Given the close timing between the journey of these Nova-tianists and the reconciliation of the Roman confessors, it would look as if Nicostratus has by now openly dissociated himself from the peace-seeking negotiations of Maximus and his com-panions, and firmly decided for the Novatianist cause—as so he was to continue (see n. 11 to *Ep.* 28). In his reply, *Ep.* 52.1.2, Cyprian assumes he has been stripped of his clerical rank (*dia-conio sanctae administrationis amisso*). Novatus here appears iden-tified as a Novatianist supporter: we do not know if he ever switched back allegiances on his return to Carthage to support his formal presbyteral colleague, Fortunatus, soon to be ap-pointed a rival bishop in Carthage (parties of Felicissimus and Privatus). In *Ep.* 52.2.5 he is identified (by Cyprian) with a rigorist (Novatianist) position. See further n. 32 to *Ep.* 14; n. 4 to *Ep.* 41.

5. *patronae suae carnali cuius rationes gessit fraudes et rapinas fecisse.* Cornelius, it happens, echoes words used by Cyprian about Felicissimus' financial peculation (*fraudes et rapinas, Ep.* 41.1.1); he was sent a copy of that *Ep.* 41 (see n. 32 to *Ep.* 45).

The phrasing *patronae suae carnali* is a trifle unexpected. Are we to understand some implied contrast between the mistress who has freed Nicostratus from physical bondage (*patrona carnalis*) and the spiritual *patrona* of the church (who frees from the slavery of error and sin)? Cf. D. D. Sullivan, *The Life of the North Africans as Revealed in the Works of St. Cyprian* (Washington 1933) 21. In any case the implication is that Nicostratus is of freedman status. To his *patrona*, by law and by custom, he would still owe services, duties, and gratitude. Not only has he committed a grave crime before the law (that of embezzlement), he has abused into the bargain his position of trust and the benefits he has been granted by his *patrona*. For further reading on the Roman freedman, see J. A. Crook, *Law and Life of Rome* (London 1967) 50 ff.; A. M. Duff, *Freedmen in the Early Roman Empire* (2nd ed., Oxford 1958) ch. 3; K. Hopkins, *Conquerors and Slaves* (Cambridge 1978) 115 ff.; S. Treggiari, *Roman Freedmen during the Late Republic* (Oxford 1969) 68 ff., 215 ff. The Council of Elvira was to lay down the regulation not long hence that *liberti* could not be promoted to clerical rank whilst their *patroni* still lived (to exercise rights over them), can. 80. See Hefele-Leclercq 1.2.263.

The early church regarded *fraudes et rapinas* as a particularly grave delict. Some examples include Pliny, *Ep.* 10.96; Tertullian, *De pudic.* 19.25 and *Adv. Marc.* 4.9.6; Gregory Thaumaturgus, *Ep. canon.* 2 ff. There is a splendid example in Hippolytus, *Philos.* 9.12.1 ff.—the future pope Callistus, slave of the Christian Carpophorus, engaged in the banking business set up by his master—and who embezzled his deposits. See also F. E. Brightman in H. B. Swete (ed.), *Essays on the Early History of the Church and the Ministry* (London 1918) 359 ff.

If the alleged fraud dates to Nicostratus' diaconate, can he have been fully employed in the church's services (in the way Cyprian required in *Ep.* 1) whilst managing, it appears, the financial books of his *patrona?* See n. 21 to *Ep.* 1.

6. *ecclesiae deposita non modica abstulisse.* The accusation is not simply that he absconded with church funds used for charitable works and almsgiving; rather, he purloined *deposita*. This is glossed in *Ep.* 52.1.2 by Cyprian as *viduarum ac pupillorum depositis denegatis.* That is to say, the church acted as safe-deposit and trustee for the savings and incomes of widows and minors

and it was with these funds in particular, on which the weak and defenceless depended, that Nicostratus was alleged to have so wickedly decamped. A similar charge is to be levelled against Novatus (*Ep.* 52.2.5: *spoliati ab illo pupilli, fraudatae viduae, pecuniae quoque ecclesiae denegatae*) and Felicissimus (*Ep.* 59.1.3: *pecuniae commissae sibi fraudator*). It must be appreciated that to "deny a deposit" was one of the most shamefully dishonourable actions a man might perpetrate in the pagan Roman calendar of sins.

Pliny's famous letter (*Ep.* 10.96) already reveals this community role of the church in providing safe-keeping for deposits (*ne depositum appellati abnegarent*); Callistus was similarly entrusted with deposits from widows and brethren (see Hippolytus, *Philos.* 9.12.1). And an African council had earlier laid it down that clerics should not become the *legal* guardians of minors; this was apparently to avoid some of the financial and legal entanglements that could result from a formalized role for clerics as trustees of orphans. For the Roman legal arrangements on *deposita* generally, see J. A. Crook, *op. cit.* in n. 5 above, 209 f.; and on Christians in banking activities generally, see R. Bogaert in *Ancient Society* 4 (1973) 239 ff.

Embezzlement of church funds generally was a rich source for scandal and abuse. Examples are Polycarp, *Ad Phil.* 11 (the presbyter Valens and his wife embezzle church funds); Apollonius *ap.* Eusebius, *H.E.* 5.18.6 ff. (the Montanist prophets and martyrs indulge in robberies and in making gain from the poor, the orphaned, and the widowed); and see further n. 4 to *Ep.* 41.

Given his functions, a deacon was especially vulnerable to the charge of financial fraud. In the case of Nicostratus we need only suppose that he may have retained with him church funds entrusted to his care (after all, he no doubt considered he was with the church). Cornelius devotes most space to assassinating the character of Nicostratus: he was a confessor and still loyally supporting Novatian.

7. *Evaristum vero cum auctore schismatis fuisse.* So Hartel's text. It is an odd way of phrasing a charge, and there is much warrant for reading with G. Mercati, *art. cit.* above, 2.235; *cum auctor schismatis fuisset* ("seeing he was one of the instigators of

the schism"). Clearly Evaristus is an episcopal supporter of Novatian's; we know of at least three such in Italy (his consecrators)—Cornelius *ap.* Eusebius, *H.E.* 6.43.8 f. There is a chance, the level of likelihood depending on the correct reading, that Evaristus may have been one of these. See also on Trofimus at *Ep.* 55.2.1; H. J. Vogt, *Coetus Sanctorum* (Bonn 1968) 48 f.

8. Compare Cornelius *ap.* Eusebius, *H.E.* 6.43.10, on Novatian's consecrators: "One of the bishops not long afterwards returned to the Church, bewailing and confessing his fault; with whom we had communion as a layman.... And as for the remaining bishops, to these we appointed successors, whom we sent into the places where they were" (tr. J. E. L. Oulton). See also *Ep.* 68.3.1 on the (later) replacing of another Novatianist bishop, in Arles. Zetus is otherwise unknown.

9. *Novatus vero ea hic designavit malitia et inexplebili avaritia sua qualia illic apud vos semper exercuit.* The text here could well be faulty, many mss reflecting the words of *Ep.* 52.2.3 and recording *maiora et graviora* before *designavit*, with the consequential variation *quam quae* for *qualia*. See for discussion G. Mercati, *art. cit.* above, 2.231. This would render the sense: "he has perpetrated here graver and more serious crimes than those which he. . . ." Cyprian expatiates on the depravities practised by Novatus in Carthage at *Ep.* 52.2.5.

10. *duces et protectores.* Most translations overlook the ironical military overtones of the phraseology here.

11. *iste schismaticus et haereticus.* See n. 10 to *Ep.* 49.

12. *bene vale, frater carissime.* On this form of salutation, see n. 24 to *Ep.* 49.

LETTER 51

Contents: Cyprian responds with thankfulness to God at the glad news that the Roman confessors have returned to the Catholic Church, their brilliant honour and glory undimmed. His people, too, join with him in celebration at the happy return of the heroes who have now pointed the way for others to follow. This has meant that in Carthage already some who were led astray have now seen the light.

Date and circumstances: The letter manifestly responds to *Ep.* 49; it will follow closely on receipt of that letter (see introductory note to *Ep.* 49 for approximate dating to mid-251).

Cyprian avoids direct comment on the unusual step announced by Cornelius, the complete reinstatement of the Roman confessors (*Ep.* 49.2.5). He makes it more than abundantly clear, however, that he approves (see n. 5 below); after all, he had himself carefully left it open—for a time—for supporters of Felicissimus' *factio et seditio* to return to his following, without penalty and without recriminations, and that included five of his presbyters. And Cyprian can now report immediately successful results of that reinstatement, viz., return to the Church of Novatianist supporters in Carthage (§2.2).

1. *agere . . . maximas gratias . . . Deo patri omnipotenti et Christo eius Domino. . . .* Cyprian pays Cornelius the compliment of echoing closely an opening turn of phrase in *his* letter, *Ep.* 49.1.1: *Deo omnipotenti et Christo Domino nostro gratias agimus.*

2. *excepimus Maximum presbyterum et Urbanum confessores cum Sidonio et Macario.* Macarius does not occur in *Ep.* 49, though the expression in *Ep.* 49.2.2: *et plerique fratres qui eis se adiunxerant* certainly could allow for this additional member. As likely as not, however, the brief note *Ep.* 53 (from these confessors) came along with *Epp.* 49 and 50—and the writers of that note included, by name, Macarius. In the report on these events which Cornelius wrote to Fabius of Antioch, Cornelius lists the reconciled confessors as Maximus, Urbanus, Sidonius, and Celerinus (Cornelius *ap.* Eusebius, *H.E.* 6.43.6). The latter does not appear to be the confessor of *Epp.* 21 and 22, 37 and 39; could this Celerinus have had Macarius as an auspicious "christian name"? Cf. P. Nautin, *Lettres et écrivains chrétiens des IIe et IIIe siècles* (Paris 1961) 162 n. 1.

3. *schismatico immo haeretico furore deposito.* See n. 10 to *Ep.* 49 on the language here, the present formulation making it clear that *haereticus* is even more horrendous than *schismaticus* (cf. n.

38 to *Ep.* 43; n. 18 to *Ep.* 3) and explaining why, when the two words or their derivates are used together, *haeresis/haereticus* often comes, climactically, second. For further discussion see Bayard 182 ff.; Watson 294.

4. *nec temptarentur caritatis adque unitatis fide qui victi robore et virtute non fuerant.* The translation I give is the best I can make out of the text provided, but I am not altogether convinced that the Latin is sound here.

5. *ecce incolumis et immaculata laudis integritas, ecce incorrupta et solida confitentium dignitas.* Cyprian's sentiments here are couched both emphatically and dramatically, and for good measure he repeats the idea more than once in what follows: there can be no doubt (it goes by rhetorical implication) that the confessors have been rightly reinstated, unaffected as they are by the disease of heresy, to the contagion of which they unwittingly let themselves be exposed. Cornelius' message in *Ep.* 49 has been received and understood.

6. *summo ut scribitis gaudio et clerus et plebs.* Cyprian refers to the scene described in *Ep.* 49.2.3 ff., where Cornelius uses the term *populus,* not *plebs* (see n. 22 to *Ep.* 49). Benson 161 n. 1 mistakenly refers this to the Carthaginian church (and deduces, in the absence of bishops, that there the Council is no longer in session).

7. *ad litteras vestras quas de eorum confessione misistis laetatus sit omnis fratrum numerus.* The *confessio* here refers to the confessors' declaration quoted *verbatim* by Cornelius in *Ep.* 49.2.4 (where see nn. 16 f.). Cornelius uses the term *professio* to describe it (§2.5). For the use of *fratres* here (inclusive of both clergy and laity) cf. nn. 15 and 18 to *Ep.* 45.

8. An allusion to Luke 15.7.

9. *quod sibi communicationem confessorum sequi videretur.* An important incidental remark, highlighting the popular view that confession and martyrdom provided the guiding signs to the true Church (hence the strong need felt to refute claims made by non-orthodox groups that they could boast of their own *martyrs*). See also introductory note to *Ep.* 15. We can now appreciate the importance to Cornelius of winning over the allegiance of the Roman confessors. Cyprian goes on to claim that, as a

result of this news, among Novatianist sympathisers in Carthage *lux* [sc. of truth] *omnium pectoribus infusa est.* It is permitted to believe that the *omnium* is an exaggeration of hope. The Novatianist church in Carthage could certainly boast of its own bishop by the following summer (see *Ep.* 59.9.2). Cyprian is in fact responding to the aspiration voiced by Cornelius in *Ep.* 49.3.2.

10. *bonos et gloriosos Christi milites non potuisse diu aliena fallacia et perfidia extra ecclesiam detineri.* Cyprian's wording here strongly suggests that we should not pull the reconciliation of these confessors too far down into the second half of 251. Could he have used the expression *non . . . diu* of their period of estrangement if it had lasted embarrassingly all the time from late March throughout the summer and well down into the autumn of 251 (as some would place it)? See introductory note and n. 14 to *Ep.* 49.

LETTER 52

Contents: Cyprian assures Cornelius that he is alerting his brethren, as requested, to the iniquities of the recently arrived Novatianists, notably of Evaristus (seeking to create fellow castaways), of Nicostratus (seeking to escape from his guilt-laden conscience and to be able to adopt a pose as a true confessor), and above all of Novatus, (being driven mad with remorse for his very many crimes, which are enumerated). But despite his machinations the mercy of God will eventually secure the return of all those who have been planted in the Lord's commandments.

Date and circumstances: This letter is Cyprian's reply to Cornelius' *Ep.* 50 (as *Ep.* 51 was to his *Ep.* 49). As *Epp.* 49 and 50 arrived together (§1.1), Cyprian will have penned this reply at the same time as he wrote *Ep.* 51, that is to say, about mid-year 251. The letter is, in form, an extended commentary on *Ep.* 50. There Cornelius had specified the enormities of Evaristus, Nicostratus and Novatus. Cyprian deals with these three in turn, merely expanding with rhetorical amplitude the information provided by Cornelius on the first two (from Italy), but adding new and damning testimony on Novatus (from Africa).

To our thinking this prolonged invective, although colourfully executed and sustained with zest and verve, may seem tasteless and unfortunate, especially as Novatus was an old personal enemy of Cyprian's. But a glance at classical polemic (e.g., Cicero's *Philippics*) will quickly reveal that Cyprian is merely obeying the rules expected in rhetorical abuse; and R. G. M. Nisbet (ed.), *M. Tulli Ciceronis in L. Calpurnium Pisonem oratio* (Oxford 1961) Appendix VI, will disclose the standards of untruth allowable within the genre. Little wonder, therefore, that some passages (see nn. 15, 17, 19 below) have caused difficulties of credence or interpretation. *Mendaciuncula*, as Cicero calls them, were proper inventions for this sort of oratorical writing. But Cyprian is not just indulging his flair for verbal abuse. He is supplying what ammunition he can for the campaign to discredit the principal followers of Novatian. For to desecrate their image is to undermine their claims to be the church of the holy and the pure. It was all in a good cause, and he renders his services with some distinction. See also the discussion in H. J. Vogt, *Coetus Sanctorum* (Bonn 1968) 140 ff. ("Cyprians Polemik"). Furthermore, Cyprian had to go to some lengths to defend his earlier dealings with the previous Novatianist legates in Africa. By this letter he is also now assuring Cornelius in no uncertain terms of the reception and credibility which these newly arrived Novatianists will be receiving in Africa.

Cyprian's overall tone is sanguine. He even ends his letter (§4) arguing that the schismatics generally must be temporarily absent from the Church. That mood of confidence derives from the return to the Church of the Roman confessors.

Pacian exploited this epistle when composing his three anti-Novatianist letters, ML 13.1051 ff. Cf. n. 19 below.

1. *Et cum diligentia et cum dilectione fecisti . . . festinato ad nos mittendo Niceforum acoluthum.* A characteristic Cyprianic letter-opening; he proceeds to elaborate, chiastically, the services of

dilectio (good news) and of *diligentia* (warning news), referring to the contents of *Epp.* 49 and 50 respectively. On the messenger Niceforus, see n. 34 to *Ep.* 45, and *Ep.* 49.3.1 and n. 21 thereto.

2. *adversus Novatiani et Novati novas . . . machinas.* Cyprian does not wince from wordplay, especially as here the root *nov-us* came richly laden with connotations of anarchy, terrorism, revolution, and radicalism for the Roman ear. For similar wordplay with proper names, cf. *Ad Novat.* 2; *Ep.* 74.2.4: *necdum quoque Marcion Ponticus de Ponto emersisset;* and see further C. Mohrmann, *Études sur le latin des chrétiens* (3 vols., Rome 1961–1963) 1.289 ff. As so often Cyprian also exploits the military metaphors latent in his language, *machinas* signifying "siege-engines" as well as "machinations."

3. *haereticae pravitatis nocens factio.* That is, the party of five Novatianist emissaries announced by Cornelius in *Ep* 50.1.1.

4. *quibus et didicimus et docere adque instruere ceteros coepimus.* Cyprian neatly and diplomatically reassures Cornelius that his request to disseminate his words of warning (*invigiletur ergo ut omnibus episcopis nostris et fratribus innotescat, Ep.* 50.1.1) is being promptly implemented. Cyprian now goes on to reflect the format of *Ep.* 50.1.2 expatiating on the atrocities and depravities of the three Novatianists singled out by Cornelius.

5. For these (alleged) criminal activities of Nicostratus, see n. 6 to *Ep.* 50.

6. *quasi mutasse sit hominem mutare regionem, confessorem se ultra iactat et praedicat.* Note the proverbial expression, of which Horace's formulation is famous: *caelum non animum mutant qui trans mare currunt.* For other examples, see A. Otto, *Die Sprichwörter . . . der Römer* (Leipzig 1980; repr. Hildesheim 1965) 61 (no. 286). There is a similar neatly turned adage adorning the conclusion of §3: *quasi evasisse sit poenam praevenisse sententiam.* This letter is showing the signs of careful elaboration. Observe also the claims being made by this Novatianist Nicostratus to be a confessor: *pace* Bayard, we are manifestly dealing with the Roman confessor Nicostratus. See n. 1 to *Ep.* 28.

7. *Christi confessor nec dici nec esse iam possit qui ecclesiam Christi negavit.* We catch an interesting glimpse into the difficulties which the churches were especially experiencing in this

year: the church could not be defined simply and solely as the church of the confessors and the martyrs. It was nonetheless still important to claim the spiritual allegiance of the confessors and martyrs (Cornelius *ap.* Eusebius, *H.E.* 6.43.20, goes out of his way to assert that Moyses repudiated Novatian before his martyr's death). It was also important to deny (as here) the genuineness of the claims made by any rival. To blacken the character of such a claimant (again, as here) was a favoured technique. Compare Apollonius *ap.* Eusebius, *H.E.* 5.18.5 ff. (discrediting Themiso, Alexander, and other alleged Montanist martyrs): Anonymous *ap.* Eusebius, *H.E.* 5.16.20 ff. (refuting the claim made by Montanists that the presence of many martyrs is proof of the power of the prophetic spirit among them); *De unit.* 20 ff.

8. Eph. 5.31 f. omitting the words *et adhaerebit uxori suae.* See Fahey 480, 491 f. comparing a similar omission in Tertullian, *Adv. Marc.* 5.18.9. Cyprian now elaborates, by means of this proof-text, the proposition he has just stated, viz., that the confessor of Christ must be with Christ and *ipso facto* with His church. He signals the importance of the text cited for his argument by surrounding it with phrases of attribution, even adding (unusually) a further, emphatic variation: *sancta sua voce testetur.*

9. *Novatus . . . rerum novarum semper cupidus.* See n. 2 above on Cyprian's penchant for wordplay (*Novatus . . . novarum*) and see n. 32 to *Ep.* 14, n. 4 to *Ep.* 41 on Novatus' previous career in turbulence.

10. *avaritiae inexplebilis rapacitate furibundus.* Cyprian deliberately dilates upon Cornelius' phrase in *Ep.* 50.1.2 (*inexplebili avaritia*), exploiting a fashionable—*bundus* formation (cf. n. 29 to *Ep.* 45).

11. *quasi haereticus semper et perfidus omnium sacerdotum voce damnatus.* In this character-depiction Cyprian, for rhetorical effectiveness, uses *semper* three times. Its employment here is, however, rather inapposite. Strictly Novatus has been condemned locally but once, earlier this year at the African synod of 251: see *Ep.* 45.4.1 with n. 30 thereto. When swept along by abusive flow Cyprian steers his course for effects, little concerned by such constraining accuracies.

12. Observe the dating-indicators. The confessors did not join the Novatianist cause until Novatus was over in Rome (*de ecclesia illo incitante discesserant*). They were not formally reconciled until Novatus had departed from Rome. See n. 4 to *Ep.* 50.

13. *qui apud nos primum discordiae incendium seminavit*. So Hartel, but there is a persistent ms tradition which adds *et schisma* (in a variety of cases) before *incendium*. See *Ep.* 43.2.1 ff. rehearsing the events here alluded to (but there Felicissimus rather than Novatus is the focus of attention).

14. *in ipsa persecutione . . . alia quaedam persecutio nostri fuit*. For the sentiment here (echoing *Ep.* 43.2.2, 4.2), see n. 11 to *Ep.* 43. There is considerable ms support for reading *nostris* rather than *nostri*, but such a use of *nostri* = "our people" is unusual for Cyprian; cf. n. 10 to *Ep.* 18; J. Schrijnen and C. Mohrmann, *Studien zur Syntax der Briefe des hl. Cyprian* (2 vols., Nijmegen 1936–1937) 1.158.

15. *qui Felicissimum satellitem suum diaconum nec permittente me nec sciente sua factione et ambitione constituit*. A notorious passage. Has Novatus presumed to ordain Felicissimus a deacon, or has he rather assigned Felicissimus (already a deacon) to be his own diaconal assistant? There are several ingredients here which suggest the latter interpretation.

(1) The description of Felicissimus' activities in *Ep.* 41 strongly suggests, but does not by any means establish, that Felicissimus was already a deacon. See n. 4 to *Ep.* 41.

(2) The appointment here is rephrased at the end of this section (*adversus ecclesiam diaconum fecerat*). Unfortunately that does not help. Cyprian is there being demonstrably misleading; *fecerat* need not mean what it appears to mean. See discussion in n. 17 below.

(3) Cyprian viewed deacons as appointed specifically to be the servants of and to be at the disposition of their bishop. See n. 17 to *Ep.* 3. The bias of Cyprian's indignation here is accordingly personal—*nec permittente me nec sciente:* Novatus was interfering with and ordering about his servant, his minister.

If, however, Novatus had *ordained* a new deacon we might have expected a different sort of indignation and more vehement outcry. In that case, not only had the bishop not been consulted but neither had Novatus' fellow presbyters nor the other deacons, let alone the rest of the clergy and the whole body of the laity (contrast the cautious appointment even of lowly lectors in *Epp.* 38 and 39). And more than just consultation and permission was wanted of the bishop: the *ordinatio* ceremony required the imposition of the hands of the *bishop* alone; see Hippolytus, *Trad. apost.* 8; V. Saxer, *Vie liturgique et quotidienne à Carthage vers le milieu du troisième siècle* (Vatican City 1969) 80 f. Under such circumstances of illicit ordination Cyprian's language remains unnaturally tame. And it would also be implied by that language that if Cyprian had been consulted and given his permission, Novatus could have so ordained a deacon: that would require a clear parallel, which I have failed to trace.

In all probability, therefore, Novatus has appropriated for himself the services of Cyprian's deacon Felicissimus, and in that arrogation of a bishop's prerogatives lies for Cyprian, the bishop, the essential outrage of Novatus' usurpation (*nec permittente me nec sciente*). See n. 13 to *Ep.* 5, and n. 2 to *Ep.* 34 on the close association there can be between an individual presbyter and a particular deacon. Will Novatus have made this appropriation of Felicissimus' services after *Ep.* 43 (unmentioned there) but before his departure, not long afterwards, to Rome?

There has been much discussion. See, e.g., Benson 115 f.; J. A. F. Gregg, *The Decian Persecution* (Edinburgh-London 1897) 187 f.; P. A. Leder, *Die Diakonien der Bischöfe und Presbyter und ihre urchristlichen Vorläufer* (Stuttgard 1905) 237 ff.; Ritschl, *Cyprian* 173 f.; F. E. Brightman in H. B. Swete (ed), *Essays on the Early History of the Church and the Ministry* (London 1918) 402 f.; G. S. M. Walker, *The Churchmanship of St. Cyprian* (London 1968) 97 n. 69; A. Vilela, *La condition collégiale des prêtres au troisième siècle* (Paris 1971) 266 f., n. 59; etc.

There is some uncertainty with the text: there is manuscript evidence for reading *satellitem suum suum diaconum*, a reading which would emphasize Novatus' appointing Felicissimus as his own (instead of, properly, Cyprian's) deacon. I am unsure of the exact significance of the phrase *sua factione et ambitione* (obviously to stand in parallel contrast with *nec permittente me nec sciente*). Can Cyprian be playing with the primary and the extended meanings of the word *factio* ("by his own doing and contrivance")? Compare *fecerat/fecit* in n. 17 below.

16. *quoniam pro magnitudine sua debeat Carthaginem Roma praecedere, illic maiora et graviora commisit.* In the latter clause Cyprian could be reflecting Cornelius' own words in *Ep.* 50.1.2 (where see n. 9). The former clause might be forced to yield the proposition that, as likely as not, the Roman *church* also, like the city, was perceptibly larger than the Carthaginian church (a fact we might surmise on *a priori* grounds anyway). See Introduction in ACW 43.40 f.

17. *istic adversus ecclesiam diaconum fecerat, illic episcopum fecit.* Nicely pointed rhetorical effect, but how far is it accurate? In the second clause, certainly, *fecit* is misleading. There were three consecrating bishops of Novatian (Cornelius *ap.* Eusebius, *H.E.* 6.43.8 ff.); Novatus' role must have been as *agent provocateur* in the enterprise (one of the two procurers who secured the services of the consecrating bishops?). As *presbyter* he would also participate in the ceremony of consecration (cf. the Roman confessors as Novatianists *paterentur ei manum quasi in episcopatum inponi, Ep.* 49.1.4). But it is only in a removed sense that he can be truthfully said to have "made" Novatian bishop. This leaves ample room for doubt that the first clause may not be equivalently misleading: "making" Felicissimus deacon against the church *could* simply disguise appointing Felicissimus (already a deacon) to specific diaconal tasks within their splinter church, Novatus assuming a role and authority which belonged properly only to the bishop. As usual in Cyprian's polemic, factual specificity yields to verbal effectiveness.

18. For this catalogue of crimes, see n. 6 to *Ep.* 50. Cyprian chooses to see in Novatus' restless *furor* ("raving madness") his (classical) punishment for his enormities.

19. These charges are reasonably specific; we are left to doubt how far they may be figments of a fine lurid imagination. However, the very classical nature of the charges (unnatural *impietas* towards an ageing *paterfamilias,* the horrors of unburied

death, violent assault producing the abortion of one's own child) all suggest at the least a certain literary pedigree. Cyprian had been, professionally, a teacher of rhetoric.

Observe an incidental touch of the male-oriented society: the deaths of his father (not mother) and of his unborn son (not daughter) frame the charges and heighten the grossness of the impiety.

Novatus, a presbyter, at some stage was married, though we cannot tell if the alleged incident occurred before or after his ordination to the presbyterate. On married clerics at this time, see nn. 6 and 15 to *Ep.* 1. The nature of the assault on that wife (*uterus uxoris calce percussus*) puts Novatus in a special class of tyrannical monsters: the mad Persian king Cambyses kicked his pregnant sister-wife in her belly, causing her death in childbirth (see Herodotus 3.32); the emperor Nero in a sudden fit of anger similarly caused the death of his pregnant wife by a blow with his heel (see Tacitus, *Ann.* 16.6); the emperor Domitian forced his niece Julia to abort his child by her, as a result of which she died (see Suetonius, *Dom.* 22; Juvenal, *Sat.* 2.32 f.; Pliny, *Ep.* 4.11.6). And note the discussion by F. J. Dölger in AC 4 (1934), 54ff. (where, by a slip, he makes the offender not Novatus but Felicissimus). A blow with the heel (*calce*) may sound strange to our ears, but the Romans kicked with the heel, the toes being relatively unprotected.

Pacian made the most of this spectacular copy, e.g., *Ep.* 2.3: *Novatus, inquam, patre prodito, ecclesia derelicta, partu uxoris effuso; Ep.* 3.19: *post interceptam pecuniam pupillarum atque viduarum, miseri parentis et partus uxoris parricidam. . . .*

20. *damnare nunc audet sacrificantium manus cum sit ipse nocentior pedibus* etc. Observe the casual way in which Cyprian identifies the unyielding penitential stand now characteristic of the Novatianists. This is, however, the first time we meet a clear allusion to such a difference with Cornelius: events have moved swiftly (including the Roman Council of 251?). See introductory note to *Ep.* 49 and compare the companion passage in *Ep.* 54.3.1 ff. In the case of Novatus himself there is a startling volte-face from the (laxist) penitential position with which he was associated in *Ep.* 43 (esp. §§2.1 ff). Are his tergiversations possibly to be

explained in terms of a desire to follow "the church of the confessors"? For confessors associated with his earlier allegiance, see *Ep.* 43.2.1 f. *(corrupisse quorundam confessorum mentes).*

For this contrast between feet and hands, compare *Ep.* 64.4.1 f.

21. *hanc conscientiam criminum iam pridem timebat.* By itself this sentence could well be rendered: "He was long tortured by the fear that these crimes should become common knowledge." But the general context suggests a more subjective meaning for *conscientiam* ("consciousness"). For a useful study of *conscientia* in Cyprian, see Watson 283 n. 2. For the (vague) time-span of *iam pridem* in Cyprian, see n. 7 to *Ep.* 1.

22. *ut qui eici de ecclesia et excludi habebat.* There is some uncertainty whether the grammatical construction here implies compulsion ("he must be thrown out") or simply futurity ("he was going to be thrown out"). This question is discussed by Bayard 256 f.; J. Schrijnen and C. Mohrmann, *Studien zur Syntax der Briefe des hl. Cyprian* (2 vols., Nijmegen 1936–1937) 2.24 f.

23. *iudicium sacerdotum voluntaria discessione praecederet.* Note the plural *sacerdotum.* Was the inquiry to be held before a Council of bishops, therefore? If the imminent investigation was forestalled by the advent of persecution, was the case to come up on the agenda of a post-Easter Council meeting in 250? The case of Felicissimus *et al.* in 251 may provide some parallel: they were first excommunicated by a local church committee (including invited bishops), their sentence being later endorsed, after investigation, at the conciliar meeting of 251. See n. 11 to *Ep.* 41. A similar timetable may have been envisaged in the case of Novatus. For discussion see n. 4 to *Ep.* 1, n. 18 to *Ep.* 34. We ought to allow that some inquiry was to be held about Novatus; but we may still suspect that the *gravamen* of the complaints may have been rather on matters of indiscipline (he had opposed Cyprian's election as bishop) than of immorality.

24. *ut veteratoris perniciosum latus fugiant.* Another echo of Cornelius' words in *Ep.* 50.1.2: *lateri suo semper iunctos,* but Cyprian here is referring to Novatus, not Novatian. Cf. nn. 10 and 16 above. Once again Cyprian draws out military overtones in his language *(latus).*

25. *neque enim potest perire nisi quem constat esse periturum.* Cyprian's thinking here is that only the really wicked can and will persist as schismatics; the rest will, eventually, be drawn back and be reunited to the Church. For a re-formulation of the same argument, see *Ep.* 66.8.1.

26. Matt 15.13.

27. *solus episcopis derelictis cum schismaticis et haereticis in furore remanere.* Observe the very characteristic concepts of Cyprian's: to abandon the Church is essentially to abandon the bishops of the Church, and not to be with those bishops is to be beyond sanity and salvation (whether as schismatic or as heretic being insignificant in importance). On *cum schismaticis et haereticis,* see n. 10 to *Ep.* 49.

LETTER 53

Contents: The Roman confessors report to Cyprian that they have been reconciled with Cornelius and with all of his clergy amid much enthusiastic acclaim by the entire brotherhood.

Date and circumstances: There is nothing to suggest that this brief note from the Roman confessors was not penned at the same time as Cornelius was (he avers) dashing off his announcement of the same events, *Ep.* 49, and that it, therefore, was delivered to Cyprian by Niceforus along with *Epp.* 49 and 50. For (approximate) dating in 251 see accordingly *Ep.* 49 intro.

The function of the note was not only formally to respond to Cyprian's *Ep.* 46. It was also to give clear assurance from the Roman confessors themselves that the glad news as reported by Cornelius was indeed genuine and true. Even in so brief a document the emphases are pointed: (1) no recriminations are to be made about the past, (2) peace is made with Cornelius (now acknowledged as bishop) and with the *entire* clergy (*universo clero*), (3) these events are welcomed with popular, indeed universal, celebration (*universae ecclesiae, omnium caritate*). Cornelius had put stress on all these points also; this is a text of which he would have approved.

We can imagine similar notes were at this same time being widely disseminated from the now reconciled Roman confessors. Dionysius of Alexandria, for example, had written to them in their Novatianist phase. He also wrote them two further letters on their return to the Church (see Eusebius, *H.E.* 6.46.5). Was one of those two (lost) letters in response to a letter similar to this *Ep.* 53? Cyprian's response to this letter is *Ep.* 54.

1. *Cypriano fratri Maximus Urbanus Sidonius Macarius s.* Is it too subtle to see here and in the salutation with which the letter opens (*frater carissime*) a touch of the charismatic and privileged status which the confessors may well have perceived for themselves? They do not give Cyprian any clerical title (in earlier letters from Rome, *Epp.* 30, 31, 36, he was consistently entitled *papa*) and he appears to be placed somewhat on an equal footing with them. But, on the other hand, Maximus does not give himself his own clerical rank either (*presbyter*); and they show a distinct sense of etiquette in putting the bishop's name first in their address and themselves second. By contrast, the Carthaginian confessors who wrote *Ep.* 23 impertinently placed themselves first and their *papa* second (*universi confessores Cypriano papati s*). In fact, the Roman confessors may be responding strictly to the form of address of *Ep.* 46 to which this note is formally the reply. For further analysis and discussion, A. A. R. Bastiaensen, *Le cérémonial épistolaire des chrétiens latins* (Nijmegen 1964) 14 ff., 21 f., 24 ff.

On Maximus, Urbanus and Sidonius, see n. 1 to *Ep.* 28, n. 1 to *Ep.* 46; on Marcarius, see n. 2 to *Ep.* 51.

2. *omnibus rebus praetermissis et iudicio Dei servatis.* The phrasing is framed vaguely but Cornelius' letter, *Ep.* 49, makes clear what is intended. The confessors are reported to have requested *ut ea quae ante fuerant gesta in oblivionem cederent nullaque eorum mentio haberetur* (§2.2); and Cornelius distinctly echoes the confessors' sentiments here in his description of their reception back into their community, *omnia ante gesta remisimus Deo omni-*

potenti in cuius potestate sunt omnia reservata (§2.5). The agreement was to let bygones be bygones, and for God alone to pass judgment on them.

3. *quod . . . cum Cornelio episcopo nostro pariter et cum universo clero pacem fecisse.* The wording carefully includes Cornelius' status; he is now fully and explicitly acknowledged as their bishop in Rome. And trouble is taken to underscore the unanimity amongst the clergy of Rome over their return (*cum universo clero*). Cornelius exploits a similar line of propaganda with Fabius of Antioch, *ap.* Eusebius, *H.E.* 6.43.11 ff.: his church has the allegiance of all 154 Roman clergy. In fact *universus clerus* is a trifle tendentious: at least six presbyters are not included (Novatian, and his five supporting presbyters; see Cornelius *ap.* Eusebius, *H.E.* 6.43.20—do these include the Maximus of *Ep.* 44 n. 2, the deacon Nicostratus [see *Ep.* 50 n. 4] and possibly the deacon Augendus [see *Ep.* 44 n. 2]?).

On the other hand, the confessors themselves do not appear exactly contrite in this statement. They have placed the blame squarely on the *perfidia* and *loquacitas* of Novatian rather than on themselves (*Ep.* 49.2.4). They therefore emphasize the positive arguments for their return—the *pax* and *utilitates* that will beneficially accrue to the church. They are motives that may induce others to follow their lead.

On the vulgar Latin construction, *quod* + infinitive, used here, see J. Schrijnen and C. Mohrmann, *Studien zur Syntax der Briefe des hl. Cyprian* (2 vols., Nijmegen 1936–1937) 2.98 f. It is eschewed by Cyprian.

4. *cum gaudio etiam universae ecclesiae prona etiam omnium caritate . . . certissime scire debuisti.* The emphatic repetition and stress is unmistakeable: it should be absolutely clear that their return has been greeted with universal acceptance and universal popularity by the Roman brotherhood. Cornelius in *Ep.* 49 was at pains to underline the same message: he did not force the reconciliation himself—rather, the initiative came from others and their whole community, clergy and laity, enthusiastically pushed forward the cause. There is also in the background a suggestion of the notion that God's people are the spokesmen of God's will, the *vox populi* reveals the *iudicium Dei* (see n. 6 to *Ep.*

43 on this concept); that sanctifies the action that has been taken.

5. *oramus te, frater carissime, multis annis bene valere.* A noticeably un-Cyprianic subscription (both *oramus* and *multis annis* are uncharacteristic). This is discussed by A. A. R. Bastiaensen, *op. cit.* in n. 1 above, 19 f.

LETTER 54

Contents: Cyprian's former delight at the Roman confessors' stand for their faith has now been equalled by his jubiliation at their return to the Church. For that step is tantamount to another profession of faith, and they are returning to the true source of their glory, leading others, as they should, in the right direction for charity and peace. Cyprian's profound distress at being cut off from them is now at last at an end. They must not be scandalized by tares within the wheatfields of the Lord: they will be sorted out at the Lord's own harvesting. It is a wicked presumption of pride for men to seek to winnow and thresh themselves; rather, they ought to adopt moderate measures. A reading of the treatises *De lapsis* and *De unitate* will convey Cyprian's thinking on these matters. They will approve especially of the latter pamphlet as by their return they are enacting Cyprian's description of the unity of charity and peace which it contains.

Date and circumstances. The letter is Cyprian's delighted response to *Ep.* 53; it belongs in the company of *Epp.* 51 and 52, as his replies to *Epp.* 49, 50, and 53, respectively. See introductory note to *Ep.* 49 on dating to about mid-251. Cyprian will not have long delayed composing these replies after the receipt of such letters.

A notable feature of the letter is a plea for *mitis iustitia* (§§3.1 ff.), for tempered moderation in dealing with sinful men. This is supported by abundant biblical imagery—wheat and tares, winnowing fan and threshing floor, vessels of precious metals and vessels of clay, the Lord's rod of iron—and accompanied by liberal abuse of those who presume otherwise. Novatian and his party have now emerged with a definable ecclesiological and disciplinary position. Cyprian's present letter marks an important movement seen for the first time with sharp clarity in the correspondence: the visibly widening gap between the (primitive) conception of the Church as a society of saints and the (developing) view of the Church as a school for sinners.

There is unmistakeable reference to Cyprian's two treatises *De lapsis* and *De unitate* in §3.4. That is precious information for the approximate dating of those documents, but attempts to attain any finer precision stir up a whole nest of problems (outlined in n. 15 below).

1. *Cyprianus Maximo presbytero item Urbano et Sidonio et Macario fratribus s.* Observe *presbytero*, even though it did not figure in the *salutatio* of the letter to which Cyprian now replies (*Ep.* 53). With some diplomatic adroitness Cyprian manages to acknowledge formally but *en passant* the reinstatement of Maximus to his former clerical rank.

2. The reference is to *Ep.* 53.

3. Cyprian first wrote of those glad tidings and of those battle honours in *Ep.* 28.

4. *nec alieni erroris vel potius pravitatis participem fieri.* Cyprian cheerfully exploits sibilants and plosives for scornful effects. *Alienus* here seems stronger than merely "of another": cf. *Ep.* 51.2.2: *aliena fallacia et perfidia extra ecclesiam detineri.* Can he be intending the sense of "insane" (a variant of *furibundus* and the like)? Cf. *Ep.* 59.13.4: *illis percussa mens et hebes animus et sensus alienus est.* For the less violent sense of "unholy," "profane," cf. *Ep.* 69.2.1: *alienis et profanis; Ep.* 55.8.5: *quisque . . . profanus est, alienus est, foris est.*

5. *erant de acie tropaea referenda.* What are these *tropaea?* J. Carcopino in *Studi in onore di Aristide Calderini e Roberto Paribeni* (Milan 1951) 1.385 ff., and *idem, Les fouilles de Saint-Pierre et la tradition* (2nd ed., Paris 1963) App. I, 255 ff. esp. 273 ff. has argued that they are physical signs of blows, beatings, etc., i.e., the scars of sufferings, comparing, *inter alia*, Prudentius *Peris-*

teph. 5.397 ff. (of Vincent's *body*): *sed nulla dirarum famis / aut bestiarum aut alitum / audet tropaeum gloriae / foedare tactu squalido.* But C. Mohrmann, in VC 8 (1954) 154 ff. and esp. 161 f. argues convincingly for a fully metaphorical usage here. *Tropaea* signify virtually "the glorified confessors in person." They are to bring back the fruits of their victory, which is their honour and glory, to the true source of that victory.

6. *ecclesiae veritas et evangelii ac sacramenti unitas.* This is typically opaque and elusive Cyprianic phraseology where, as so often, a qualifying epithet, for emphatic effect, is transformed into an abstract noun. Particularly fugitive is the significance here of *sacramenti* in *sacramenti unitas.* De Ghellinck *et al., Pour l'histoire du mot "sacramentum"* (Louvain-Paris 1924) 1.164 ff. argue for "[unity in] the profession of faith [e.g. as at baptism]." It does not seem at all necessary to be so specific.

7. *vos de carcere prodeuntes schismaticus et haereticus error excepit . . . quando milites Christi non ad ecclesiam de carcere redirent.* The confessors appeared to have left their Roman prison heading straight for the Novatianist schism. Should that bring down their release to a time when the formal split was already effected (? late March 251, or so: see introductory note to *Ep.* 44)? Or rather on their release did they openly join the Novatianist side in the unseemly canvassing and electioneering that (it was later charged) preceded the appointment of the new pope? The latter seems more probable especially as they can be described as having supported Novatian "right from the beginning" (κατ' ἀρχάς, Cornelius *ap.* Eusebius, *H.E.* 6.43.5).

8. The allusion is to Matt. 13.25. Cyprian is soon to repeat the present argument and allusion in *Ep.* 55.25.1 in favour of more lenient treatment of sinners: it is only God on judgment day who can make the appropriate separation. The text had already been so exploited by Callistus; see Hippolytus, *Philos.* 9.12.22 f. There is a parallel argument in *Ad Novat.* 2.9: the Church is the ark of Noah *in qua non tantum munda animalia sed et immunda.* By contrast, Novatian clearly argued that the Church must be holy and that this can be achieved only by the holiness of its members. Of course Cyprian was elsewhere prepared to allow separation of the good and wicked before the

final day; and, against Cyprian, Augustine vigorously argued from the same parable of Matthew in favour of the Church's duty to root out (excommunicate) except when there is any fear of involving the innocent as well; see *Contra epist. Parm.* 3.13; *De bapt.* 4.12.18; *Contra Cresc.* 2.34.43; *Contra Gaudent.* 2.3.3 ff.; etc. In other words, we have here a fairly typical sample of Cyprian's somewhat opportunistic exploitation of his biblical text from which he drew metaphorically rich, rhetorically impressive, but not necessarily logically impeccable *ad hominem* arguments; cf. M. Bévenot in *Dublin Review* 228 (1954) 167; and on the history of the variable exploitation of this parable of the tares, R. H. Bainton in *Church History* 1 (1932) 67 ff.; J. S. Alexander in JTS 14 (1973) 512 ff. What is of importance here, however, is the clear implication that the Novatianists were already identified with the purist view of the church and the rigorist discipline for penitence against which Cyprian is now marshalling his arguments: see n. 13 to *Ep.* 49. The remark of Ignatius of Antioch to the Romans (*ad Rom.* 4.1) is justly famous on the present theme: "God's wheat I am, and by the teeth of wild beasts I am to be ground that I may prove Christ's pure bread" (tr. J. A. Kleist in ACW 1.82).

9. 2 Tim. 2.20.

10. An allusion to Apoc. 2.27 f.; cf. Ps. 2.9—There is the same congeries of references to "stubble" and "vessels" in *Ad Novat.* 1.6 f. Cyprian's illustrations here appear especially pointed as Novatian declared that he and his followers were gold (*aurum certe se suosque quos colligit esse pronuntiat, Ad Novat.* 1.6) and the Novatianists referred to the repentant lapsed as *ligna, faenum, stipulam* (cf. 1 Cor. 3.12), *Ad Novat.* 7.1.

11. John. 13.16. There follows an allusion to John 5.22, where Cyprian's text read: *pater . . . omne iudicium filio dedit.* See Fahey 381.

12. Cyprian continues to exploit the allusion to Matt. 13.24 ff. (see n. 8 above) with which he opened this section of biblical reflections, along with Matt. 3.12.

13. *Dei patris pietatem ac misericordiam cogitantes.* A very clear example of *pietas* used in the sense of "pity" (a "Christianism").

See, for example H. Pétré, *Caritas. Étude sur le vocabulaire latin de la charité chrétienne* (Louvain 1948) 251 ff.

14. *diu multumque tractatu inter nos habito, iusta moderatione agenda libravimus.* A description of the protracted and no doubt painful proceedings of the Council meeting of 251. Cf. *Ep.* 55.6.1: *Scripturis diu ex utraque parte prolatis temperamentum salubri moderatione libravimus.* The description here is intended to emphasize the weighty deliberations that preceded the just and moderate decisions reached; the conclusions were neither hasty nor ill-considered.

15. *lectis libellis quos hic nuper legeram et ad vos quoque legendos pro communi dilectione transmiseram.* From the description which follows it is clear that Cyprian is referring to his two treatises, *De lapsis* and *De ecclesiae catholicae unitate.* (Translated by M. Bévenot, the two are in ACW 25.) We are thus provided with a *terminus ante* for the two works. It would be helpful if we could narrow the dating further. Does the language here assist?

It is generally assumed that Cyprian now encloses copies of the two works and forwards them to Rome for the first time. This requires the pluperfect *transmiseram* to be interpreted as an "epistolary present" (see, e.g., M. Bévenot in JTS 28 [1977] 357 n. 1). Unfortunately, that is counter to Cyprian's epistolary habits. Whenever Cyprian records a current enclosure elsewhere, he invariably uses the preterite (e.g., *Epp.* 20.2.1, 25.1.2, 26.1.3, 27.2.1, 27.3.2, 32.1.1, 35.1.1, etc.) The pluperfect here is quite exceptional; accordingly, in the light of Cyprianic usage, it would naturally be interpreted as "I have already sent." We ought to conclude, therefore, that the copies of the two treatises have already been forwarded to Rome.

But if they were already despatched, how long ago? Here the preceding clause, *hic nuper legeram,* could be invoked (although *nuper* is too elastic in Cyprian to be helpful; see nn. 7 and 27 to *Ep.* 1). For it has often been urged that the reading was at the African Council convened, it is assumed, not too long after Easter 251. That is certainly feasible in the case of *De lapsis,* but the piece itself is composed and presumably was originally delivered as a sermon to Cyprian's congregation. It may well have been read out *also* at the Council meeting, though it was clearly not a programmatic statement for that Council's agenda (e.g., the special, mitigating, penitential arrangements arrived at for *libellatici* are not even suggested). Cyprian wrote to Rome a lost letter conveying the Council's decisions; the *De lapsis* could well have been an attachment to that document.

However, in the case of the *De unitate* there are grounds for doubting that it was completed until formal schism was apparent in the Church, in Rome, that is to say, late March/early April. That would still be in time for the Council—but only just (started meeting at end of April?). The dispute is in full spate whilst the Council is in session. But it remains controversial whether we need to conclude that the completion must be pulled down even further, until Cyprian had *decided* on the Roman schism, against Novatian and for Cornelius, that is to say, until shortly before *Ep.* 44 (i.e., mid-year), when the Council was no longer in session (see *Ep.* 45.1.3; and see introductory note to *Ep.* 44). I find it hard to believe that we *must* so conclude. The description of the illicit bishops in *De unitate* 10 reflects as much the charges that were levelled against Cornelius as those that became fixed against Novatian. Compare *De unitate* 10 with the charges implied against Cornelius in *Ep.* 44.3.2, *Ep.* 45.3.1, *Ep.* 48.4.1; and see further n. 21 to *Ep.* 48. If, in fact, the *De unitate* missed the presumed reading before the Council and subsequent attachment to the Council minutes, it could indeed have been conveyed even *earlier* to Rome by Caldonius and Fortunatus, attached to the lost letter which they were carrying about schism and which urged on the Romans—adherents of Novatian and Cornelius alike—return *ad catholicae ecclesiae unitatem* (*Ep.* 45.1.1). The references in the *De unitate* to illicit bishops are indeed so generalized that neither party could reasonably take offence; each could welcome them as confirming his description of his opponent. Still it remains true to say that the *De unitate* appears to be directed basically against the local Carthaginian threat of schism and for the benefit of a general congregational audience there. One thing we can assert, Cyprian's relative order for the two treatises (*De lapsis* coming before *De unitate*) reappears in Pontius, *Vit Cyp.* 7.5, in the so-called Cheltenham List of A.D. 359–365, and a sermon of Augustine

(ML Suppl. 2.611). This order, we can reasonably presume, at least marks chronological sequence.

There is much literature—and many unresolved problems—on these questions. For earlier literature, see H. Koch, *Cyprianische Untersuchungen* (Bonn 1926) 79 ff., and esp. 107 ff. on this passage. On later literature, see M. Bévenot in *Analecta Gregoriana* II (1937) 73 ff. and in JTS 28 (1977) 357 f. See also U. Wickert, *Sacramentum unitatis. Ein Beitrag zum Verständnis der Kirche bei Cyprian* (Berlin-New York 1971) 25 ff.

ADDITIONAL NOTES

(p. 112 *Ep.* 29 n.11) For recent discussion see V. Saxer, *Vie liturgique* ... (Vatican City 1969) 78; A. Vilela, *La condition collégiale* ... (Paris 1971) 31Off; A. Faivre, *Naissance d'une hiérarchie* (Paris 1977) 158ff. and *idem, Revue des sciences religieuses* 50 (1976) 102ff. There is earlier discussion at some length in Dodwell, *Dissertatio cyprianica* vi (pp. 28ff. in 1682 edition of Pearson and Fell).

(p. 156 *Ep.* 34 n.2) Note that the word *Didensis* is garbled in a number of MSS and that its relation to some presumed ancient city of "Dida" is entirely conjectural. There is further discussion by N. Duval in *Mél. école fran. Rome* 89 (1977) 848f., n.3.

(p. 182 *Ep.* 38 n.9) For other evidence suggesting local courts might exercise capital powers, see E. Schürer, *History of the Jewish People in the Age of Jesus Christ* (rev. ed., Edinburgh (1979) 2.219f., n.80 and F. Millar in *Journ. Rom. Stud.* 71 (1981) 80f. For evidence that local magistrates might exercise summary powers of expulsion see Paulus *Sent.* 5.21.1 (itinerant soothsayers) with an example in W. Dittenberger, *Sylloge Inscriptionum Graecarum*[4] (Hildesheim 1960) 2 No. 799 (Cyzicus) and consult further A. N. Sherwin White, *Roman Society and Roman Law in the New Testament* (Oxford 1963) 77f.

(p. 192 *Ep.* 39 n.15) For further recent reading on Christians and Roman military service see now J. Helgeland in ANRW 23.1 (1979) 724ff. esp. 752ff. (evidence of Cyprian) and L.J. Swift in ANRW 23.1 (1979) 835ff.

(p. 199 *Ep.* 40 n.6) The other problematic use of *sacerdos* in Cyprian occurs in *Ep.* 67.4.3 where see n.13 and cf. n.10 to *Ep.* 43.

(p. 238 *Ep.* 45 n.14) Dr G.F. Diercks reports, by letter, that all the MSS he has consulted read here *fratres nostros cum litteris redigendos* ("*our* brethren should be sent back with letters") and not just *fratres* only (as in Hartel's text). This reading implies that Cyprian is sending out his own brethren whom he wants to report back to Carthage with the letters of recognition gathered from the individual bishops: they will then be forwarded to Rome. Cf. n. 18 to *Ep.* 48.3.2 and n.2 to *Ep.* 55.1.1f.

(p. 268 *Ep.* 49 n.6) In the following sentence I translate Hartel's text *ista quae per legationem mandaverant* ("the message they had delivered through their spokesmen"). But virtually all MSS record *mandaveram* ("the message which I had instructed through my spokesmen"). If that is the corrent reading, we gain an even clearer picture of Cornelius' managing the affair; he had dictated himself in advance, *via* envoys, the formulae the confessors were publicly to declare on their return to the fold. Cf. n. 16 below.

(p. 276 *Ep.* 49 n.22) For further discussion of *populus/plebs* in Cyprian see Watson 257; H.H. Janssen, *Kultur and Sprache* ... (Nijmegen 1938) 60ff., 65ff.; J. Schrijnen and C. Mohrmann, *Studien* (2 vols. Nijmegen 1936–1937) 1.57 ff.

(p. 301 *Ep.* 54 n.15) Note especially *Epp.* 14.7 and 45.4 with preterite verbs for items currently enclosed (*misi, transmisi*), pluperfect verbs for items previously despatched (*miseram*).

INDEXES

1. OLD AND NEW TESTAMENT

2. AUTHORS

3. LATIN WORDS

4. GENERAL INDEX

absolution, 132, *see* penitential discipline
Alexander, bishop, 12
altars, 239 f.
Apostates, *see lapsi*
Armenia Minor, 97
Augendus, 60, 61, 200 ff., 208, 209, 211, 242 ff.
Augendus, confessor, 79, 208, 268, 278
Augendus, Novatianist deacon, 67, 208, 226, 247 f., 296
Aurelius, lector and confessor, 14, 15, 52, 56, 108, 110, 177 ff., 181 ff., 183, 186, 193, 195

Babylas, bishop, 12
Biblical majuscule, 184
bishops, 14 f., 40, 107, 137, 145 ff., 154, 158 f., 166, 179, 207, 256, 262, 294; and charitable funds, 207; and deacons, 289; consecration of, 229, 269 f.; election of, 216; powers of, 219; succession of, 146 f.
bishop, of Rome, 74, 76 ff.

Caecilian, presbyter, 112
Caldonius, bishop, 59, 61, 67, 69, 72, 75, 76, 202, 208, 209, 210, 222, 224, 228 ff., 233 ff., 256, 268, 302
Callistus, pope, 155, 280, 281, 299
Capsa, 96
Carthage, 217; clergy of, 106 ff., 109, 141, 159, 195
catechists, 113 f.
catechumens, 112
Celerina, martyr, 55, 190 f.
Celerinus, Roman confessor, 283
Celerinus, lector and confessor, 6, 9, 14, 15, 48, 54 ff., 96, 101, 108, 110, 126, 170 ff., 171, 172, 177, 181, 182, 183, 187 ff., 195
certificates of forgiveness, 9; *see libelli pacis*
certificates of sacrifice, *see libelli*
charitable funds, 205, 280
Christians, and military service, 191 f.; popular hostility towards, 197
church, Numidian, 258; in Armenia, 12, 97; in Carthage, 8 ff.; in Sicily, 6; in the East, 11; in Roman, 6 ff., 67, 114, 117, 168
clergy, appointments of, 290; clerical office, 180; elections of, 114; laicisation, 274; married, 198, 292; probation of, 113 f.; translation of, 196; of Carthage, *see*

Carthage, clergy of; of Rome, *see* Rome, clergy of
confessors, 110, 187, 212, 247, 284, 288; Carthaginian, 171; Roman, 33 ff., 48 ff., 99 ff., 114, 117, 170, 249, 262 ff., 295 ff., and clerical office, 180; and intercessory powers, 137; release of, 182
confiscations, 205
Conon, bishop, 12
conscience, 121
consuls, 174
Cornelius, pope, 7 f., 11, 15, 16, 17, 67, 69 ff., 74, 76, 80, 82, 86, 95 f., 96, 97, 101, 102, 103, 118, 131, 146, 213, 223 ff., 224, 234, 245 ff., 249, 251 ff., 262 ff., 277, 283, 285, 296; consecration of, 228 f.; and penitential discipline, 263; election, 237, 273; objections to election, 261 f.
council, African, 10, 11, 17 f., 160, 212, 222, 228, 238, 239, 242, 252, 263 f., 274, 288, 293, 301 f.; Italian, 18, 229, 263 f., of Antioch, 96; of Arles, 198; of Carthage, 397, 157; of Elvira, 139, 157, 280; of Hippo, 393, 157; of Nicaea, 198, 274
Cyprian, of Carthage, and Carthaginian clergy, 107 f., 141, 155 f., 178, 186 f., 195 f., 201, 206, 211, 213, 242 f.; and Novatian, 244 f.; and Roman confessors, 133 ff., 265, 297 ff.; and Rome, 9, 13, 16 ff., 115, 161, 162, 169 f., 229 f.; and charitable funds, 10, 13 f., 59, 202; and clerical appointments, 114, 184; and confessors, 180 f.; and *De lapsis*, 213, 301; and *De unitate*, 201 f., 213, 301; and divine inspiration, 197; and ecclesiastical commission, 200 ff., 208 f.; and flight, 160; and his *provincia*, 258; and laity, 178, 212, 216; and pagan hostility, 219 f.; and polemic, 286; and powers of bishops, 145; and recognition of Cornelius, 225 f., 231, 233 ff., 244 f., 251 ff., 255, 261, 278, 302; and role of bishops, 294; election as bishop, 215; in hiding, 142, 172, 177, 219; relations with clergy, 14 ff.; relations with confessors, 9; visit to Hadrumentum, 255

De lapsis, 301
De unitate, 301
deacons, 156, 204, 214, 281, 289

311